Allies at Odds

VIETNAM
America in the War Years

Series Editor
David L. Anderson
California State University, Monterey Bay

The Vietnam War and the tumultuous internal upheavals in America that coincided with it marked a watershed era in U.S. history. These events profoundly challenged America's heroic self-image. During the 1950s the United States defined Southeast Asia as an area of vital strategic importance. In the 1960s this view produced a costly American military campaign that continued into the early 1970s. The Vietnam War was the nation's longest war and ended with an unprecedented U.S. failure to achieve its stated objectives. Simultaneous with this frustrating military intervention and the domestic debate that it produced were other tensions created by student activism on campuses, the black struggle for civil rights, and the women's liberation movement. The books in this series explore the complex and controversial issues of the period from the mid-1950s to the mid-1970s in brief and engaging volumes. To facilitate continued and informed debate on these contested subjects, each book examines a military, political, or diplomatic issue; the role of a key individual; or one of the domestic changes in America during the war.

Volumes Published

Melvin Small, *Antiwarriors: The Vietnam War and the Battle for America's Hearts and Minds*

Edward K. Spann, *Democracy's Children: The Young Rebels of the 1960s and the Power of Ideals*

Ronald B. Frankum, Jr., *Like Rolling Thunder: The Air War in Vietnam, 1964–1975*

Walter LaFeber, *The Deadly Bet: LBJ, Vietnam, and the 1968 Election*

Mitchell K. Hall, *Crossroads: American Popular Culture and the Vietnam Generation*

David F. Schmitz, *The Tet Offensive: Politics, War, and Public Opinion*

Seth Jacobs, *Cold War Mandarin: Ngo Dinh Diem and the Origins of America's War in Vietnam*

Joseph A. Fry, *Debating Vietnam: Fulbright, Stennis, and Their Senate Hearings*

Allies at Odds

America, Europe, and Vietnam, 1961–1968

Eugenie M. Blang

ROWMAN & LITTLEFIELD PUBLISHERS, INC.
Lanham • Boulder • New York • Toronto • Plymouth, UK

Published by Rowman & Littlefield Publishers, Inc.
A wholly owned subsidiary of The Rowman & Littlefield Publishing Group, Inc.
4501 Forbes Boulevard, Suite 200, Lanham, Maryland 20706
http://www.rowmanlittlefield.com

Estover Road, Plymouth PL6 7PY, United Kingdom

British Library Cataloguing in Publication Information Available

Library of Congress Cataloging-in-Publication Data
Blang, Eugenie, 1964–
  Allies at odds : America, Europe, and Vietnam, 1961–1968 / Eugenie Blang.
     p.   cm. — (Vietnam : America in the war years)
  Includes bibliographical references and index.
  ISBN 978-1-4422-0922-0 (cloth : alk. paper) — ISBN 978-1-4422-0923-7 (electronic)
  1. Vietnam War, 1961–1975—Diplomatic history. 2. Vietnam War, 1961–1975—
United States. 3. United States—Foreign relations—France. 4. United States—Foreign
relations—Germany (West). 5. United States—Foreign relations—Great Britain. 6.
France—Foreign relations—United States. 7. Germany (West)—Foreign relations—
United States. 8. Great Britain—Foreign relations—United States. I. Title.
  DS557.7.B57 2011
  959.704'32—dc22
                                                                    2010047436

♾™ The paper used in this publication meets the minimum requirements of American
National Standard for Information Sciences—Permanence of Paper for Printed Library
Materials, ANSI/NISO Z39.48-1992.

Printed in the United States of America

For Dirk

Contents

Acknowledgments

I am deeply grateful that David Anderson chose to include my study for his series: *Vietnam: America in the War Years*. David's encouragement and support greatly aided in the completion of this book. I am also indebted to Edward Crapol, who in a sense is the father of this study, as he suggested that I investigate the French, British, and German response to U.S. policy in Vietnam for my dissertation. Ed was also instrumental in clarifying the scope and structure of this book. I am very thankful. Niels Aaboe, Sarah David, Naomi Burns, and Janice Braunstein at Rowman & Littlefield have made the publication process so much easier than anticipated. I deeply appreciate their guidance and assistance. My family on both sides of the Atlantic has also steadfastly encouraged me through the years of research and writing. My greatest debt is to my best friend and wonderful husband, Dirk Morton. Dirk's love, thoughtful insights, and uplifting humor made writing this book a more joyful experience.

Introduction

The United States has not fully learned that the political advice or criticism of less powerful friends who share a common heritage does not necessarily denote hostility or envy or malice—or even bad judgment.

—George Ball, *The Discipline of Power*[1]

The American decision to invade Iraq in 2003 led to a deep rift in transatlantic relations. While British Prime Minister Tony Blair supported U.S. President George W. Bush, French President Jacques Chirac and German Chancellor Gerhard Schröder condemned the Bush policy in no uncertain terms. Even before military actions began, millions of Europeans took to the streets in protest of America's Iraq policy. European intellectuals started a media campaign to arouse a common European sentiment to be followed by a joint and truly European policy to counterbalance the United States. It seemed that the cherished ties between Europe and America fostered since the end of World War II had frayed beyond repair.

Yet, this was not the first time that the transatlantic allies found themselves at odds. France, Britain, and Germany had disagreed with U.S. policy before. The most profound discord between the United States and the three European countries occurred forty years before the Iraq War over the growing American involvement and subsequent military intervention in Vietnam. In order to better understand the divergent views on Iraq, a closer study of the interallied debate over America's Vietnam policy will provide insight and detail for why the European allies do not always support a strategy that Washington defines as essential for its national security and hence for that of its allies.

This book examines America's Vietnam policy from 1961 to 1968 in an international context by focusing on the United States' relationship with its

European partners France, West Germany, and Great Britain. The European response to America's Vietnam policy provides an analytical framework to assess this important chapter in recent American history within the wider perspective of international relations. Equally significant, the respective approaches to the "Vietnam question" by the Europeans and Americans reveal the ongoing challenge for nation-states of transcending narrowly defined state-centered policies for a global perspective pursuant of common goals among the transatlantic allies.

During the Kennedy and Johnson administrations, Great Britain, France, and West Germany perceived the growing American military involvement in South Vietnam as misguided, dangerous, and unwanted. Did European "criticism" of America's role in Vietnam, to use Ball's phrase quoted above, "denote hostility or envy or malice?" While some envy of America's superpower status affected all three European countries, their anxiety over U.S. policy in Vietnam first and foremost resulted from both a concern for their respective national self-interest and a pragmatic, realistic assessment of the situation in Southeast Asia. European leadership feared that the crisis in Asia portended a decreasing American interest in European affairs and a possible reduction of American troops that might leave Western Europe more vulnerable to potential Soviet encroachment. The Europeans also worried that the conflict in Vietnam might escalate into a major Asian and perhaps even world war, thereby endangering the security of Western Europe.

In light of these profound concerns, the failure of France, West Germany, and Great Britain to significantly influence American policy making is intriguing and of historical importance. Disregarding European concerns, the United States unilaterally embarked on a strategy of escalation to secure a non-Communist South Vietnam. Had Washington listened more closely to European advice, the quagmire in Vietnam might have been averted. In addition, the United States was forced to fight in Vietnam without its European allies. Whether European troops might have improved the military situation in South Vietnam cannot be assessed, but European assistance would have certainly reinforced America's Vietnam policy both in the court of world opinion and within the United States. A joint Western position proved essential to secure the independence of South Korea during 1950 to 1953, but ten years later American leaders were unable to form a similar alliance with the West Europeans to defeat Communism in South Vietnam.

Why, then, was a mutualistic transatlantic approach to the Vietnam question unattainable? First, the Europeans missed the opportunity to develop a joint, well-coordinated critical response to U.S. policy in Vietnam. The Europeans were hampered by a centuries-old paradigm of state interest that precluded any unified strategy aimed at American decision making. Reliance upon "nationalistic" ideologies prevented the French, Germans, and British from moving beyond their individual agendas to come to an understanding with each other regarding the American role in Vietnam. The Vietnam "question" became a lesson for the Europeans about their impact on global politics. Second, unilateral advice and expressed misgivings from the Europeans were ignored by Washington. All three European powers had a grander imperialist past but were reduced to secondary rank in global affairs following the Second World War. Britain and France, especially, had profound experience in the affairs of Asia, convincing them that the American policy in Vietnam was mistaken and portended little chance of success. While some of their advice may have been valid, their behavior still exhibited patterns of a bygone era. The United States was less inclined to follow suggestions of European states that, until recently, had exploited third world nations for their self-interest. Britain, France, and even more so West Germany were in fact "less powerful friends." In light of the worldwide obligations of the United States, the European positions appeared parochial and detrimental to America's effort in South Vietnam. Washington was even more dismayed by the fact that European misgivings over the Vietnam question left the United States fighting alone in Southeast Asia, while at the same time America also provided for the security of Western Europe.

A closer analysis of the motives and approaches taken by Paris, Bonn, and London is necessary in order to define the respective national agenda of each country. What were the forces and factors that brought about such an ineffective European response to Washington's Vietnam policy? It was neither "hostility" toward the United States nor "bad judgment" but rather self-interest. All three powers had to adapt to the bipolar world while trying to restore influence with the superpowers and thus enhance their national status. Also, policy makers in Paris, Bonn, and London faced a domestic audience that was reluctant to endorse the American policy in Vietnam. While most Europeans appreciated American military protection and were grateful for American economic aid after the Second World War, the U.S. escalation of the conflict in Vietnam led to concern and criticism of Washington.

France analyzed America's policy on Vietnam through the prism of its own long and ultimately disastrous experience in Indochina. Indochina, with France's other colonies, had been cherished as manifestations of French greatness and world power status. While France's role in Europe diminished after 1871, its colonial empire remained an obvious expression of *grandeur*. After 1945, France spent considerable resources and manpower to retain Indochina. Supported by the British and events of the Cold War, Paris recast its effort to retain control over Indochina as a struggle against Communism. Since 1950, France received substantial financial and military aid from the

United States in the conflict against Vietnamese insurgents led by Ho Chi Minh. Charles de Gaulle, who had initially advocated the retention of Indochina, changed his views after 1954.

When de Gaulle returned to power in 1958, he endeavored to convey France's hard-learned lessons in Asia to Washington by urging U.S. leaders not to become bogged down in the jungles of Vietnam. When his advice went unheeded, de Gaulle used the increasing difficulties of the United States in Southeast Asia as an opportunity to enhance the role of France in global affairs. The French president sought closer relations with third world countries, particularly those of the former French Empire. Toward these nations de Gaulle depicted his country as a trustworthy friend genuinely interested in promoting their well-being. De Gaulle's rhetoric presented France as an alternative to what he characterized as the ideologically driven interference of the Soviet Union and the United States. By pursuing this foreign policy, de Gaulle hoped to restore France once more to a position of *grandeur* in the world—replacing Cold War ideology with French nationalism. French envy of the United States was certainly a factor in de Gaulle's foreign policy. But de Gaulle also relied on the American nuclear shield to protect his country and could not afford an outwardly hostile policy toward the United States. Regardless of his own ambitions, he genuinely tried to save the Americans from undertaking a doomed Vietnam policy. Despite a decade of tensions with Washington, de Gaulle provided good judgment on Vietnam.

The Federal Republic of Germany had far more immediate goals to deal with than a struggle of distant people in Southeast Asia. The necessity of American military protection, the status of the former German capital Berlin, and the issue of German unification topped the agenda of West German foreign policy making. Berlin suffered physical division in 1961 with the construction of the wall, and reunification seemed further postponed by increasing East-West tensions over the crisis in Southeast Asia. Consequently, the Vietnam conflict became a major policy dilemma for Bonn. If Washington continued to be distracted by events in Southeast Asia, what would happen to the German agenda? Yet, open opposition to the widening American role in Vietnam was impossible because West Germany—still not a fully sovereign state at the time—relied on Washington's goodwill for survival and possible German reunification in the future. But West Germany could also not afford to antagonize the French, who increasingly opposed Washington's course in Vietnam. France, too, was one of the allied powers needed for any progress toward German unity.

Great Britain, apprehensive of losing its role as "special ally" to the United States, was painfully aware of the need for American military protection. But the crisis in Southeast Asia ran counter to British goals and realities. During the 1950s and 1960s, London was overseeing the demise of its colonial empire yet still hoped to play a global role as leader of the Commonwealth. Britain did facilitate the return of French forces to Indochina after the Second World War. In 1954, Britain cochaired the Geneva Conference with the Soviet Union ending the First Indochina War. By the 1960s, British forces and resources were clearly strained by commitments in Malaysia, Aden, Cyprus, and the turmoil in Rhodesia. Economic difficulties within the United Kingdom further precluded additional British military engagements elsewhere. Britain neither desired to participate in an uncertain effort in Vietnam nor wished to risk its own security in Europe. In addition, British leaders were apprehensive about negative reactions within the United Kingdom and the Commonwealth to America's role in Vietnam. Hence, London attempted to find a peaceful political solution to the Vietnam problem through quiet but solid diplomatic initiatives. By doing so, Harold Macmillan, Alec Douglas-Home, and Harold Wilson aspired to remain a "special ally" of the United States while carefully balancing British economic limitations with the country's political obligations toward its Commonwealth partners.

Obviously, the basis and aims of foreign policy making differed among the three European powers. Nevertheless, their approach to global issues and the U.S. Vietnam policy was rather similar. French, German, and British foreign policy decision making was founded on an ideology of nationalism, the notion that the nation's best interest was paramount. The divergent European views on the Vietnam problem were due to the respective interpretation of the threat posed by Communism. Regarding the Sino-Soviet split, Macmillan keenly remarked that so-called Communist countries demonstrated similar political and ideological dilemmas that marked Europe's history. De Gaulle always referred to "la Russie," refusing to use the term Soviet Union because to him ideologies were temporary while nations were not. Konrad Adenauer believed that the Soviet Union would ultimately have to relinquish its hold on the East Germans because the reality of freedom and prosperity in the West would prove far more desirable than a rigid planned economy. The Soviet Union was threatening in the eyes of Western Europeans because it represented a totalitarian system, taking the guise of Marxist ideals, and bent on extending its influence further into Western Europe. Soviet goals vis-à-vis Western Europe were not new historically. Ever since the days of Czar Peter the Great, Russian interest lay toward the West.

American policy making was also driven by self-interest, but its objectives differed profoundly from those of the Western Europeans. Propelled into the role of leader of the Western world by the Second World War, it became America's self-assumed duty and burden to defend the freedom of its allies against the Communist threat. John F. Kennedy and Lyndon B. Johnson were guided by the demands of domestic politics and by a different ideological view on global affairs than were the Europeans. While the Europeans pursued agendas of national self-interest aimed at retaining or enhancing their roles in global affairs, the Cold War dogma of the free world versus Communist oppression pervaded the mind-set of Americans and foreign policy advisers. After the "loss" of China in 1949, the stalemate in Korea in 1953, and a dissatisfactory political settlement for Laos in 1962, for Washington Vietnam became the front line in the continuing Cold War struggle. According to the American doctrine of containment, South Vietnam simply could not be abandoned because its fall might open the floodgates to Communist expansion in the entire region. A lack of American determination in Southeast Asia might also backfire politically at home. Republicans as well as "hawks" within the Democratic Party insisted that the United States had to stand up to any Communist encroachment. Presidents Kennedy and Johnson were unwilling to risk potential political defeat at home. Therefore, they chose to expand America's commitment against Communism in South Vietnam with tragic consequences for both countries.

The first chapter of *Allies at Odds* focuses on President Kennedy's decisions that led to a far greater American advisory and military role in South Vietnam. Within the administration and among some members of Congress, concerns were raised whether the president's strategy was indeed the best course for the United States or if it would be wiser to negotiate a settlement. The following three chapters provide a closer look at the European background to the Vietnam problem. Examining France's long history in Indochina and its humiliating loss of the colony in 1954 helps to better understand the position of President de Gaulle that an American military escalation in Vietnam might lead to defeat. To West German Chancellor Konrad Adenauer, regaining West German sovereignty, preserving the unity of Berlin, and ultimately ending the German division were far more important than the brewing conflict in Southeast Asia. Yet, Bonn was obligated to pay greater attention to events in Vietnam since it could not afford to alienate first France and after 1954 the United States in their commitment to the region. Adenauer grew increasingly suspicious of President Kennedy's policy of détente and flexible response toward the Soviet Union and therefore turned to France to counterbalance the United States. Like France, Great Britain had extensive experience in Asia as a colonial power. The United Kingdom played a crucial role in helping the French reestablish control over Indochina after the Second World War and indirectly assisted the French in their struggle against Ho Chi Minh and his Vietnamese insurgents. Yet, as a result of Britain's own struggle against Communist insurgents in Malaysia and ever-expanding costs to maintain a global role east of Suez, Britain concluded that a negotiated settlement would be the preferable solution for the Vietnam conflict.

Chapters 5 to 8 analyze President Johnson's decision to escalate the war in Vietnam and his efforts to win French, West German, and British support for his Vietnam policy. But none of the three European powers was willing or able to back Johnson's policy. De Gaulle consistently insisted on a negotiated settlement. West German Chancellor Ludwig Erhard officially supported Washington's Vietnam policy because he hoped that approach would garner a reciprocal response from the United States in his quest for German unity. But de Gaulle's opposition to America's Vietnam policy and divisions within Erhard's own party between those favoring Paris and those supporting a pro-American course burdened the chancellor. Intensifying American demands for Germans to do more in Vietnam led to the offset payment crisis and hastened the fall of Erhard. British Prime Minister Wilson refused to provide any military aid to Vietnam and instead set out to initiate a diplomatic solution. Wilson faced considerable opposition to America's course in Vietnam within his own Labour Party and throughout the British Commonwealth. However, like previous prime ministers, he could not afford open antagonism with the special partner in Washington, since British security, and in a lesser degree the stability of its currency, depended upon American support.

Chapter 9 addresses the Johnson decision in March 1968 to seek a negotiated settlement with North Vietnam and then President Nixon's effort to listen more closely to America's European allies. The promise of a political solution for Vietnam certainly lessened tensions between the transatlantic allies. Differing views and interests persisted, although in times of serious crisis the allies stood side by side. The terrorist attacks against the United States on September 11, 2001, exemplified the deep bond between the allies. Europeans were equally shocked and its people and governments expressed emotional solidarity with the United States. Perhaps the French headline stating "We are all Americans" best summed up how genuine European support for America was. The Europeans quickly joined President George W. Bush in the military campaign to oust the Taliban from Afghanistan and to bring the plotters of September 11 to justice. But the American policy to topple the regime of Iraqi dictator Saddam Hussein once again caused a deep rift in transatlantic relations. The split within Europe over how to respond to the Iraq problem once more prevented a joint European position that might have impacted Washington's decision making.

Chapter 1

The United States
and the Vietnam Conundrum

The origins of America's engagement in Vietnam were based on guidelines defined by National Security Council (NSC) Resolution 68 written in 1950. NSC 68 furthered the Truman Doctrine by postulating American reaction to even limited expansion of Communism. During the previous years, Washington remained officially neutral in the French Indochina war, but with the victory of Mao Zedong in China in 1949, Southeast Asia became a major focus of American foreign policy making. The Korean War further validated American suspicions that the Soviet Union and Communist China intended to conquer and dominate Asia, and therefore American aid to the French was increased. President Dwight Eisenhower continued Harry Truman's commitment to the French effort to defeat Communist guerrillas in Indochina. Although Eisenhower refused direct American military intervention or the use of nuclear weapons to save the French in Indochina, he nevertheless restated the importance of the region for American security interests.

Following the Geneva Settlement in 1954, Eisenhower was unwilling to renounce American influence in Southeast Asia and hoped that the newly created Southeast Asia Treaty Organization (SEATO) and indirect American support to the government of Ngo Dinh Diem would be sufficient to secure the viability of South Vietnam.[1] Washington consequently embarked on a "nation-building" policy in South Vietnam, which centered on President Diem. This policy worked quite well until 1959. By then domestic opposition to the repressive Diem regime intensified, leading to the formation of the National Liberation Front (NLF) in 1960.[2] Progress in South Vietnam proved rather precarious, but Eisenhower remained committed to Saigon based on the conviction that Communism had to be contained. Accordingly, American security interests were at stake in Vietnam. If South Vietnam fell, so would the rest of Southeast Asia, endangering the entire Pacific Rim and the United States.

In December 1960, President-elect John F. Kennedy was briefed by President Eisenhower on global challenges facing the United States. In Southeast Asia, Laos was of immediate concern. Kennedy decided against U.S. military intervention and appointed Averell Harriman to find a political solution.[3] In 1962, another Geneva Conference, under the cochairmanship of Great Britain and the Soviet Union, neutralized Laos. But repeated violations of the agreement by North Vietnam left a sour taste in Kennedy's mouth and also raised concerns for the safety of South Vietnam. Kennedy's Republican opponent, Richard Nixon, called the Laotian settlement an "unqualified disaster." Following the Bay of Pigs debacle in 1961, politically, Kennedy could not afford a similar failure in South Vietnam.[4]

As congressman, Kennedy favored American support for South Vietnam. He was intensely critical of the French during the First Indochina War but quickly endorsed the new leader of South Vietnam, Diem. Interestingly, his comments on French policy in Indochina were right on the mark for the future American role as well—but perhaps as president Kennedy did overlook his own assessment of April 1954. At the time, Kennedy could not possibly foresee a French victory because the French pursued an outdated policy based on colonial interests and failed to promote a "strong native non-Communist sentiment," which was the basis for any success in Vietnam. Unless the Vietnamese were willing to fight for their independence, a "military victory, even with American support . . . is difficult, if not impossible, of achievement."[5]

Where the French failed, Americans could do better. In 1953, Kennedy met Diem and was immediately impressed with the South Vietnamese politician. As a founding member of the American Friends of Vietnam, Kennedy fervently defended Eisenhower's commitment to South Vietnam. To Kennedy, that country was the "cornerstone of the Free World in Southeast Asia" and a "proving ground for democracy." The United States was the "godparent" of South Vietnam and had a moral obligation to stand by Saigon. Failure to do so would profoundly blemish the American image in all of Asia and also hurt American strategic interests.[6]

By 1961, South Vietnam was not on the road to democracy, nor was its survival assured. Days after his inauguration, Kennedy received an alarming report from General Edward G. Lansdale who, as a CIA agent, played a major part in the implementation of American policy in South Vietnam from 1954 to 1956. According to his information, the Communist insurgency was growing in numbers, and many Vietnamese were disgruntled with Diem's authoritarian leadership, partly a result of the unconditional American support for the South Vietnamese leader. Lansdale recommended an American "emergency treatment." Otherwise, Saigon could do no better than "postpone eventual defeat." Kennedy immediately approved forty-two million dollars in aid for South Vietnam.[7] The president also adopted a counterinsurgency plan for Vietnam already under discussion during the last year of the Eisenhower administration. A National Security Action Memorandum on Vietnam (NSAM 52) authorized infiltration and harassment operations against Viet Cong (VC) guerrillas, even in North Vietnamese territory. A special task force of the army—the Green Berets—was created and trained in counterinsurgency. Kennedy also further increased the number of American "advisors" to South Vietnam beyond the officially allowed limit of 685 under the 1954 Geneva agreement.[8] While Kennedy did not want another war in Asia, he was also resolved not to lose in South Vietnam.

How important was Vietnam to Washington? French President Charles de Gaulle called it a "rotten country" and warned Kennedy in May 1961 not to make the same mistakes as the French had during the First Indochina War. British Prime Minister Harold Macmillan also urged against further involvement, while the West Germans pleaded for American help to maintain the freedom of Berlin. But for Washington, Berlin and South Vietnam had become symbols that demonstrated American determination to draw the line against Communist aggression. As Vice President Lyndon B. Johnson put it after he returned from his first visit to Saigon,

> We must decide whether to help these countries to the best of our ability or throw back the towel in the arena and pull back our defenses to San Francisco and a "Fortress America" concept. More important, we should say to the world in this case that we don't live up to treaties and don't stand by our friends. This is not my concept. I recommend that we move forward promptly with a major effort to help these countries defend themselves.[9]

Kennedy's own 1960 campaign propaganda had accused Eisenhower of softness against Communism, and Kennedy frequently referred to the infamous "missile gap" by stating that the United States was falling behind in the arms race against the Soviet Union.[10] Once Kennedy assumed the presidency, it was apparent that abandoning South Vietnam would most likely backfire politically at home.

Republican opponents were also closely watching Kennedy's moves. In May 1961, Nixon gave a speech on foreign policy issues in Chicago that indirectly addressed Vietnam, once again reminding Kennedy not to be or appear weak on Communism: "Whenever American prestige is to be committed on a major scale we must be willing to commit enough power to obtain our objective even if all our intelligence estimates prove wrong. Putting it bluntly, we should not start things in the world unless we are prepared to finish them."[11]

President Kennedy (left), French President de Gaulle (center), and Jacqueline Kennedy (right) in 1961. De Gaulle privately warned Kennedy not to become bogged down in Vietnam. Courtesy of the John F. Kennedy Presidential Library.

Whatever farsighted advice de Gaulle and Macmillan had to offer, Kennedy had to follow through with what he had promised as a presidential candidate. He had to maintain the image of being a determined warrior against Communist encroachment, thereby preempting possible criticism by the Republican Party and hard-line Democrats.

The majority of Kennedy's advisors also recommended expanding the American effort in South Vietnam. General Maxwell Taylor and presidential advisor Walter Rostow visited Vietnam in the fall of 1961 and judged the situation serious. Diem was increasingly losing support, and the morale among the South Vietnamese was dismal. They concluded that more American aid, including the deployment of eight thousand American ground troops, might turn the tide in Vietnam. Like Eisenhower, Kennedy rejected the idea of sending American combat troops but, at the same time, refused a negotiated settlement. Negotiations over Vietnam would obviously evoke a storm of protest from the Republicans and hawks within the Democratic Party. Given the domestic situation, the president favored a middle course of providing more financial assistance and advisors to South Vietnam.[12]

By approving additional military and economic support, Kennedy took the first steps along an increasingly slippery road in Vietnam. As de Gaulle had predicted, Washington soon discovered that American assistance to Saigon was not sufficient to subdue the insurgents. Diem's autocratic rule facilitated the appeal of the Viet Cong. However, Kennedy continued his support of Diem and, in November 1961, affirmed that the United States would not tolerate Communist aggression in South Vietnam.[13] By the end of 1962, the number of American military advisors in South Vietnam had increased from 3,200 to 11,500, with more than one hundred killed or wounded. Kennedy held fast on his approach of limited response, though victory in South Vietnam was remote. The Viet Cong modified their strategy to respond better to superior American–South Vietnamese weaponry, and Diem himself became a growing obstacle to American success. To make things worse for Kennedy, the American media increasingly focused on the failures of the South Vietnamese leader, whose behavior gave them ample opportunity for criticism.[14]

AMERICAN VOICES OF DISSENT: CHESTER BOWLES, JOHN KENNETH GALBRAITH, MIKE MANSFIELD, AND GEORGE BALL

The press was not the first to question the American policy in Vietnam. Some of Kennedy's advisors came to similar conclusions to de Gaulle's and Macmillan's, urging a rethinking of the U.S. commitment in South Vietnam. Chester Bowles, John Kenneth Galbraith, Mike Mansfield, and George Ball moved beyond the paradigm of containment and falling dominoes. They provided a realistic assessment of the strategic importance of South Vietnam for the United States and regarded the current American policy there as being futile and misguided. These four important advisors urged an American disengagement and supported a political solution of neutralizing Vietnam.

As early as February 1961, then Undersecretary of State Bowles suggested neutrality as a possible solution for all of Southeast Asia.[15] A nonaligned Southeast Asia would allow the United States to move beyond the rigid confines of the SEATO treaty by enlisting broader international support for Washington's policy in Vietnam and preventing Ho Chi Minh from interfering in South Vietnamese affairs.[16] The proposal to neutralize Vietnam fell on deaf ears. Some members of the State Department even indicated that Bowles's proposition played into the hands of the Communists.[17]

After the Taylor-Rostow mission to Vietnam of October 1961, Bowles again introduced his idea of neutralization. According to Bowles, a deployment of U.S. ground troops would only result in "a full-blown war of unpredictable dimensions." The White House responded negatively to Bowles's suggestions.[18] Soon Bowles found himself removed from the inner circle of Kennedy's advisors through his "promotion" as special presidential representative for Asian, African, and Latin American affairs.[19] In this new capacity, Bowles continuously kept a close eye on Vietnam and, during 1962, disagreed even more vociferously with the administration's policy. Bowles was convinced that Ho Chi Minh was primarily driven by nationalistic goals and that his version of Communism was as independent from Moscow as that of Marshal Tito's in Yugoslavia. Bowles pointed out that Vietnam had struggled for centuries against the Chinese, and Ho now cleverly used the Sino-Soviet antagonism to get weapons from both sides but did not welcome any direct Chinese interference in his country.[20] Bowles urged his superiors to appreciate the complexity of the Vietnam situation and reassess U.S. policy in Vietnam. Bowles wrote to Kennedy in May 1962 after another visit to Southeast Asia: "If there ever was a need for an 'agonizing reappraisal,' it is here and now. This reappraisal must look far beyond counter-guerrilla tactics and fortified townships to the political factors which in the long run prove decisive. American history is replete with tragedies born of our failure to relate our military efforts to political objectives."[21] In order to restore peace, South Vietnam had to become truly independent and prosper economically, and its government had to respect the cultural, political, and religious differences of its peoples.[22] American support of South Vietnamese self-determination not only would make the U.S. presence in that country permissible but also assured the nations of Asia that the United States entertained no hegemonic ambitions in the area. This approach might facilitate an understanding with the Soviet Union on securing the neutrality of Southeast Asia, while also precluding any intervention in the region by the People's Republic of China (PRC).[23]

This time, the White House and Secretary of State Dean Rusk responded favorably to Bowles's proposal. Bowles refined his ideas for a "Peace Charter for Southeast Asia" in the summer of 1962. He concluded that fighting must cease immediately and that the entire region should then be neutralized under United Nations supervision, including the withdrawal of all foreign forces. Neutrality and territorial sovereignty should be guaranteed by the United States, Great Britain, France, the Soviet Union, China, India, Pakistan, and perhaps Japan, who were also to provide further economic and political aid to Southeast Asia.[24] Bowles's proposal reflected the basic British and French point of view, and they might have endorsed it. But the charter was soon dismissed by the State Department, which judged his initiative as being "unrealistic, impractical and premature."[25] Deeply disappointed, Bowles commented: "Our present course of action within a rigid political and military framework dominated by Diem is very likely to fail, and for this failure we may eventually be called upon to pay a heavy price, both in Asia and here at home."[26]

Kennedy was unwilling to consider neutralization because it might lead to the unification of Vietnam under a coalition government, which he equated with the loss of South Vietnam to the Communists. Washington could not perceive that a neutralized and perhaps socialist Vietnam might not affect the Cold War balance. Most importantly, Kennedy might have to face serious repercussions at home if he agreed to a negotiated settlement on Vietnam in adhering to the 1954 Geneva agreement.

John Kenneth Galbraith, who succeeded Bowles as ambassador to India in 1961, also regarded the growing American involvement in Vietnam as ineffective and self-defeating. The Harvard economist was chosen to facilitate better U.S. relations with India and its Prime Minister, Jawaharlal Nehru. From Delhi, Galbraith counseled Kennedy on economic questions, but the ambassador also expressed his views, sometimes on request by the president, on events in South Vietnam.[27] Galbraith viewed Vietnam with profound concern and maintained that President Diem had alienated his people "to a far greater extent than we allow ourselves to know." He argued that Washington's view was distorted because American policy makers only listened to the "ruler's account" and that of the American officials committed to Diem.[28]

Galbraith experienced conditions firsthand during a visit to South Vietnam in November 1961. Although Saigon appeared lively and bustling to Galbraith, it was a city "in a modified state of siege." American personnel were constantly accompanied by well-armed bodyguards, and most United States Operations Mission (USOM) members were stuck in Saigon proper. The military briefings disclosed an intriguing numbers game to the economics professor. About 15,000 opposition forces controlled many areas around Saigon, facing 250,000 Army of the Republic of Vietnam (ARVN) troops. Even more astonishing was the claim by an American officer that the Viet Cong had suffered seventeen thousand casualties in 1961. When questioned, the U.S. advisors could not account for these discrepancies. To Galbraith, the military briefing appeared clearly "as a clue to the state of things."[29] Kennedy should use caution in interpreting the military's statistics from Vietnam.

Politically, South Vietnam was "certainly a can of snakes," due mainly to President Diem. Galbraith maintained that the Vietnamese leader was far more concerned with preventing a coup against him than protecting his people

from the Viet Cong. The incompetence of local administrators, in addition
to the lack of centralized control over the ARVN and insufficient knowledge
about the moves of the opponent, made the situation even worse.[30]

Like Bowles's, Galbraith's assessment was disregarded. Nevertheless, the
ambassador urged Kennedy to reconsider current U.S. policy toward South
Vietnam:

> We are increasingly replacing the French as the colonial military force and will
> increasingly arouse the resentments associated therewith. Moreover, while I
> don't think the Russians are clever enough to fix it that way, we are surely play-
> ing their game. They couldn't be more pleased than to have us spend our billions
> in these distant jungles where it does us no good and them no harm. Incidentally,
> who is the man in your administration who decides what countries are strategic?
> . . . What strength do we gain from alliance with an incompetent government
> and a people who are so largely indifferent to their own salvation? . . . But it is
> the political poison that is really at issue. The Korean War killed us in the early
> 50's; this involvement could kill us now.[31]

Galbraith recommended that Kennedy resist demands to commit American
combat forces to Vietnam. Even a small deployment would lead to further engagement, while many South Vietnamese would eventually go "back to their
farms," leaving the actual fighting to the Americans. Kennedy should also
uphold civilian control in Saigon and most importantly "keep the door wide
open for any kind of political settlement." If Hanoi was giving "any indica-
tion to settle, we should jump at the chance."[32] Galbraith acknowledged that a
negotiated solution for Vietnam might result in strong criticism by American
conservatives and their press, but the alternative of growing involvement was
far more disconcerting.[33] According to Galbraith, the only feasible solution to
Vietnam was an international conference that enforced the Geneva Accords
of 1954. Otherwise, the United States would find itself in a "major, long
drawn-out, indecisive military involvement." Washington supported a weak,
ineffectual government in Vietnam and was in danger of replacing the French
as "the colonial force and bleed[ing] as the French did."[34]

Like Bowles, Galbraith was unable to convince the president to seek a political solution in South Vietnam. In response to the Galbraith memorandum,
the Joint Chiefs completely rejected the idea of negotiations because the
United States had already made "a well-known commitment to take a forth-
right stand against Communism in Southeast Asia." A reversal of American
policy would have "disastrous effects" not only in Southeast Asia but also for
American credibility around the globe. However, the voices of dissent were
not completely without impact. In 1962, Kennedy authorized Averell Harriman to talk privately with the North Vietnamese foreign secretary during

the Laos conference in Geneva, but Harriman received no positive feedback. Since North Vietnam was not interested in a negotiated settlement, Kennedy sided again with the majority view of his advisors to pursue the military campaign against Communism in Vietnam.[35]

Another voice of caution was that of Senator Mike Mansfield. As a member of both the House and subsequently the Senate, Mansfield established himself as an expert on Asia. In 1953, Mansfield and Kennedy were invited to meet fellow Catholic and promising leader Diem. Both senators were impressed by the Vietnamese politician. Like Kennedy, Mansfield endorsed Eisenhower's Indochina policy.[36] The French defeat at Dien Bien Phu dismayed Mansfield, and he partly blamed Eisenhower's indecisiveness in providing additional support to the French as one of the reasons for their defeat.[37]

Mansfield drew a different conclusion from the French loss than most of Washington's policy makers. He believed that freedom in Southeast Asia could only be preserved by the effort and determination of its peoples. The United States should not perpetuate colonialism by any power but rather support indigenous governments that truly represented their people. Any military alliance for Southeast Asia should be primarily composed of Asian, not Western, nations. Conflicts in Southeast Asia, Mansfield maintained, needed to be solved by the United Nations and not the United States.[38]

Mansfield's assessment in 1954 defined the core of the senator's view on Southeast Asia for the next twenty years. He persistently abided by his own 1954 recommendation, the exception being his vote for the Tonkin Gulf Resolution ten years later. In 1954, and later, Mansfield opposed American intervention in Southeast Asia because he feared it would lead to another major, even world, war:

> I was never in favor of intervention; and I am opposed to it now. I think it would be suicidal. I think the worst thing that could happen to the United States would be to have our forces intervene in Indochina and then bog down in the jungles there. For in that case we think there would be war in Indochina, but also war in Korea, and a third world war would commence in Asia, and no doubt would involve the countries of Europe.[39]

Until 1960, Mansfield strongly supported Diem, whom he regarded as a savior of his country offering an Asian solution to the problems at hand. But the senator increasingly disagreed with the American strategy in South Vietnam and conveyed his concerns to Kennedy in September 1961. Instead of increasing military assistance or even deploying U.S. combat troops, Mansfield suggested that Washington win the goodwill of the Vietnamese people. He argued that the difficulties in South Vietnam were a result of the severe lack of morale of its people; hence Washington needed to foster greater unity and purpose in the fight against Communism.[40] Unlike Bowles and Galbraith, the senator was not yet ready to write South Vietnam off. However, the South Vietnamese not only had to prove their determination to stand up to the Communists but also needed to do the actual fighting:

> While Vietnam is very important, we cannot hope to substitute armed power for the kind of political, economic, and social changes that offer the best resistance to Communism. If the necessary reforms have not been forthcoming over the past seven years to stop communist subversion and rebellion, then I do not see how Americans combat troops can do it today. I wholeheartedly favor, if necessary and feasible, a substantial increase of American military and economic aid to Vietnam, but leave the responsibility of carrying the physical burden of meeting communist infiltration, subversion, and attack on the shoulders of the South Vietnamese, whose country it is and whose future is their chief responsibility.[41]

Mansfield was the original proponent of "Vietnamization," the policy later adopted by President Nixon. This was not America's war to fight. In a commencement address at Michigan State in 1962, Mansfield deplored Washington's move toward a broader, more dangerous commitment in Vietnam. American ground troops might only lead to a prolonged and costly conflict. Mansfield maintained that the United States should employ the services of the United Nations and also engage SEATO to find a diplomatic solution for Vietnam, using the neutralization accord for Laos as a model.[42]

With numerous reports of progress in South Vietnam during 1962 reaching the United States, it was politically unwise for Mansfield and other Democratic skeptics of America's Vietnam policy in Congress to mount any opposition to Kennedy's course. Nevertheless, they maintained doubts about the constitutionality of a growing involvement in Southeast Asia. Ultimately, Mansfield and his colleagues deferred any action because they accepted the executive's prime authority in foreign policy.[43] Challenging the president on Vietnam would backfire politically, and given the crises over Berlin and Cuba, the great majority of Americans would probably not understand, even less follow, the suggestions of a handful of senators.

In late 1962, at Kennedy's request, Mansfield visited Vietnam for the third time. While there, his doubts about actual progress against the Viet Cong and regarding Diem's leadership ability were confirmed. On arrival, he was briefed by Ambassador Frederick Nolting, who depicted the situation as improving and maintained that the United States provided sufficient means to facilitate an ARVN victory against the Communists. A meeting with President Diem was even more unproductive in the eyes of the senator. But Mansfield was looking for other opinions as well and found them in American reporters stationed in Saigon. The journalists gave Mansfield a far less optimistic briefing on the realities in South Vietnam, explaining that victory was more elusive than ever.[44]

Upon his return to Washington, Mansfield filed two reports: one for the public and a private one for the president. The public report criticized Diem's leadership but reaffirmed the American commitment to the country.[45] The confidential assessment was much more pessimistic. Mansfield disagreed with official estimates that the rural South Vietnamese could be won over within a year through a strategic hamlet program. It would take additional American aid, responsive Vietnamese leadership, and years of patient work to stifle Viet Cong support in the countryside. While Diem still possessed leadership potential, his abilities were increasingly undermined by the influence of his power-hungry brother, Ngo Diem Nhu. Despite these difficulties, the senator saw a good chance for success with Kennedy's Vietnam program, provided the situation in South Vietnam did not change dramatically.

Mansfield adamantly opposed a larger American military commitment and argued that the United States should continue its support but not go beyond the position of helping the Vietnamese help themselves:

> To ignore that reality will not only be immensely costly in terms of American lives and resources but also might draw us inexorably into some variation of the unenviable position in Vietnam which was formerly occupied by the French. We are not, of course, at that point at this time. But the great increase in American commitment this year has tended to point us in that general direction and we may well begin to slide rapidly toward it if any of the present remedies begin to falter in practice.[46]

Kennedy discussed the report with Mansfield, and while displeased with the senator's assessment, the president in fact shared some of the senator's concerns. Yet, to the Kennedy administration, a diplomatic solution as recommended by Mansfield was not a viable political option. Neutralization of Vietnam would only facilitate a Communist takeover. Moreover, another fact-finding mission by Roger Hilsman and Mike Forrestal convinced Kennedy that the United States was probably winning but more slowly than expected.[47]

In August 1963, Mansfield tried one more time to warn the president against further escalation in Vietnam. The senator was wary of the dangers of U.S. involvement and believed that Kennedy was coming closer to a point of no return that might result in a conflict of at least Korean proportions. Like Bowles and Galbraith, Mansfield argued that Washington needed to reevaluate its vital security and global interests. He argued that the importance of Vietnam had been overemphasized in the past, placing it at the core of American foreign policy making, while, in fact, it was only of peripheral significance to the United States.[48] Therefore, any unilateral engagement in South Vietnam was self-defeating and might only do more damage than good. Again, the senator's concerns were not fully heeded by the president.[49]

Mansfield was shocked by Diem's assassination and even more so when Kennedy suffered the same fate three weeks later. The death of Diem and the growing American involvement in the quagmire of Vietnam reinforced Mansfield's conviction that the United States was pursuing a policy that was not only futile and costly but also damaging to the country's essential interests. He remained a voice of reason and caution during the following decade.

Undersecretary of State George Ball was not an expert on Southeast Asia as he had focused for most of his life on foreign policy in Europe, particularly France. In Europe, he became a close friend of Jean Monnet, the inspirational force behind European integration, and learned to appreciate the French point of view on international politics that influenced Ball's thinking on Vietnam.[50] Ball was initially uncertain about Kennedy's views on foreign policy. He soon appreciated the president's intelligence and pragmatism but noted that Kennedy often lacked a long-term vision of a particular policy.[51] In the fall of 1961, Ball replaced Bowles as undersecretary of state and hence had to expand his field of expertise. Vietnam was one of the problems placed on Ball's desk.[52] As a result of both the Korean War and the French debacle in Indochina, Ball concluded that the United States should "rigorously avoid land wars in Asia." He advised Kennedy along these lines on Laos and urged the president not to overcommit American forces in needless conflicts in Asia.[53]

In South Vietnam, according to Ball, the situation was both serious and hopeless. Ball was rather bewildered by his colleagues' views on Vietnam because they lacked any profound historical knowledge about that country. Their estimates echoed what he had heard in France ten years earlier: a better coordinated effort, additional money, and more troops would eventually pay off.[54] Ball was dismayed by the findings of the 1961 Taylor-Rostow mission and completely disagreed with their recommendations. He expressed his concerns to Secretary of Defense Robert McNamara, pointing out that committing combat forces would lead to a "protracted conflict more serious than Korea" for the United States. The French had learned the hard way about the toughness of the Vietnamese opponent, and unlike Korea, the task in Vietnam was not one of simply repelling an invasion but rather defusing a revolutionary situation in which any Western involvement might be equated to some form of colonialism. McNamara did not share Ball's point of view and endorsed the Taylor-Rostow report.

A few days later, McNamara changed his mind about troop deployments and partly concurred with Ball's position. To send U.S. forces without a greater Vietnamese effort was unwise, as American soldiers obviously "could not accomplish their mission in the midst of an apathetic or hostile population."[55] Ball conveyed his misgivings about the American Vietnam strategy to Kennedy, indicating that any deployment of U.S. combat troops would be a "tragic error." Once troops were committed, the process could not be reversed and might lead to a futile and costly war: "Within five years we'll have three hundred thousand men in the paddies and jungles and never find them again. That was the French experience. Vietnam is the worst possible terrain both from a physical and political point of view."[56] Kennedy did not appreciate Ball's argument, calling it "crazy." The predicted escalation was simply not "going to happen." Perhaps the president was impressed by Ball's argument after all, since he decided against combat deployments a few days later.[57]

The rebuke by Kennedy signaled to Ball that his advice was neither heeded nor desired, and he focused on policy matters where he could make his "influence effectively felt." He probably remembered the fate of his predecessor, Bowles. While harboring doubts in private, Ball remained loyal to the president in public. In an April 1962 speech, Ball completely endorsed America's course in Vietnam, calling a potential loss of South Vietnam an event of "tragic significance" for the West in Asia. He added that failure to assist South Vietnam would have severe repercussions around the world and serve only to further encourage Communist aggression: "How we act in Viet-Nam will have its impact on Communist actions in Europe, in Africa and in Latin America. Far from easing tensions, our unwillingness to meet our commitments in one tension area will simply encourage the Communists to bestir one in another." The struggle in Vietnam could not be solved overnight, and it would take years of effort but it was a "task that we must stay until it is concluded."[58] When some of the press interpreted the speech as an irrevocable commitment to Vietnam, the White House was enraged. Ball had seemingly gone from one extreme to the other.[59]

Ball also played an important role in sanctioning the November 1963 coup against Diem by endorsing two telegrams by Ambassador Henry Cabot Lodge, who had replaced Nolting, recommending the replacement of Diem. Ball was certainly not the final authority to give a green light to the overthrow of Diem, but as did his superiors, he shared responsibility in American acquiescence to the coup against the South Vietnamese leader.[60] Ball denied any responsibility for the military putsch and maintained that the August telegram had not triggered the overthrow of Diem. He regarded the events of early November as being an entirely Vietnamese operation.[61] The facts proved otherwise. Nevertheless, Ball's account serves as an important example of the way he and other officials tried to reconcile their profound concerns about developments in Vietnam during a time when "dominoes" and "containment" dominated American thinking. Ball was much more outspoken against the American policy in Vietnam during the Johnson administration and more willing to confront that president than others. But, then too, he found it difficult to balance his personal convictions on Vietnam with his loyalty to the president. Ball's ambition to play an important role in American foreign politics further complicated his convictions.

The voices of dissent reinforced and reflected the concerns Kennedy heard from Paris and London. While the Europeans' advice might be discarded because of their colonial past or parochial views, the unwillingness of Kennedy to consider the opinions of skeptics within his own administration indicates that the president was troubled about any domestic fallout from Vietnam and trusted his immediate counsel that the American strategy in Vietnam would succeed.

CONTINUOUS COMMITMENT TO VIETNAM

The coup against Diem in November 1963 was a turning point in American policy making on Vietnam. The U.S. decision to sanction the coup manifested the failure of previous efforts at improving the situation in Saigon. The summer 1963 Buddhist crisis revealed the bankruptcy of the Diem regime and brought South Vietnam into the limelight of both the American and European media. Diem remained unyielding to demands of religious freedom and claimed that the Buddhist protest was sparked by the Viet Cong. In June 1963, the media coverage of the self-immolation of a Buddhist monk in Saigon, and the subsequent suppression of Buddhist rallies by Diem, aroused world opinion and unified opposition to Diem in South Vietnam.[62]

Kennedy warned Diem that the treatment of the Buddhists was unacceptable and, unless the situation improved, the United States would dissociate itself from Diem. Kennedy authorized American personnel in Saigon to talk to dissident South Vietnamese military leaders. Between late August and September 1963, American pressure mounted on Diem to dispose of his brother and adopt a program of political reform.[63] Though the administration had second thoughts about a possible coup, the president and most of his counsel remained determined not to pull out of Vietnam since a withdrawal would ultimately result in a Communist takeover in Southeast Asia. Kennedy publicly confirmed his belief in the "domino theory" during a NBC television interview in September: "I think the struggle is close enough. China is so large, looms so high just beyond the frontier, that if South Vietnam went, it would not only give them an improved geographic position for a guerrilla assault on Malaya, but would give the impression that the wave of the future in Southeast Asia was China and the Communists."[64] A week earlier, the president explained in a CBS interview that the Vietnamese were the "ones who have to win it or lose it." Yet, he immediately contradicted this statement by pointing out that it would be a "great mistake" for the United States to withdraw and hinted that a change in "policy, and perhaps with personnel," might increase the chances of success in South Vietnam, signaling to Diem that time was running out.[65]

A fact-finding mission by Taylor and McNamara indicated that further military progress had been made against the Viet Cong but regarded Diem as the major obstacle in political reform.[66] While Kennedy opposed a coup for the time being, events in Saigon progressed precisely toward that end. The American ultimatum on Diem was interpreted as a sign of support for Vietnamese military leaders to go ahead with their plans to oust Diem. Washington made no move to thwart such action, nor did the embassy or the CIA team in Saigon.[67] On November 1, 1963, Ngo Dinh Diem and his brother Nhu were overthrown in a military coup and killed the next day. Kennedy was dismayed and deeply shocked when he heard about Diem's murder, although he was fully aware of a planned coup.[68] "To bear any burden, pay any price" had come to a tragic first conclusion in South Vietnam. Only three weeks later Kennedy, too, paid the ultimate price.

Why did Kennedy disregard the advice of both members of his administration and foreign leaders, as well as his own assessment of the challenges in Vietnam of almost a decade earlier? First of all, there is Kennedy's view that by backing Diem he was helping a government that offered a real alternative to Communism and, with American assistance, would succeed in the process of nation building.[69] Robert Kennedy later admitted that this faith in both Diem and the American ability to build a viable government in South Vietnam was misguided. The younger Kennedy acknowledged his initial support of the policy in Vietnam during his brother's presidency. But shortly before his own death in 1968, he wrote that it was perhaps "never really possible to bring all the people of South Vietnam under the rule of the successive governments we supported."[70]

Second, Kennedy's own campaign proposal to stand firm against Communism might have trapped him in the growing Vietnam quagmire. He had accused the Eisenhower administration of not doing enough to contain Communism. Kennedy pointed to the "loss of China" as American failure to prevent Communist victory leading to even more dangers in the global struggle to secure freedom. As president, Kennedy was unwilling to risk similar domestic criticism and refused to disengage from South Vietnam. In addition, the neutralization of Laos made it necessary in the eyes of the administration to hold firm in South Vietnam to prevent further Communist successes in Southeast Asia. Although Kennedy was determined to hold South Vietnam, he persistently rejected a major commitment of U.S. ground troops.[71]

Finally, Kennedy's Vietnam policy was affected by an inability to completely and realistically assess the situation in Saigon. As McNamara pointed out, the administration was seldom satisfied with information received from Vietnam, which led to frequent fact-finding missions and consultations with senior officials in Saigon. Even these missions resulted in an overly optimistic assessment on the progress made in South Vietnam. Part of the blame rested with the South Vietnamese who gave inaccurate information to the Americans, hoping that their reports depicted what the U.S. government wished to hear. On the American side, military commanders and many politicians alike misunderstood the nature of the conflict by viewing it solely in terms of the Cold War, the containment of Communism, and the resulting global commitments of the United States.[72]

The luxury of hindsight and the views of those critical to the American engagement in Vietnam from 1961 to 1963 offered alternative approaches, particularly negotiation with the Viet Cong, or even Hanoi. But throughout his presidency, Kennedy rejected both negotiations and a reduced commitment because he believed that American assistance could actually tip the balance in favor of the West. Political pressure at home made it nearly impossible to abandon South Vietnam.[73]

Public opinion polls and the media generally supported the president's view. Soviet gains in space technology, the alleged missile gap, and Communist activities in the third world created a sentiment affirming the global American commitment to resist Communist aggression. Up to the second half of the 1960s, most Americans favored an interventionist role by the United States, although the great majority was rather uninformed about the war in Vietnam.[74] With few exceptions, the media also regarded Vietnam in the context of the larger Cold War struggle against Communism. Most journalists condoned the coup against Diem and focused on the general relief expressed by most Vietnamese over the "fall of the House of Ngo."[75] Journalists revealed that pressure from Washington, despite official disclaimers of any responsibility, "had effectively encouraged the overthrow of the Diem regime." The overall tenor of the press reaction to the coup was not shock about the death of Diem but rather whether Communism could be defeated in Vietnam:

> In the last analysis, though, the success or failure of U.S. policy toward South Viet Nam will have to be judged on pragmatic grounds. The aim of that policy is to speed a successful end to the war against the Communists. To achieve that, the U.S. is now clearly committed to back General Minh with even more money, and if necessary even more American lives. If it works, if Minh does

manage better than Diem, if the U.S. is thereby enabled to pull out of Vietnam sooner, then the policy will be a triumph. But these are a lot of ifs. And if they turn sour, the outcome could affect the cold war balance and U.S. political life for a long while to come.[76]

Senator Mansfield and a number of journalists believed that Kennedy was preparing to change course in Vietnam, or was at least doubtful about current strategy, and that he might have accepted a negotiated settlement after the 1964 presidential elections.[77] Information coming from Saigon and the critical assessments of French President de Gaulle, British Prime Minister Macmillan, and various American advisors might have caused considerable doubt about the American commitment to South Vietnam. However, Kennedy made no effort to modify his policy but hinted that he would consider a reassessment after he was reelected in 1964. He never seriously considered a withdrawal from South Vietnam but continued to pursue the avowed objective of training the South Vietnamese to defend themselves against Communist aggression. Rusk summarized Kennedy's position:

> We took for granted that the United States had a treaty commitment to South Vietnam and that South Vietnam's security was important to the security of the United States. We also took for granted that if we failed "to take steps to meet the common danger," our network of collective security treaties throughout the world might erode through a judgment made by the Communists that these treaties were a bluff. At no time did we say to ourselves, "We will put in X number of men but no more. If the other side continues to escalate, then we'll just pull out." At no time did we think that the American people would not support an effort to prevent Southeast Asia from going Communist.[78]

Chapter 2

France and Indochina

For France, the year 1940 marked more than four hundred years as a colonial power. But the same year brought national humiliation with the German invasion of most of France. The German conquest made the maintenance of the French Empire extremely important to French leaders, be that the Vichy government of Marshal Henri Petain or the Free French under General Charles de Gaulle.[1] For France, her colonial acquisitions and speed of conquest during the nineteenth century clearly related to the country's strategic standing in Europe. In times of relative weakness, colonies gained in importance. The occupation of Tonkin, the nucleus for Indochina, in June 1885 was no exception. Jules Ferry, French foreign minister and prime minister in 1881 and 1885, addressed France's diminished position in Europe, resulting from her defeat in the Franco-Prussian War in 1871 and German Chancellor Otto von Bismarck's alliance policies that isolated France internationally. In order to restore French greatness, or *grandeur*, "it was up to the republic to erase the stigma of defeat first by safeguarding and then by enlarging the fields of French expansion outside of Europe."[2] Africa and Asia increasingly took center stage of European attention for both economic and strategic reasons. Therefore, it was in the vital interest of France to acquire colonies in Africa and Southeast Asia. As Ferry told the Chamber of Deputies in 1885, for France not to play the role of colonial power would mean an abdication of France's standing as a great power. Ferry admonished opponents of his policy of "self-extension," unable to believe they would willingly relinquish France's great power status: "Say that you want a France that is great in everything . . . a great country exercising her influence on the destiny of Europe; and that she should extend that influence around the world and carry everywhere possible her language, her mores, her flag, her arms, and her genius."[3] In addition to the necessity of colonies as a constituent element of

French *grandeur*, politicians from the late nineteenth century to the 1930's emphasized France's mission to export her "superior" civilization. In 1931, Albert Sarraut, who had extensive experience as minister within the French Empire and government, argued that French leadership was needed more than ever to guide and elevate the indigenous populations in Africa and Asia. The colonies were viewed not as regions to be exploited but rather as "integral parts of the French state, which through scientific, economic, moral, and political progress, are going to be encouraged to accede to the highest destinies."[4] In language that forecast later speeches of General de Gaulle, Sarraut exclaimed that "France does not oppress, she liberates; she does not exhaust, she enriches; she does not exploit, she shares."[5] This sentiment also shaped the French desire to maintain her colonial empire after 1945. Yet, in Indochina, and Vietnam in particular, French justification for her colonial rule increasingly met with resistance.

FRANCE IN INDOCHINA

As a country, Vietnam is at least as old as France, as Vietnamese recorded history dates back to 208 BCE. Its early history was dominated by the Chinese, who brought their institutions and Confucianism to Vietnam. Although Vietnam incorporated many Chinese customs, its people refused political assimilation into the Chinese Empire. For centuries, the Vietnamese rebelled against Chinese rule. These efforts ultimately led to Vietnamese independence in 939 CE. A subsequent effort to bring the Vietnamese under the direct control of the Dragon Throne failed due to ferocious resistance led by Le Loi in 1428, a wealthy landowner, who became Vietnam's greatest emperor.[6]

The first Europeans to come to Vietnam were Portuguese traders in 1535, followed by Catholic missionaries who left a deep imprint on Vietnam. But it was civil war in Vietnam, begun in 1613, that brought Vietnam to the attention of France. Missionaries and then traders showed increasing interest in the country's resources. The country was again unified under Emperor Nguyen Anh in 1802. For some decades, Vietnam resisted French encroachment, but in 1862, the French seized Saigon and forced Vietnam to cede the surrounding three provinces in the Mekong Delta. The next year, France established a protectorate over Cambodia. During the early 1880s, the French undertook the conquest of northern Vietnam. Despite Chinese help, the Vietnamese were defeated, and, by 1885, the French conquest of Vietnam was complete. The country was divided into two protectorates: Tonkin and Annam, and one colony: Cochinchina, in southern Vietnam.[7] In 1887, France created the

Indochinese Union comprising Vietnam and Laos and, in 1893, included Cambodia into the union.

Yet, French rule immediately met with resistance. Confucian scholar Phan Dinh Phung set an ominous example by launching a guerrilla struggle against the French. His efforts had failed by 1896 but set a striking example for other Vietnamese to follow.[8] During the 1920s, opposition to French rule spread from the Vietnamese elite to larger parts of the population. The decade also witnessed the formation of the Vietnamese National Party and the Vietnamese Revolutionary Youth League (RYL), led by Nguyen Ai Quoc, better known as Ho Chi Minh. The RYL split in 1929 and was replaced the next year by Ho Chi Minh's Indochinese Communist Party (ICP). France forcefully repressed any opposition and persecuted the Vietnamese National Party with a vengeance after they assassinated a French official.[9]

Although French repression succeeded in crushing Vietnamese resistance to colonial rule during the first decades of the twentieth century, the method of French administration in Indochina sowed the seeds for future disaster. Colonies were a means to achieve French *grandeur* and, beside economic interest, also a means to spread French civilization. Therefore, Indochina, as well as other French colonies in Africa, was ruled directly from Paris. Further, the French civilizing mission resulted in French education locally and, for qualified students, the opportunity to study at universities in France. As a result, French republican ideals reminded indigenous students of their own lack of political rights and resultant inferior status.

French centralized rule was also expensive. By the mid-1920s, Indochina had as many French officials as it took Britain to administer the vastly larger India. Most French officials had little knowledge of local culture and customs, and did not speak indigenous languages. The result of these shortcomings was a vast gap between rulers and ruled.[10]

WORLD WAR II AND THE CHALLENGE TO *GRANDEUR* IN INDOCHINA

Of course, France had no intention to relinquish what it regarded as part of greater France. After the Nazi Germany invasion of 1940, the question arose whether the colonies were indeed part of France and subject to the terms of the armistice concluded with Germany. Marshal Petain and his Vichy government accepted that the colonies were subject to the armistice stipulations. However, de Gaulle, the emerging leader of the Free French, adamantly insisted that the colonies had not been conquered and were therefore still free

French territory. Consequently, the struggle against Nazi Germany should continue from the French colonies. Most colonial administrators, though, remained loyal to Petain, and hence colonial policy was tightly controlled by the Germans.[11] Yet, de Gaulle's position inherently enhanced the status of the overseas possessions, affirming that they were vital for ultimate French victory and the restoration of her *grandeur*. The question, then, for de Gaulle was whether the colonies would be willing to contribute to this grand design while their peoples remained relegated to an inferior status.

After 1940, most colonies, including Indochina, remained loyal to the Vichy government. By then, Indochina found itself besieged by the Japanese Empire. Governor-General Georges Catroux attempted to accommodate Japan by cutting off supplies to China and, as a result of his cooperation with Japan, was dismissed in June 1940. Catroux's replacement, Vice Admiral Jean Decoux, tried to maintain the independence of Indochina from Japanese encroachment while simultaneously repressing with force any Vietnamese opposition to French rule.[12] Decoux nevertheless tried to win indigenous support against the Japanese, to whom the Japanese slogan "Asia for Asians" was obviously appealing. The vice admiral reversed previous policies by encouraging expressions of Vietnamese nationalism, yet his efforts in resisting Japanese aggression were ultimately unsuccessful.[13] In July 1941, Decoux received orders from Vichy to accommodate Tokyo by signing an agreement giving Japan the right to station troops in Tonkin. Both France and Japan were to provide for the common defense of Indochina. While the "Protocol Concerning Joint Defense" allowed France to retain de jure sovereignty over Indochina, it established de facto Japanese control in Indochina. This semblance of French sovereignty ended with the Japanese takeover in March 1945. Even as France was liberated and de Gaulle returned to Paris in August 1944, the future of Indochina as a French colony was more dubious than ever before.[14]

In 1945, the sustainability of France's colonial possession in Indochina also faced another challenge, with U.S. President Franklin D. Roosevelt's design for postwar Asia. Since the early 1940s, President Roosevelt doubted that Indochina should be returned to France and disregarded French claims to sovereignty over the colonies in Southeast Asia. Instead, Roosevelt envisioned a trusteeship under the United Nations and ultimately some form of self-determination as envisioned in the Atlantic Charter. Of course, his statements gave great hope to Ho Chi Minh and his Viet Minh.[15] De Gaulle quickly recognized Washington's opposition to the continuation of French control over her colonies. In response, de Gaulle and the Free French attempted to recast the colonies in a new liberal light. This strategy resulted in the Brazzaville Declaration of 1944.

A "NEW" APPROACH TO FRENCH EMPIRE

By 1944, the Free French had regained control over most of France's colonies from the Vichy regime with the exception of Japanese-controlled Indochina. Regaining the colonial empire was of great importance to de Gaulle in order to enhance the standing of metropolitan France. De Gaulle regarded the colonies as an extension and a manifestation of France's *grandeur* and not surprisingly reacted to the concept of self-determination of the Atlantic Charter with "distinct coolness."[16] Yet, in order to reclaim all her colonies, France had to present herself as a responsible, liberal colonial power that would grant autonomy and perhaps ultimate independence to most of her overseas possessions. In late January 1944, French colonial administrators met in Brazzaville, the French Congo, to discuss colonial reform. From the beginning, it was clear that the conference also served French propaganda purposes. One delegate argued, "Do I need to draw attention to the terms of the Atlantic Charter? While all around are rethinking the colonial world, France cannot afford to remain silent or absent. It is only just that, following the deeds and declarations of the Americans, the South Africans, and the Australians, France should also make itself heard, and act."[17] The conference focused mainly on further economic and political development of France's African colonies, but its resolutions affected Indochina as well. The results were mixed and forecast problems for France in the future. On the one hand, consensus was reached at the conference that indigenous people should have a greater say in political and economic policies, that the standards of living should be raised, and that economic productivity should be increased. The conference even called for a colonial parliament, or federal assembly, to respect "the life and local freedom of each of the territories" of the French Federation (since 1946 rechristened French Union). On the other hand, Brazzaville rejected autonomy and, as de Gaulle suggested in his opening remarks, French sovereignty of its overseas possessions should be reaffirmed. While the Brazzaville Declaration called for greater rights of the indigenous peoples, it was also abundantly clear that Paris would remain in control. Yet, many indigenous people regarded the limited concessions at Brazzaville as a first step to complete local autonomy. This was definitely the case in the colony France regarded as its most economically profitable and one of her crown jewels—Indochina.

GRANDEUR VERSUS VIETNAMESE NATIONALISM

Since 1940, in Indochina, Ho Chi Minh and his ICP sought allies in their opposition to both French colonial rule and the Japanese occupiers. In May

1941, the party established the Viet Nam Doc Lap Dong Minh, or the League for the Independence of Vietnam, better known as Viet Minh. While Ho did not abandon his ultimate goal of a socialist society, the liberation and independence of Vietnam were of even greater importance. Hence, Ho evoked strong patriotic language to gain the support of the Vietnamese people and also win sympathy from the Allied powers.[18] However, if the Allies supported a French return to power in Vietnam, then the Viet Minh had to continue the fight for the country's liberation alone, regardless of the costs.

The French Provisional Government (GPRF) was shocked by the complete Japanese takeover of Indochina on March 9, 1945, which ended any semblance of French rule in the colony. Even more disconcerting was that Emperor Bao Dai of Annam (Vietnam) on March 11, King Norodom Sihanouk of Cambodia on March 13, and King Sisavang Vong of Luang Prabang (Laos) on April 8, 1945, proclaimed the independence of their countries. By mid-April, Bao Dai had assembled his cabinet, led by Tra Trong Kim.[19]

French dismay over the events in Indochina was partly the result of Vichy Governor-General Decoux's policies, providing little information to the provisional government. Since 1944, however, the GPRF tried to gain greater insight and control over Indochina by engaging both indigenous groups and ranking officers under Decoux's command. A fact-finding mission led by François de Langlade, secretary-general of the Committee on Indochina, to Tonkin provided Paris with a clear intelligence picture of the political groups in Vietnam. Langlade described the Viet Minh as the most anti-French group and also recognized that its leader Ho Chi Minh was the previously suspected insurgent leader Nguyen Ai Quoc. Langlade described the Viet Minh as follows: "In principle this group is made up of Annamites and nationalists . . . but in reality this is the Communist Party with a nationalist label attached in order to attract and assemble the greatest number of members possible."[20] Léon Pignon, head of the Indochina division, refused to consider autonomy for any part of Indochina. Yet, in reality, French sovereignty in Indochina was extremely fragile. Even before the Japanese takeover, indigenous resistance and external opposition from the United States challenged French rule. The French government's Indochina division under Pignon, along with the father of the Brazzaville Conference Henri Laurentie, worked hard to formulate a policy for Indochina that would both allow the continuation of French sovereignty in Indochina and also appease Washington.

The result was the Declaration on Indochina of March 1945. Like the Brazzaville Declaration, it was a mix of promises of greater autonomy as well as an assertion of sovereignty in Indochina.[21] The declaration affirmed the existence of the Indochinese Federation, which was to become a vital part of the future French Union. The Indochinese Federation consisted of the five distinct regions of Laos, Cambodia, Tonkin, Annam, and Cochinchina, comprising some twenty-five million people. France promised citizenship to the Indochinese both in their respective states and in the French Union. As citizens, they could hold local and federal colonial government positions and represent Indochina within the French Union. Indochina would receive its own government, headed by a powerful governor-general, who was appointed by the French president, and a council of ministers. The ministers were chosen from the ranks of the Indochinese and resident French population by the governor and were responsible to him. In addition, the declaration called for a Council of the State, consisting of high-ranking officials, to draft laws and regulations. Last, an assembly should be elected with the power to debate laws, to vote for a budget, impose taxes, and regulate commercial relations within the Indochinese Federation. A list of civil liberties granting freedom of press, assembly, thought, and religion was included as well. Finally, the declaration followed the Brazzaville postulations of economic, social, cultural, and educational improvements.[22]

The declaration faced immediate criticism, most of it coming from the Indochinese themselves. Based on their long experience with Paris, most Indochinese wondered whether the French would this time honor their promises. People also questioned what kind of guarantees a provisional French government in Paris could provide, just weeks after the Japanese had ousted French authorities in Indochina and when World War II had not yet even ended. Three other important points were raised as well. First, commentators pointed to the problem of how a federation within a federation could possibly work. As Nguyen Quoc Dinh succinctly put it, "The formation of the French Union, the keystone of tomorrow's French imperial system, seems to have been conceived with the aim of finding a compromise between two apparently contradictory principles: the *freedom* of Indochina, which is apparently to be recognized, and the *unity* of the Empire, which is equally fundamental."[23] The answer was, of course, that the French Provisional Government and General de Gaulle, in particular, did not intend to grant full freedom to Indochina. This was obvious in the almost dictatorial powers granted to the governor-general of the new Indochinese Federation—the second point of criticism raised by opponents. Last, and equally important, was the proposed permanent division of Indochina into five regions, denying Vietnamese unity. For many Vietnamese, this was unacceptable, regardless of party affiliation. Further, following the declaration of independence by Emperor Bao Dai, Vietnam as a state already existed for many Indochinese. Although the emperor had acted on Japanese orders, it was obvious to both French and Vietnamese that French sovereignty had to be reestablished before any Indochinese Federation could be created.[24]

The French government was fully aware of opposing views to its Indochinese proclamation and knew they lacked the economic and military means to implement their plan for Indochina. Internationally, the French Provisional Government lacked any substantial support for its colonial policies. Of the Big Three—the United States, Great Britain, and the Soviet Union—only Britain expressed some empathy toward the French design in Indochina. Captain Paul Mus, a leading expert and scholar on Indochina, reported that France's chances of regaining sovereignty of Indochina were bleak. Even the Indochinese "masses" were now sufficiently educated to prevent a return to the status quo in Indochina of 1940. France had to put forth a convincing strategy to its allies in order to regain its position in Southeast Asia.[25]

The first effort by the provisional government was to talk with opposition groups in order to reach a compromise. The most important was the Viet Minh. An initial contact between Jean Roger, known by the code name Sainteny, and the Viet Minh in May 1945 indicated that the Viet Minh might be willing to help France oust the Japanese and raised hopes of future cooperation. Yet, by July 1945, the Viet Minh position hardened, insisting on complete independence for Indochina.[26] Concurrently, the Viet Minh increased its guerrilla actions against the Kim government of Emperor Bao Dai and the Japanese occupiers. Most importantly, the Viet Minh found help from the American Office of Strategic Services (OSS). While the Viet Minh needed modern weaponry, the OSS needed information about Japanese military moves, and to some extent both received what they hoped for.[27]

International events seemed to further undermine French hopes of regaining control in Indochina during July and August 1945. On July 23, the Big Three decided at Potsdam to divide Indochina at the sixteenth parallel to facilitate Japanese surrender. The North would be occupied by China and the South by Great Britain. On August 14, 1945, the empire of Japan surrendered to Allied forces, and two days later, Japan handed control of Vietnam to Bao Dai's government. The Viet Minh called for an immediate uprising of the Vietnamese people. On August 18, the Viet Minh seized the main government offices in Hanoi. Prime Minister Kim resigned on August 22, and three days later a new government, led by Ho Chi Minh, was installed. Emperor Bao Dai abdicated three days later.[28]

On September 2, Ho Chi Minh declared the independence of the Democratic Republic of Vietnam (DRV). Ho appealed to the allies to recognize Vietnamese freedom and independence after eighty years of oppressive French rule: "Vietnam has the right to enjoy freedom and independence and in fact has become a free and independent country. The entire Vietnamese people are determined to mobilize all their physical and mental strength, to sacrifice their lives and property in order to safeguard their freedom and independence."[29]

Within a month, fighting erupted in the South. British General Douglas Gracey refused to hand over authority to the provisional Committee of the South, consisting of Viet Minh representatives and other anti-French groups. After deadly riots initiated by French residents on September 23 and subsequent Vietnamese retaliation, Gracey, along with French troops just released from Japanese captivity, chased the Vietnamese resistance out of Saigon. In early October, the French returned to Saigon under the command of General Philippe Leclerc. General Gracey quickly granted Leclerc de facto control over Cochinchina. Desperate, the Viet Minh attacked French forces on October 10 but were far too undermanned and underpowered to succeed. Soon they were either arrested or forced to flee into the jungle, where Viet Minh forces and their supporters retained an advantage over French troops. On October 30, 1945, the new high commissioner for Indochina, General Thierry d'Argenlieu, appointed by de Gaulle in August, arrived in Saigon. His first order was to assume full legislative and executive powers in the South. Thus, by the end of the year, Vietnam was de facto divided, with Ho in control of Tonkin, and d'Argenlieu in control of the South. But Paris was eager to restore sovereignty in the entire country.[30]

Unlike some of his more liberal advisors, de Gaulle was determined to completely restore French sovereignty in Indochina. This desire was obvious in his choice of high commissioner. D'Argenlieu was at least equally determined to restore and retain control over Indochina. The high commissioner's obstinate policies soon proved a major cause for the First Indochina War.[31] By early 1946, the restoration of French rule in all of Indochina except Tonkin was accomplished. In the North, the Viet Minh won a landslide victory in general elections on January 6, 1946, further strengthening the position of Ho Chi Minh. Two weeks later, General de Gaulle resigned over a budget conflict with the Constituent Assembly. His departure from office, though, did not change France's Indochina policy.[32]

IN SEARCH OF A COMPROMISE

Both Ho and the French government shared one immediate goal and that was the withdrawal of Chinese troops from the territory north of the sixteenth parallel. Yet Ho resisted an unconditional return of French troops and demanded French recognition of Vietnamese independence. On the other hand, the Viet Minh leader was acutely aware of the precarious position of the DRV. Repeated pleas to the international community, and the United States in particular, to recognize his government remained unanswered. Therefore, Ho had no other choice than to negotiate with Paris. In February 1946, Ho Chi Minh reached a preliminary agreement with French government representative Jean Sainteny: France recognized the self-government of the DRV, but the DRV had to remain a member the French Union and had to accept French soldiers to relieve Chinese troops in Tonkin. This understanding formed the basis of the Preliminary Convention signed on March 6, 1946. The March Accords, however, were vague about the unity of Vietnam and only referred to a future referendum.[33]

However, Ho gained some valuable concessions from the French. In the Annex Accord, also signed on March 6, 1945, the number of French troops was limited to fifteen thousand, while the DRV fielded ten thousand troops. Vietnamese delegates were to assist the French High Command, and most importantly, all French troops would be replaced by Vietnamese troops within five years. Yet, some members of the French government were angered by the Annex Accord, leaving its future implementation doubtful.[34]

Twelve days later, French troops led by General Leclerc returned to Hanoi as stipulated by the accord. While French residents cheered, the Vietnamese population remained resentful. Ho was eager to work toward full implementation of the accords, but the French officials embarked on a policy of stalling. The key figure in obstructing the March Accords was High Commissioner d'Argenlieu. He rejected the notion of potential Vietnamese unity and insisted that Annam—the central part of Vietnam—was and should remain separate from Tonkin. He urged Paris to accept a preparatory conference in Dalat instead of allowing Ho to travel directly to France for final peace negotiations. Before Paris could respond, d'Argenlieu invited Ho Chi Minh, and the Vietnamese leader accepted a preliminary conference at Dalat.[35]

Both the Viet Minh and the French planned to control the agenda at Dalat. France was only willing to grant self-government to the DRV within the Indochinese Federation and hence would represent the country internationally, denying any semblance of sovereignty to the DRV. The French also rejected complete unity of Vietnam, but the people of Cochinchina might at some future point decide by plebiscite to join the DRV. The Vietnamese delegation insisted on full sovereignty and true independence. They claimed that Cochinchina had been part of Vietnam for centuries and a referendum would resolve a "purely administrative question concerning Cochinchinese autonomy within the Vietnamese polity."[36] Given the vast divergence in agendas, the conference ended without producing any conclusive results.

As a consequence of the failure to find any consensus at Dalat, High Commissioner d'Argenlieu took matters again into his own hands. Without consulting Paris, d'Argenlieu proclaimed the Autonomous Republic of Cochinchina on June 1, 1946. He argued that Paris had the choice of backing Cochinchina's autonomy and risking opposition by Hanoi, or allowing the unification of Vietnam. D'Argenlieu painted a dire picture of the future if Paris accepted the latter course. Hanoi would not only take over all of Vietnam but later swallow Cambodia and Laos as well. This possibility meant, of course, the end for French rule in Indochina.[37]

THE FONTAINEBLEAU NEGOTIATIONS

D'Argenlieu's increasingly independent policy in Cochinchina forecast major obstacles for the pending talks in France. The negotiations were delayed by a government crisis in France, a frequent event in the history of the Fourth Republic. Finally, Georges Bidault replaced Socialist Felix Gouin as prime minister, and the Vietnamese delegation was able to reach Paris on June 22, 1946. The conference eventually convened at Fontainebleau on July 6. As at Dalat, both sides had diametrically opposed positions. Pignon, head of the Indochina division and again a key player for the French delegation, wrote on the day before the conference, "Tomorrow's negotiations are a round in the Battle we are fighting, in which we are trying to reinstate ourselves in Indochina and they are trying to see us off. It is as simple as that. The question we should be asking ourselves at this moment is the following: do we or do we not wish to keep Indochina?"[38] French welcoming remarks were followed by a critical statement by Pham Van Dong, the leader of the Vietnamese delegation. Pham denounced the creation of an autonomous Cochinchina and the French occupation of the Governor's Palace in Hanoi on June 25. Both sides finally agreed on an agenda. Ultimately, the debate boiled down to the definition of Vietnamese independence and the status of Cochinchina. Ho Chi Minh, who was not an official member of the Vietnamese delegation, also tried to use the French media to sway public opinion toward his cause. In a press conference on July 12, 1946, Ho insisted that all of Vietnam, including Cochinchina, should be independent but accepted the notion of membership in the French Federal Union. The French response was quite vague and left details to be worked out after the French Union had been established.[39]

High Commissioner d'Argenlieu finally succeeded in his efforts to undermine the Fontainebleau talks by announcing another conference in Dalat to explore the details of Indochina's status within the French Union, excluding the DRV. At Fontainebleau, Pham Van Dong once more strongly protested, suggesting that this latest move again violated the March 1945 Accord, and suspended participation in the conference. The Vietnamese delegation left Fontainebleau after France rejected formal recognition of Vietnamese sovereignty on September 10. Clearly, the conference was a tragic failure.[40]

However, Ho Chi Minh decided to stay behind in Paris and salvage the negotiations. His efforts resulted in a modus vivendi signed on September 16, 1946, by Ho Chi Minh and Marius Moutet, the Socialist French colonial minister. The document affirmed the March 1945 Accords and called for a cease-fire in Cochinchina effective October 30, 1946; the release of prisoners; a guarantee of democratic liberties; and the resumption of negotiations in January 1947. Of course, d'Argenlieu had his doubts about the feasibility of the agreement, and Ho had his own concerns as well. The DRV president told *New York Times* correspondent David Schoenbrun that war was inevitable. Although the Vietnamese lacked modern weaponry, his people would ultimately prevail:

> It will be a war between an elephant and a tiger. If the tiger stands still the elephant will crush him with his mighty tusks. But the tiger does not stand still. He lurks in the jungle by day and emerges by night. He will leap on the back of the elephant, tearing huge chunks from his hide, and then will leap back into the dark jungle. And slowly the elephant will bleed to death. That will be the war in Indochina.[41]

While Ho was trying to salvage the Fontainebleau Conference, a second Constituent Assembly in Paris debated the constitutional structure of the French Union to administer France's colonial empire. French voters had rejected an initial constitutional draft in May 1946, which would have given inhabitants of the French Union full equality with French citizens. The second draft was more restrictive. It was clear that despite some cosmetic changes the colonies, now called Associate States, would not receive full autonomy and certainly not independence. Although the draft postulated that colonial rule should not be subject to coercion, any reference to the free consent of the indigenous populations was erased.[42] While the constitution dismissed the old notion of assimilation, it included no venues for colonial peoples to conduct their own policies. This view also reflected the attitude of the majority of the French, who given their recent experience still relished the notion of a global empire. The framers of the October constitution acted as if they still lived in a pre-1940 world.[43]

RETAIN CONTROL OVER
INDOCHINA BY ALL MEANS NECESSARY

Soon harsh realities set in. The modus vivendi of September 1946 did not last. French government officials quickly lost confidence that the modus vivendi was truly in France's best interest. General Leclerc maintained that Ho was an enemy of France and no concession should be made to the DRV. Furthermore, the general claimed, falsely as it turned out, that France had already won control over Indochina.[44] Pignon, head of the Indochina division in the Overseas Ministry, argued along similar lines. France had to build up Cochinchina as a "liberal" alternative to the DRV, and the former should serve as a basis for the future unification of Vietnam led by France. Leaving Paris for Indochina to oversee the implementation of the modus vivendi, Pignon saw only two choices: French abandonment of Indochina or a "considerable reinforcement of our military effort."[45]

The Viet Minh position hardened as well. Vo Nguyen Giap, Pham Van Dong, and Truong Chinh opposed further compromise, offering an indirect criticism of Ho's strategy in Paris.[46] Yet, Vietnamese efforts to abide by the modus vivendi initially showed signs of promise. Violence in Cochinchina decreased considerably. The Viet Minh leader in the South, Nguyen Binh, followed orders from Hanoi to cease guerrilla actions, and Saigon experienced some days of calm. However, the French continued to hunt down Viet Minh forces around Saigon, and Binh soon responded in kind. A further blow to French plans to build up Cochinchina as an alternative to Ho's DRV came on November 10, 1046, when Nguyen Van Trinh, the head of Cochinchina's government, committed suicide. Within days, the French retook Haiphong in the north, and on November 23, French forces shelled the Chinese quarter of the city, killing at least six thousand civilians.[47]

Last-minute efforts by both a new French government under Socialist Prime Minister Léon Blum and Ho Chi Minh failed to prevent further escalation. On December 19, 1946, Viet Minh forces attacked French troops throughout Hanoi, leaving some forty people dead and more wounded. Ho Chi Minh called for a general offensive the next day. The First Indochina War had begun.[48]

While there were voices of concern on both sides, the advocates for war ultimately prevailed. Admiral Pierre Barjot, acting chief of staff, strongly cautioned against a military solution for Indochina, criticizing the unauthorized actions by d'Argenlieu. In late November 1946, Barjot adamantly opposed taking French forces to Tonkin before Cochinchina was secured. He predicted that if France tried to regain the three Vietnamese regions it would take up to 250,000 troops, which would drain France of its reserves in Africa. General Georges Humbert, head of Prime Minister Bidault's military office, put the prospect of a military campaign in even starker terms. This war would be a "bottomless pit into which France would pour its inadequate manpower resources." General Leclerc argued that France simply did not have the means to enforce a military solution. And despite his earlier suspicion of Ho, he, too, favored negotiations.[49]

Ho also tried to prevent further bloodshed by reaching a settlement with
Prime Minister Blum. In mid-December, Ho contacted Blum in order to end
the growing conflict between the DRV and France. Blum also favored a political solution.[50] Their good intentions were thwarted by the violence in Hanoi on
December 19, 1946. The reaction in France to the events was outrage, and the
Viet Minh was blamed for an unprovoked attack on French forces and citizens.
Blum told the National Assembly that order had to be restored first before
negotiations could resume. However, he admitted that the days of colonial oppression had ended and that colonial peoples capable of governing should be
granted self-rule freely associated with the French Union.[51] After a whirlwind
fact-finding mission to Hanoi, Overseas Minister Moutet agreed and argued
that once the military had reestablished order "it will be possible again to look
at political problems."[52] But the events of December 19, 1946, further strengthened the position of hard-liners such as d'Argenlieu that any negotiations with
Ho and the Viet Minh would only mean further French humiliation.[53]

THE ELEPHANT VERSUS THE TIGER

The confidence of some French officials in quick military victory was over-
enthusiastic and short lived. Undoubtedly, the French response to the December 1946 attacks was forceful and swift. Ho and his government barely
escaped Hanoi, but they and the main Viet Minh forces were able to regroup
at prearranged bases in the mountains and the river deltas. French commanders increasingly faced the challenge of an enemy who blended with the local
population, fought in difficult terrain, and claimed to embody the will of the
Vietnamese people. Equally important was the desperate economic and fragile political situation in cosmopolitan France.[54]

The question, then, was how did Paris expect to succeed in Vietnam given
its very limited resources? The answer was to win support of the British and
even more importantly that of the United States. Since early 1946, Paris embarked on a concerted campaign to gain assistance for its Indochina policy
both in the United States and in Britain. The March 1945 Accords and the
Fontainebleau Conference of 1946 were cited by Paris as sincere efforts to
grant autonomy to the Indochinese people. At the same time, though, Paris
increasingly depicted Ho Chi Minh and his government as fervent Communists and also made the case that the Viet Minh were unable to govern the
country. At first, it was a difficult strategy to sell when many in Washington
and London blamed the deteriorating situation in Indochina on French intransigence and ineptitude.[55]

After December 1946, France was even more dependent on allied support,
military aid, and equipment to succeed in Vietnam. Once again, the French ef-

fort centered on recasting the Indochina conflict in terms of the Cold War. At home, though, a majority of French who followed events in Indochina still saw the conflict in terms of *grandeur* and France's civilizing mission. Even most French Communists initially refrained from criticizing the government's Indochina policy, but the position of the French Communist Party (PCF) moved to harsh opposition to the war after it left government in May 1947. The Socialist Party's position was somewhere in the middle, but insisted that order should be restored first before any negotiations were to take place.[56]

But dreams of *grandeur* did not help the French military effort in Indochina. By late 1947, the French forces controlled the cities but not the countryside, and casualties were mounting. One officer feared that it might require half a million troops to crush Vietnamese resistance. Clearly, France did not have sufficient resources to raise and supply that many troops. Eventually, Paris was able to win some tacit support and limited aid from Great Britain. Yet London, as a result of its own problems of decolonization and sensitivities of the Commonwealth countries, could not openly back France's Indochina policy. The endeavor to win Washington's support proved far more difficult. The State Department was split between conservatives and liberals—the former more willing to help France by accepting the argument that the Viet Minh were Communists, the latter opposed to France's colonial policy. Secretary of State George Marshall personified the predicament in the State Department. On the one hand, the United States recognized French sovereignty over Indochina and Washington was determined to help France regain great power status. On the other hand, Marshall complained that France was unwilling to pursue a political solution in Vietnam.[57]

As a result of unfavorable international opinion and a further decline of the situation in Indochina, French Prime Minister Paul Ramadier supported what became the Bao Dai solution. The former emperor would be again installed as head of state to present a truly Vietnamese nationalist alternative to the DRV. After lengthy negotiations, Bao Dai signed an agreement with High Commissioner Emile Bollaert in June 1948.[58] On paper the solution looked promising, particularly since it contained the magic words of Vietnamese independence and unity. But the French government, once more led by Georges Bidault following Ramadier's resignation, was unwilling to abandon Indochina.[59]

COLONIAL WAR TURNED
INTO STRUGGLE AGAINST COMMUNISM

Growing Cold War tensions between the United States and the Soviet Union, the Communist insurrection in British Malaya, and the victory of Mao Zedong in China in 1949 brought France the long-desired support it needed, most importantly that of the United States. France, under pressure from the United States and Great Britain, finally ratified the treaty with Bao Dai on June 4, 1949, making an independent and unified Vietnam official.[60] By 1950, the United States perceived the First Indochina War as part of the worldwide struggle against Communism. The United States accepted the notion of a truly independent nationalist Vietnam under Bao Dai that offered an alternative to the Communist DRV. Washington as well as London embarked on an extensive diplomatic campaign during fall 1949 and spring 1950 to persuade Asian governments to recognize the Bao Dai regime. But Washington went even further. By late December 1949, President Harry Truman approved National Security Council (NSC) 48/I, which argued that Washington must give support to anti-Communist parties in Asia and meet Communist threats "by providing political, economic and military assistance and advice" to those fighting communism in the region. While NSC 48/I urged the French to remove any obstacles for full independence for the Bao Dai government, the study asserted that "the United States should exploit every opportunity to increase the present Western orientation of the area and assist, within our capabilities, its governments in their efforts to meet the minimum aspirations of their people and to maintain internal security."[61]

The war in Indochina had become one of the battlegrounds of the Cold War. The U.S. commitment of 1950, which deepened with the outbreak of the Korean War, turned a conflict between a colonial power driven by an almost mystical idea of greatness, and the equally potent aspirations of the Vietnamese people to gain autonomy, into a much larger, Cold War–driven conflict.

That France lost the war in Indochina is common knowledge, and the details of this First Indochina War need not be traced in their entirety. France was able to control the urban centers but could not capture the countryside. The French attacked villages, killed perhaps some Viet Minh as well as innocent farmers, confiscated food and water buffalo, burned huts, and then left—and the Viet Minh returned. The Viet Minh found further assistance after Mao Zedong's victory in China in 1949. Mao granted the Viet Minh safe havens on the Chinese border and provided military advisors and better weaponry. A year later, the Soviet Union formally recognized the DRV. By then, France was forced to abandon its outlying posts near the Chinese border. At the end of October 1950, French forces were ousted from northern Tonkin after suffering thousands of casualties.

The dismal reports from Indochina, along with mounting casualties, finally aroused French domestic opinion, which, until then, was focused on rising prices, strikes, and a general feeling of distrust of the politicians of the Fourth Republic. A debate in the National Assembly in October and November 1950 was divided by those who wanted the government to prosecute the war more forcefully and those on the left who argued for negotiations with the Viet Minh. The Communists (PCF) condemned the war outright as a "dirty war."[62] Pierre Mendès-France forcefully condemned the government's strategy: "The whole concept of our action in Indo-China is wrong, because it is based both on a military effort which is insufficient and incapable of bringing about a solution by force and a policy which is insufficient and incapable of ensuring us the support of the local populations."[63] However, France's fortunes in Indochina seemed to improve with increasing military aid from the United States[64] and the appointment of General Jean de Lattre de Tassigny as supreme commander and high commissioner for Indochina in December 1950. De Lattre had sufficient credentials for the position; he was an expert soldier with no illusions about the Vietnam conflict and possessed an air of flamboyance. De Lattre was able to stop the Viet Minh assault in the Red River Delta, and although Paris refused to send regular service men, infantry from Africa and American aid in equipment gave him a momentum. In the endeavor, de Lattre lost his only son to the war in Indochina and later died of cancer in January 1952.[65] By then, some 174,000 French troops and 260,000 Vietnamese forces were engaged in the conflict. Soon malaise returned, and the war was deadlocked again. Michel Debré, a member of the Gaullist Party, summed up what many French felt: "The French people feel that this war is out of control and in the hands of destiny. . . . They have the impression that France does not know what she wants and that we are fighting aimlessly without a clear objective. What is painful is not so much the fact of fighting and accepting sacrifices; it is that we are apparently fighting without any goal."[66] After de Lattre's death, Paris tried to limit French casualties by increasing the number of Bao Dai's Vietnamese fighting for their own freedom against the Communist DRV. But Bao Dai remained a figurehead for the French and did very little to win over the hearts and minds of his people. His government, like the later one of Ngo Dinh Diem, served only the Francophile elite while doing nothing to improve the lot of the average farmer and the country as a whole.

DIEN BIEN PHU

France's Indochina war ended with the battle of Dien Bien Phu during fall 1953 and spring 1954. By then, the United States was fully committed to the struggle in Indochina, certainly not to uphold the French colonial empire but rather to hold "the line of freedom" against Communist advances in Asia.[67] In 1953, Viet Minh forces under General Giap moved into Laos, and recently appointed French commander General Henri Navarre decided to stop Viet Minh infiltration by taking positions in the valley of Dien Bien Phu near the

Laotian border. However, the French government and its people were tired of this endless conflict. Prime Minister Joseph Laniel had already intimated that, if an "honorable" settlement was possible, his government would "be happy to accept a diplomatic solution to the conflict." Laniel gave his approval for discussion of Indochina at an upcoming conference in Geneva scheduled for late spring 1954.[68] A diplomatic solution was precisely what France needed. General Navarre had seriously underestimated Viet Minh numbers, firepower, and weaponry. For Vo Nguyen Giap and the Viet Minh, Dien Bien Phu represented the last purely military stage of the three-stage people's war and served as a pawn for the upcoming Geneva Conference. The French decision to make a stand in the valley proved disastrous. The garrison was quickly surrounded by heavily armed Viet Minh forces. In desperation, the French asked for American airstrikes, even the deployment of a nuclear weapon, but President Dwight Eisenhower refused. Dien Bien Phu fell on May 7, 1954, twelve days after the Geneva Conference officially convened. More than 1,500 French-Vietnamese forces died, and the Viet Minh suffered 25,000 casualties, with nearly 10,000 killed in action.[69]

Despite forceful American appeals to continue fighting, Prime Minister Laniel and his successor Mendès-France refused. French public opinion backed the decision of the government. By May 1954, only 7 percent of the French public still supported the war and 60 percent were against it. The fall of Dien Bien Phu was a resounding and humiliating defeat for France. For many, it harbored the end of the French Empire and also exemplified what many French regarded as the shortcomings of the Fourth Republic and its leaders. Although most French had paid little attention to the Indochina war while it was being fought, its humiliating conclusion left a lasting impression. Even worse was to come in what France considered part of metropolitan France—Algeria—and it was up to the leader of the Free French, General de Gaulle, to redefine French *grandeur*, albeit without an empire.[70]

A day after the surrender at Dien Bien Phu, the Geneva Conference convened to discuss the Indochina conflict. The DRV and the Bao Dai governments and Cambodia and Laos were represented along with France, Great Britain, the Soviet Union, the People's Republic of China (PRC), and the United States. Pham Van Dong again headed the DRV delegation as he had at the Fontainebleau talks in 1946, but once more he faced major obstacles. This time, it was not France but rather the DRV's major allies—the Soviet Union and the PRC—who posed limits to what Hanoi could achieve. Both wanted an immediate end to the conflict, fearing that if the war continued, the United States might intervene directly. French Prime Minister Mendès-France was also firmly committed to ending France's war in Indochina and promised his country a satisfactory solution within four weeks.[71]

Mendès-France kept his promise, though it turned out to be a close call. He and Chinese delegate Zhou Enlai held secret talks resulting in the concept of a divided Vietnam. With Soviet arbitration, the seventeenth parallel was chosen as the temporary division line between the DRV and the Bao Dai state. French forces had to withdraw from the North and Viet Minh troops from the South within three hundred days. Free and general elections for a national government were scheduled for the summer of 1956, and a supervisory commission of Indian, Polish, and Canadian members would monitor the execution of the accords.[72]

The First Indochina War was finally over, but the Geneva Accords proved only a temporary solution, due mainly to the American response. Washington refused to sign the accords and only reluctantly promised to abide by the agreement. Soon after the Geneva Conference ended, the Eisenhower administration fully committed itself to the defense of "free" South Vietnam and its new president, Ngo Dinh Diem.[73]

For France, the Geneva Accords ended one colonial conflict, but an even more divisive one was brewing in North Africa. By 1956, the French government had granted independence to Tunisia and Morocco but not to Algeria, and Algeria's struggle for independence turned violent in November 1954.[74] The Algerian war ultimately destroyed the Fourth Republic. Facing civil unrest and a rebellious military in 1958, the French turned once more to de Gaulle for guidance and leadership to regain *grandeur*.

Chapter 3

West Germany
from the 1950s to 1963

Finding a Role in International Affairs

On May 8, 1945, a little more than seventy-four years after the proclamation of the German Empire in 1871, Germany as a sovereign state ceased to exist with the unconditional surrender to Allied forces. It was the zero hour—*Stunde Null* in German history. *Stunde Null* had multiple meanings: One was the result of total defeat in a war that had been postulated "total war" by the Nazis. On the other hand, *Stunde Null* might allow a new beginning for a Germany no longer dominated by militarism and authoritarianism. For the average German, though, *Stunde Null* meant struggling to survive; finding shelter and food; rebuilding bombed cities and factories; and hoping that fathers, husbands, and brothers who had survived the war would soon return home. For some eleven million refugees it also meant escaping the rage and rape of the Soviet Army and starting all over again.

Germany was carved into four occupation zones, and on June 5, 1945, the United States, Great Britain, France, and the Soviet Union assumed full sovereign control over Germany. During the immediate months following V-E Day, Germany's future remained unclear. What was clear, though, was that Germany had to pay a price for the murderous ambitions and crimes of Adolf Hitler. The Potsdam Conference held from July to August 1945 sought clarification over the status of Germany. Its goals were demilitarization, de-Nazification, disarmament, democratization, and decentralization. The three allies—the United States, Great Britain, and the Soviet Union—France was not invited—agreed to treat Germany economically as a single unit, and the Allied Control Council in Berlin would make unanimous decisions on issues affecting Germany as a whole. Thus, it appeared that Germany might remain a unified country and that a draconian punishment as envisaged under the American Henry Morgenthau plan had been rejected.[1]

Although Germans could not play any major role in decisions about their political future, three major approaches for a future position of Germany were discussed. First, exemplified by the Christian Democrat Jacob Kaiser, was the notion that Germany should cast itself as neutral between East and West, adopt the role of an honest broker, build bridges among the nations in Europe, and find ways to accommodate capitalism and socialism. The second approach, personified by Kurt Schumacher, leader of the Social Democratic Party (SPD), aimed at greater cooperation with the socialist and social democratic parties in Western Europe. Schumacher was both an anticapitalist and an anticommunist and rejected any accommodation with the Soviet Union. The third option was the policy adopted by Konrad Adenauer, who urged close integration of Germany with democratic nations of the West. In light of the growing division between East and West, only the last approach was feasible for West Germany.[2]

While the Potsdam Conference had envisioned joint Allied decision making for Germany, the policies of the Allies within their respective sectors of occupation varied. Most marked was the difference in the Soviet-occupied zone. Although the Soviets allowed the establishment of political parties earlier than the Western powers did, the purpose was to ensure the dominance of the Communist Party (KPD). The result was a forced unification of the KPD and SPD into the Socialist Unity Party of Germany (SED) in April 1946. Clearly, the Soviet-occupied part of Germany followed the same pattern to establish Soviet domination that all countries behind the Iron Curtain experienced.[3]

The Western Allies' policies witnessed differing goals during the early years of occupation. Most notable was the French desire to obstruct the creation of a viable German state. American and British responses to the costs of occupation and economic problems within their sectors, along with the intensifying Cold War, led to the creation of the Bizone in December 1947. France eventually agreed to the creation of a Trizone in March 1948, after the United States began to pour millions of dollars of aid into Western Europe as part of the Marshall Plan. By June 1948, the three Western Allies agreed that Germans should have the opportunity to create a "free and democratic form of government."[4] The Western allies introduced a new currency in June 1948 to end the rampant inflation of the reichsmark. The launch of the deutsche mark resulted in a serious Cold War crisis when the Soviet Union blocked surface access to Berlin on June 24, 1948. The West responded with Operation Vittles—the immense airlift of whatever goods Berlin needed to stay alive.[5] While the Soviet blockade of Berlin was ultimately abandoned, the division of Germany into two states was sealed.[6] In July 1948, the Allies asked the minister presidents of the states within the Trizone to convene a constituent assembly to write a constitution for Germany. The resulting

Basic Law provided the constitutional framework for a democratic Federal Republic of Germany (FRG).[7] After voter ratification and consent of the Allied council, the FRG was officially proclaimed in May 1949. The new country still had only limited sovereignty—the Western Allies retained supreme authority based on their declaration of June 1945. By October 1949, another German state was formed—the German Democratic Republic (GDR). To the new West German Chancellor Adenauer now fell not only the task to rebuild confidence for West Germany but also the challenge to devise a course to reunify Germany.

ADENAUER

Adenauer dominated the political life of the FRG during the first two decades of its existence. Elected chancellor in September 1949, Adenauer remained in office until his resignation in October 1963. Adenauer was already seventy-three years old when he became chancellor, and his experience encompassed the turmoil of modern German history. Born on January 5, 1876, in Cologne to a middle-class family, he grew up in the German Empire dominated by Prussia. As a Catholic and Rhinelander, Adenauer became an opponent of everything Prussian, especially its militaristic tradition and behavior, which he later blamed for the First World War and labeled the "evil spirit of Europe." Adenauer felt more at home with the culture of Western Europe than that of the East.[8] Adenauer also strongly opposed socialism and communism and believed that only a democratic market economy would serve the best interest of the people. He pursued these policies as the hugely popular major of Cologne from 1917 until he was removed from office by the Nazi Party (NSDAP) in 1933. He was reelected major of Cologne in 1945. After a few months, he was dismissed by the British because of "lack of energy and incompetence." Adenauer joined the newly formed Christian Democratic Party (CDU). In 1949, Adenauer was chosen as president of the parliamentary council that had the task of writing a new German constitution. This prominent position gave him national recognition and paved the road to his election as first chancellor of the Federal Republic with the majority of one vote—his own.[9]

As chancellor, Adenauer was the prime architect of West German foreign policy, which during the early years of the Federal Republic revolved around the goals of obtaining security, political sovereignty, and economic recovery. Like Charles de Gaulle, Adenauer was a pragmatic realist. The German chancellor certainly did not subscribe to any sublime idea of German greatness, but he did whatever he could to regain sovereignty and international respectability for his country. Adenauer's policy was quite successful. In 1955, the Allied High Commission relinquished most of its control over German foreign policy by ending the state of occupation, and shortly thereafter, West Germany became a partner in the defense for Western Europe by joining the North Atlantic Treaty Organization (NATO).[10]

Adenauer's foreign policy was based on three basic assumptions. First, international politics were defined by the antagonism existing between the free Western and the Communist world, the German division being one of the core examples of this conflict. Second, although Western Europe's future was primarily determined by the Soviet threat, it was still influenced by its recent past, which made it potentially an anti-German system. Third, the Western European democracies relied heavily on the United States for their survival in this antagonistic system.[11] The solution for Adenauer was both a solid relationship with the United States and full integration of West Germany into Western Europe, which closely matched American policy toward Germany. Since 1947, the United States placed prime importance on both West Germany's economic recovery as well as the integration of West Germany into the Western European state system in order to contain any revisionist German ambition. The United States quickly appreciated Adenauer's capable leadership and regarded the chancellor as a guarantor for West German stability.[12]

Moreover, to Adenauer, European integration prevented any alliance of France with the Soviet Union, a union that had proved devastating with the breakdown of Bismarckian foreign alliances in the 1890s. Adenauer never forgot this lesson of history and did everything to prevent hostile coalitions against Germany.[13] In addition, a West Germany fully integrated into a strong Europe, perhaps even the "United States of Europe," might prevent any American-Soviet settlement over Germany without consulting European powers or West Germany. Moreover, another Potsdam conference—a settlement by the allied powers on Germany but without German participation—was a constant concern for Adenauer.[14]

West German foreign policy hence had to be built on two pillars: European integration and friendship with the United States on whose protection West Germany had to rely for its survival. But dependency on the United States, in addition to Allied restrictions on German sovereignty, allowed Adenauer only limited room to maneuver. Therefore, Adenauer viewed European integration as a potential venue toward a more independent German foreign policy. A French-German understanding and partnership could become the cornerstone for a unified Europe. Adenauer emphasized the European pillar of his foreign policy each time he felt the United States might return to a more isolationist policy, neglect what he regarded as prime German interests, or focus too much on crises in Asia. The ultimate goal of this two-pronged strategy was German reunification.[15]

During the 1950s, Adenauer's course complemented the policy of the United States toward both the Soviet Union and West Germany, a policy resulting into "double containment," which meant to restrain further ambitions of not only the Soviet Union but Germany as well. West Germany as a member of NATO and the European Economic Community (EEC) no longer posed a threat to Europe and the world at large, and East Germany was fully embedded within the Warsaw Pact. West and East Germany proved their loyalty to their respective alliances and became the focal concern for the European policy of both the United States and the Soviet Union; despite short periods of tension, these alliances guaranteed stability in Europe.[16]

WEST GERMANY AND SOUTHEAST ASIA

In light of the challenges facing West Germany, Adenauer, as well as his successor Ludwig Erhard, would have probably preferred that conflicts in Southeast Asia had never occurred. These distant wars distracted its major allies, France and the United States, from what both chancellors aimed to ultimately achieve—German unity. Bonn's Vietnam policy reflected the limitations on West German foreign policy, imposed for the necessity of maintaining strong relations with the Western Allies, and the constitutional framework of West Germany. Since the Basic Law did not allow for any military involvement beyond the scope of NATO, Bonn had to insist on strict military neutrality in both Indochina wars, while at the same time present itself as a faithful ally of first the French and later the United States in their respective engagements in Vietnam. Moreover, the Federal Republic was determined to assure its allies and third world nations that it had made a clear cut with the German past and had become a reliable and stable partner.[17]

Already in 1953, the Bao Dai government in Saigon was interested in diplomatic relations with the Federal Republic, yet Bonn proved reluctant due to the uncertain political conditions in Vietnam at the height of the First Indochina War. The Federal Republic was only willing to consider trade negotiations. In 1955, Bonn sent a trade commissioner to Saigon and after five years finally established full diplomatic relations with South Vietnam. Based on the West German position that it was the sole legal representative of the German people, Bonn maintained until the early 1970s that the Saigon government represented all of Vietnam, hence dismissing the factual division of the country.[18] During the first half of the 1950s, Bonn observed the events in Indochina but was primarily focused on gaining more political initiative as a reliable ally in the West. However, the Adenauer administration was fully aware of the international importance of the conflict in Asia; the conflict became directly connected to the German question during the Berlin Conference in early 1954, where the settlement of the First Indochina War was the prime concern. While an understanding could be reached on Indochina resulting in the Geneva Conference later that year, the Berlin Conference was once more inconclusive on the issue of German unification.

In addition, the war in Indochina touched French-German relations and had to be considered by Adenauer in order to form a durable friendship with Paris and integrate the Federal Republic into the EEC. The French military effort in Vietnam also presented a major obstacle in the planned creation of a European Defense Force (EDF). Adenauer strongly supported the EDF since it would give additional assurances to German security. Ultimately, the overcommitment of French forces in Indochina resulted in the French veto of the EDF in August 1954.[19] Another obstacle for Adenauer was the fact that German nationals were serving in the French Foreign Legion in Indochina, which resulted in vehement protest by the SPD. Adenauer downplayed the role of Germans in Indochina by stating that they were only aiding in the international struggle against Communism.[20]

Following the French withdrawal from Indochina in 1954, the United States assumed major responsibility for the survival of South Vietnam, and again, West Germany had to use caution to not appear unreliable to its Western allies. If Bonn completely supported the United States' Vietnam policy, France's feelings might be hurt because Paris stood fully behind the Geneva Accords prohibiting any foreign interference in Vietnam. Yet, on the other side, Germany depended on American protection and therefore could not afford to be critical of American policy in Southeast Asia. Adenauer subsequently endorsed Washington's policy in Southeast Asia since the U.S. policy of containment ensured the viability of West Germany as well.[21]

Following the proclamation of the South Vietnamese Republic in 1955, the Diem government increasingly pressured Bonn to establish diplomatic contacts. The Federal Republic finally opened a general consulate in Saigon in 1957.[22] By then, Adenauer regarded any deepening of relations with South Vietnam in terms of American commitment to that country. He and his advisors felt assured that the U.S. obligation to South Vietnam would continue.[23]

As the formation of the Southeast Asia Treaty Organization (SEATO) in 1954 signaled, Washington was determined to contain Communism in Southeast Asia, making any independent West German approach toward Vietnam unthinkable. Clearly, Adenauer was unwilling to risk any disturbance in German-American relations, which until 1958—the death of John Foster Dulles—were particularly tight. In 1955, the GDR recognized North Vietnam and sent a diplomatic delegation to Hanoi. This precluded any bilateral relations between Hanoi and Bonn based on the West German Hallstein Doctrine of nonrecognition of any country that maintained ties with the GDR.[24] Since Bonn accepted the American position that Vietnam was part of the global fight against Communism, it was impossible for the Federal Republic to even consider any contacts with North Vietnam. While France established diplomatic relations with North Vietnam, any West German contact would have been regarded as an unfriendly act by Saigon and probably Washington as well.

Adenauer firmly supported President Dwight Eisenhower's policy in Indochina. The chancellor dismissed de Gaulle's criticism of the American strategy and proposed West German humanitarian aid to as well as political contacts with Saigon. In the fall of 1958, Vice Chancellor Erhard visited Southeast Asia, affirming West Germany's commitment to the global fight against Communism. He was concerned about the increasing influence of the Communist Eastern European states in Cambodia, Laos, and North Vietnam and emphasized that the West had to intensify its effort to prevent a Communist takeover in Asia. Erhard expressed his sympathy to President Ngo Dinh Diem, who as a fellow Catholic was trying his best to eradicate the scourge of war from his country. While any military contribution by the Bundeswehr was impossible, Erhard conveyed that it was West Germany's moral obligation to ease tensions in Asia and aid the countries in the region in their struggle against Communist aggression.[25]

By 1960, however, the Adenauer administration received increasingly pessimistic assessments on South Vietnam. West German Ambassador Alexander von Wendland described the situation in South Vietnam as rapidly deteriorating. Communist attacks against the Diem government had increased to a level not seen since 1955, and most of the population was critical of their leader. Even worse, Diem's own military officers had become restless. Washington, too, showed growing concern about Diem. However, as von Wendland commented, at the time, the West had no other choice than to support the South Vietnamese president, or it would face a Communist victory.[26]

Bonn's views changed somewhat in late 1961. The major reason was West Germany's increased empathy for another divided country after the construction of the Berlin Wall in August 1961. The Berlin crisis seemed to once more confirm Eisenhower's domino theory, and hence Bonn felt obligated to further assist South Vietnam against Communist aggression. In addition, the neutralization of Laos evoked fears of additional Communist successes in Cambodia and Thailand. Further, Bonn worried that the United States might reconsider its policy toward Germany and reduce its military presence in Europe. As a consequence, Bonn quickly approved a DM50 million credit to South Vietnam.[27] In 1962, the federal government restated that West Germany was observing with profound concern the valiant fight by the freedom-loving people of South Vietnam against Communist aggression.[28] West Germans indeed empathized with the hardships of the people of South Vietnam and appreciated the dilemma of a divided country. German concern for Saigon also demonstrated the sincerity and concern of the Federal Republic for the third world in general, in hopes of winning wider sympathy and respect for West Germany.

In summary, by 1962, the Adenauer government had accepted the American position that the defense of South Vietnam was vital in the global struggle against Communism and hence that West German freedom was indirectly defended at the Mekong River. However, within the Bonn government, the debate continued on how much Bonn should contribute to the survival of South Vietnam. In general, Bonn was more than willing to make public statements of support and provide some development aid. This position left Bonn vulnerable to demands by the United States and to French criticism. Since the FRG had publicly accepted U.S. policy in Southeast Asia, Washington augmented its pressure on Bonn during the coming years to do more for South Vietnam. However, based on his critical assessment of American policy in Vietnam, de Gaulle attempted to draw Bonn into his orbit by presenting France as an alternative to the United States. Bonn found itself in the dilemma of having to steer a course without alienating its major allies.

ADENAUER, KENNEDY, AND DE GAULLE

From 1961 to 1963, French President de Gaulle succeeded in forming closer ties with Adenauer, mainly due to the policies of President John F. Kennedy. With the election of Kennedy, a new generation came to power in Washington, and they brought with them a different perspective on global issues. While the status of Berlin was definitely a concern, the Kennedy administration was looking for a fresh approach in American-Soviet relations in order to focus on the problems in Latin America and Southeast Asia. Facing a Soviet nuclear arsenal that directly threatened the United States, Kennedy proposed a novel defense strategy of "flexible response." Instead of an immediate American nuclear retaliatory response to a Soviet attack on Europe, conventional troops would be used first, hoping for a diplomatic solution, and if that failed, the United States would then employ its nuclear weapons. This approach deeply worried Adenauer since he feared the new strategy might invite a Soviet attack on the Federal Republic, leaving the country in ruins before an American response would occur.[29]

During Kennedy's first months in office, it was unclear to an apprehensive Adenauer how this "young man" would conduct American policy toward

Kennedy (left) and Adenauer formed cordial relations but remained apprehensive of each other's policy goals. Courtesy of the John F. Kennedy Presidential Library.

Germany. In 1951, Kennedy had visited the Federal Republic but was more impressed by the SPD leader Schumacher than with Adenauer. Six years later, Kennedy wrote that Adenauer was a "shadow of the past" and that the Eisenhower administration should focus on potential successors to the old chancellor. Still, during the presidential campaign of 1960, he felt that Adenauer's policies were too narrow-minded and that, like Eisenhower, the chancellor was a "relic of the Cold War," unable to adapt to the changes in Europe and the world. Hence, he viewed the Federal Republic as a difficult partner, and Adenauer's preference for Richard Nixon during the campaign definitely did not help to facilitate American-German relations.[30]

Bonn noted with some concern that the American president had not mentioned Berlin in his inaugural address. Further, Kennedy frequently used the term "West Berlin" instead of "Berlin," tacitly admitting he would not challenge a division of the city. Kennedy considered Soviet pressure on Berlin since 1958 as a test of NATO's sincerity and perhaps an effort to neutralize West Germany that might lead Germany on a dangerous "nationalistic and independent course."[31] The president was not willing to relinquish Western Allied rights in their sectors but at the same time would not risk a major war by going beyond the defense of West Berlin. He was also less adamant about the right of self-determination of all Berliners, free access to the city, and close ties between West Berlin and the Federal Republic. The first encounter with Adenauer in April 1961 was friendly but reserved; Kennedy proved a polite host and good listener. However, Berlin was only a minor issue, with both sides working on contingency operations in case of another blockade of the city and most of the meetings focused on problems within NATO.[32]

During the summer of 1961, the question of Berlin gained further urgency. In early June, President Kennedy met Soviet Premier Nikita Sergeyevich Khrushchev in Vienna, and both Germany and Southeast Asia were major topics on the agenda. The two leaders failed to agree on a settlement for Germany or Berlin. Khrushchev once more threatened that he would conclude a separate peace with East Germany, to end the three-power status for West Berlin. In July, President Kennedy declared that, if necessary, the United States would defend West Berlin with force, and Great Britain and France reaffirmed the Western Allies' rights in Berlin as well.[33]

Kennedy's advisors viewed the Berlin crisis in a wider geopolitical context, indicating that Khrushchev perhaps deliberately intensified tensions over the former German capital to gain concessions in other areas of the world, particularly in Southeast Asia. Admiral Arleigh Burke, chief of Naval Operations, explored this connection in a memorandum to the Joint Chiefs of Staff in June 1961. He emphasized that Khrushchev was embarking on a risky course over Berlin since the Soviet premier was fully aware that the viability of Berlin represented an essential element of American credibility within NATO and Western Europe. Admiral Burke was convinced that despite Khrushchev's belligerent language the Soviet leader was not seeking a war over Berlin and might "envision a relaxation of the Berlin crisis in exchange for an understanding that the U.S. would not forcefully resist further Communist expansion in Southeast Asia."[34] The American commitments to both Berlin and Southeast Asia also affected military planning in Washington: in order to appear firm but not too fixated on either issue or overextend the American military, troop deployments to Berlin should occur only if the crisis further intensified. Clearly, the president should not play into Khrushchev's hand by focusing solely on Berlin but rather reassure America's Asian allies that the United States had no intentions to disengage from the region.[35] Senator Hubert Humphrey (D-MN), in a memorandum to the president, also saw Berlin connected to wider global issues. He urged Kennedy to tell both the American people and the world that the division of Berlin was an example of what Soviet policy would mean for Southeast Asia. The United States had to stand by its commitments around the globe:

> People needed to be reminded that what happened to Berlin—its division—and what happened to Germany—its division—has happened to Viet Nam, has happened to Korea, is happening to Laos, that the Soviet Union is seeking to divide and cut up. . . . We must make it crystal clear . . . that we are not afraid, that our commitments are real and will be honored.[36]

The division of Berlin and Germany could not be solved by war since it would only destroy Berlin and transform Europe into the "battleground of civilization's last hour." In the end, the German question had to be settled by the Germans themselves. The root of the problem obviously lay in Moscow, not Germany. The possibility of military confrontation should be used only to exert pressure on Moscow, and hence the United States had to reiterate its resolve to stand firm on Berlin. American resolve combined with the demand of free elections for Berlin, and the right of German self-determination would also have a tremendous impact in the third world where people were caught in the power struggle between the United States and the Soviet Union.[37]

President Kennedy agreed with his advisors to be adamant in the question of Allied legal rights in West Berlin and access to the city. He expressed his determination to defend West Berlin, but only West Berlin, in a report to the nation on July 25, 1961. Kennedy implicitly recognized the partition of Berlin in stating that the "endangered frontier of freedom runs through a divided Berlin."[38] The threat to West Berlin was not an isolated problem but part of a worldwide threat of Communism.

> We face a challenge in Berlin, but there is also a challenge in Southeast Asia, where the borders are less guarded, the enemy harder to find, and the danger of communism is less apparent to those who have so little . . .West Berlin . . . has now become—as never before—the great testing place of Western courage and will, a focal point where our solemn commitments stretching back over the years since 1945, and Soviet ambitions now meet in basic confrontation.[39]

The American objectives in dealing with Berlin were to find a satisfactory solution without war or further increase in tensions with the Soviet Union; a solution was needed that might result in growing cooperation with Moscow by finding a stable modus vivendi in Central Europe. The independence of West Germany and its integration with the West needed to be assured, and West Berlin ought to have the right of self-government and "sufficiently close association with West Germany to make it economically viable," including free access to the city.[40] The crisis should also be a handled in such a way as to present a clear message to the Soviet Union, America's allies, and the world in general that "we are a united people, confident of our capabilities and realistic in the understanding of German and world problems" and willing to act firmly and faithfully to American commitments by facing risks in a reasonable manner.[41]

The policy of guaranteeing protection to West Berlin ran counter to the position of Adenauer and also of Berlin's Governing Major Willy Brandt. Both hoped to maintain the freedom and right of self-determination for the entire city and prevent Berlin from being divided.[42] However, Washington desired more flexibility in its German and Berlin policy. Once tensions over Berlin subsided, the United States and the Soviet Union would be able to negotiate global issues and arms reductions.[43] While the Kennedy administration was not willing to recognize the East German regime of Walter Ulbricht, it was prepared to "encourage" West Germans to seek contacts and open discussion with East Germany on a variety of issues.[44]

During the summer of 1961, the Kennedy administration was at odds over what to do in Berlin. While Kennedy's White House advisors proposed negotiations with Khrushchev, the State Department and former Secretary of State Dean Acheson urged to remain absolutely firm, even if it meant war. Kennedy favored negotiations. The United States should insist on its rights in West Berlin but was willing to discuss the Berlin question in the wider context of European security, which might implicitly lead to the recognition of the GDR and the Oder-Neisse border. The president fully accepted Soviet control over East Berlin, though Berlin was still legally a jointly occupied city, and would not challenge the Soviet position by military means. While he understood the concern of the Berliners, he felt that neither the United States nor its allies were prepared to risk a possible nuclear war over the unity of the city.[45] Kennedy was aware that his position might lead to debate or even opposition within the Western alliance and the Federal Republic. Therefore, in early August 1961, Kennedy sent Secretary of State Dean Rusk to Europe to sound out the American allies about their respective positions. French President de Gaulle forcefully rejected the idea of negotiations with the Soviet Union since this approach would be seen as a first step of surrendering Berlin.[46]

Meeting Adenauer at the chancellor's summer vacation residence in Italy, Rusk expressed his administration's trust in West Germany. Adenauer agreed to negotiations on Berlin, but he was deeply worried about statements made by Senators William Fulbright and Mike Mansfield in favor of American troop withdrawals from Europe and their proposal to declare Berlin a free city under UN command. To Adenauer, these comments by prominent senators definitely sent the wrong signals to Khrushchev. Adenauer also pointed out that, despite the saber-rattling stand of Khrushchev, the Soviet leader was quite vulnerable when it came to the sluggish Soviet economy. The chancellor suggested an economic embargo of the Soviet Union in case the Berlin negotiations proved futile.[47] Flexibility was one thing for Adenauer, but the freedom and security of Berlin was too serious a matter for policy experiments. He hoped the United States would stand by its commitments to the entire city and use economic pressure on Moscow to defuse the time bomb of Berlin.[48]

BERLIN, 1961

On August 13, 1961, the East German government, with approval from Moscow, began to build barricades and barbed-wire fences to stop the ever-growing flow of refugees to the western half of Berlin. The events caught the Kennedy administration by surprise, and his advisors were uncertain how to interpret the action of East Berlin since the construction of barricades might simply be another means to control the flow of refugees and might not infringe Western Allied rights. Kennedy's Berlin task force went into session but reached no conclusive plan of action for the time being, and it took Washington four days to send a note of protest to Moscow. Secretary Rusk emphasized that the wall was merely a tool directed against East Germans, and in West Germany, Adenauer simply pointed to the Allies' responsibility for the city.[49] Only Governing Mayor Brandt frantically tried to convince the allies to do something against the construction of the wall.

Most West Germans were shocked and angry as well. Newspapers ran the headlines "Der Westen Tut Nichts" [The West Does Nothing], but nobody knew how to prevent the obvious wait-and-see policy of the Allies and Chancellor Adenauer. Adenauer decided not to visit the city immediately and continued on the campaign trail for the federal elections. He added more fuel to the fire when he met with Soviet Ambassador Andrei Smirnov on August 16, describing the conversation as an improvement in German-Soviet relations and agreeing that the Federal Republic would take no measures to harm German-Soviet relations.[50] Meanwhile, Kennedy responded to Brandt by urging West Berlin to keep its calm and frankly admitted he was not willing to risk war over West Berlin; while he regretted the division of the city, most measures contemplated "bore no comparison to the enormity of what had happened." However, Kennedy sent 1,500 additional troops and, to boost morale in West Berlin, also deployed Vice President Lyndon B. Johnson and the organizer of the Berlin airlift of 1948, General Lucius D. Clay.[51]

Ultimately, the Berlin crisis did not seriously undermine West German–American relations in the long run, but for the next two years, a lack of confidence on both sides was apparent. Adenauer continued to oppose any American policy that, in order to reach a security and arms agreement with the Soviet Union, was willing to implicitly recognize the GDR and the Oder-Neisse border.[52] The chancellor insisted that Bonn had equal status as a NATO member in any negotiations with the Warsaw Pact.[53] Adenauer later admitted there had been no alternative response to the wall other than nuclear war, which nobody wanted. Brandt and the SPD became strong supporters of Kennedy's "grand design" in lessening tensions with the Soviet Union. Brandt demonstrated more willingness to accept the American position than Adenauer.[54] As in the United States, everyone in Germany was terrified of a potential nuclear war during the Cuban missile crisis of 1962. In 1963, West Germans and Berliners cheered with enthusiasm when President Kennedy visited the country and affirmed the American commitment to West Berlin with his famous "Ich bin ein Berliner" speech.[55]

But the Berlin crisis of 1961 also made clear a difference in perspectives that resulted from each country's historical experience. West Germany experienced again its dependency on the United States for survival and the limitations for West German policy due to this dependency. The West German agenda was just one of many global challenges facing the Kennedy administration. To Washington, European security as well as a rapprochement between both superpowers could only be achieved by accepting the status quo in Europe, which implicitly meant accepting the German division.[56]

Adenauer's concern about American support and reliance after the construction of the Berlin Wall led to another turn toward Europe, particularly France. Adenauer and de Gaulle had established good personal relations since their first meeting in 1959, and France's rejection of any negotiation over Berlin that would change the status of the city had reassured the German chancellor. In December 1961, Adenauer met again with de Gaulle, and cross-Atlantic relations were a top priority for the chancellor. He was worried that too many people were involved in American foreign policy, and he rejected the view of the State Department that the United States had no disagreement with the Soviet Union, while the latter threatened the security of the Federal Republic. Adenauer hoped that France would play a more active role in supporting West Germany against the interests of both the United States and Great Britain.[57] He found a receptive listener in de Gaulle who

German Chancellor Konrad Adenauer (left) and French President
Charles de Gaulle signed the historic Franco-German Friendship
Treaty in 1963. Courtesy of the German Information Center.

rejected any negotiations in regard to Berlin and Germany as a whole that might lead to a change of status quo, or even neutralization, which would threaten French security as well. France opposed any contacts between the United States and the Soviet Union over Germany since, for de Gaulle, the Soviet Union was ultimately trying to break up the Western alliance.[58]

Two months later, both expressed again their dissatisfaction with American foreign policy. De Gaulle and Adenauer agreed that a joint policy in the major issues would have a more profound effect on Washington, Moscow, and also London. While there was no question that Europe needed the Atlantic alliance and the United States, the United States also needed the support of the Western Europeans and that the latter should have a stronger voice in the decisions of NATO.[59] In the summer of 1962, Adenauer pressed the issue of French-German relations, proposing permanent consultations between both countries on major issues of European, defense, and global politics. His underlying concern was a potential U.S.-Soviet understanding on Berlin without consulting West Germany. Adenauer also expressed his concerns about a British entry in the EEC, a move favored by Washington, but clearly opposed by de Gaulle.[60] In September 1962, during a triumphant visit to West Germany, de Gaulle finally agreed: West Germany and France should conclude an agreement that stressed their mutual interests and coordinate their foreign policy in regard to Berlin, East-West relations, defense, and relations to the third world.

THE FRANCO-GERMAN
TREATY AND AMERICAN REACTIONS

This understanding finally resulted in the Franco-German Friendship Treaty signed on January 22, 1963. The treaty was a milestone in French-German relations, which had been dominated by hostility and war for almost a century. It expressly stated that the increased cooperation between France and the Federal Republic was a first step on the path to further political union among the EEC member states and that the other members would be regularly informed about French-German consultations. Washington was shocked and uncertain what the treaty meant for the future. Only days before signing the treaty, de Gaulle had vetoed the British entry into the EEC to the dismay of both Harold Macmillan and Kennedy. The French-German treaty seemed to Washington another sign of France's increasingly independent and sometimes antagonistic policy and that now West Germany might become unpredictable as well.[61] Adenauer had no intentions to become an unreliable partner to the United States; rather, it was his concern about American reliability that made the Franco-German treaty indispensable. As he told de Gaulle in Paris for the signing of the treaty,

> I am quite concerned about the United States. I do not know which defense strategy might be adopted since everything seems to change quickly there. . . . The United States obviously had no intentions to mislead anyone intentionally, but nobody could know what the Americans might think tomorrow. This was quite disconcerting. Germany was immediately facing Russia and France was directly in line behind Germany. The danger for Western Europe had become very considerable. In regard to the changing American strategic thinking nobody could be sure whether the political strategy might change as well, resulting in a possible general *malaise*.[62]

Adenauer hoped that de Gaulle could use his political influence and experience with President Kennedy to better present the European point of view and also that of the Federal Republic. He was aware that, while some Germans enjoyed a good reputation in the United States, overall German-American relations still lacked profound understanding and appreciation. Apparently, Americans had developed a sincere empathy with Berlin yet not with Germany as whole. The United States needed a better understanding of the European position, and any advice de Gaulle could offer to the Kennedy administration would surely help transatlantic relations.[63]

Adenauer's view and actions were obviously not shared by Kennedy. Shortly before the treaty was signed, the president sent Undersecretary of State George Ball to Adenauer to inform him about Kennedy's plan to create the Multilateral Nuclear Force (MLF), which would provide a greater voice for Europe in the use of nuclear weapons. Although Adenauer agreed to participate in the MLF, he expressed his doubts about the American concept to de Gaulle.[64] Washington was baffled and infuriated by Adenauer's vacillating course. Kennedy openly expressed his criticism of the Franco-German treaty to German Ambassador Karl Heinrich Knappstein. Secretary Rusk was also worried where Germany was heading. Rusk had no intention of forcing Bonn to choose between Washington and Paris, but Bonn could not possibly prefer "fifty French bombs over fifty thousand American missiles."[65] Washington's message to Bonn was clear. West Germany's policy initiatives remained limited. On the other hand, Adenauer made his point by demonstrating that West Germany, despite its restrictions, had to be accepted by Washington as a political force.

By 1963, Adenauer had become disillusioned with Washington and turned increasingly toward France. This move fit perfectly into de Gaulle's design of *grandeur* because he hoped that with West German support he could further his quest for leadership in Europe and an independent policy of France in the world. Since Adenauer left office in October 1963, it remains uncertain how he might have responded to the American military escalation in Vietnam as chancellor. Two years after his resignation, Adenauer maintained that military escalation in Vietnam was a grave mistake. The war in Vietnam was senseless. Washington should have listened to French advice and sought negotiations since the Americans could not win the war in Southeast Asia.[66] In August 1966, Adenauer repeated this assessment to the *New York Times* and urged for an American withdrawal from Vietnam. He argued that Europe was the prime region of interest for the United States. If Washington neglected Europe, the Soviet Union might have the opportunity to gain control over West Germany and France.[67] His opinion did not affect Washington and was not shared by his successor Erhard.

Chapter 4

Britain and Indochina

We Have Experience in These Matters

Great Britain experienced a taste of the difficulties in Vietnam firsthand in 1945. British troops under General Douglas Gracey cleared out Japanese soldiers in the southern part of Vietnam and helped restore French colonial rule. As a colonial power, London did not question the legitimacy of French imperialism, since Britain, too, had a strong interest in maintaining her own dominions, which stretched from Central America to Africa and Asia.[1] The British shared French fears that the Roosevelt and Truman administrations might insist that all colonial powers relinquish their possessions, not just the French in Indochina. After signing the Atlantic Charter in August 1941, Prime Minister Winston Churchill quickly pointed out that the charter's third point, conveying the right of self-determination and self-government, did not apply to Britain's overseas possessions. In February 1944, London concluded an Anglo-French Protocol of Mutual Aid with Charles de Gaulle's Free French government guaranteeing cooperation in overseas affairs. London also believed that French rule in Indochina would preserve an important buffer between China and British colonies to the south from Burma to New Zealand and Australia. In addition, the British government supported the French agenda to reclaim Indochina in order to regain a strong and friendly partner in the reconstruction of postwar Europe.[2]

Despite British military and political support of the French, London realized that without U.S. assistance French and British resources were too scarce to reestablish French control in Indochina. Therefore, London did what it could to convince Washington that a French-controlled Indochina also served U.S. strategic and economic interests, allowing for a stable Southeast Asia.[3] Harry Truman was certainly more receptive to a French return to Indochina than Franklin D. Roosevelt, yet little aid and support was forthcoming, and Washington embarked on a policy of neutrality during 1945 and 1946. Britain did more, and its forces under General Gracey helped to crush Vietnamese opposition to French rule and facilitated the return of French authorities and troops in October 1945. In January 1946, Gracey handed his post in Saigon over to French General Philippe Leclerc.[4]

By then, Britain was dealing with a far more important issue in regard to her empire—granting independence to India. For some two hundred years, Britain had ruled the vast subcontinent, and after the loss of the American colonies, India became the crown jewel of the British imperial possessions. Although Prime Minister Churchill had refused to grant India independence, the new Labour Party government of Clement Attlee, elected in August 1945, was committed to do just that. Given Attlee's ambitious domestic reform agenda, fervent Indian nationalism, and sectarian violence between Muslims and Hindus, retaining India would be far too costly. However, the unity of India could not be preserved, and on August 15, 1947, India and Pakistan became independent states. Both countries joined the British Commonwealth, created in 1939.[5] The independence of India and Pakistan had a snowball effect for other British possessions seeking self-determination and independence. In 1947, Britain turned its mandate in Palestine over to the United Nations, leading to its partition and the creation of the state of Israel in 1948. The same year, Burma (now Myanmar) and Sri Lanka gained independence. A year later, the Republic of Ireland achieved its complete independence, while Northern Ireland remained part of the United Kingdom.[6]

In the spring of 1948, Britain also faced a Communist insurgency in Malaya. Malaya was especially important because of its rubber and tin production, which brought badly needed pounds to the sagging British economy. Some ethnic Chinese had turned to Communism before World War II and fought ferociously against the Japanese occupiers during the war. British efforts to disarm those Chinese-Malay forces after the war were only partly successful, and several thousand of them launched guerrilla attacks against rubber plantations and tin mines. Britain was ultimately successful in crushing the Communist insurgency by isolating the rebels from the indigenous population, using "new settlements" where the British won the collaboration from local and ethnic Chinese opposed to the rebellion—a method later tried unsuccessfully in Vietnam. The rebels also lacked any support of the Malay population and any considerable assistance from Communist countries. By 1954, most of the insurgents had been defeated, and in August 1957, the British handed control over to the Federation of Malaysia.[7]

A general trend is apparent from British acceptance of dissolution of empire: once London realized that the costs of resisting nationalist movements were too high, it settled on a peaceful transfer of sovereignty. As a result, most newly independent nations joined the Commonwealth, and the Commonwealth in turn was transformed from a white-dominated organization to a diverse assembly of sovereign states. Though Britain lost its empire, it was able to retain cordial and important relations with the newly independent states.[8] The importance of the Commonwealth was evident during Prime Minister Harold Wilson's response to the American escalation in Vietnam. Most Commonwealth members in Africa and Asia were troubled by the conflict and influenced Wilson's decision to find a negotiated settlement.

THE ATTLEE GOVERNMENT AND VIETNAM: 1945–1952

While the United Kingdom was making important steps to grant independence to its overseas possessions, the Attlee government continued to support the French efforts in Indochina. But not every member of Parliament (MP) of his Labour Party approved. Foreshadowing the intraparty strife that Wilson would encounter during the 1960s, leftist MPs strongly criticized Attlee, charging that his government helped restore "repressive colonial rule" in Indochina. The chairman of the Labour Party, Harold Laski, asked his government to recognize the negative impact British policy would have "upon colonial peoples all over the world." Laski claimed it was tragic that Britain was restoring French rule in Indochina, thus abetting a policy that crushed the hopes of indigenous people.[9] However, Attlee stuck to his course. Primarily, he did so because of the strategic and economic importance of a stable Indochina. The British did encourage the French to respond to Vietnamese grievances and accept reform. After fighting between the French and the Viet Minh broke out in late 1946, London responded more cautiously to the French request for assistance. Given Labour Party concerns and also outright opposition from India and Burma, London ruled out any major effort to help Paris. Instead, it sought to convince Washington to become more engaged in Southeast Asia.[10]

The outbreak of the Communist insurrection in Malaya in June 1948 led to an increase of British assistance to the French. London feared the spread of Communism would threaten pro-Western governments in Southeast Asia. A possible victory by Ho Chi Minh against the French in Vietnam raised the specter of Communist victories in Burma, Laos, and Cambodia, and might worsen the situation in Malaya. Equally worrisome was the fact that Ho Chi Minh's Democratic Republic of Vietnam (DRV) had established offices in Bangkok, Singapore, and Hong Kong—the latter two still ruled by Britain.[11] London augmented intelligence sharing and aid to France and urged Washington to do more. Yet, wary of domestic and Asian moderate leaders' opinion, the Attlee government defined its assistance in terms of the struggle against Communism and made clear that it was not abetting French colonial aspirations. As a consequence, Britain, after initial doubts, supported quasi-autonomy granted by the French to Vietnamese Emperor Bao Dai. By accepting the French endeavor to recast the conflict in Indochina as part of the global Cold War contest against Communism, London hoped to win American financial and material assistance. It would serve two purposes: a stable non-Communist Indochina and hence greater security for Britain's possessions and former colonies, such as India and Burma. Undersecretary Sir William Strang of the Foreign Office phrased his government's position succinctly: "We have a part to play in this area [Southeast Asia] which can best be played by no other power. . . . It can best be played by a combination of British experience and United States resources."[12]

The Truman administration reassessed its Indochina policy after the Communist victory in China in October 1949. While the French refusal to grant greater autonomy still angered many in the administration, the State Department increasingly regarded French despotic rule in Indochina as a lesser evil to a Communist victory of Ho Chi Minh. This shift was obvious in two papers of the National Security Council (NSC)—NSC 48/1 and NSC 48/2, which stated that the United States should help Southeast Asian nations gain "peace, national independence and stability." In late 1949, the Attlee government decided to unconditionally recognize the Bao Dai government of Vietnam and did so on February 7, 1950, followed a few hours later by the formal recognition from the United States.[13] Britain's desire to protect her own interests in Southeast Asia and skillful redefinition of colonial struggles as part of the Cold War fight against Communist expansion had helped persuade Washington to assume a far greater role in Indochina. The outbreak of the Korean conflict was the final push needed to convince Washington that the conflict in Indochina was part of the global struggle against Communist aggression. Truman and Eisenhower acted accordingly. In 1954, the United States covered more than 80 percent of the cost of the French Indochina war.[14]

THE CHURCHILL AND EDEN
GOVERNMENTS AND VIETNAM: 1952–1956

When Churchill returned to power in 1952, he and his foreign secretary Anthony Eden viewed Indochina as one of the most dangerous and acute problems for the immediate future. The conflict in Indochina was turning into a proxy war between the United States and the People's Republic of China (PRC). The Churchill government hoped for a French victory for a similar reason that the Attlee administration had—the security of British Malaya and fear of possible Communist attacks on Thailand and Burma. Both countries exported important foodstuffs to Malaya, and without those supplies the fight against Communist insurgents would have proved far more difficult. London also worried that a Communist victory in Vietnam might result in a direct military assault on Malaya. This scenario would then require even more British troops, stretching the country's financial and military resources to the point that other important British defense commitments in the Middle East and Western Europe were to suffer. Before Washington officially adopted the "domino theory" in 1954, London was already worried in 1952 that a Communist victory in Vietnam would have serious consequences for Southeast Asia and beyond. However, the Churchill government was equally concerned about a full-scale American intervention in Indochina, leading perhaps to a large-scale war with the PRC. Thus, the best outcome would be a French victory in Vietnam.[15]

Another potential casualty of the Indochina conflict was the planned European Defense Community (EDC). Like German Chancellor Konrad Adenauer, Churchill strongly supported the creation of the EDC, which would allow for West German rearmament—albeit safeguarded by the EDC—to counterbalance the Soviet threat and an important Western European venue for its own defense. The French government signed the treaty in May 1952, but French Defense Minister Rene Pleven immediately informed Eden that the French parliament would not ratify the treaty as long as France's military resources were drained in Vietnam.[16]

During 1952 and 1953, London hoped that the French would increase their efforts to win the Indochina war. But the Churchill administration refused military aid to the French in Indochina or to supplement French troops with British forces in the EDC. While Britain supported the EDC, it rejected the notion that her troops would be subject to a supranational force. Thus, Britain wanted a European defense for Western Europe to contain any German military ambition but also keep her own forces under British control. London's vague commitment left the Churchill government without any leverage to convince by then war-weary France to do more in Indochina. France did make one more effort, and the result was the debacle of Dien Bien Phu.[17]

The British position shifted during the Geneva Conference of 1954. It was clear that France was losing the war, but more worrisome was that Washington signaled the possibility of direct American intervention to save Vietnam. Eden abandoned the "domino theory" and instead preferred a political solution to prevent an American intervention, which he feared might lead to a wider war, perhaps even a direct U.S.-Soviet conflict.[18] Therefore, the Churchill government supported a diplomatic solution and refused an American proposal to intervene jointly in Vietnam. Britain chaired the Geneva

Conference with the Soviet Union, and the final settlement included international guarantees to adhere to the neutralization of Vietnam. However, Churchill agreed to join the American-sponsored defense community for Southeast Asia (Southeast Asia Treaty Organization [SEATO]), designed to forestall further Communist aggression in the region.[19]

Churchill and Eden expected Eisenhower to abide by the Geneva agreement and were sorely disappointed when Washington decided to embark on nation-building in South Vietnam. London had grave concerns about the viability of the Ngo Dinh Diem government, concerns initially shared by Washington, yet Eisenhower and Secretary of State John Foster Dulles were firmly committed to backing the premier by late 1954. London, as it turned out, rightly feared that the United States would encourage Diem to cancel the planned 1956 nationwide election that Britain strongly favored regardless of the possibility of a Viet Minh victory. According to London, failure to adhere to the Geneva Accord might lead to further conflict and, if the United States intervened militarily, the possibility of a wider war.[20] However, with Diem consolidating his control over South Vietnam, Prime Minister Eden reluctantly agreed to support the South Vietnamese leader in 1956.

Churchill's and Eden's policy during the First Indochina War set the pattern for their successors of how to respond to the growing American role in Indochina. While Britain refused to intervene in Vietnam militarily, no British leader felt at liberty to openly challenge the U.S. policy in Vietnam. The United Kingdom relied on American military protection for her security, but this safety net might be weakened if Washington engaged in a major war in Southeast Asia. London discerned a twofold scenario in case conflict intensified in the Far East. First, U.S. primary interest would shift from Europe to Asia, leaving Europe more vulnerable to Soviet encroachment. Second, the American commitment to defending Southeast Asia could explode into a major, perhaps even world, war. These prospects were dismal, but London also had to consider maintaining its "special relationship" with the United States. The partnership with Washington became even more important after Great Britain was denied entry into the European Economic Community (EEC) by France's President de Gaulle in 1963. Britain hence had to find a policy that accommodated its national self-interest without alienating the United States. In addition, British prime ministers from Harold Macmillan to Harold Wilson had to face intensifying domestic opposition to the American policy in Vietnam.

HAROLD MACMILLAN (1961 TO OCTOBER 1963)

During the early 1960s, Prime Minister Macmillan followed the framework set for Vietnam by Churchill and Eden. Admittedly, Communism threatened Southeast Asia, but in the final assessment, it was in the best interest of neither the United Kingdom nor the United States to pursue a policy of greater involvement. Subsequently, Macmillan tried to discourage President John F. Kennedy from a greater commitment in Southeast Asia. Macmillan, born in 1894, had been in government service since 1939. He became prime minister in January 1957, after the Suez Crisis, which had caused a serious strain in Anglo-American relations. The conservative leader enjoyed a very cordial relationship, even friendship, with President Eisenhower, and he was somewhat concerned whether this mutual understanding would continue with Kennedy—a man a generation younger than himself. Soon these doubts were dispelled, and both leaders developed good personal relations, despite the different approaches each leader adopted toward Southeast Asia.[21]

Macmillan strongly favored a political solution for Indochina. In February 1961, he sent David Ormsby-Gore to the newly inaugurated Kennedy to convey British concern about the American role in Southeast Asia in general and the current crisis over Laos in particular. The English ambassador openly criticized the American role in Laos and accused the United States of backing a corrupt government, a policy that could lead to serious consequences for the Kennedy administration in the future.[22] Less blunt, but in essence not that different, was the advice of Macmillan when he met with Kennedy a month later. Macmillan indicated that America's allies were unwilling to support any major American intervention in Laos. Britain also could not subscribe to an "unlimited commitment" to the region.[23]

The prime minister looked at Indochina in not so much ideological but rather more pragmatic, historical terms. The once solid Communist alliance had apparently been breaking apart since the late 1940s when Marshal Tito had sought his own independent version of communism in Yugoslavia. More importantly, in the early 1960s, Moscow and Beijing were at odds over both ideology and foreign policy. The Sino-Soviet split demonstrated that, although both the Soviet Union and the PRC adhered to communist ideology, they also acted according to self-interest, which led to the cessation of diplomatic relations between both countries in late 1961. Macmillan concluded, "These developments made it clear to me even at the time that the old lessons of history were once again proving true. Ideological agreement led no more on the Communist side to automatic cooperation than it did among the nations of Europe in the sixteenth and seventeenth century."[24] Turning to history, Macmillan traced the background to the current situation in Indochina. Obviously, French colonial rule did not bring the same benefits to the region that Britain left her former possessions. India was a good example. Despite the "grave injury of partition," British rule gave India and Pakistan "a legacy of efficient local, provincial and central administration."[25] In Indochina, the situation was clearly different. Although granted formal but not actual independence, the new states of Cambodia, Laos, and Vietnam experienced "confusion and internal weakness, coupled with the unrelenting pressure under Communist direction."[26] British Foreign Minister Eden had worked "tirelessly" to end the conflict in 1954, because British interests were not served by war in Southeast Asia.[27]

In 1960, when the civil war in Laos became a focal point of the Eisenhower administration, the prime minister grew anxious about a potential American intervention. Macmillan feared that American involvement might lead to a wider conflict, eventually including the PRC and the Soviet Union. Consequently, London urged a cease-fire and was strongly opposed to any direct Western interference. Macmillan and his cabinet were also uncertain about American aims in Laos and feared that Britain could be dragged into an open-ended conflict.[28]

In his first meeting with Kennedy in March 1961 in Key West, the British leader expressed his concern about Indochina and Laos, in particular, and warned Kennedy of "the danger of being sucked into these inhospitable areas without a base, without any clear political or strategic aims and without any effective system of deploying armed forces or controlling local administration."[29] Macmillan clearly did not want to engage Britain in a widening conflict in Southeast Asia. But as a SEATO member, London might still face the decision to follow the American lead and send British troops. Hence, he had to convince Kennedy that a major military operation in landlocked Laos was futile. Macmillan presented three options for the Americans in Laos. First, they could set up a puppet regime, which "would be useless and corrupt," eventually forcing the United States to get more deeply involved in Laotian politics. Second, the United States could intervene directly, with "bigger and bigger" armies. Third, the Americans could stay out. To Kennedy, the first option was too close to imperialism and hence not feasible. The other two possibilities required more deliberation. However, Macmillan felt that Kennedy was not keen on intensifying the American role, and neither leader wanted to proceed in Laos unilaterally.[30] In turn, Kennedy pressured Macmillan to agree that it might be politically necessary "to do something" in Laos, before the West lost more ground to the Soviet Union. Yet Macmillan made it clear that his government was not willing to do more than "join in the appearance of resistance" and again emphasized that the geography and conditions in Laos made it a dangerous place to fight.[31]

In a letter to Queen Elizabeth II in September 1961, Macmillan addressed his misgivings and concern about the American course in Laos. He particularly deplored the striving of some members of the U.S. State Department, including Americans stationed in Laos, to sabotage negotiations seeking to

President Kennedy (left) and British Prime Minister Harold Macmillan developed a genuine friendship, although Macmillan privately tried to dissuade Kennedy from further escalation in Vietnam. Courtesy of the John F. Kennedy Presidential Library.

neutralize the country. Apparently, the American officials favored a military solution involving SEATO. Macmillan told the queen that, if he promised support to Washington, the United Kingdom might be asked to intervene militarily if a limited intervention became necessary. The British leader was relieved to learn that President Kennedy decided against the use of force soon after their Key West meeting.[32]

Laos demonstrated the dangers of the Cold War world and, moreover, the possibility of the use of nuclear weapons. Britain would seriously undermine her self-interest by endorsing or even contributing militarily to an unnecessary showdown in Southeast Asia. Already, by the summer of 1961, Macmillan reconsidered his promised support to the United States in case of a SEATO intervention. He regarded his approval given to Kennedy at Key

West as "lapsed" and looked upon the entire operation as "more and more unreal."[33] It was obviously far better for London to end conflicts in Southeast Asia through diplomacy and negotiations. London's insistence that Laos was not worth risking a major war did help influence American decision making in finding a negotiated settlement.

The crisis was finally solved at the conference table in the summer of 1962, affirming the neutrality of Laos and the formation of a coalition government. Despite recurring violations of the 1962 settlement by the Pathet Lao and their North Vietnamese allies, the episode made clear that Great Britain was hesitant to commit military forces to fight in the jungles of Southeast Asia. Foreign Secretary Douglas-Home—Macmillan's successor in office in 1963—expressed the profound relief of the British government over the peaceful solution in Laos in a speech before the United Nations. Lord Douglas-Home pointed out that the other alternative might have been warfare between the great powers. He added that both sides realized the difficulty of containing a military face-off and fortunately chose to talk, instead of escalating the conflict. War would have devastated Southeast Asia and perhaps the rest of the world.[34]

Yet the possibility of renewed conflict in Southeast Asia worried British leaders. Kennedy demanded British financial contributions to rebuild Laos. Reluctantly, London provided more than one million pounds. While pleased that Britain had regained its traditionally good understanding with the United States, the special relationship was not without hazard. Douglas-Home noted, "I think that our policy of close co-operation with the Americans in South-East Asia has been the right one. It is more likely we should have been faced with a local war in the area in 1960 or 1961 if we had not been able to persuade the Americans to take the right line. The risk of a disaster in Vietnam, Laos, or even Cambodia is still considerable."[35]

Though the Laotian crisis was solved at the conference table, Prime Minister Macmillan was increasingly troubled about the American involvement in South Vietnam. In December 1961, Washington deployed helicopters, planes, and four hundred additional men to Saigon to assist the South Vietnamese military in the struggle against the Viet Cong. At the time, Macmillan did not foresee "any more grave developments" but admitted in hindsight that this arrangement was the first step leading to a "long and inextricable entanglement" of the United States in Southeast Asia.[36]

The prime minister also believed that American military operations were inadequate "to deal with this kind of infiltration" by Vietnamese Communists. Macmillan relied on Britain's own experience with Communist insurgents in Malaya. The British combined political and military actions to crush the Communist opposition. Macmillan maintained that the situation in

Vietnam was different because the United States neither had efficient control over the South Vietnamese government nor offered a political alternative to those opposed to Diem. Unless the great majority of the local population could be engaged in the struggle, the Americans had no real basis on which to build a successful policy.[37]

THE BRITISH ADVISORY MISSION IN VIETNAM

Under pressure by the Kennedy administration to do more in Vietnam, in July 1961 London concluded a bilateral agreement with the Diem government to establish the British Advisory Group in South Vietnam, better known as the British Advisory Mission (BRIAM). Concerned about the deteriorating situation in South Vietnam, Britain had already proposed plans to President Diem in 1960 to establish an advisory mission. The goal was to share British experience gathered in counterinsurgency fighting in Malaysia and help train South Vietnamese forces to defeat its own insurgency. The initial response both in Saigon and Washington was negative. To Saigon, the offer evoked the specter of colonialism, and Washington did not welcome British criticism of its strategy in South Vietnam.[38] BRIAM was led by Robert Thompson and two other officers who had ample experience in counterinsurgency. Its scope was rather limited since Washington was opposed to any activities that interfered with its Military Assistance Advisory Group (MAAG). However, Thompson and his superiors envisioned a wider role. Douglas-Home thought BRIAM could help remedy the situation because the United States faced difficulties fighting the insurgency on its own. Douglas-Home concluded that the mission "might tip the balance against a very expensive war."[39]

Soon after his arrival in Saigon in September 1961, Thompson devised an ambitious plan to pacify the Mekong Delta. The plan required substantial civilian and military cooperation, the construction of fortified villages, and the use of already existing self-defense corps in order to isolate and exterminate insurgents. After initial concern, the United States endorsed Thompson's strategy. However, successful implementation was hindered by the South Vietnamese leadership. Diem's brother Nhu was put in charge of the Strategic Hamlet Program. Strategic hamlets were indeed built, but they displaced the local population and the program did not include any social or economic reform. Nhu's sole goal was to extend his control over the rural population. The British Ambassador to Saigon Henry Hohler strongly urged his government in the summer of 1962 to disassociate itself from the Strategic Hamlet Program, and London accepted the advice. The program ended in failure, driving more of the rural population into the arms of the Viet Cong.[40]

The BRIAM mission itself did not meet its goals. It was undermanned and underfinanced, and although Thompson in various visits to Washington found high-level approval of his ideas, Washington did not back Britain sufficiently to have an impact on Diem. Instead, Diem and his brother Nhu used elements of Thompson's strategies to increase their control over Vietnamese farmers. BRIAM also faced questions and criticism in Parliament. Parliament insisted that it should have more information and oversight over any British involvement in counterinsurgency operations in South Vietnam.[41]

GROWING CONCERN IN PARLIAMENT

In February 1962, the United States sent four thousand additional troops to Vietnam. Macmillan deplored that move because he regarded the government of South Vietnam as weak and ineffective and unable to unify the people against the Viet Cong. Obviously, additional American troops could not solve the problems of the Diem government.[42] But Britain's concern over the consequences of an expanded American commitment to Vietnam required an open exchange with the United States administration. Macmillan chose to express his apprehension privately to Kennedy, refusing to publicly challenge American policy. However, this diplomatic approach encountered domestic opposition in Parliament.

Several members of Parliament, most of them Labour MPs, wondered whether Macmillan might commit Great Britain to the American policy in Vietnam. In March 1962, the House addressed the recent increase in American personnel. Parliament learned that American pilots participated in bombing operations in South Vietnam, and some members expressed their anxiety about a possible escalation of the conflict. They also questioned the legality of the American involvement and inquired about the British position toward Vietnam and the government's willingness to end the fighting through diplomatic means. Peter Thomas, joint undersecretary of state for foreign affairs, was asked whether Britain would address Vietnam in the UN Security Council. He replied negatively.[43] MP William Warbey regarded American participation in bombing raids as a considerable deterioration of the situation in South Vietnam, leading to a dangerous and "inflammatory" development in Southeast Asia. He accused the United States "of military intervention in a civil war which the Americans themselves have provoked by their sabotage of the Geneva Agreement."[44] Thomas strongly disagreed with Warbey and stressed that the United States was simply responding to a call for help by the Saigon government. Thomas also emphasized that the "threat to peace in Vietnam" was not a result of American activities but rather aggression from the North Vietnamese government, which was encouraging and supporting an "insurrectionary movement" in the South.[45]

Thomas, though, agreed that the situation in Vietnam was serious. His government awaited further information from the International Control Commission (ICC) before Britain decided on any political action. Labour MP Wilson was not satisfied with the government's position. He could not comprehend why Britain did not take responsive action as cochairman of the Geneva Conference. Wilson argued that the appropriate policy was to put "pressure on all concerned" and that the Geneva agreement had to be adhered to.[46] Two years later, as prime minister, Wilson would face similar questions and criticism from his Labour MPs, who repeatedly reminded him of his statements as opposition leader. However, Macmillan's government was withholding from Parliament its conviction at that time that negotiation over Vietnam would be counterproductive. While North Vietnamese infiltration of the South accelerated, American military support to Diem might help stem the tide.[47]

Later, in March 1962, Undersecretary Thomas again had to defend his government's policy on Vietnam to attacks from MPs. Several MPs expressed their concern over the differing positions of the two Geneva chairmen, from London and Moscow, on the Vietnam conflict, which obviously prevented a joint approach for a diplomatic settlement.[48] MPs Fenner Brockway, Harold Davies, and Christopher Mayhew were also worried how the conflict affected British obligations to SEATO, perhaps even leading to a British military engagement. Moreover, they inquired whether the British government, as cochair of Geneva, was discussing with Washington its military aid to South Vietnam, hoping that London urged the United States "not to go beyond operational military training" of South Vietnamese troops.

Thomas made clear that the United Kingdom had no responsibility to Saigon. He was less certain how the present situation affected British obligations within SEATO but hoped that Britain would not be forced to intervene militarily. Indeed, London was in close contact with Washington over events in Vietnam but not as Geneva cochair. Labour MP Konni Zilliacus demanded stronger assurances that Great Britain would not be drawn into the Vietnam conflict or even a war with China because of the continuous American assistance to Diem:

Is the hon. Gentleman aware that American intervention in South Vietnam, whatever may be the allegations concerning North Vietnam help or otherwise to South Vietnam, is contrary to the Charter and might involve us in war? Will the hon. Gentleman at least give the same warning that Mr. Eden, as he then was, gave to Mr. Dulles over Dienbien-phu, if American military action in Vietnam results in war with China, we will dissociate ourselves from such a war and will refuse to be involved in it?[49]

Secretary Thomas was unable to give such assurances, citing the need to await the ICC report before deciding on further action.

The ICC report arrived in the summer of 1962 and recommended the immediate withdrawal of all American personnel and the end to any American weapon shipments to South Vietnam. The Soviet Union sent a note to Macmillan asking him to condone the findings of the commission. American actions, according to the Soviet note, were in obvious violation of the Geneva agreement, and the United States, together with South Vietnamese authorities, was the "main culprit" in preventing nationwide elections in Vietnam with the goal of uniting the country.[50] Moscow suggested that Britain join in a statement as cochairman of the Geneva agreement that demanded the immediate withdrawal of the United States from the region. Some MPs backed the Soviet suggestions, but Edward Heath, speaking for the government, strongly rejected the Soviet point of view. Heath considered North Vietnam solely responsible for the present dangerous situation in Vietnam. Not Washington, but Hanoi, violated the 1954 accords in its attempt to overthrow the Saigon government.[51]

The discussions in Parliament illuminate domestic concern about events in Vietnam. Like Macmillan, MPs were deeply anxious about further military escalation, particularly a war with the PRC. Consistent with British policy since the 1950s, they believed that Britain could not and should not support any policy leading to war in Indochina. Several MPs strongly attacked the U.S. engagement, which they charged violated the Geneva agreement and risked a major war. In their view, Britain should bring the issue before the UN Security Council and dissociate itself from the dangerous American policy. Parliament was increasingly divided between supporters and critics of the American policy.

Prime Minister Macmillan expressed his doubts of the American strategy repeatedly in consultations with American leaders during the Kennedy presidency. He hoped that solid advice and also Britain's own experience in the Far East might influence American thinking and allow a reevaluation of the engagement in South Vietnam. Macmillan strongly rejected any British troop deployments to Vietnam and ultimately favored a negotiated settlement following the example of Laos. In addition, British global security interests drained Britain's resources. British troops were stationed in West Germany, Kenya, southern Arabia, and the Far East. In 1963, the United Kingdom spent almost two billion pounds on defense, about a tenth of the gross national product.[52] Britain simply could not afford another major military engagement.

SIR ALEC DOUGLAS-HOME
(OCTOBER 1963 TO OCTOBER 1964)

After seven years at the helm, Macmillan resigned as prime minister in October 1963 due to health problems. His last days in office saw a decline of general support for his Conservative Party. Foreign secretary Douglas-Home, heir to an old and distinguished Scottish family, was invited by Queen Elizabeth II to form a new government on October 18, 1963. Born in 1903, Douglas-Home had served in the British government since 1951 and became foreign minister in 1960.[53]

Douglas-Home represented the ambiguities of Britain after 1945. Britain had to come to terms with its loss of empire and global status. Douglas-Home supported the British decision to build its own nuclear force and favored an independent course toward the two superpowers. Communism was an obvious threat to Western security, but Britain also had to play an autonomous role in global affairs, albeit within the framework of the North Atlantic alliance.[54] Douglas-Home accepted the limits of British global power but insisted that the United Kingdom continue to be a special partner, though with lessened influence, of the United States. Britain faced the dilemma to fulfill its military commitments while it barely had the resources to do so. London could no longer maintain its prestige by military might but had to resort to diplomacy in maintaining prestige throughout the world.[55] Douglas-Home held firm in his belief that the United Kingdom should not become engaged in South Vietnam. As foreign minister, Douglas-Home expressed this conviction to Kennedy on several occasions, pointing to the British commitment in Malaya and Singapore. Britain did not have sufficient forces to intervene in Vietnam, but even if it had Douglas-Home maintained that the "country would swallow up almost any army, as indeed it swallowed the French and then the American." Moreover, public opinion in Britain was against British intervention or outright endorsement of the American role in Vietnam.[56]

As Prime Minister, Douglas-Home had a rocky start. Rumors persisted that he was handpicked by Macmillan and not really up to the job. His status as peer was also seen as an impediment. How could a Scottish aristocrat understand the problems of the poor and underprivileged in Britain? Labour leader Wilson even labeled Douglas-Home the "scion of effete establishment." The prime minister responded by disclaiming his peerage, leaving it to his son, and transformed himself from the Earl of Home into Sir Alec.[57] Yet problems persisted, and the British economy was clearly in decline while the pound was losing value. Douglas-Home underestimated the economic difficulties in Great Britain that aided the Labour victory in 1964. In foreign policy, the prime minister faced crises ranging from Cyprus and Rhodesia to, once again, Malaya that further strained British finances. Economics and self-interest clearly dictated that Britain could not embark on any major foreign policy operations in Southeast Asia.[58] Both Cyprus and Southeast Asia complicated Anglo-American relations, and despite attempts to conceal their differences, defense planners were at odds on how to proceed.[59]

Douglas-Home's first visit to the United States as prime minister was the sad occasion of Kennedy's funeral in late November 1963. Three months later, he returned to meet with Lyndon B. Johnson. The prime minister received a warm welcome, and Johnson reaffirmed the close relations between both countries despite recent differences in opinion. Douglas-Home emphasized that Britain and the United States shared the same goal of worldwide peace. Regardless of sometimes contrary approaches—British sale of buses to Cuba being one—Douglas-Home maintained that it was his sincere desire to "keep as close as we can" to the United States as partners and as allies since the "peace of the world" depended on their understanding.[60] In his conversation with Johnson, the main topics were Vietnam and Malaysia. The meeting resulted in a compromise; both sides agreed they were facing similar problems in Southeast Asia. While the United States recognized the British position to maintain the independence of Malaysia against encroachment from Indonesia, Douglas-Home announced his support for the American policy in Vietnam.[61]

The prime minister also agreed to explore the French position on Vietnam and to discuss with President de Gaulle the French proposal calling for the neutralization of both Vietnams. Douglas-Home was interested in the American progress in Vietnam but received the bad news that the situation was not improving. Johnson emphasized that it was crucial the United States and Britain concurred on Southeast Asia in adopting a policy that offered both the "olive branch and arrows," instead of the vague and counterproductive French neutralization proposal.[62] Both leaders agreed on the need to assist the free nations in that area in maintaining their independence and reaffirmed their defense commitment to the region:

> The Prime Minister and the President gave special consideration to South-east Asian matters and to the problem of assisting free states in the area to maintain their independence. . . . The Prime Minister reemphasized the United Kingdom's support for the United States policy in South Vietnam. The President reaffirmed the support for the peaceful national independence of Malaysia. Both expressed their sincere hope that the leaders of the independent countries in the region would by mutual friendship and cooperation establish an area of prosperity and stability. . . . Both Governments reaffirm that in all these fields

[Southeast Asia and Latin America] their aim remains [to] solely achieve and safeguard the integrity and stability of the countries of the free world on the basis of full independence.[63]

To Douglas-Home, the visit was a success. Washington finally accepted the British position on Malaysian security, and the American role in Southeast Asia was defined solely in terms of assistance. Douglas-Home also hoped that in the future Britain would be closely consulted by Washington on all global issues.[64] Like France, Britain was not willing to be dominated by the United States and wherever possible expressed its independence and sovereignty. However, Johnson was angered by Douglas-Home's insistence to send nonmilitary machinery to Cuba in defiance of the American embargo and henceforth distrusted British leaders.

The events in the Tonkin Gulf in early August 1964 surprised Douglas-Home in the middle of his summer holidays. The first news was not too worrisome since Washington described the attack on the *Maddox* as an "isolated incident." Though the United States increased naval patrols in the gulf, along with a protest note to the United Nations, the situation did not appear serious.[65] A second attack two days later led to retaliatory airstrikes against North Vietnam and a congressional resolution on Southeast Asia. On August 4, 1964, Johnson informed Douglas-Home of the attack and the retaliatory air raids. The American president expressed his determination to "take all measures necessary to prevent such attacks and protect our forces." Johnson assured Douglas-Home that the American goal in Southeast Asia remained unchanged and focused on maintaining peace and security. Johnson promised to stay in close contact and continuously inform the prime minister of future developments.[66] Douglas-Home and his foreign secretary R. A. Butler expressed their full support for Johnson's actions:

As regards to the North Vietnamese attacks on United States naval forces, H.M. Government made their position clear in the Security Council when they supported the action taken by the United States Government, in accordance with the inherent right of self-defence recognized by Article 51 of the charter of the United Nations. They share the desire of the President of the United States to avoid risk spreading the conflict.[67]

Britain was not alone in its support of the American reaction to the Tonkin Gulf attack. Bonn showed "full understanding," and New Zealand and Australia also responded favorably. In Canada and France, approval was mixed with caution. However, not all British papers endorsed the American course in Vietnam. The *Manchester Guardian* actually went so far as to question the circumstances of the attack on the *Maddox* and accused Washington of having manufactured the entire crisis so that it could implement airstrikes planned months earlier.[68] The *London Times* commentary on the events also expressed some concern while it dismissed the "furious responses" of Beijing and Hanoi to the American airstrikes. Danger could arise if either Beijing or Hanoi claimed the Tonkin Gulf as territorial waters or if Washington changed its strategy:

> If President Johnson had announced that he was henceforth carrying the war by land, sea, and air into North Vietnam, or even was going on with air raids indefinitely, then more of the allied peoples would have qualms and doubts. It is true that some Americans would like to broaden the war in that way . . . yet the answer is not to let American or any other foreign servicemen invade or bomb North Vietnam indefinitely. Such an action, in China's doorstep, would almost certainly bring more havoc than profit.[69]

Times editorialists argued that the best course for saving South Vietnam was to expand on the current approach, which included military aid and training, economic support, and confidence-building measures for the Vietnamese people. Without such help, South Vietnam would be lost. Military escalation by either Washington, which seemed unlikely for the time being, or Beijing would only make matters worse. The place to settle the tensions in Southeast Asia was the UN Security Council and not the battlefield.[70] The *Times* summed up the thinking of many British citizens and their government when editorialists held that the American response to the attack in the Tonkin Gulf was justified, but any further escalation had to be prevented.

In light of Britain's costly global commitments, the country could not afford any major military effort to fight the insurgency in South Vietnam, as some in Washington desired. The majority of the British public and a considerable number of MPs were also opposed to such a course. While a non-Communist South Vietnam might provide a security barrier against Communist encroachment to Commonwealth countries in Asia, British experience in South Vietnam left profound concerns about whether the Diem government pursued the right strategy to defeat the insurgency and North Vietnamese infiltrators. British governments after World War II depended on the special relationship with the United States and, economically and politically, could ill afford a rift with Washington. Hence, British leaders Macmillan and Douglas-Home chose a quiet, diplomatic approach in order to influence presidents Kennedy and Johnson. The task to manage domestic opposition to escalation in Vietnam, maintain a global role for Britain, and foster the special relationship with Washington proved to be even more challenging for Prime Minister Wilson.

Chapter 5

Lyndon B. Johnson and Military Escalation in Vietnam, 1964–1968

Vietnam was undoubtedly a troubling issue for John F. Kennedy, but the conflict was far from consuming all of Kennedy's attention. The struggle in Southeast Asia, while unexpected and clearly unwanted, would become the overriding concern for Lyndon B. Johnson. He was less interested than Kennedy in the intricacies of foreign policy making. Johnson's dream was the "Great Society" that guaranteed civil rights, social security, welfare, health care, and education to all Americans.[1]

Johnson's experience in foreign policy was rather limited, but like Kennedy, he firmly believed that America could not give in to Communist aggression. He argued that the United States had to remain vigilant and faithful to its commitments. Otherwise, the free world might experience another "Munich" by caving in to dictators. Johnson maintained that third world countries, aided by American tutelage and assistance, could learn to appreciate the benefits of Western democracy and become partners in the conflict against Communist totalitarianism.[2] To Johnson's dismay, the South Vietnamese proved unwilling to fully accept Western democracy and way of life because they had their own long history and culture, which they cherished over the American-imposed model.

More important for Washington was domestic pressure not to surrender another country to Communist rule. Kennedy feared that a withdrawal from Vietnam would lead to "another Joe McCarthy Red scare," but Johnson's dilemma was even more profound. He deeply wanted to enact profound domestic reforms but could not afford losing South Vietnam:

> I knew from the start that I was bound to be crucified either way I moved. If I left the woman I really loved—the Great Society—in order to get involved with that bitch of war on the other side of the world, then I would lose everything at

home. All my programs, all my hopes to feed the hungry and shelter the home-less. All my dreams to provide education and medical care to the browns and blacks and the lame and the poor. But if I left that war and let the Communist take over South Vietnam then I would be seen as a coward and my nation seen as an appeaser, and we would both find it impossible to accomplish anything for anybody around the globe.[3]

Johnson quickly despised the conflict in Vietnam but trapped himself with his commitment to pursue his slain predecessor's policies. Instead of securing domestic harmony, his decision to escalate the war in Vietnam divided the country to a degree not experienced since the Civil War. One of the casualties was Johnson's own career. In March 1968, he announced that he would not run for reelection and declared a bombing halt on North Vietnam.[4] By then, Kennedy's limited commitment of more than sixteen thousand advisors to South Vietnam had grown into a large-scale war with more than half a million U.S. troops deployed and thousands killed or injured. Despite the massive firepower of the United States, no end to the fighting was in sight.

THE BACKGROUND: JOHNSON

Born in the hill country of southwestern Texas in 1908, as the oldest of five children, Johnson came from a very different background than the affluent and nine-years-younger Kennedy. Of lower middle-class background, John-son was encouraged by his mother to attend Southwest Texas State Teachers College. There he quickly enjoyed college politics. In 1928, he taught for nine months in a predominantly Mexican American elementary school in Cotulla, Texas. Johnson then returned to college, graduating in 1930. For a short time, he taught high school in Houston but jumped at the first chance to enter poli-tics. In 1931, he left for Washington as a congressional aide for Representa-tive Richard Kleberg and ably used this position to study the intricacies of Congress. Four years later, he became Texas's director of the National Youth Administration. In 1937, Johnson was elected to the House of Representa-tives, and after an unsuccessful first attempt in 1941, he was finally elected to the Senate in 1949.[5] Following Pearl Harbor, Johnson served for a year in the Navy, earning a Silver Star, before being called back to Washington by Franklin D. Roosevelt.

As senator, Johnson rapidly rose through the ranks. He was elected party whip in 1951, minority leader in 1953, and majority leader in 1955. In the Senate, Johnson proved his talent as a consummate politician, earning him national recognition as one of the most effective and powerful leaders in the Senate's history. Johnson was instrumental in bringing down Senator Joseph

McCarthy, and he was also the driving force behind the passage of the civil rights bills of 1957 and 1960. He generally supported the Eisenhower administration in foreign policy issues but opposed American airstrikes to help the French at Dien Bien Phu in 1954. Overall, Johnson prodded his Democratic senators to pursue a responsible and constructive course during the Eisenhower years.[6]

Johnson's status and achievements made him a potential candidate for the presidency in 1960.[7] But Johnson started late in the presidential race and eventually settled for number 2—becoming vice president, with the election of Kennedy. Johnson hoped he could play a substantial role as vice president yet was never fully part of the Kennedy inner circle.[8] Johnson attended both cabinet and National Security Council (NSC) meetings and represented his country abroad. Hence, he was well informed about foreign policy issues, such as Vietnam, which he had visited in 1961.[9]

EARLY DECISIONS: NOVEMBER 1963–MARCH 1964

The Johnson administration dealt with the aftermath of Dallas by first ensuring a smooth transition and bringing Kennedy's domestic program to fruition. Johnson kept the entire Kennedy cabinet and many of Kennedy's advisors, assuring the country that he would continue his predecessor's course. In foreign policy issues, he relied heavily on the advice of Kennedy's men.[10] Like most foreign policy issues, Vietnam was dropped in the background for the time being—of foremost importance was Kennedy's domestic agenda, which was approved in the following months by Congress.

Soon Vietnam required Johnson's attention. At the end of 1963, North Vietnam intensified its infiltration into the South, also deploying regular military units. The National Liberation Front (NLF) stepped up its political and military operations and received better arms and equipment from the North.[11] Johnson was unwilling to let South Vietnam fall to the Communist North. He felt obligated to continue Kennedy's policy and stand firm against Communist aggression because it was America's duty as leader of the free world. But he was also concerned about his image at home.[12]

Within days of assuming office, Johnson had to make his first decision on Vietnam. On November 24, 1963, Johnson met with Secretaries of State and Defense Dean Rusk and Robert McNamara, as well as Ambassador to Vietnam Henry Cabot Lodge, to discuss the situation in Vietnam, and received mixed answers. The president made it abundantly clear that he was determined to win in South Vietnam and would not allow that country to become another China. He demanded that his generals and officials get the job done and give him breathing space for his domestic program.[13] While he expected positive results, Johnson had no intentions to go beyond the current American role in Vietnam.

The result of that discussion was Johnson's first National Security Action Memorandum on Vietnam (NSAM 273), which was approved on November 26, 1963. It stated that the central objective of the United States in South Vietnam was "to assist the people and Government of that country to win their contest against the externally directed and supported Communist conspiracy."[14] Johnson was aware that Ngo Dinh Diem's assassination had not solved the domestic problems in South Vietnam and that the new government lacked in competency. Despite these odds, McNamara and the president hoped to turn the tide, ending the American commitment by 1965.[15] NSAM 273 also proposed covert operations, already suggested in May 1963, in which South Vietnam was to perform "hit-and-run" attacks against North Vietnam, with secret American military assistance (Oplan 34A).[16] The memorandum was clearly not a change of previous American policy. It promised continuous support for the new South Vietnamese government, led by General Duong Van Minh, but at the same time reaffirmed that the war could only be won by the South Vietnamese themselves, assuming there was no major change in the political situation in Saigon.[17]

But McNamara's visit to Vietnam in December 1963 was dismaying. Unless prevalent trends were reversed, South Vietnam might quickly become neutralized or, even worse, be taken over by the Communists.[18] McNamara recommended a greater role for U.S. advisors in Saigon's decision making.[19] The bad news from Vietnam worried some members of Congress who were critical of further American involvement in Vietnam. Senator Richard Russell (D-GA), chairman of the Armed Services Committee and longtime friend and mentor of Johnson, suggested that the president reach an understanding with Saigon, allowing for a quick American withdrawal from the country, without losing face in world opinion.[20]

Senate majority leader Mike Mansfield was more direct, urging the president in January 1964 to reexamine the U.S. policy in Vietnam. Mansfield felt that the United States was close to the "point of no return" in Southeast Asia, heading toward escalation. In Vietnam, America again displayed a tendency already evident during the Korean War "to bite off more than we were prepared to chew."[21] The administration had to assess whether it was truly in the interest of the United States to continue its involvement and pay for it "with blood and treasure," only to discover later that the initial commitment was shortsighted. The solution of the conflict was ultimately a Vietnamese responsibility, and Johnson needed to work for a peaceful settlement between North and South Vietnam, involving diplomatic consultations with France, Great Britain, India, and perhaps even Russia.[22]

When Johnson asked his leading cabinet members for advice, they strongly discouraged a political settlement or neutralization, since it would only be the first step to an ultimate Communist victory, and emphasized that the United States had extended security interests in the region.[23] However, Mansfield lobbied for neutralization in the Senate. He asserted that American national interest did not require the United States to take on prime responsibility for Vietnam, sacrificing "a vast number of American lives." Americans were in Vietnam solely to help "improve the Vietnamese military."[24] The conflict in Vietnam was essentially a matter among Vietnamese and could only be solved by them; it should never become an American war:

> Indeed, we might ask ourselves: Do we ourselves, in terms of our national interest as seen in the juxtaposition to the cost of American lives and resources . . . prefer another Vietnamese type of involvement or a Korean type of involvement in these and other countries and elsewhere in southeast Asia? . . . Are we to regard lightly the American casualties which would certainly be involved?[25]

Even more critical of the administration's Vietnam policy was Senator Wayne Morse (D-OR), who urged Johnson to immediately withdraw from Southeast Asia. The American role in Vietnam since the 1950s had not been justified and would not stand the test of history, Morse thought.[26] Morse also found support in senators Allen J. Ellender (D-LA) and Ernest Gruening (D-AK). The administration was shocked, as well as angered, by the senators' comments. It felt betrayed by the Democratic majority leader and was concerned by the possible reaction to Mansfield's comments in Saigon. A public debate over Vietnam could give the impression that the United States was wary of the conflict, leading to the collapse of the Saigon government.[27]

But also, Johnson was not willing to make Vietnam an American war. McNamara testified to the House Armed Services Committee that continuous U.S. training and supplies would be sufficient to allow the Army of the Republic of Vietnam (ARVN) to succeed against the Communist insurgents. He added, "I don't believe that we as a nation should assume the primary responsibility for the war in South Vietnam. It is a counter-guerrilla war, it is a war that can be only won by the Vietnamese themselves. Our responsibility is not to substitute ourselves for the Vietnamese, but to train them to carry on the operations that they themselves are capable of."[28] Increased turmoil and violence in South Vietnam quickly proved that American support was insufficient to turn the tide against the insurgents. Johnson reached another fork in the road and once more intensified his country's commitment to South Vietnam.[29]

NSAM 288: PREVENT THE FALL
OF SOUTH VIETNAM AT ALL COSTS

As a result of the deteriorating conditions in South Vietnam, the Joint Chiefs proposed a change in policy, requiring considerable expansion in the American effort. The new policy, as adopted in NSAM 288, not only called for a larger commitment but also redefined the American objectives in Vietnam. A Communist victory in South Vietnam had to be prevented at all costs; otherwise, the rest of Southeast Asia and even the Pacific Rim might fall under Communist dominance.[30] South Vietnamese military forces must be further augmented, and the United States needed greater control over the Saigon leadership. The Joint Chiefs of Staff also favored direct action against North Vietnam. Johnson opposed escalation and targeting North Vietnam since it might lead to increased guerrilla activity against the South, which the Khanh government was too weak to repel. Even worse, American escalation might result in direct Chinese or Soviet intervention. But the president approved of extending covert operations to block North Vietnamese infiltration and conducting retaliatory raids against the North (Operation Plan 34A).[31]

NSAM 288 presented a major step toward American escalation. But Johnson still refused to deploy U.S. troops. After all, 1964 was an election year, and while most Americans accepted the current policy, it was uncertain how they would react to another war in Asia. By accepting the position that Vietnam had to be held at all costs, Johnson had moved closer to the "point of no return." In April 1964, Johnson sounded out sentiments of Congress on possible expansion of the American role in Vietnam. He informed congressional leaders about the new policy in an NSC meeting.[32] Johnson faced only one opposing voice, in Senator Morse, who favored a negotiated settlement under United Nations supervision.[33] Another NSC meeting found even greater consensus in condemning European unwillingness to back America's Vietnam policy. Although the Europeans provided some symbolic aid, it seemed that they "really do not give a damn about Communist aggression in Southeast Asia."[34]

The debate and decisions of spring 1964 showed that Johnson was determined to draw the line in South Vietnam in the Cold War against Communism. On the other hand, Johnson did not want another Korean War possibly involving China or the Soviet Union. It was also unclear whether the United States would find appreciable support among its allies if the conflict escalated. Consequently, Johnson endorsed a middle course, hoping that American aid and guidance would be sufficient to enable a South Vietnamese victory. As Johnson put it, "American boys should not do the fighting that Asian boys should do for themselves."[35] But the challenge was whether the "Asian boys" could do the fighting well enough to attain American objectives.[36] One option was no longer seriously discussed by most of Johnson's advisors—withdrawing from Vietnam. They accepted the assumption that Vietnam was vital to American foreign policy and that a Communist victory would have the feared trigger effect on the entire region.

During the critical spring of 1964, Johnson lacked incisive advice to reexamine his Vietnam policy. McNamara and the Joint Chiefs not only condoned the military actions adopted but also argued for an intensified commitment. Undersecretary Ball was the only voice in the administration questioning the "domino theory," and he counseled against further escalation. To Ball, the problem lay not so much in Johnson, who was anxious to avoid an irrevocable commitment, but rather in the fact that he inherited and listened to Kennedy's advisors who failed to critically reassess the conflict in Vietnam.[37] Ball admitted that it might have been difficult for Johnson to disengage within months after Kennedy's death since it would appear that Johnson was rejecting Kennedy's foreign policy. Such a move would undoubtedly lead to domestic repercussions and accusations of Johnson being soft on Communism by handing over South Vietnam.[38] Nevertheless, to Ball, a change in American policy was feasible and could be made at any time, even if the stakes were high:

> I never subscribed myself to the belief that we were ever at a point where we couldn't turn around. What concerned me then [in late 1963] as it did much more intensely even later was that the more forces committed, the more we were committed to Vietnam, the more grandiloquent our verbal encouragement of the South Vietnamese was, the more costly was any disengagement.[39]

According to Ball, Johnson's concern regarding his domestic agenda and his lack of experience in Asian politics prevented the president from critically appraising America's Vietnam policy. Consequently, Johnson was pulled along by events in Vietnam, instead of formulating a long-term strategy of his own, leaving the president without much room to maneuver. Johnson listened to Ball's opinions challenging the administration's view on Vietnam. However, Johnson did not heed Ball's advice but rather used him as a devil's advocate against the war hawks.[40] The obligation to continue with Kennedy's course, along with pressure from the hawkish Republicans, limited his view and options toward the unfolding events in Vietnam. Johnson admitted his dilemma in his memoirs: "Certainly I wanted peace. I wanted it every day of every month I was in the White House. All through 1964 and after, I hoped and prayed the men in Hanoi would sit down and negotiate. But I made it clear from the day I took office that I was not a 'peace at any price' man. We would remain strong, prepared at all times to defend ourselves and our friends."[41]

Success in Vietnam became even more elusive during the late spring and early summer of 1964. The United States had to expand its efforts to save South Vietnam. Johnson also needed congressional support for an upgraded commitment. His advisors concurred. In May 1964, William Bundy, assistant secretary of state for East Asian affairs, prepared a first draft for a congressional resolution that authorized the president, upon request by South Vietnam or Laos, to use all measures, including the deployment of armed forces, for their defense against Communist aggression.[42] Johnson was not yet willing to make such a fundamental decision. He was also concerned about his critics in Congress and decided to wait for the time being.[43] But he sounded out congressional opinions in a series of meetings with key senators reviewing American policy in Vietnam. The president assured the senators that he had no intention of escalating the war but that congressional support was needed to demonstrate to Hanoi the American determination to prevent a takeover of South Vietnam and Laos.[44]

Uncertainty about the future course in Vietnam continued to plague the administration during early summer 1964. The presidential campaign was intensifying, and Johnson wanted to prevent Vietnam from becoming a major issue. Yet, he had to convey the image of effectively handling the Communist threat in Southeast Asia and avoid Republican criticism. Republican presidential candidate Barry Goldwater of Arizona strongly opposed Johnson's domestic program, which he denounced as far too "liberal." He attacked every aspect of Johnson's Great Society as "state paternalism." To Goldwater, "collectivism and the welfare state" were the greatest threat at home, while Communism was the "foremost enemy around the world."[45] While the federal government should only have a minimal role in domestic politics, the United States definitely needed to adopt a more aggressive position with foreign policy.[46]

According to Goldwater, the United States could not afford to lose the Cold War with the Soviet Union. Only victory over Communism would allow an acceptable peace with the Soviet Union. The United States had to become superior to the Soviet Union, politically, economically, and militarily. Moreover, America needed to pursue an offensive strategy in the fight against Communism and encourage its allies to do the same. Peoples around the globe should join together in defeating the Communists, and the United States needed to support their efforts, if necessary by military means. In Southeast Asia, South Koreans and Vietnamese ought to cooperate with Taiwanese to liberate the entire region. To Goldwater, bombing North Vietnam would demonstrate the American resolve. He summed up his attitude in his acceptance speech as the Republican presidential candidate: "Extremism in the defense of liberty is no vice, and . . . moderation in the pursuit of justice is no virtue."[47] Richard Nixon, in less extreme language, generally concurred that Johnson was not doing enough in Vietnam. He believed that Johnson's policy of restraint would not succeed and more had to be done to defeat Communist aggression in Asia.[48] While many Americans in 1964 showed little interest in Vietnam, the Republicans were ready to make the conflict a campaign issue.

Anxious that Vietnam might undermine his domestic goals, Johnson asked his good friend Senator Russell for advice. Russell described Vietnam as a "damn worse mess." The senator had been apprehensive about American commitment to Vietnam since 1954, and he feared that the conflict might lead to a war with China. When Johnson asked how important Vietnam really was for the United States, Russell responded that it was worth "a damn bit" with the exception of the psychological impact a withdrawal might have. Russell and Johnson agreed that the United States was bound by the Southeast Asia Treaty Organization (SEATO) treaty to defend South Vietnam. Johnson was ambiguous about the views of his advisors, yet he did not have any choice but to see things through. He was worried he would be forced to send U.S. soldiers and face American public opposition to a war it might not comprehend.[49]

Russell believed it was a mistake to get further involved because the United States was already "in the quicksand up to our very necks." Johnson suggested that the senator recommend an American withdrawal in Congress aimed at preempting criticism from the Goldwater camp. Unfortunately, Russell was unwilling to comply since he was not persuaded by either choice—withdrawal or escalation. Johnson repeated his concerns over the future course in Vietnam to his National Security Advisor, McGeorge Bundy: "I don't think it's worth fighting for and I don't think we can get out. And it's just the biggest damn mess. . . . What the hell is Vietnam worth to me. . . . What is it worth to this country?"[50]

By June 1964, Johnson preferred to hold the line. Most of his counsel favored the idea of a three-step approach: increased pressure on Hanoi, followed by an urgent warning to Ho Chi Minh to end his support of the Viet Cong, and if Ho did not comply, the bombing of North Vietnam.[51] Again, Johnson put escalation on hold, based on his own doubts and campaign considerations.[52] At the same time, he was busy finding European support for American actions in Vietnam but failed to overcome British and French reservations.

AUGUST 1964: TONKIN GULF
AND THE CONGRESSIONAL RESOLUTION

On August 2, 1964, and again two days later, the American destroyers *Maddox* and *Turner Joy* were attacked by North Vietnamese torpedo boats.[53]

President Johnson decided not to retaliate but rather to send a firm note of protest to Hanoi that threatened grave consequences in case of another unprovoked assault. He also ordered continued patrols in the Tonkin Gulf.[54] After the second attack on American vessels, the president authorized the launch of Navy aircraft to bomb a number of North Vietnamese coastal installations.[55] The North Vietnamese attacks enraged Americans and gave President Johnson the congressional carte blanche to increase the U.S. involvement, eventually leading to the deployment of combat troops and the Americanization of the war.

On August 4, 1964, President Johnson informed congressional leaders about the second assault in the Tonkin Gulf and asked for a resolution to sanction retaliatory bombing of North Vietnamese military targets. The resolution was presented to the House of Representatives the next day and passed unanimously on August 7. The Senate debate took several hours, and the resolution was adopted with only two votes dissenting (senators Gruening and Morse) and ten senators abstaining. The Tonkin Gulf Resolution gave the president the right to take all necessary measures to repel any armed attack on U.S. forces and, in addition, far-reaching powers "to take all necessary steps, including the use of armed force, to assist any member or protocol state of the Southeast Asia Collective Defense Treaty requesting assistance in defense of its freedom."[56]

Although the resolution was passed by an overwhelming majority, the debate in the Senate reflected profound concerns about the increasing American commitment to Vietnam. Some speakers fully endorsed a hardening position toward and, if necessary, attacks on North Vietnam, yet the great number of debaters worried about the administration's Vietnam policy and the broad powers given to the president by this congressional resolution.[57] The somber mood of the debate foreshadowed the debate the United States would face during the next eight years. While many senators lamented the lack of European support of America's Vietnam policy, in August 1964, they raised the same issues as European observers.[58]

Senators Gaylord Nelson, Daniel Brewster, Chester Cooper, Al Gore Sr., Frank Church, Robert Bartlett, and Richard Russell viewed the situation as a dangerous turning point on a treacherous road toward a full U.S. military commitment.[59] The concern was undoubtedly shared by the French and the British. But unlike the Europeans, the senators felt compelled to respond to the attack on American vessels. American honor was at stake and this, at least for the time being, justified a limited military response.[60] Senator Church (D-ID) summarized the dilemma he and many of his colleagues faced. He believed that America's Vietnam policy was fundamentally flawed and lacked a realistic assessment of American national interest, but he had to support the congressional resolution and give Johnson the powers he asked for. Congress shared the responsibility for the current situation, because it had willingly funded the policy in Southeast Asia and thereby acquiesced to decisions made by Eisenhower, Kennedy, and Johnson. Church concluded, "We must accept the consequences of our own actions. We must now face the fact that the difficulties in which we find ourselves are our responsibility, in having chosen to pursue [an] action which exposed us to such hazards."[61] The overall tenor revealed that many senators rejected any military action that went beyond limited retaliatory strikes. Although aware of the powers given to President Johnson, the overwhelming number of senators debating the resolution did not want a wider war and hoped that Johnson received this message by displaying caution and restraint.[62]

THE ROAD TO ESCALATION:
SEPTEMBER 1964–FEBRUARY 1965

Johnson used restraint until his victory at the polls. Washington was trying to prevent any incident that could be used by Hanoi to escalate the war. For the time being, De Soto patrols were put on hold and 34A operations were suspended.[63] In several campaign speeches, Johnson restated that he had no intention to escalate the Vietnam conflict and presented himself as the candidate for peace, attacking the belligerent stand of Goldwater. But in Saigon, events were further unraveling. On August 7, General Nguyen Khanh announced a state of emergency, resulting in press censorship and restriction of civil liberties, and devised a new constitution giving him almost unlimited powers. These measures resulted in widespread demonstrations during the second half of August. For weeks, the government was in turmoil, and coup rumors, street protests, and efforts to find some kind of compromise paralyzed the Saigon regime.[64] Ambassador Maxwell Taylor discerned two choices for the United States: continue the passive course as advisor or assume a more active role to carry the counterinsurgency program to success. The first option was unacceptable because it would eventually force the United States to abandon South Vietnam.[65]

Since early September 1964, Johnson's advisors also discussed systematic airstrikes against North Vietnam, its supply lines, and deployment of U.S. ground troops to South Vietnam.[66] The military brass, with exception of Army Chief of Staff General Harold K. Johnson and Admiral Grant Sharp, were in favor of air attacks on North Vietnamese targets, with the goal to break Hanoi's will to fight, and prepared a list of more than ninety select targets in the North.[67] President Johnson was reluctant to escalate and rejected

President Lyndon B. Johnson (right) and Undersecretary George Ball. Ball was an opponent of military escalation in Vietnam. LBJ Library Photo by Yoichi Okamoto.

airstrikes for the time being. Again, he asked his cabinet whether Vietnam was truly worth all the effort; yet, his advisors and the Joint Chiefs insisted that the United States could not afford to lose South Vietnam. Johnson finally approved the recommendation allowing for retaliation in the form of extensive airstrikes, if the North Vietnamese or Viet Cong assaulted U.S. forces or South Vietnam.[68] This was another step toward all-out war.

Ball tried to avert impending disaster. Dominoes and containment simply did not apply to Vietnam. He argued that American policy makers were solely concerned with "how" they could succeed in Vietnam but never asked "why" they were engaged in Vietnam in the first place, and why they persisted pursuing a war that they were less and less likely to win. Ball fully agreed with Charles de Gaulle's assessment, with whom he discussed Vietnam during a visit in June 1964 in an effort to win France's support for Johnson's policy.[69] Deeply worried about the consequences of "tit-for-tat" escalation, in October 1964 Ball sent a sixty-seven-page memorandum to Rusk and McNamara describing the dangers of a further expanded American engagement. Ball noted that the political structure in South Vietnam was increasingly disintegrating and that he could not foresee the formation of any government that could unify its people, or mobilize its military, to successfully defeat the insurgents. Based on the situation in South Vietnam, the United States had four policy alternatives: continue along current lines, take full responsibility for the war, engage in aerial attacks on North Vietnam, or pursue a political settlement.[70] Ball obviously preferred negotiation with the goal of guaranteeing the viability of South Vietnam, thus allowing for an American disengagement. His assessment closely resembled the analysis of Britain's counterinsurgency specialist Robert Thompson and of French President de Gaulle. According to Ball, the administration had to realize that Vietnam was unlike Korea in 1950. Despite infiltration from the North, many countries regarded the conflict as a civil war, which did not require or justify intervention by any foreign power.[71] A deeper American involvement in Vietnam could lead to serious repercussions within the international community. The Western allies already expressed concerns about Washington's commitment to their own security:

> Our allies believed that we were "engaged in a fruitless struggle in South Vietnam" and feared that if we became too deeply involved "in a war on the land mass of Asia," we would lose interest in their problems. What we had most to fear was "a general loss of confidence in American judgment that could result if we pursued a course which many regarded as neither prudent nor necessary."[72]

Most disturbing to Ball was the possibility of U.S. military actions against North Vietnam. He rejected the notion that bombings would not lead to further escalation but insisted that the United States had to eventually make the next step and deploy ground troops and, with it, increasingly lose any initiative in the war.[73] Once the United States was on the "tiger's back," it could no longer choose when to get off and this ride could lead to a major conflict involving China and possibly the Soviet Union:

> Nobody was prepared to concede that any particular step would require any further step. This was kind of a standard assumption which I kept repeating again and again was a false assumption. . . . You go forward with this further step, and you will substantially have lost control. Finally you're going to find the war is running you, and we're not running the war.[74]

The next years proved Ball correct both on Vietnam and allied reaction to America's escalation of the conflict. But he, like the Europeans, failed to impress his superiors. Rusk and McNamara were shocked and dismissed the political solution promoted by Ball. To them, negotiations without guarantees to South Vietnamese independence would have the same result as unconditional withdrawal, leading to a Communist victory in South Vietnam and the potential fall of Cambodia and Indonesia. Both believed that negotiations at this time would be seen as a sign of weakness. Hanoi had to first realize American determination by stopping its infiltration into the South and its support of the Viet Cong.[75] Neither Hanoi nor the Viet Cong were willing to cease their struggle. As long as they refused to do so, Washington was also not willing to retreat. Despite continuously bad news from South Vietnam, most of Johnson's counsel simply could not perceive the possibility that the United States might fail in Vietnam. Yet, by making every American response contingent on North Vietnamese and NLF action, Washington placed itself on the defensive, further limiting its freedom of action.

On November 1, 1964, the Viet Cong attacked the American base at Bien Hoa, near Saigon, killing four Americans and destroying five B-57 bombers. The Joint Chiefs recommended immediate airstrikes against the North, but Johnson decided against it. Yet pressure on the administration to approve additional military action continued. On the same day McNamara met with Earle "Bus" Wheeler, chairman of the Joint Chiefs of Staff, who expressed the deep concerns of his colleagues, suggesting that the situation in South Vietnam required intensified military operations including airstrikes over both North and South Vietnam. Wheeler pointed out that, if the president decided against further action, it would be better for the United States to withdraw from Vietnam.[76] Wheeler placed his finger at the core of the issue. The United States must either employ its military might without restriction and fight for complete victory in Vietnam or decide to call it quits. Limited military reaction would simply not succeed. De Gaulle made the same point when he told Ball that, unless the United States was willing to take the war all the way to North Vietnam and even China, negotiations were the only feasible solution.

Still uncertain what to do, Johnson ordered the creation of a working group headed by Assistant Secretary of State William Bundy to assess policy options. The group admitted that the conflict did not fit the traditional framework of Communist aggression but was to a large degree a domestic struggle. Hence, U.S. military assistance might not prevent the fall of South Vietnam.[77] Despite this assessment, the Bundy group upheld the "domino theory." The fall of South Vietnam could "unravel the whole Pacific and South Asian defense structures."[78] The group also worried about the impact American failure in Vietnam would have abroad.[79] But as long as the United States maintained its image of a strong, determined nation, the fallout from a debacle in Vietnam might be acceptable to American friends and allies. In Europe, Great Britain and Germany sympathized with American policy, whereas with France "we are damned either way we go."[80] American prestige in Europe depended on the U.S. conduct in Vietnam: "Our key European allies probably would now understand our applying an additional measure of force to avoid letting the ship sink; but they could become seriously concerned if we get ourselves involved in major conflict that degraded our ability to defend Europe and produced anything less than an early and completely satisfactory outcome."[81]

The Bundy group was correct but failed to follow its own analysis in its recommendation for what Washington should do next. The committee favored a combination of military pressure and negotiation and sought a compromise between hard-liners and critics of further escalation. The report illustrated the self-imposed quagmire of Washington. South Vietnam could not fall, but all-out war to defend its independence was a dismal alternative as well. Nobody was satisfied with the group's recommendations. The Joint Chiefs preferred the full use of American military might to gain a victory on the battlefield.[82] Ambassador Taylor and General Westmoreland wanted to give Saigon more time to reorganize, but hoped to use the threat of bombing North Vietnam to make Hanoi more amenable to a settlement. Ball rejected the entire argument as another example of wishful thinking and "bureaucratic casuistry" that turned logic upside down and completely disregarded the realities in South Vietnam.[83] President Johnson was deeply frustrated with both the developments in Saigon and the multitude of opinions and advice from his staff. He was anxious about the consequences of stepped-up military operations and felt his landslide victory against Goldwater did not give him the mandate for all-out war in Vietnam.[84] Nevertheless, Johnson inched step-by-step further toward escalation. On December 1, 1964, he accepted a two-phase program. Phase I insisted that the Saigon government finally solve its internal quarrels and adopt a program of reform before considering further military operations. Phase II authorized the U.S. Saigon mission to develop jointly with the South Vietnamese plans for reprisal operations. Despite the admonitions of Ambassador Taylor, the leaders in Saigon did not comply, and the question of airstrikes was back in the debate. Yet, for the time being, the president only agreed to continue the Oplan 34A mission and ordered armed reconnaissance flights over Laos, Operation Barrel Roll, to strike at North Vietnamese infiltration routes, with both measures aimed at increasing the pressure on Hanoi.[85] Once more, Washington moved closer to an "endless entanglement," as de Gaulle had told Kennedy, in the hope that each step would turn the tide.

In Congress, a few voices of concern about the dangers of escalation could also be heard. Most outspoken was Senator Mansfield, who sent a memorandum to the president in early December 1964 warning of the dangers of further military action. The United States was in a similar position to that of France in the early 1950s, when South Vietnam was without a truly legitimate government, held together only by foreign support. In addition, the military situation was turning worse, and Mansfield feared that the fighting would spill beyond the borders of South Vietnam.[86] He recommended negotiation involving both Chinese and European mediation. If the administration rejected this course, it would face a long-term commitment to South Vietnam, possibly a larger Asian war. Such commitment must be explained to the American public "in no uncertain terms" so that the nation was fully aware of what might lie ahead.[87] Mansfield made quite clear that he was against any attacks on North Vietnam, a sentiment that was shared by the majority of his colleagues. According to a poll by the Associated Press, only seven out of eighty-three senators favored the deployment of American ground forces and bombings of North Vietnam, while a considerable number of senators preferred a political settlement.[88] Again, this disparity between the official line on the importance of Vietnam and the unwillingness to sacrifice American lives to defend that Southeast Asian country is intriguing. But it is also a reflection of American democracy in general. The commitment to a global role had to be defended at home. Another Korea-like war was not what many senators and American citizens aspired to.

Mansfield's recommendations were discarded by Johnson's counsel, which increasingly favored attacking North Vietnam using the full might of American power to force a change in Communist policy. They were joined by conservative voices who demanded a greater military effort in Vietnam. Their criticism evoked Johnson's fear that a Democratic president could not survive failure in Vietnam, since it was the general belief at the time that Democrats were "soft on Communism abroad." Moreover, Johnson worried that his Great Society would be derailed by congressional attacks on his performance in Vietnam. He felt that giving up in Vietnam would make things even worse domestically.[89] He addressed the situation in Vietnam in his State of the Union address in January 1965, pointing out that America had pledged its support to South Vietnam ten years ago and was not willing to break that promise. Ultimately, America desired peace in Southeast Asia, but it could only be achieved "when aggressors leave their neighbors in peace."[90]

McNamara and Bundy were determined not to fail in Vietnam. They favored the military option outlined in a memorandum submitted to the president in January 1965, which argued for sustained reprisals against the North. They were fully aware of the consequences of their suggestions but believed that the current policy would not lead to success and thus advised the president to approve increasing American military operations:

> Both of us understand the very grave questions presented by any decision of this sort. We both recognize that the ultimate responsibility is not ours. Both of us have supported your unwillingness, in earlier months, to move out the middle course. We both agree that every effort should still be made to improve our operations on the ground and to prop up the authorities in South Vietnam as best as we can. But we are both convinced that none of this is enough, and the time has come for harder choices.[91]

Not every cabinet member agreed with these recommendations. Rusk opposed any military action that would expand the war into North Vietnam, and his concerns were duly noted by McNamara and Bundy. While Rusk firmly stood behind the American commitment to South Vietnam, he believed the United States should continue the present course, advising the South Vietnamese to help themselves. Rusk argued,

> I believed we should persevere with our policy of advising and assisting the South Vietnamese and playing for breaks, rather than risking a major escalation if one could be avoided. At this stage, in late 1964, the stakes were high enough that we couldn't simply withdraw, but neither did I want us to go all out fighting a guerrilla war. Unless the South Vietnamese themselves could carry the major burden, I didn't see how we could succeed.[92]

McNamara and Bundy won the debate. Following a Viet Cong attack on an American airbase near Pleiku and a U.S. helicopter base at Camp Holloway on February 6, 1965, Johnson decided to escalate. On February 8, Johnson endorsed a strategy of reprisals against North Vietnam and indicated his willingness to send a substantial number of American ground forces to secure American bases in South Vietnam.[93] Another Viet Cong attack in Qui Nhon two days later that killed twenty-three Americans further strengthened Johnson's determination. He authorized an expanded bombing campaign of North Vietnamese targets, Operation Rolling Thunder.[94] On February 26, 1965, Johnson approved sending two marine battalions to Vietnam. They landed near Da Nang on March 8. On April 1, 1965, Johnson authorized the deployment of two more battalions, increasing the level of U.S. troops to more than thirty-three thousand men. He also expanded their mission from base security to active combat.[95]

The subsequent escalation of America's war in Vietnam has been told and analyzed in minute detail by historians. Despite the growing number of American troops, Washington did not win the war. Domestic and European skeptics who warned against escalation were proved correct, although nobody relished the fact. Vietnam was an unnecessary war that extracted a far too high price from all combatants. Johnson indirectly admitted the failure of his Vietnam policy in March 1968 and withdrew from public service. Certainly, he was not the only one to blame for the quagmire in Vietnam, but he was responsible for escalating the war.

The conflict might have been avoided long before marines set foot on Vietnamese soil in March 1965. De Gaulle's insistence on retaining Indochina in 1945 led to the First Indochina War. Harry Truman's fear of losing France to the Communist Party, reinforced by pleas for American help by French Prime

Minister Paul Ramadier, resulted in growing American aid to the French struggle in Indochina. Mao Zedong's victory in China in 1949, and the Korean War, brought Southeast Asia to the forefront of American policy making. Thence, containment, falling dominoes, and national security defined the American foreign policy paradigm from Truman to Johnson. Eisenhower took the next step by solidifying U.S. commitment to Diem's Vietnam in 1954. Kennedy inherited this commitment and, against his better judgment, not only reaffirmed but also expanded America's role in Vietnam. His concern about losing his political mandate at home prevented any profound reassessment of the situation in Vietnam and its actual importance for the United States and the free world. Neither he nor Johnson heeded the voices of dissent among their advisors. Also, they did not acknowledge British, French, and German concerns about America's Vietnam policy. We must again ask, why?

The answer is complex. First, the ideological paradigm of containment confined American policy makers. With the acceptance of the status quo in Europe, Cold War "proxy wars" were fought in the third world. South Vietnam became another battle line, as had West Germany and South Korea, where the United States was determined not to allow further Communist encroachment. Second, ideological thinking not only affected American policy makers but also pervaded American public opinion, partly as a result of public relations campaigns by American leaders. Cold War rhetoric of "free world against Communist oppression" was convincing and catching. Third, the combination of Cold War ideology and the belief that South Vietnam was the domino that could not fall petrified American bureaucracy. Officials in Washington and Saigon provided information they thought Washington wanted to hear.[96] Last, there was what C. Vann Woodward described as a "commitment to American pride" rooted in a "legend of invincibility." Based on America's historical experience of victorious wars, defeat by a far less powerful enemy was unthinkable.[97] The consequences of these various factors were tragic for both the Americans and the Vietnamese. Until the Vietnam War, whenever American might was employed during the twentieth century, victory ensued. South Korea, albeit a bitter struggle, was secured for the West. In Latin America, the Monroe Doctrine had become reality. Johnson's reaction to turmoil in the Dominican Republic proved the point. U.S. Marines prevented a "leftist putsch" in April 1965.[98]

Since U.S. Marines had successfully turned the tide in the Dominican Republic, why could they not do the same in Vietnam? The conflict in Vietnam went beyond any previous American experience. Regardless of reports from American officials in the country, every fact-finding mission by high-ranking members of both the Kennedy and Johnson administrations brought back news of further deterioration. In light of the self-imposed restriction to only secure South Vietnam but prevent a wider war, neither Kennedy nor Johnson considered negotiations or even disengagement a valid option but allowed the United States to become enmeshed in the quagmire of Vietnam. Washington's course led to a major crisis with its Western European allies, France, Great Britain, and West Germany. The Europeans disagreed with the U.S.'s Vietnam policy, and all three refused to support America's efforts in Vietnam.

Chapter 6

De Gaulle's Response to American Policy in Vietnam, 1961–1966

On August 31, 1966, French President Charles de Gaulle strongly criticized the American war in Vietnam in a speech to a supportive crowd in Phnom Penh, Cambodia. He accused the United States of outright aggression in Vietnam and urged the withdrawal of all American forces to allow for a negotiated settlement of the conflict. While leaders in Great Britain and the Federal Republic of Germany also had misgivings and doubts about America's involvement in Vietnam, neither dared to challenge Washington as openly and publicly as France. Why, then, did de Gaulle?

As discussed earlier, France had extensive and painful experiences in Vietnam, as the colony gained its independence in a bloody and costly war. Based on the French experience in Indochina, de Gaulle urged Washington against extending its commitment to the region. His advice went unheeded by both presidents John F. Kennedy and Lyndon B. Johnson. The question is, why? Two related factors contributed to divergent French and American views. First, de Gaulle approached foreign policy based on an ideology of superiority that depended for its maintenance on the restoration of French *grandeur*, a larger international role and voice for France. Washington placed far greater emphasis on Cold War ideology and regarded the Vietnam conflict first and foremost in terms of the struggle against Communism. Second, de Gaulle steadfastly insisted on an independent policy for France in Europe and globally by directly challenging American leadership of the Western alliance. Washington was obviously bewildered by the mixed signals coming from Paris and was therefore less inclined to seriously consider de Gaulle's advice concerning Vietnam.

De Gaulle's character and upbringing shaped his policy. He was born in November 1890 into a patriotic family and grew up cherishing the images of France's past. In 1909, he joined the French military and graduated from

St. Cyr a lieutenant in 1912. Wounded twice during the First World War, he was awarded the Legion of Honor medal. After the war, he moved up the ranks slowly. His superiors certainly acknowledged his intelligence, but his egotistical behavior impeded smooth promotion, and he only made colonel in 1937. De Gaulle observed the rise of Hitler with growing concern and recommended an improved defense strategy against the increasingly aggressive Germany, but his advice was discarded by his superiors. His fears became reality when Hitler attacked France in the summer of 1940. In London at the time of the French surrender, de Gaulle found himself cast in the role of leader of the French resistance.[1]

Years spent as the leader of the Free French left a profound mark on de Gaulle and laid the foundation for his policy toward Great Britain and the United States during the 1960s. Although supported by Britain and the United States, de Gaulle was excluded from most major decisions during the war and feared that French interests were not sufficiently acknowledged.[2] The general interpreted the "haughty" Anglo-American attitude during the war as insults on French honor. De Gaulle was determined more than ever to restore France to great power status. His first effort toward this goal was short lived. With the establishment of the Fourth Republic in January 1946, de Gaulle resigned from office and left a burdensome legacy in Indochina to his successors.

During the Second World War, de Gaulle was unwilling to grant Indochina independence and quickly reaffirmed French sovereignty there in 1945. His position had clearly changed by 1954. By then, de Gaulle regarded colonialism as a burden to France. Conflicts within the empire drained the strength of the French military in distant wars while its main purpose, to secure France proper, was undermined. Moreover, France could not possibly become a major player in Europe or globally as long as she was distracted and weakened in the colonies. In Vietnam, it was evident that France was unable to maintain her influence by force, and for de Gaulle, it was more important to focus on Europe first. Only from a solid base in Europe could France then expand her role in global politics through diplomatic and economic support of her former colonies and other third world countries.

In 1958, de Gaulle was back at the helm of French politics. He replaced the bankrupt Fourth Republic with his own creation—the Fifth Republic. A new constitution gave wide powers to the president, particularly in foreign policy. Taking advantage of his increased mandate, de Gaulle ended French intervention in Algeria and facilitated Algerian independence in 1962. Domestically, de Gaulle restored stability, ending the rapid succession of cabinets that marked the Fourth Republic. The Fifth Republic gave de Gaulle the basis to continue the policy he envisioned for France during his first years in power: independence and *grandeur*. The major obstacle to his grand design was what de Gaulle defined as "Anglo-Saxon dominance," the policies of Great Britain and the United States. Regarding the Soviet Union, de Gaulle desired a policy of cooperation and reaffirmation of historical ties between both countries.[3]

The growing conflict in Vietnam revealed to de Gaulle potential short-comings in American leadership of the Western alliance. The American commitment in Vietnam also offered de Gaulle an opportunity to assert his country's role in world affairs. France could assume the part of champion of the nonaligned world. By supporting the independence of third world countries politically and economically, de Gaulle hoped to provide an alternative to these new nations, "freeing" them from the Cold War contest between the United States and the Soviet Union.[4] Greater influence around the globe might allow France to become a third force, while not quite a superpower. Once again, the base for France's greater role was Europe. De Gaulle preferred a multipolar over the bipolar world and hoped that France and Europe as well as the People's Republic of China (PRC) would create a new balanced power system going beyond the nuclear stalemate between the United States and the Soviet Union.[5]

From 1961 until his resignation from office in March 1969, de Gaulle steadfastly reiterated his conviction that the Vietnam conflict could only be ended through a negotiated settlement providing for the withdrawal of all foreign forces and the neutralization of the entire country. He argued strongly against further U.S. escalation of the conflict. Initially, de Gaulle attempted to influence American policy making on Southeast Asia through confidential advice. When this approach failed, he went public in criticizing the United States. Although de Gaulle addressed concerns shared by Great Britain and West Germany, neither country endorsed his views.

The French refusal to sanction American policy on Vietnam led to a crisis and a turning point for the transatlantic alliance. De Gaulle challenged the United States on Vietnam and skillfully utilized the Vietnam controversy to question American predominance in the Western alliance. His withdrawal from the North Atlantic Treaty Organization (NATO) command in 1966 exemplified the rift between France and the United States.[6] De Gaulle's policy of independence certainly dismayed Washington. He dismissed the Cold War framework of American policy makers and questioned American leadership in the alliance. As a consequence, he failed to change American policy on Vietnam but left Washington fighting in Southeast Asia without his country's support. The United States eventually learned that de Gaulle's assessment on Vietnam was correct. Even more importantly, subsequent American administrations realized that the United States needed the support of its European allies as much as the Europeans needed American protection.

The situation in Indochina in 1960 offered France the opportunity to embark on the role of honest broker. In Laos, to the dismay of the Eisenhower administration, France supported the neutralists led by Prince Souvanna Phouma. A year later, France refused to participate in any intervention by Southeast Asia Treaty Organization (SEATO) forces.[7] For Vietnam, de Gaulle soon adopted the same policy of advocating neutralization, coupled with the demand of withdrawal of all foreign forces.

DE GAULLE'S DIPLOMATIC APPROACH: 1961–1964

Kennedy's election gave de Gaulle new hope that he might influence American foreign policy making. Dwight Eisenhower had increased the American commitment to Indochina, but conflicts in Laos and South Vietnam nevertheless intensified. Perhaps Kennedy was more amenable to de Gaulle's suggestion of a political settlement for the entire region. In March 1961, Jacques Chaban-Delmas, president of the National Assembly, was scheduled to visit the United States. Before leaving, he received instructions from de Gaulle, who asked Chaban-Delmas to report what impression President Kennedy made. De Gaulle added, "See him and tell him not to get caught up in the Vietnam affair. The United States could lose its forces, but also its soul."[8]

Kennedy listened and agreed in principle to the political settlement in Laos but rejected a similar solution for Vietnam. De Gaulle was concerned about the growing crisis in South Vietnam, and he repeated his advice during Kennedy's visit to France in May 1961. Kennedy indicated that Western intervention in Southeast Asia might be necessary to stop further advances of the Communist forces. De Gaulle refused to directly interfere in South Vietnam and rejected Kennedy's plan to establish a barrier against the Soviet Union and the PRC in Indochina. The general argued that military intervention was a hopeless endeavor that would ultimately do more to strengthen the Communists than destroy them. He warned Kennedy,

> You will find that intervention in this area will be an endless entanglement. Once a Nation has been aroused no foreign power, however strong, can impose its will upon it. You will discover this for yourself. For even if you find local leaders who in their own interest are prepared to obey you, the people will not agree to it, and indeed not want it. The ideology which you invoke will make no difference. Indeed, in the eyes of the masses, it will become identified with your power. That is why the more you become involved out there against Communists, the more the Communists will appear as champions of national independence, and the more support they will receive, if only from despair. We French have had experience of it. You Americans want to take our place. I predict that

you will sink step by step into a bottomless military and political quagmire, however much you [spend] in men and money. What you, we and others ought to do for unhappy Asia is not to take over the running of these states ourselves, but to provide them with the means to escape the misery and humiliation which, there as elsewhere, are the causes of totalitarian regimes.[9]

Hindsight validates de Gaulle's prediction. He correctly assessed the appeal of nationalism in Southeast Asia, having experienced its power both in Europe and within the former French colonial empire. As de Gaulle noted, ideologies were temporal and simply another tool to justify a nation's self-interest and self-determination.[10] Based on this assessment, the only successful way for the West to influence events in Southeast Asia was an indirect approach through economic aid and political support. Obviously, de Gaulle did not want to see Communism succeed in Southeast Asia, but military intervention was undoubtedly the wrong way to defeat the Communist insurgents. Also, de Gaulle was not willing to relinquish the French role in her former colony, and the best way to maintain ties was through economic aid to help improve the viability of South Vietnam.

However, Kennedy could or would not perceive the turmoil in South Vietnam within de Gaulle's framework. In fact, Kennedy regarded the conflict in Vietnam primarily in terms of the ideological battle of the Cold War. Although the United States already provided ample economic and military aid, Kennedy hoped that a concerted Western policy might further prevent Communist successes. Western support of American strategy in Vietnam would further justify Kennedy's policy and score some points in Congress. In Asia, it was necessary to realize the dangers of a North Vietnamese thrust into Laos and South Vietnam, an operation that in American eyes was backed by Moscow. In addition, Beijing might also become involved in Indochina, further encouraging Communist insurgents in South Vietnam. To meet the Communist challenge, the West had to adopt a joint strategy for the upcoming conference on Laos and, in case the conference failed, a contingency plan for Indochina. Washington believed that an "increased understanding from the international community" would actually accelerate a settlement in Vietnam.[11]

Washington appreciated the considerable role France still played in South Vietnam. National Security Advisor McGeorge Bundy suggested the formation of joint U.S.-French committees to find solutions for the complex problems in South Vietnam. More importantly, Washington hoped to "eliminate past cross purposes in Southeast Asia" and obtain an "urgent high-level effort to concert UK-French-US position on Vietnam."[12] De Gaulle was receptive to these suggestions, favoring closer consultations as well.[13] But de Gaulle expected Washington to recognize the French position on Indochina as a prerequisite for any French support of America's policy in Vietnam. He rejected Western intervention and favored the neutralization of the region. The French president was unwilling to give up his own policy on Indochina simply to placate the Americans.

The general's position was difficult for Washington to comprehend or accept since it ran counter to American perceptions. Over Laos, at least, a political settlement could be reached, with both the United States and the Soviet Union as guarantors of that country's neutrality. Yet the issue of Vietnam proved more problematic and ultimately more divisive in future French-American relations. De Gaulle insisted on complete neutrality for both Vietnams, allowing for closer ties between North and South, eventually leading to the peaceful unification of the country.

In 1962, President Kennedy was not ready to acquiesce to de Gaulle's policy of neutralizing Vietnam. The State Department duly noted de Gaulle's "distaste" for President Ngo Dinh Diem and worried over French support of Cambodia's Prince Sihanouk, who pursued a neutral course between East and West. In November 1962, presidential advisor Walter Rostow met with Jean-Claude Winkler, special envoy to de Gaulle, to devise a strategy to convince the French president of the validity of the American approach in South Vietnam. A recent attack by the PRC on India served as a pertinent example of overall Communist aggression. According to Rostow, the incident in the Himalayas should make it more than obvious to de Gaulle that "the containment of China can be conducted along the lines similar to the containment of Russia in Europe."[14] Washington was certain its policy of stemming the tide against Communism in Vietnam would lead to positive results and hoped to gain de Gaulle's support.[15]

The general refused to join ranks. In turn, Washington was unwilling to accept French obstinacy to a concerted Western policy in Southeast Asia. While both sides agreed that South Vietnam should not fall into the hands of the Communists, their respective approaches to prevent the loss of South Vietnam differed profoundly. A possible understanding was further complicated by a strong conviction—both in Paris and Washington—that their policies exclusively promised success. Kennedy reiterated his view that only Western support could save Vietnam in a meeting with French Foreign Secretary Maurice Couve de Murville in May 1963. The president, deeply concerned about the nuclear ambitions of China, reiterated his obligation to preserve the independence of South Vietnam to guarantee the freedom of the entire region. Couve de Murville believed that China did not intend to take over Southeast Asia and only desired to establish a "buffer region" to protect itself from the United States. If the French view proved correct, the best recourse was to "achieve a political solution to the problems in the area."[16]

In private with Kennedy, and then publicly in the summer of 1963, de Gaulle expressed his misgivings about the American involvement in Vietnam. At a press conference on August 29, 1963, the French leader maintained that only the Vietnamese people could determine their future and choose the path to independence as well as internal peace and harmony. France was willing to do everything within its power to facilitate the Vietnamese struggle for domestic stability and peace:

> The French Government is following with attention and emotion the grave events occurring in Vietnam. The task accomplished in the past by France in Cochin China, Annam and Tonkin, the ties she has maintained with the country as a whole, and the interest she takes in the development explains why she understands so well and shares so sincerely in the trials of the Vietnamese people. In addition, France's knowledge of the merits of this people makes her appreciate the role they would be capable of playing in the current situation in Asia for their own progress and to further international understanding, once they go ahead with their activities independently of the outside, in internal peace and unity and harmony with their neighbor. Today more than ever, this is what France wishes for Vietnam as a whole.[17]

For de Gaulle, the best way to achieve peace in Vietnam was the neutralization of the country in accordance with the 1954 Geneva agreement and the solution for Laos reached in 1962. The French leader instructed his ambassador in Saigon, Roger Laloulette, to convey de Gaulle's vision of a peaceful settlement to Diem and his brother Ngo Diem Nhu who, facing mounting pressure from the United States, were receptive to the French proposal of negotiations with the Viet Cong and even Hanoi.[18]

Washington was disturbed by de Gaulle's comments and was anxious to learn what the general's long-term policy for Vietnam entailed. The Americans were also concerned about possible contacts between Nhu and North Vietnamese leaders as well as French knowledge of or acquiescence to such talks.[19] In fact, the French mission won cooperation from the Indian chair of the International Control Commission (ICC) and employed ICC Polish delegate Mieczyslaw Maneli to open a venue for dialogue with Saigon and Hanoi. To the chagrin of Washington, both sides came close to an agreement, but the possibility of an internal Vietnamese settlement ended with Diem's assassination.[20] While Kennedy was well aware of de Gaulle's position ever since their 1961 summit, he still did not "understand just how General de Gaulle envisages the development of a unified and neutral Vietnam without the successful development of a strong non-Communist society" in South Vietnam.[21] The American president maintained that South Vietnam still needed "external support and cooperation" to establish a viable noncommunist society.

Further, he could not conceive of how, "in the face of Communist subversion," a withdrawal by the West would lead to any acceptable solution. Washington was certain that de Gaulle's plan of neutralization would have no "other result than the abandonment of Vietnam to the Communists."[22] If de Gaulle perceived other venues of solving the crisis in South Vietnam, Washington was willing to listen. Actually, Washington was less willing to listen than to convey its point of view or at least to stop de Gaulle from meddling in the affairs of Vietnam. Not surprisingly, de Gaulle continued to pursue a policy he regarded as proper. He reaffirmed the right of self-determination of third world countries in a late September 1963 speech. To Washington, de Gaulle's policy remained unpredictable in terms of how he would proceed on Vietnam.[23]

By October 1963, Kennedy received reports that de Gaulle was "exploring possible deals with Communist China and North Vietnam" and also considered diplomatic recognition of the PRC. A CIA report conceded that Paris might be discussing terms of a negotiated settlement in Beijing and Hanoi. The CIA regarded the chances of success for such a diplomatic solution as slim and doubted that de Gaulle had a "grand design" for the Far East.[24] Even if de Gaulle lacked a "grand design," his opposition to the American commitment might diminish the chances of success in South Vietnam. The French leader was little impressed by American concerns and adamantly contended that Washington's approach would only lead to a military quagmire and defeat.[25]

By the fall of 1963, Washington and Paris were deeply entrenched in their respective positions on Vietnam. The United States believed it had to defend the free world from Communist encroachment in South Vietnam. De Gaulle regarded the conflict in Vietnam as both a struggle for self-determination as well as domestic opposition against the corrupt Saigon regime. Foreign intervention would only make things worse. Therefore, it was advisable to reach a political solution as quickly as possible. The general also worried about the possible increase of East-West tensions as a consequence of a deepening American engagement in Vietnam. Obviously, he could not envision a victory should the United States become bogged down in the jungles of Southeast Asia. In addition, de Gaulle's opposition to Washington's Vietnam strategy gave him the opportunity to pursue an independent foreign policy and enhance France's image in the third world. A greater role in international affairs would also improve France's position in Europe. Both to the Western Europeans as well as to Moscow and its allies, France again demonstrated leadership and national independence.

THE WIDENING GAP: DE GAULLE AND JOHNSON

From 1961 to 1963, Paris and Washington developed different approaches to the increasing problems in South Vietnam based on their respective foreign policy paradigms. Each side tried to convince the other of the validity of its view to ending the conflict in Southeast Asia. Although Kennedy deployed a growing number of personnel and military equipment to South Vietnam, he remained reluctant to commit the United States fully in the struggle against the Communist insurgents. Kennedy's refusal to send American ground troops left the door still open for de Gaulle's concept of a negotiated settlement. Diem's overthrow in early November 1963 ended the possibility of an internal Vietnamese settlement for the time being. Three weeks later, Kennedy was assassinated and Lyndon Johnson became president. During 1964, the situation in Vietnam further deteriorated, and the Johnson administration gradually expanded the American commitment to Vietnam, resulting in the deployment of ground forces in March 1965.

De Gaulle refused to reconsider his initial assessment on Vietnam. Consequently, both Washington and Paris grew more intransigent in their approaches to solve the problems of the region. De Gaulle's opposition to the American course in Vietnam became more outspoken and damaging to Washington. The Johnson administration tried to contain the potential fallout of French policy both in Southeast Asia and within the Western alliance by continuing to persuade de Gaulle of the effectiveness of the American strategy in Vietnam. De Gaulle remained unconvinced and persistently insisted on a political settlement and the neutralization of that country.

To the French leadership, Johnson appeared reserved and inscrutable—in essence quite the contrary to Kennedy, who was always willing to engage in open discussion. French Foreign Secretary Couve de Murville described Johnson as a "cunning politician" from the South, who had made his name in Congress but was virtually unknown outside of the United States. Accordingly, Johnson assumed office unprepared but with the determination to lead his country and control its policy.[26]

Johnson had misgivings about de Gaulle as well. The French leader had privately complained that the United States entered both world wars rather late and wondered whether the Americans would be reluctant to support freedom in Europe in the future. Understandably, Johnson was apprehensive to meet the French president following Kennedy's funeral in November 1961. While both leaders generally agreed on overall policies, their encounter was dampened by a minor diplomatic spat over the planned de Gaulle visit to the United States in May 1964.[27] De Gaulle's proclaimed confidence in American support in case of Soviet aggression sounded hollow to Johnson. French desire of a closer organization of Europe, first economically and then politically, worried Washington even more. To Johnson, it was unclear what the French president intended to do in Europe.[28] Johnson later expressed his ambiguous feelings about de Gaulle that were overshadowed by the Vietnam controversy:

> In the years that followed, when de Gaulle's criticism of our role in Vietnam became intense, I had many occasions to remember that conversation. The French leader doubted—in private, at least—the will of the United States to live up to its commitments. He did not believe we would honor our NATO obligations, yet he criticized us for honoring a commitment elsewhere in the world. If we had taken his advice to abandon Vietnam, I suspect he might have cited that as "proof" of what he had been saying all along: that the United States could not be counted on in times of trouble.[29]

The missed opportunity of a good personal rapport between both leaders was caused not only by the character and style of the new American president but also, according to the French assessment, by Johnson's insufficient interest in the affairs of Europe. With the mounting difficulties in Vietnam, Johnson's foreign policy focus shifted almost exclusively to Southeast Asia. In addition, Johnson faced a multitude of domestic problems, which became even more urgent from 1965 onward, when civil rights, racial tensions, and domestic opposition to the war in Vietnam increasingly challenged and undermined Johnson's "Great Society."

Johnson displayed an interesting mixture of distrust and respect for de Gaulle. He described their peculiar relationship in very American terms, those of baseball. He saw himself "as the power hitter" whose rival, de Gaulle, was trying to outplay him, yet Johnson "would just lean back and let the ball go in the catcher's mitt."[30] Despite increasing tensions with France because of de Gaulle's contradictory policies and American escalation in Vietnam, Johnson rejected a more forceful approach in counteracting French policy. He instructed his administration to abstain from any public criticism of de Gaulle in the hope that he could outlast the old general and prevent further damage in the Western alliance.[31]

The Vietnam conflict did not allow Johnson to neutralize the general. Since Johnson was unwilling to change course over Vietnam, de Gaulle had to find other means to pursue French interests in Southeast Asia and increase French status in the world. Consequently, de Gaulle explored new venues to facilitate a political settlement for Vietnam. The obvious solution was a rapprochement with the PRC. France did not recognize the PRC in 1949 because of its own Indochina war. In 1963, global conditions had changed while war was still ravaging Vietnam. China was a major force in Asia, and de Gaulle postulated that no political solution could be found for Vietnam without including Beijing. The PRC proved receptive to French overtures during the Geneva Conference on Laos in 1961–1962. In late October 1963, de Gaulle sent China expert Edgar Faure to Beijing to investigate the prospect of diplomatic relations. Chairman Mao Zedong and Prime Minister Zhou En-lai were openly pleased with the idea, and negotiations finally led to full diplomatic recognition of the PRC by France in January 1964.[32]

Paris was fully aware that the French decision would perturb Washington, but de Gaulle remained firm. It was a mistake for the United States to continue a policy of nonrecognition of the PRC. While Mao's regime was totalitarian and despicable, China's increasing role in Asia could simply not be discounted. French recognition of Beijing served two purposes: one affected Europe; the other might bring new initiatives to the conflict in Southeast Asia. The Sino-Soviet split offered new opportunities for Western Europe to play the China card against Moscow. In Southeast Asia, de Gaulle sought a modus vivendi that would neutralize Vietnam. This solution presented the only possible alternative to further military escalation but required Chinese consent. The basis of any productive Western relations with Beijing was the recognition of this vast country. Admittedly, de Gaulle had no guarantee that the Chinese might actually agree to the neutralization of Vietnam but, in his opinion, it was at least worth the effort. Given the profound domestic challenges facing Beijing, Chinese leaders might be willing to accept the neutralization of Vietnam.[33]

The Khanh government in South Vietnam fumed over de Gaulle's decision and resolutely criticized the recognition of Beijing. From Saigon's perspective, the French move further condoned Communist aggression. Saigon took issue with de Gaulle's interference in Vietnam's business. Government officials called de Gaulle's policy illusionary and considered it just another French effort to restore her influence in Southeast Asia, this time with the help of Beijing. France was undermining the struggle of the South Vietnamese against Communism, and Saigon contemplated breaking diplomatic relations with Paris.[34]

Washington also deplored the French decision, calling it an "unfortunate step, particularly at a time when Chinese Communists are actively promoting aggression and subversion in Southeast Asia and elsewhere." A Senate resolution asked the French not to recognize Beijing or face grave consequences in Franco-American relations. Secretary of Defense Robert McNamara told journalists that countries that recognized the PRC were aiding Communist expansion in Southeast Asia. He was also afraid that Paris's decision would be followed by the French-speaking nations in Africa. Recognition of the PRC might upset the balance of nations against Communist China in the United Nations, complicating the American role in that assembly. But de Gaulle was encouraged by the mostly positive response to his decision in the rest of the world, particularly in Asia.[35]

France had again a voice in world affairs. The general would definitely not reverse his views on Vietnam in order to placate the United States and undermine his strategy of *grandeur*. Publicly, de Gaulle defended his decision to recognize China in the overriding context of the conflict in Vietnam and in China's role in Asia as a whole: "There is no political reality in Asia . . . which does not interest China. Neither war nor peace is imaginable on that continent without China's becoming implicated. Thus it is absolutely inconceivable that without her participation there can be any accord on the eventual neutrality of Southeast Asia."[36] France had to recognize this vast country of seven hundred million people to further French involvement in matters of international importance: "It is clear that France must try and understand China while China must also be willing to hear what France has to say." Only with Chinese participation was the neutralization of Southeast Asia possible.[37]

The policy of neutrality for Vietnam was rejected by Washington since it would allegedly only lead to a Communist victory. All of Johnson's principal advisors opposed de Gaulle's concept as detrimental to American objectives in Vietnam. None of them gave more than a cursory glance at the French proposal. Only a few voices of dissent favored the French position. Washington's aim was to convince Americans and the world that the United States would stand by its commitment to South Vietnam.[38] This would prove more difficult than anticipated.

THE AMERICAN EFFORT TO CONTAIN DE GAULLE

The Johnson administration grew apprehensive over the ramifications de Gaulle's ideas had in Europe and also in South Vietnam. Although the Khanh government in Saigon strongly rejected the idea of negotiations, not all South Vietnamese were opposed to French suggestions.[39] General Nguyen Khanh claimed that French agents were plotting to assassinate him and were also cooperating with the Viet Cong. The Viet Cong, in fact, did react positively to de Gaulle's ideas and issued an official communiqué that approved "President de Gaulle's proposal to establish a regime of neutrality in South Viet-Nam."[40] Washington needed to take action to prevent further damage by de Gaulle and once again adopted the strategy of friendly coercion.

During the spring and summer of 1964, Johnson explored ways of influencing de Gaulle's position in Washington's favor. Ambassador to Paris

Charles Bohlen and Henry Cabot Lodge in Saigon as well as CIA advisors set out to develop an approach to contain de Gaulle. Bohlen characterized the French president as "highly egocentric and with touches of megalomania" but argued against any direct criticism of the French leader by the Johnson administration.[41] Bohlen recommended that Washington present a clear political objective and course of action in Vietnam to de Gaulle and request his cooperation in that policy.[42] Johnson concurred with the ambassador. Hence, it became Bohlen's task to work directly with de Gaulle and win him over to the American point of view.

Johnson asked Lodge to reassure the South Vietnamese government that Washington was determined to "stop neutralist talk wherever we can by whatever means we can."[43] Further, Johnson hoped that Lodge could give advice on how to handle the French president. Lodge immediately went to work by devising a strategy that might change de Gaulle's mind. De Gaulle had to understand that American goals in Vietnam were profoundly different from French objectives during the First Indochina War. The United States was not seeking an exclusively military solution, which by itself had no chance of success, but was sincerely endeavoring to improve the lives of the Vietnamese people. Moreover, American and French interests in Vietnam were not so different. The American effort to strengthen South Vietnam was "directly to the advantage" of French doctors, teachers, and businessmen in that country. French nationals could play a significant role in the overall progress in South Vietnam by aiding the American commitment. Given the still considerable French influence in South Vietnam, Washington had to convey to de Gaulle that neutralization at the present was counterproductive to both countries' objectives in Vietnam:

> France has an influence in Viet-Nam way beyond what it contributes in the way of men, weapons, and money. This is because French is still the Western language which is possessed by the largest number of Vietnamese . . . at the present, the so-called people who count in Viet-Nam read French newspapers; in particular, they read background news stories which the Agence France Presse gets from the Quai d'Orsay. Some are impressed by it and others are infuriated by it, and altogether no good purpose is served. If what is desired is the eventual neutralization of Indo-China or of Viet-Nam, the way not to do it is to create the furor which these statements out of Paris create. General de Gaulle is thus a very influential figure in Viet-Nam and, unwittingly, in a way which is defeating his own stated purpose.[44]

All de Gaulle needed to do was to modify his time schedule for neutralization and postpone it for some future time. Lodge suggested de Gaulle take a look back into France's own history during 1940 and 1944. Had Washington adopted neutralization for France then, France might have suffered Nazi

occupation far longer. As in the 1940s, Americans continued to oppose neutralization because such policy only facilitated hostile attacks.[45]

Johnson urged Bohlen to seek an appointment with de Gaulle as soon as
possible and inform the French president that the United States, after thor-
ough consideration, rejected the idea of disengaging from Vietnam or initiating negotiations at the present time. Based on Lodge's recommendation,
Johnson told Bohlen what he expected de Gaulle to do:

> What we actually want from de Gaulle is a public statement, prior to the SEATO
> meeting [April 13–15, 1964], that the idea of "neutralization" does not apply to
> the attitudes or policies of the government in Vietnam or its friends in the face of
> the current communist aggression. We want him to state that he does not favor
> "neutralization" of this sort at the present time. We are not asking him to drop
> his idea for all eternity. What we want is a statement that he does not think it
> applies now.[46]

Bohlen could use whatever argument he felt was most convincing, but Johnson stressed in no uncertain terms that he expected de Gaulle to comply with
his wishes and, as an ally and friend, "adopt an attitude of cooperation rather
than obstruction" in this area of vital interest to the United States.[47]

On April 2, 1964, Bohlen finally met with de Gaulle. During forty-five
minutes of discussion, Bohlen failed to convince the general of the validity of
the American Vietnam strategy. De Gaulle flatly refused to reject neutralization for Vietnam. He disagreed with the American prognosis that the Khanh
government was winning the war against the Communist insurgents. The
French leader pointed to the similarities of both the French and American
Indochina conflicts. He asserted that the South Vietnamese had "no taste for
this war" and therefore were unable to meet the challenge of the Communist
insurgents.[48] Bohlen did not concur with de Gaulle's assessment. The French
struggle differed profoundly from the American efforts. France had fought a
colonial war, while the United States assisted South Vietnam against foreign
aggression. The ambassador implied that de Gaulle surely did not favor a
Communist victory. Indeed, the general did not want to see a Communist
takeover in Vietnam but questioned American strategy. He doubted whether
the United States could even obtain military stabilization in the country and,
unless Washington changed course, would eventually suffer the same debacle
as France had a decade earlier.

According to de Gaulle's judgment, the best solution was the neutralization of Vietnam through another Geneva conference that included Beijing. If
Washington was unwilling to consider negotiations, then it had to be willing
to "really carry the war to the North and if necessary against China."[49] The
latter alternative was disconcerting but presented a more clearly defined

policy. De Gaulle regretted that France and the United States had not done more to coordinate their policies in Southeast Asia. Bohlen responded that the United States had in fact strongly supported France in Indochina from 1949 onward. Regardless, de Gaulle declined to support the American policy in Vietnam because neutrality was the "only way out to the US other than engage in major hostilities against North Vietnam and China."[50]

The French leader rejected Bohlen's view that neutralization would lead to further Communist advances. Although de Gaulle could not guarantee Communist, particularly Chinese, cooperation in a peace conference, he repeated that the sooner the United States "went for neutralization the better off they would be." Bohlen, quite displeased, ended the conversation by pointing out that Washington would be considerably disappointed by de Gaulle's intransigence. The general unfortunately missed a "good opportunity" to work closely with the United States on the situation in Vietnam.[51] But de Gaulle saw no reason to reverse his views.

Bohlen left the meeting dismayed over his failure to impress de Gaulle. Although Bohlen later questioned the war in Vietnam, in 1964 he concluded that de Gaulle was misinformed and did not comprehend the seriousness of the Communist threat in Vietnam, a feeling that was shared by Lodge.[52] The answer was simple, de Gaulle was not misinformed. Unlike Washington, he did not perceive the conflict in Vietnam in terms of Cold War ideology. To him, conditions in Vietnam had not changed since the First Indochina War. Now, as ten years ago, the Vietnamese were fighting for independence and for a government that truly represented the people's interests. By supporting a corrupt regime, the United States only provoked Vietnamese resistance.

The SEATO conference in Manila of April 1964 further exacerbated the French-American rift over Vietnam. Dean Rusk met with Couve de Murville to discuss the situation in South Vietnam, quickly learning that the French position was as resolute as ever. To the French foreign minister, the problems in South Vietnam were essentially political. He suggested returning to the provisions of the 1954 Geneva agreement that prohibited foreign interference in Vietnam. If these provisions were obeyed, Vietnam could obtain independence, nonalignment status, and reunification. In fact, nonintervention affected both North and South Vietnam because the North was also not independent but rather ruled by outside forces.[53] Couve de Murville believed that Saigon could not defeat the Communist insurgents unless the United States escalated its commitment. He told Rusk, "If you tell me military victory, I will say that is fine. But if the war is not extended to the North and if U.S. forces do not participate, there is not likely to be a military victory in Viet-Nam. The South Vietnamese people are out of the game. All you have is a professional army supported from outside."[54] But even escalation might not succeed. Once again, Couve de Murville alluded to his country's experience. In 1962, France controlled most of Algeria but still lost the battle. He reminded Rusk that victory was impossible "without the people."[55] Couve de Murville also maintained that the situation in Vietnam was further complicated by Beijing. Washington needed to consider Chinese interests and influence in the region. For centuries, China had coveted Southeast Asia, but in 1964, any imperialist aim was impeded by the immense domestic difficulties within China. Thus, Beijing might be interested in any negotiated solution for Vietnam provided it did not threaten the PRC. Hanoi would have to follow suit and, at least for the time being, agree to "leave South Vietnam alone."

Rusk was curious to learn what argument could induce China to accept neutralization at the present since it had been reluctant to do so in the past. The French answer was very simple; Beijing implicitly regarded the American presence in Vietnam as a potential threat to China proper. Couve de Murville stressed that the Chinese were "terrified" by U.S. personnel in Vietnam.[56] Given the last two hundred years of Western imperialism in and around China, even a few hundred Americans stationed in Vietnam might be a potential threat to Beijing.

The meeting between Couve de Murville and Rusk was as unproductive as that of Bohlen and de Gaulle. While each side remained friendly and polite, they were far from reaching common ground. The French foreign minister acknowledged the divergence in opinion but agreed with his American counterparts to keep the matter confidential. During the SEATO conference, Couve de Murville was obliged to present the French view unequivocally, making news headlines. He refused to embrace a joint communiqué endorsing the American policy in Vietnam. Such an act of defiance had never occurred before in the history of the alliance. Couve de Murville explained to his colleagues that France could not support the American course because this policy would lead only to defeat. South Vietnam might fall, or even worse, the conflict could escalate, which was far more damaging for all involved. The SEATO members firmly opposed the French position. They refused to even consider neutralization because all were convinced that the United States would prevail in South Vietnam.[57]

Washington and Paris could only agree to disagree.[58] To Paris, the American position in Vietnam was obviously misguided. Likewise, the French view seemed misguided to the Americans. Couve de Murville recounted numerous discussions with Rusk, who exemplified the thinking of the Johnson administration. Accordingly, Rusk was convinced that the United States fought a good fight for a just cause, namely, the battle against world Communism. He did not distinguish between the Soviet and Chinese Communism, ignoring the conflict between these two countries. Regarding Vietnam, Couve de Murville maintained that Rusk also proved incapable to understand the determination of many South Vietnamese to resist American intervention. In addition, Paris alleged that American intervention only intensified the already difficult situation in South Vietnam.[59]

Rusk grew increasingly irritated about the French attitude and regarded de Gaulle as living a dream of France's past glory. The French had failed in Vietnam because they were a declining power that had tried in vain to uphold a colonial empire. He admitted that the American commitment was not without peril, but Washington was willing to accept the risks in order to succeed against Communism.[60] To the French, any military intervention in Southeast Asia would prove futile. But Washington was increasingly determined to use military means to end the conflict in Vietnam. As the conflict in Vietnam approached a new phase, so did Franco-American relations. Since Washington refused to listen to de Gaulle, the general escalated his attacks of America's Vietnam policy.

DE GAULLE RECALCITRANT: SUMMER 1964 TO 1968

For Washington, a diplomatic solution was not feasible as long as the Viet Cong and North Vietnamese troops intensified their attacks on the Saigon government. Johnson and most of his counsel rejected the French view as being mistaken. For the administration, neutralization was only the first step toward a Communist victory in Vietnam, endangering all of Southeast Asia. The loss of South Vietnam would have serious repercussions for American leadership not only in the free world but also at home. Further criticism by de Gaulle was hence both unwelcome and damaging.

In June 1964, Johnson attempted once more to gain French approval of his Vietnam policy. This time he chose the skeptic among his advisors on Vietnam, George Ball, to convey the American position to de Gaulle. Ball, like the French president, favored an American withdrawal from Vietnam, but Johnson predicted correctly that Ball would loyally defend American policy.[61] Johnson instructed Ball to elucidate the American commitment to a free and independent South Vietnam. More importantly, Johnson counted on French cooperation to prevent "doubts between our two Governments, and even division of purpose" that could play into Communist hands and lead to further escalation in Vietnam. The American leader expected full French support in case he had to use military force:

> In the event that the United States should find itself forced to act in defense of peace and independence in Southeast Asia, I am confident that I could place reliance upon the firmness of General de Gaulle as a friend and ally, as America

properly did in the Cuba crisis of '62, and if by any chance I am wrong in this
point, it is a matter of importance that we should know it now.[62]

Ball met de Gaulle on June 5, 1964. The undersecretary explained that
Johnson was interested in de Gaulle's comments and advice on the situation in Southeast Asia. While both countries desired a viable government in
South Vietnam, they differed over methods and procedures. Washington and
Paris agreed in fact that a Communist takeover in Southeast Asia would be a
"catastrophe for the whole free world." Ball blamed Hanoi for the guerrilla
activities in South Vietnam and claimed it was Ho Chi Minh not Washington
who decided on further escalation.[63] The United States, according to Ball, had
no ambition of establishing military or political control in Southeast Asia.
But if American aid to Saigon failed to lead to significant progress, Washington was resolved to "bring increasing military pressure on Hanoi in order
to change the Communists' course of action."[64] Ball argued that Washington
did not prefer military action and still hoped for a political solution. But Ho
Chi Minh had to fully understand American determination. The last statement
was perhaps a hint to de Gaulle to utilize his diplomatic channels with Beijing
and convey the sincerity of the United States in holding its ground in South
Vietnam.

According to Ball, French and American views conflicted the most on the
PRC. Washington did not expect Beijing to accept a solution for Vietnam that
contained the spread of Communism. Past experiences demonstrated that the
Communists could only be stopped by a countervailing force. The United
States could not abandon Saigon, even after a political solution was reached,
until the South Vietnamese government was strong enough to control the
entire country.[65]

De Gaulle listened patiently and took note of the American "hope" to
defeat the insurgency. Yet he believed chances of success were faint. The
French leader then repeated almost verbatim what he had told Kennedy in
May 1961: the United States could not win this struggle despite its military
might. The conflict was not a military but a political and psychological challenge, affecting not only the government of General Khanh but also the entire
Vietnamese people. De Gaulle explained to Ball, "I do not mean that all of
the Vietnamese are against you but they regard the US as a foreign power
and a very powerful foreign power. The more the US becomes involved in
the actual conduct of military operations the more the Vietnamese will turn
against us, as others will in Southeast Asia."[66]

De Gaulle did not deny that the United States had the military might to
destroy Hanoi, Canton, and even Beijing. But what would the consequences
be of such a strategy? For de Gaulle, it was obviously not worth the risk to
allow events to proceed that far. Vietnam was a "rotten country" for the West

to fight in, which France had learned with much sorrow. If the United States decided to escalate the war in Vietnam, France refused to have any part in it, as "an ally or otherwise." The message to Johnson was abundantly clear: no French support for any policy other than negotiations as proposed by de Gaulle.[67]

De Gaulle also doubted that present American support to Saigon could lead to success. Washington had to realize that its involvement in Vietnam was futile and thereby come to the conclusion that a political settlement was the only decent way out of the quagmire. A political agreement could not be reached without China and other regional powers. Regarding China, de Gaulle was doubtful whether the American view of an aggressive, expansionist country was correct. Nevertheless, the United States should have contact with Beijing to gain a better understanding of "what China was up to."[68] Ball interjected that diplomatic overtures to either Beijing and Hanoi at present would undermine the will of Saigon to combat the insurgents. Even if conditions in South Vietnam were more agreeable toward peace talks, Washington questioned strongly whether the Communists would fully honor an agreement.[69]

De Gaulle maintained that U.S. diplomatic efforts alone might not bring the expected results. He suggested a conference of the major Western and Asian powers to positively affect world opinion. International guarantees to uphold a settlement would preclude further North Vietnamese aggression. De Gaulle recognized American concerns but argued that all "policy involves risk. If it is a policy that does not involve risk there is no choice of policy."[70] The present American course was unfortunately self-defeating, and as French experience had shown, it did not have any chance of success. Despite his assurance of empathy with American hardship, Ball received the impression that de Gaulle was patiently waiting for events in Southeast Asia to develop as he predicted: "He is confident that they will. He is certain no improvements will result from the present efforts. He probably envisages that some time in the not distant future we will begin to consider seriously his suggestions of a conference. He quite likely assumes that we will then ask the French to take soundings with the Chinese and North Vietnamese."[71]

De Gaulle's refusal to fall in line triggered another round of diplomatic debate between Paris and Washington on American policy in Vietnam. On July 1, 1964, Rusk met with French Ambassador Hervé Alphand in yet another effort to find consensus.[72] Once more, the discussion led nowhere. Both sides repeated the same arguments, but the tone of the debate sharpened. Alphand blamed American interference in South Vietnam since 1954 for the current difficulties. Rusk discarded this view and demanded that France help create a viable government in South Vietnam. Paris should publicly recognize the need for a continuous American presence in Vietnam: "Standing aside

and equating the U.S. with Communist presence was definitely not helpful."[73] As soon as Hanoi and Beijing would "leave Southeast Asia alone,"
the Americans could withdraw. Rusk asked Alphand to inform the Chinese
that the United States was determined to protect the independence of South
Vietnam.[74]

Rusk then became "brutally frank" and in scarcely veiled terms charged de
Gaulle with rejecting America's Vietnam policy in the false belief that Washington threatened to diminish French influence in Southeast Asia. According
to Rusk, the United States did not seek to challenge French power and welcomed an "extension of French influence in Southeast Asia, in Africa, and
other parts of the world." Alphand angrily rejected Rusk's allegations and
stated that nobody in the French government feared American predominance
at the cost of French prestige. The ambassador emphasized that the global
role of the United States had been a "good thing" and had helped in securing
peace in the West. Nevertheless, American policy making led to the deep
U.S. involvement in Southeast Asia, which was obviously not a good idea.[75]

Rusk strongly disagreed and attacked the parochial perspective of the
Europeans. The United States looked beyond the confines of the Atlantic,
and as a Pacific power, the security of Asia was of equal importance to that
of Europe: "To us, the defense of South Vietnam has the same significance
as the defense of Berlin." The French ambassador dismissed the comparison
between Berlin and Vietnam as erroneous. The loss of Berlin would seriously
threaten Western security while failure in Vietnam would not endanger the
Western world.[76] Rusk was obviously frustrated with the inconclusive discussion and once more demanded outright French support: "The secretary [Rusk]
said that the appearance of a division of the West in regard to Southeast Asia
had a definite bearing on the problem and made a solution more difficult. He
said that the French should tell the North Vietnamese that they must leave the
South Vietnamese alone and that France will oppose them if they continued
their interference."[77] Rusk expected that the French would also emphasize
to Beijing the need to refrain from further support of Hanoi. If the Chinese
refused, then Paris should also oppose the PRC. Ultimately, a persuasive
French stand against the Communists would truly allow the neutralization
of Southeast Asia. A nonaligned Southeast Asia would probably turn toward
Paris, increasing the French role and influence in the region.[78]

The intense debate did not change de Gaulle's mind. With every contact
between American and French diplomats, the gap between the two powers
widened, increasingly preventing any mutual agreement concerning Vietnam.
The more Washington intensified its commitment to South Vietnam and im-
plored de Gaulle to support U.S. policy, the more obstinate de Gaulle became
in his refusal to follow America's lead. Ball and Rusk identified the basic

motivation of de Gaulle in his desire to pursue an independent foreign policy. Regarding Vietnam, the French president, unlike Washington, also enjoyed the leisure of waiting for events to turn in his favor. Events did play into the hands of de Gaulle. He was probably not deeply interested in the fate of the Vietnamese but rather focused on how his government could benefit from the turmoil in Vietnam. France now maintained relations with China and offered an alternative from the Cold War conflict to third world countries. Both were important elements for de Gaulle's policy in Europe and the world. But the French leader also worried over the possibility of another large-scale war in Asia, a sentiment that was shared by London and Bonn. A major war in Asia might refocus American attention away from Europe, possibly leading to the withdrawal of U.S. troops in Europe. Therefore, Europe might be more vulnerable to the Soviet Union. Last, as were British Prime Minister Harold Wilson and German Chancellor Ludwig Erhard, de Gaulle was apprehensive of being drawn into an Asian war. Europe could live with the fall of South Vietnam but not the fall of West Berlin.

Consequently, de Gaulle became increasingly outspoken about the American course in Vietnam. At a July 23, 1964, press conference, de Gaulle addressed Vietnam at length and criticized American policy. He regretted that the 1954 Geneva Accord had not been adhered to for long. The United States quickly established itself as the protector of the Diem regime in the sincere effort to combat Communism. When Diem tried to end the civil war, he faced American objection and was replaced by military rule. Other coups followed as the Vietnamese grew less inclined to support a cause pushed on them by a foreign power. Frankly, he argued, the United States could not desire a wider conflict but should logically want a political solution. De Gaulle proposed a Geneva-type conference, including all major powers, to end the bloodshed in Vietnam.[79]

French intelligence indicating that Johnson contemplated augmenting American troops in Vietnam made de Gaulle even more pessimistic about the prospects for peace in the region. He was encouraged to hear that the secretary-general of the United Nations, U Thant, also favored a political solution for Vietnam and was asking other countries to do likewise. By the end of July 1964, the Soviet Union, China, Cambodia, North Vietnam, and the Viet Cong all expressed their interest in a peace conference.[80] However, Washington and Saigon refused to consider a conference for the time being. Saigon issued a statement denouncing the idea of another Geneva conference and neutralization as contrary to the self-interest of Vietnam. General Khanh added that he was committed to pursue the fight for freedom and independence against the insurgents despite "colonialist [i.e., French] and Communist efforts." He also appealed to his allies to expand their aid in light of growing Viet Cong aggression. Johnson backed Saigon by increasing the American personnel in South Vietnam from sixteen to twenty-one thousand under the mantle of further military advisors and technicians.[81]

The Tonkin Gulf incident of August 1964 and initial American bombings of North Vietnam led to Johnson's decision in March 1965 to send U.S. Marines to Da Nang. To Paris, this was a turning point that further exacerbated conditions in Vietnam. A month before American ground troops arrived in Vietnam, French Foreign Secretary Couve de Murville had another meeting with Rusk and Johnson. Couve de Murville was distressed about the Tonkin Gulf incident, aerial attacks on North Vietnam, and rumors that Washington might send substantial military units to Vietnam. He urged Rusk to consider a political solution and suggested the withdrawal of all foreign forces so that the Vietnamese could finally determine their future without any foreign interference. Rusk was not inclined to listen.[82]

President Johnson openly expressed his annoyance to Couve de Murville for anyone desiring negotiations. In a long monologue, he presented the French foreign minister with his views on the situation in Vietnam. According to him, the Viet Cong grew increasingly aggressive, causing serious incidents that also involved Americans. The United States had to fight back to prevent another Korea. Johnson did not desire further escalation, but he had to decide which military response was appropriate for each incident: "We are going to keep them guessing and use appropriate means in response to their aggression. We don't want to move to escalation, but if the others do it, we will do whatever is required on the basis of the wisest military judgement. We would like to have everybody else's help in our efforts and we haven't had much help from others."[83]

Johnson was merely honoring a commitment made by his predecessors to assist South Vietnam in establishing a viable government. He only desired that the Viet Cong stop its aggression and allow peace to return in South Vietnam. But negotiations were presently unrealistic. Saigon had first to improve its bargaining position. Johnson openly wondered what de Gaulle would do if he were in the same situation, facing attacks on his people and installations. He also pointed out that he was under growing domestic pressure from Republicans to respond more forcefully to Communist aggression in Vietnam. Unless Johnson secured sufficient support from his European allies, the American public as well as Congress would maintain doubts about European reliability and the purpose of the Western alliance in general.[84] Couve de Murville was neither intimidated nor convinced by the president's arguments. Although he understood the problems the president was facing, Couve de Murville insisted that a political settlement was the only way out of the American dilemma. The French politician refuted point by point Johnson's views about the current situation in Vietnam, calling them misguided, unrealistic, and unconvincing.[85] Johnson could obviously not count on French support. But to Couve de Murville, it was also apparent that he had no chance of changing Johnson's mind. Once more, both sides were deadlocked.[86]

On March 1, 1965, de Gaulle made public his intention to cooperate with Moscow in finding a negotiated settlement for Vietnam. His announcement came only days after Johnson stated that the time was not yet ripe for negotiations. Washington was deeply angered by the French initiative. Accordingly, de Gaulle violated the spirit of SEATO, which had been created to defend Southeast Asia against Communist aggression.[87] But de Gaulle's proposals received some favorable responses in South Vietnam. The civilian government of Dr. Pham Huy Quat was contemplating negotiations as well. Sources close to the government revealed that his cabinet, under public pressure to reach a peaceful solution, was willing to establish contact with the Viet Cong to conclude a cease-fire. However, it was uncertain whether this was just another political move or a serious effort to secure peace for South Vietnam.[88] Quat soon changed his mind. He told the press that his country would continue to fight Communist aggression and demanded that the National Liberation Front (NLF) cease all hostilities before any settlement could be reached. Quat also attacked any foreign power that demanded a return to the Geneva Settlement since, he claimed, the great majority of the Vietnamese thought otherwise. The Buddhist movement defied the government position and demanded the withdrawal of all foreign forces from South Vietnam.[89] While the South Vietnamese were divided on how to react to the Viet Cong, Washington was increasing its pressure on the insurgents in Vietnam. The bombings of North Vietnam continued as part of the desire to negotiate only from a position of strength. Washington dismissed the notion that the conflict in Vietnam was basically a civil war but instead increased its pressure on Hanoi.[90]

On March 8, 1965, two battalions of marines landed in Da Nang. Soon, other marines and army troops followed. The United States had begun the Americanization of the war in South Vietnam. Washington now faced the dangers of an unlimited commitment, which de Gaulle had described to Kennedy in 1961; by pouring in more and more troops, it hoped to turn the tide but would find itself riding the tiger's back. Paris opposed the American escalation and intensified its criticism of Washington's Vietnam policy. This course eventually led to outright accusations that the United States was primarily responsible for the war in Vietnam.

Although contacts between both countries continued, France and the United States were evidently "hostile allies." The tensions between both countries would only ease with the beginning of peace talks on Vietnam in 1968. While other Western Europeans initially endorsed the American escalation in Vietnam, despite private concerns, the French position remained consistent, labeling American policy as gravely mistaken. Unlike the British Prime Minister Wilson, de Gaulle was not willing to handle the issue of Vietnam solely through diplomatic channels but rather chose to present his case to the media.

In the spring of 1965, Couve de Murville related to the Soviet ambassador that France was more determined than ever to reconvene the Geneva Conference and end the conflict in Vietnam. While Washington was seeking Western support for a widening war in Southeast Asia, France was talking to Cold War opponents, Moscow and Beijing, in order to find a political solution. The French opposition to American escalation in Vietnam found the approval of UN Secretary-General U Thant and other Western governments, Canada, for example. India, Poland, and the Soviet Union, representing the unaligned world and the Warsaw Pact, also condemned the American course as a violation of the Geneva agreement, calling for an end of hostilities.[91]

A visit by Ball to Paris in early September 1965 renewed speculations that the Americans might be willing to consider talks over Vietnam. But President Johnson was not interested in any French mediation and sent Ball to reiterate American goals and policy in Vietnam. North Vietnam was also unwilling to begin any negotiations as long as American troops remained in the South. Nevertheless, de Gaulle insisted that military force could not end the conflict and urged the return to the 1954 settlement.[92] The buildup in Vietnam continued and, with it, French opposition to America's policy in Southeast Asia.

Later, in September 1965, Couve de Murville addressed the General Assembly of the United Nations on Vietnam. He pleaded for the admission of the PRC to the United Nations. Without Beijing, the agonizing problems of Southeast Asia could not be solved satisfactorily. Couve de Murville once again insisted on a political settlement for the Vietnam conflict. But such a solution was only feasible if all foreign powers involved in Vietnam ended their interference.[93] According to Couve de Murville, the war not only had bloody repercussions in Vietnam but also seriously hurt its neighbors Cambodia and Laos, which were also torn apart by opposing factions. In the sole interest of the people of Southeast Asia and world peace, France was willing to use all her experience, influence, and goodwill to work for a peaceful settlement and the reconstruction of Vietnam. The French government once more reaffirmed that it did not support any "war of aggression" in Vietnam and opposed foreign interference by North Vietnamese, Chinese Communists, as well as the United States.[94]

The Vietnam conflict allowed de Gaulle to pursue his "grand design" in enhancing the French position in the world. He continued to seek contacts with North Vietnam leading to the resumption of diplomatic relations with

Hanoi in July 1967.[95] De Gaulle also sought better relations with Moscow in order to promote French leadership in the West. In April 1965, the Soviet foreign secretary, Andrei Gromyko, visited Paris with both sides agreeing on their opposition to the American role in South Vietnam. De Gaulle used the occasion to publicly distance himself from Washington and present France as an honest friend and supporter of the third world:

> Yes, we are helping these countries, and they rely on France as a result. In their view the contrast between us and the United States has become immense: while we are helping them, the Americans are using all their brilliant new technological inventions to exterminate in the most horrible ways thousands of these poor long suffering Vietnamese, who merely want to be left alone.[96]

In the summer of 1965, de Gaulle visited the Soviet Union, hoping to increase his status as the leader of Western Europe and creating a counterbalance to Washington. The rapprochement with Moscow culminated in 1966 in the joint Soviet-French declaration of friendship that constituted a virtual nonaggression pact.[97]

ALL-OUT "WAR" AGAINST THE UNITED STATES: WITHDRAWAL FROM NATO AND THE PHNOM PENH SPEECH

On March 7, 1966, de Gaulle wrote to Johnson that France appreciated the achievements of the Atlantic alliance and the essential role of the United States by securing its members' freedom. However, the world and France had changed considerably since the signing of the NATO treaty in 1949. Because France no longer required foreign forces on her soil for defense, France would "reassume on her territory the full exercise of her sovereignty." All NATO forces had to leave within thirteen months.[98] Forewarned of de Gaulle's move by Ambassador Bohlen, Johnson remained calm and accepted the decision by offering France a leading role in the alliance if de Gaulle changed his mind.[99]

De Gaulle did not change his mind. On March 11, 1966, Paris sent an aide-mémoire to Washington, elaborating the decision to resume its full sovereignty. Most importantly, Europe was no longer the center of international crisis. The threat of conflict lay now in Asia where the Alliance was "obviously not implicated."[100] De Gaulle's reasoning to disengage from NATO was the war in Vietnam along with American demands to give at least moral support to its policy there and the infringement on French sovereignty by NATO.

To Washington, the French withdrawal along with the recent overtures to Moscow indicated that de Gaulle was set on a neutralist course between the

two blocs, which might have serious repercussions in Europe.[101] Ambassador
Bohlen blamed de Gaulle and his policy of *grandeur* for this new affront to
the United States. Regardless, Washington would be unable to alter French
policy. Bohlen commented that the current NATO crisis revealed two "diametrically" opposed ideas toward the conduct of foreign relations:

> On one hand de Gaulle is fanatically a proponent of the idea of independence;
> that the nation-state is the sole enduring, viable entity in international relations;
> that this entity is uncompromisable and multilateral arrangements tend to limit
> its freedom and independence. On the other hand is the concept espoused by
> the US and other states in the modern world which considers all nations, even
> the most powerful, as inter-dependent in their relations with other like minded,
> particularly allied states.[102]

While the French would not find fault with the first part of the statement, they
disagreed profoundly with the second. Interdependence meant nuclear sharing and an equal voice in the alliance, yet Washington had refused to comply
with these French demands.[103]

Washington, albeit angered by the French decision, was hopeful that once
de Gaulle had gone U.S.-French relations would revert back to normal. Yet,
the resentment over de Gaulle's decision was obvious in Bundy's statement
to the Senate Foreign Relations Committee in June 1966. Bundy regarded
de Gaulle's policy as disappointing, "costly in its pride, wasteful in its lost
opportunities, irrelevant in much of its dramatics." Both countries could still
reach an understanding on larger issues, but Bundy dismissed the French
claim that it presented an alternative to a bipolar world. De Gaulle's leadership had failed to unite West Germany or attract other Western European
countries:

> The notion of leadership in a third world was simply unreal; this heady wine
> did not survive its first voyage. The recognition of China was a gesture with
> no practical result. And the present specter of a deal with Moscow is sheer
> fantasy—as far beyond French power as it is contrary to French intentions. . . .
> We have many differences with France, but none that we cannot endure. The
> most painful may be the quite special French position toward Vietnam, but in
> the light of the French past there, it is not surprising that there should be some
> differences between us. The French attitude is not helpful, but it is understand-
> able and marginal.[104]

Even if Americans regarded the French view on Vietnam as marginal, de
Gaulle was not impressed and continued his criticism of American Vietnam
policy. From mid-1965 to 1966 onward, he expressed his misgivings to all
foreign diplomats, particularly Americans. The conflict not only was devas-

tating to Vietnam but also poisoned the international climate by augmenting the fear of another world war. Moreover, the war in Vietnam demonstrated that the United States refused to accept the sovereign decision of other nations.[105] De Gaulle could perceive only one solution for Vietnam—the immediate halt of the bombing against North Vietnam and negotiations.

Washington did not comply, and de Gaulle decided to take the offensive. He chose the occasion of his state visit to Cambodia to express his position on the conflict in Vietnam.[106] Upon his arrival to Phnom Penh on August 31, 1966, de Gaulle laid out what was to follow. He told Prince Sihanouk that he appreciated Cambodia's policy of independence and neutrality as a promising precedent for the entire region. Vietnam deeply troubled both de Gaulle and Sihanouk. The two leaders defended the resumption of diplomatic relations with North Vietnam as a venue to explore new possibilities of peace and gather further information about the future intentions of Hanoi. Moreover, Sihanouk shared de Gaulle's pessimism about the outcome of the Vietnam conflict and was apprehensive of further escalation.[107]

Although the prospect of peace was distant, de Gaulle could not resist the opportunity to voice his opinion on the Vietnam War. To a cheering crowd of one hundred thousand, he congratulated the Cambodians for defending their independence from both the Communist Khmer Rouge and the United States and for saving "their lives and souls." Unfortunately, the people of South Vietnam still suffered from outside intervention. The United States interfered in a civil war. American attacks on North Vietnam, inching closer to Chinese territory, endangered peace not only in Asia but also in the world at large. Hence, American policy was increasingly criticized by the peoples of Europe, Africa, and Latin America.[108]

De Gaulle endorsed the Cambodian policy of neutrality as the solution for all of Indochina and condemned those who aspired otherwise. France had learned from its own painful experience not to fight the will of the people. The French leader advised all combatants, particularly the Americans, to accept the lessons of history. Washington lacked clearly defined political objectives, and the Vietnamese resented American intrusion in their domestic affairs. The peoples of Indochina should demand an explanation of why the Americans were fighting in their countries in the first place. He could not discern any valuable reason for the American policy in Vietnam. The general also understood that the peoples of Asia were unwilling to submit to a policy dictated by a nation on the other side of the Pacific.[109]

Why did the United States resist a peaceful settlement and refuse to accept the Geneva Accord of 1954? Why did it oppose the right of self-determination for the peoples of Indochina? The path of negotiation was complicated and arduous, and would require the eventual withdrawal of all American

forces, but it was the only way to secure peace. While the chances for negotiation were presently remote, de Gaulle appealed once again to the United
States to listen to reason and not condemn the world to worse afflictions. De
Gaulle felt obligated to voice his opinion because of France's earlier experience in Indochina and the strong ties she still maintained in the region. But
it was also out of a deep and old friendship with the United States that de
Gaulle was obliged to remind the Americans of their long-cherished belief in
independence and self-determination of all nations.[110]

De Gaulle argued that Washington still had the opportunity to change
course and heed the advice he had repeatedly offered regarding Vietnam.
Now was the time for the United States to renounce a policy that only hurt
the United States and that it could not justify. Washington should accept a
settlement endorsed by the major international powers to restore peace to
Indochina and guarantee prosperity to this important region. To continue its
military engagement would only hurt American pride, contradict American
ideals, and undermine its national interest. The president believed that a diplomatic settlement of the conflict in Vietnam was also in the best interest of
the West and would serve to restore the credibility of the United States as a
great and benign nation in Europe and Asia.[111]

While a peaceful solution was de Gaulle's most sincere desire, he refused
to mediate the conflict, believing that such effort did not promise any chance
of success. Instead of France, Cambodia might be better situated to initiate
negotiations and offer her service as a model of independence in Southeast
Asia.[112]

It was de Gaulle at his best. Foreign Minister Couve de Murville was
deeply impressed by the wisdom and clairvoyance expressed by his "glorious
and venerated" president advising Asia and the world on restoring peace in
Southeast Asia. De Gaulle was close to having the best of both worlds. He
presented the solution for war-stricken Vietnam, speaking only in terms of
"friendship and respect" for the United States. At the same time, he directly
accused Washington of imperialism. But de Gaulle refused to take any active role in mediating the conflict and tossed this thankless task to the Cambodians.[113] Washington was infuriated by de Gaulle's attempt to blame the
United States for the war in Vietnam. President Johnson, in public at least,
again remained calm. But he was worried about a domestic backlash to de
Gaulle's speech. French accusations might either intensify opposition to the
war or push Congress toward a more isolationist policy in Europe. Within a
week, Johnson responded to de Gaulle's challenge in a press conference. The
United States was more than ready to withdraw from Vietnam if Hanoi did
so as well. However, Hanoi was not listening and mainly spoke about war.
Johnson emphasized that the world should not only scrutinize the American

role in Vietnam but also focus on the deeds of the aggressor, North Vietnam and its allies.[114] The French responded with another attack on America's Vietnam policy. Couve de Murville used a speech to the General Assembly of the United Nations to reiterate the main points de Gaulle made in Phnom Penh.[115]

In October 1966, the French foreign minister met again with Johnson. Although storm clouds were gathering between Paris and Washington, the American president was surprisingly pensive during their ninety-minute private meeting. Instead of demanding direct French support, Johnson employed a much more subtle approach to convey his views. He told the Frenchman about his life, his hopes and worries, and his endeavor to reform American society. But most of all, he addressed his sorrows over Vietnam and the dreadful responsibility the war had caused. Virtually day and night he was busy supervising the progress of military operations in Vietnam. On the day of Couve de Murville's visit, Johnson selected bombing targets in the Hanoi area, profoundly aware of the casualties and hardships his decision caused. The president's monologue undoubtedly touched Couve de Murville. He was impressed by Johnson's inner turmoil. But the foreign minister also worried that Johnson was unable to follow his moral instincts because he received biased information on Vietnam. Johnson's advisors dismissed any strategy other than war, which precluded a meaningful appreciation of the French proposal to seek a negotiated solution.[116] Johnson's inner turmoil quickly evaporated, and he made clear that he was irritated by French contacts with Hanoi. He hoped that de Gaulle would cease his efforts to find channels for negotiations without consulting Washington first.[117] After two years of inconclusive discussions with the French, the American leader recognized that de Gaulle would remain obstinate. The only question was who could outlast the other.[118]

The low point in Franco-American relations was reached in 1966. Both sides remained diametrically opposed to the future course in Vietnam, and neither was willing to make concessions to the other side. De Gaulle stated in October 1966 that the war in Vietnam not only threatened world peace but also forced France to pursue an independent policy vis-à-vis the United States. French independence should not be interpreted as either isolationist or hostile by Washington; rather, it meant that "we decide ourselves what we have to do and with whom." France had surrendered to foreign dominance during the Second World War and the Fourth Republic. She had almost lost her soul and identity but, under de Gaulle's lead, was no longer willing to be a mere tool in the hands of outsiders, be that Washington, Moscow, or any other nation.[119] Both Washington and Paris also thought they could outlast the other side and ultimately prevail. By the end of 1966, Johnson predicted that a showdown was indeed coming and the day of "reckoning" with de Gaulle was quickly approaching.[120]

Yet the day of reckoning did not come in terms of outlasting de Gaulle but rather through events in Vietnam that undid Johnson. Although the Tet Offensive in early 1968 was a military victory for American forces, the joint Viet Cong–North Vietnamese forces delivered a profound psychological defeat to the United States. Johnson accepted the consequences in March 1968 by announcing that he was not seeking reelection and ordered an end to the bombing of North Vietnam, opening the path for negotiations. Paris greeted Johnson's decision as a first step in the right direction and commended his political courage. The bombing halt was a positive sign that the United States finally considered de Gaulle's proposal of a negotiated settlement. Paris was selected by Hanoi and Washington as the meeting place for peace talks. For Johnson and de Gaulle, their "cold war" over Vietnam was over, although the war in Vietnam would linger on for five more years.[121] Both leaders resigned from office due to domestic opposition and would not live long enough to see the end of the Vietnam War.

Chapter 7

Ludwig Erhard

Bonn, Washington, Paris, and the Problem of Vietnam, 1964–1966

In an interview with the *New York Times* in August 1966, former chancellor of the Federal Republic of Germany (FRG) Konrad Adenauer urged Lyndon B. Johnson to disengage from Vietnam. Both the Erhard government and the Social Democratic Party (SPD) deplored Adenauer's frank statement and, taking the opposite position, strongly endorsed America's Vietnam policy.[1] The spat between Adenauer and Ludwig Erhard on the "Vietnam question" reflected their differing approaches to West German foreign policy making. Both chancellors were affected by limitations on West German sovereignty in international relations. Adenauer and Erhard were committed to securing American protection, achieving German unity, and maintaining the freedom of Berlin. Both were afraid that German goals might become of secondary importance to the Western allies in a climate of détente. Following the Berlin crisis, Adenauer tried to expand the German role in transatlantic relations by strengthening Bonn's European base, most notably through close cooperation with France. Erhard rejected this policy and regarded the United States as Germany's principal ally. He hoped that loyal support of Washington would result in new initiatives on the German question. But Erhard could not dismiss France's role in achieving unification. The "Vietnam question" intensified the German dilemma of how to pursue the quest of unity when its major allies, Washington and Paris, were at odds over the conflict in Southeast Asia. Erhard's faithful support of Washington precluded an unconstrained German voice regarding the Vietnam conflict, and he chose to fully endorse American policy in Southeast Asia. By doing so, he alienated Charles de Gaulle and found himself increasingly pressured by Johnson to participate in the American effort in Vietnam. America's conflict in Southeast Asia and Bonn's response to it not only complicated relations between Germany, the

United States, and France but also impeded progress on the issue of German unification.

Erhard regarded the United States as Germany's principal ally. He was skeptical of Adenauer's advances to de Gaulle and even more suspicious of the general's quest for leadership in Europe. Bonn could not lose the friendship and protection of the United States. First and foremost, Bonn had to prove its loyalty to Washington. Then, Erhard hoped he could win stronger American support for German unification. This easy equation proved unrealistic. Erhard neglected the second pillar Adenauer saw as important for German foreign policy making—the European angle.

Erhard's pro-American policy limited the options for Bonn and soured relations with de Gaulle. The Vietnam conflict complicated German-American understanding, resulting in American demands to directly aid the U.S. endeavor in Vietnam. The war in Vietnam also affected the general spirit of détente with the Soviet Union and overshadowed East-West relations. The German question no longer topped the international agenda with both superpowers accepting the status quo in Germany.

Unlike Adenauer, Erhard was far better versed in economics than in the intricacies of foreign policy making. Erhard was born on February 4, 1897, in Fürth, Bavaria. He served in the First World War and was seriously wounded in France. He obtained his PhD in economics and sociology at the University of Nuremberg. He taught there until 1942, when he was dismissed because he refused to join the National Socialist German Workers' Party (NSDAP) but found employment in the private sector. From 1945 to 1947, Erhard worked as advisor to the allies and also as minister of economics in the Bavarian government.[2] He was appointed professor of political economy at the University of Munich but continued to work as advisor and then secretary for economics in the combined American and British zone. In 1948, Adenauer successfully urged Erhard to join the Christian Democratic Party (CDU).[3] As Adenauer's minister of economics, Erhard quickly proved his program of a social-market economy successful. Yet his relations with Adenauer soured. While Adenauer pursued European integration based on the core of German-French understanding, Erhard desired to move beyond these limitations and engage all Western European countries. Adenauer prevailed until 1963, when Erhard replaced him as chancellor.[4]

ERHARD'S FOREIGN POLICY: "COURTSHIP WITH UNCLE SAM, COLD SHOULDER TO MARIANNE"

Erhard and Foreign Secretary Gerhard Schröder felt that a reevaluation of German relations toward Washington and Paris was necessary. Both believed

German Chancellor Ludwig Erhard. Erhard steadfastly supported Lyndon B. Johnson's Vietnam policy. Courtesy of the German Information Center.

that the German-French Friendship Treaty (1963) not only caused resentment within the European Economic Community (EEC) but also affected the indispensable goodwill of the United States. Only the United States could guarantee German security. The new chancellor rejected Adenauer's strategy to gain greater leverage vis-à-vis Washington by playing the French card. Unlike Adenauer and de Gaulle, Erhard had no doubts about the reliability of the American commitment to Europe. He concluded that German security interests did not conform to those of France and required a continuously strong bond with the United States. The United States was also the more promising partner in the quest for German unity. But Bonn needed to assess the current policy of détente between the United States and the Soviet Union.

Rapprochement between Washington and Moscow appreciably limited the danger of a nuclear Armageddon but implicitly recognized the status quo in Germany.

Erhard failed to conceive new strategies for Germany. He lacked an understanding of the larger global picture and the importance of the European angle to broaden German options. Unification would not fall into Germany's lap simply by reiterating the German desire to overcome division.[5] Generally, Erhard's foreign policy framework revolved around the Bonn-Washington-Paris triangle, which, to him, prescribed the boundaries and possible opportunities for West Germany. Erhard soon discovered that his tenuous balancing act between Washington and Paris was further complicated by the war in Vietnam.[6] During the next years, Erhard tried—ultimately unsuccessfully—to win the Western powers for new initiatives for German unification. President Johnson acknowledged the desire for unification, but his Vietnam policy did not allow for additional complications in the relations with the Soviet Union. Across the Rhine, de Gaulle offered Erhard participation in France's *force de frappe* and greater independence from the whims and demands of Washington, but Erhard steadfastly stood with the United States. Erhard's reliance on Washington eventually resulted in growing difficulties in his own party, the CDU, which split into factions favoring either the Atlantic alliance or closer ties to France. This debate increasingly undermined Erhard's leadership and contributed to his fall in 1966.[7]

Within days after his election, Erhard outlined his departure from the Adenauer policy to Dean Acheson and Dean Rusk. While the German-French understanding was essential to European reconciliation, the German-American cooperation was of even greater significance for the security and survival of Europe.[8] Erhard worried that West German interests might be ignored in the rapprochement between the two world powers. Despite lessening tensions between the United States and the Soviet Union, any solution of the German question appeared remote. Also, Erhard was concerned over rumors that Washington might reduce its troops in Europe. The Americans reassured the chancellor that Washington was sensitive to German anxieties. But Rusk stressed that Bonn had to cease viewing world affairs solely from a German perspective.[9]

A month after Erhard's election, South Vietnam made headline news with the overthrow and assassination of Ngo Dinh Diem in November 1963. Bonn hardly took notice, and the events were not discussed in the cabinet.[10] Vietnam was not yet a major concern for German foreign policy makers, but the growing American commitment to that Asian country and subsequent French opposition to the American policy in Southeast Asia not only increasingly forced Bonn to take a stand regarding Vietnam but also required strategies to accommodate both allies. The German goal of unification necessitated the support of both the United States and France, along with that of Great Britain. Additionally, the opposite view of the former two on Vietnam created problems for Bonn on how to placate both sides in order to win assistance for any initiative on Germany. Bonn decided to approve the American position in Vietnam, partly to demonstrate its loyalty, yet was also anxious about the repercussions of a Communist victory in South Vietnam for American policy in Europe.

In early November 1963, Washington asked Bonn to establish diplomatic relations with the new government in Saigon of General Duong Van Minh, which was seconded by a personal request by the Vietnamese general. While the United States supported the new government, Washington was reluctant to be the first Western country to recognize Minh—to avoid any suspicion of American involvement in the coup against Diem. Hence, Washington desired Bonn to take the lead and endorse Minh.[11] Bonn complied with the American request mainly because Minh enjoyed American backing. But Bonn also worried that a lack of Western support might aggravate the situation in South Vietnam and perhaps even tempt Saigon to negotiate with Hanoi, leading to even greater chaos in the region. Despite justified doubts about the legitimacy and viability of the new regime, the situation in South Vietnam required Bonn to immediately recognize the Minh government.[12]

Saigon soon demanded more from Bonn. West Germany, according to General Minh, should not only increase its financial contribution to South Vietnam but also use its influence on Paris to prevent de Gaulle from interfering in Vietnamese affairs. The U.S.-French disagreement over policy in Vietnam further undermined his country's struggle against Communist aggression. Minh pleaded with Bonn to apply its influence as closest ally to France by urging Paris to end its detrimental policy of neutralization.[13]

The Vietnamese request troubled German ambassador to Saigon, Alexander von Wendland. He was uncertain about American aims in Vietnam and even more confused of what to make of French contacts with the People's Republic of China (PRC), aiming at diplomatic recognition. Wendland opposed any German interference in the French-American debate over the possible neutralization of Vietnam. Circumstances in South Vietnam might actually require neutralization to save Saigon unless significant progress could be made in the coming months. The other alternative was further escalation and major war.[14]

Obviously, Bonn had doubts about the American role in Vietnam but chose to pursue the course of the most loyal ally and back Washington. The French refusal to endorse the American commitment created a stir of anger in Washington. Yet, as the German ambassador to Washington, Karl Heinrich

Knappstein, observed, France enjoyed substantial latitude in the United States. Francophile President John F. Kennedy was more than willing to reconcile the differing views based on a "certain understanding of de Gaulle's position." Bonn could only benefit by improving U.S.-French relations.[15] The German-French treaty had shocked Washington, but the Americans increasingly appreciated the advantages of Franco-German reconciliation and believed that Bonn was now in the position to influence French foreign policy making. However, Bonn still had to earn complete trust by the Americans.[16] The problem for Bonn was how to change de Gaulle's mind and deliver what Washington expected.

BONN'S "CHINA CARD"

The Erhard government was aware of its limits vis-à-vis Washington, but the question remained whether Bonn could pursue other venues to further German self-interest. The Sino-Soviet conflict presented such a window of opportunity. French overtures to Beijing offered new prospects for the Federal Republic as well. Following French reasoning, Bonn hoped that friendly relation with the PRC might add to its bargaining position with the Soviet Union regarding German unification and the recognition of West Berlin as part of the FRG. But the conflict in Vietnam was a major obstacle for any bilateral understanding with the PRC. Washington considered China the source of Communist aggression in that region. In addition, taking sides in the Sino-Soviet conflict might appear as meddling in a "family conflict" and could backfire.

The only feasible course for Bonn was to establish economic ties with the PRC. Direct diplomatic relations were impossible for two reasons. First, diplomatic relations with Beijing not only confirmed the division of China but also might undermine Bonn's claim of sole representation of the German people. Second, and more importantly, an understanding with Beijing might be unacceptable to the United States.[17] Yet the China angle was too promising to dismiss.

The PRC also desired further recognition in the West. The broader the support for the PRC in the West, the better the chances were to be accepted into the United Nations, despite American opposition. In May 1964, Beijing officials conveyed its interest in tentative talks with the Federal Republic. The Chinese proposed a trade and cultural agreement, with discussion of other pertinent questions, and accepted confidential talks. While a trade agreement was promising, Bonn remained reluctant to the exchange of officials.[18] Bonn was dodging the question of any German recognition of the PRC, but further discussions with the Chinese could be advantageous to Bonn's overall goals.

Bonn could probe the Chinese view on the German question and possibly use the Sino-Soviet conflict to pursue negotiations on unification:

> We should not miss any opportunity to assess how the Sino-Soviet conflict might be utilized for the solution of the German and Berlin question. This [is] of even greater importance now since our Western allies realized that a new approach [on Germany] has no chance of success in Moscow. Every opportunity to gain greater room to maneuver has to be pursued. Most of all, we have to explore whether and how far Beijing might be willing to downplay or even reassess its relations with the Soviet Occupied Zone.[19]

While Bonn was hoping to win the Chinese for its position, the Foreign Ministry was concerned about American objections to any German-Chinese understanding. Therefore, Bonn developed a "defense strategy" toward Washington. Five North Atlantic Treaty Organization (NATO) members, including Great Britain and France, maintained diplomatic ties with the PRC while Bonn was only considering trade relations. More important, the West could not miss the opportunity given by the Sino-Soviet tensions. Also, Western Europe could assume the role of mediator with Beijing in lessening global tensions. For West Germany, in particular, contacts with the PRC served to explore additional venues on the German question. Last, the American ambassador to Warsaw, John Cabot, had maintained close but ultimately unsuccessful contacts with PRC ambassador Wang Ping-nan. Accordingly, the United States could not object to any exploratory German consultations with Beijing.[20]

The Chinese were certainly interested in negotiation with Bonn, as a first secret meeting in Bern revealed. Tsui Chi-yuan, head of the PRC delegation in Switzerland, was eager for a trade agreement and quite disappointed to learn that Bonn had not yet made a final decision. Tsui emphasized that his government conducted its own independent policy to foster world peace, implicitly referring to Sino-Soviet relations, and Beijing was solely guided by the concerns of its own people. German consul in Switzerland Niels Hansen was delighted by the Chinese position and pushed hard for the recognition that Bonn represented Berlin internationally. Tsui remained reluctant, though he regarded the German division as abnormal. Beijing favored unification through negotiations between the two "parts" of Germany, which made perfect sense since the PRC hoped for a similar solution with Taiwan. Beijing saw no reason to break diplomatic relations with the German Democratic Republic (GDR) but promised to refrain from interfering in inner-German affairs provided that Bonn followed the same policy of noninterference in the conflict with the Soviet Union.[21] Senior official Franz Krapf recommended that Washington be informed about the recent talks. He did not foresee any

American opposition regarding a trade agreement since contacts with Beijing were helpful toward a solution of the German question and did not damage American interests.[22]

In July 1964, Hansen again met with Tsui in Bern. Hansen was worried about press reports on Sino-German contacts and suggested further meetings should be held at a secure place. Tsui was quite displeased with recent statements by Chancellor Erhard rejecting closer ties to the PRC. Tsui feared that Bonn, like the United States, had adopted a hostile course toward Beijing. Thus, further Sino-German negotiations appeared futile. Hansen replied that Bonn was still interested in a trade agreement, downplaying the press reports along with Erhard's comments, and Tsui agreed to continue talks in secrecy.[23] The talks went nowhere because Erhard lacked the political courage to continue the China angle. He rejected any approach that endangered the precious relationship with the United States. Since Erhard did not pursue the China angle to its fullest, it is hard to predict what might have happened in terms of an American response to this German initiative. The conflict in Vietnam, along with Erhard's deference to Washington, ended the German rapprochement with Beijing.[24]

BONN, WASHINGTON, PARIS,
AND THE PROBLEM OF VIETNAM, 1964–1965

The short-lasting Chinese interlude demonstrated that Erhard's policy making was self-restricted by the overriding need of a solid friendship with the United States. Erhard's courtship of Washington increasingly alienated de Gaulle. The French president had placed high hopes on comprehensive relations with West Germany and a more independent Europe under his own leadership. Consequently, de Gaulle was thoroughly disappointed in Erhard's new course. De Gaulle even labeled Erhard as subservient to the United States. Erhard was deeply offended, but he insisted that his pro-American course was the best way to serve West German interests. The first encounter with Johnson in Texas seemed to prove Erhard correct.

Meeting on the Johnson ranch shortly after Christmas 1963, both leaders started off well. Erhard reaffirmed his complete trust in the United States and pledged his unequivocal support to the president.[25] Johnson was primarily concerned with domestic problems and relations with the Soviet Union. The president promised to closely consult Erhard on any questions of détente with the East.[26] The chancellor worried that an improvement in East-West relations might result in diminished American interest in German unification and lead to the recognition of the status quo. Johnson assured Erhard that

Germany like any other nation enjoyed the right of self-determination and should stand firm in pursuing the goal of reunification. But then Johnson quickly addressed what was important to him. Bonn had to contribute to the costs of U.S. troops stationed in Germany, and Erhard should expand his defense budget to some DM20 billion. West Germany had to pay its offset dues for American military protection.[27] This first encounter established a pattern that would continue during the following years. Erhard eagerly assured his loyalty to the United States, hoping to gain concessions and backing on vital German concerns. Johnson was pleased to find an encouraging voice in Erhard, but German issues were and remained secondary on Johnson's foreign policy agenda as long as Bonn fulfilled its financial obligations to the United States.

Events in Asia soon preoccupied the Americans and the French and increasingly affected Bonn. In early 1964, France established diplomatic relations with the PRC. Bonn opposed this decision because it ran counter to Bonn's agenda. Any recognition of the Chinese division might undermine Bonn's claim to solely represent the German people, and more important, the French decision intensified tensions between Paris and Washington.[28] De Gaulle justified the recognition to Erhard by pointing to the possible benefits both for Vietnam and Western Europe. On Vietnam, de Gaulle repeated the position previously expressed to Washington; the conflict could only be solved through negotiations.[29] Erhard disagreed with de Gaulle. The German leader accused Beijing of actively promoting aggression and Communist expansion in Southeast Asia. Erhard considered the French recognition of the PRC as premature. He was concerned with the possibility of Beijing and Moscow ending their disagreements once they realized the West was exploiting the split of the Communist world. After all, Communism threatened free countries around the globe, and Erhard concurred with the American position that the free world could only stand up to aggression if it fought the enemy jointly.[30] Erhard was less concerned about the actual motives of the Chinese, with whom Bonn was negotiating as well, than the negative repercussion of the French recognition of the PRC for West Germany.

De Gaulle dismissed Erhard's repetition of the American point of view. He refused to placate Washington merely to present a unanimous front within the NATO alliance. While Paris was open to debate, it also reserved the right to express and pursue its self-interest within NATO or elsewhere. Bonn could not refute this argument because West Germans also hoped for a more influential role within NATO. At the same time, Erhard could not officially endorse the French position regarding the PRC and Vietnam given his own policy goals to secure the protection and goodwill of the United States.[31]

By early 1964, Vietnam had become another issue on which France and the Federal Republic agreed to disagree. Interestingly, Bonn and Paris, at least unofficially, were not completely at odds over Vietnam and China. The German ambassador to Saigon doubted that an American victory in South Vietnam was achievable, and in secret, Bonn was also seeking closer ties to Beijing.[32] Despite his differences with Paris, Erhard was acutely aware that he had to maintain a constructive dialogue with de Gaulle because further deterioration in French-German relations might torpedo chances for progress toward unification.

To Bonn, the French diplomatic recognition of the PRC and its fallout for the Atlantic alliance put West Germany on the spot.[33] What could Bonn do to facilitate French-American relations? Bonn found de Gaulle's "Grand Design," a Europe from the Atlantic to the Ural, appealing, but this unified Europe might result in an isolationist policy in Washington. West German policy goals depended both on American and French cooperation. Bonn had to work for reconciliation between Paris and Washington:

> Only if we have Washington and Paris on our side, can we accomplish our objectives. . . . We have to prevent with all means available any further deterioration in French-American relations. We cannot remain passive to de Gaulle's actions nor can we actively side with the Americans. The first option would cause extensive harm to German-American relations, while the second would de facto nullify the French-German Friendship Treaty.[34]

West Germany was not and could not be in a position to choose only one of its Western partners if unification was to become reality, but the French-American antagonism over Southeast Asia undermined Bonn's own "grand design."

Bonn also realized that the German question was currently of only marginal importance to American foreign policy makers. Washington was more interested in solving Cold War conflicts outside of Europe and, perhaps later, might address the thorny issue of German unity.[35] For Erhard, unification remained the prime goal, and he hoped for a more active American approach regarding Germany. In return, the chancellor completely accepted Johnson's position on Vietnam.[36] Soon Erhard realized that his endorsement covered not only American "technical" support to South Vietnam but also possible U.S. airstrikes on industrial targets in North Vietnam. The other alternative to those air attacks was U.S. military intervention to prevent the collapse of South Vietnam.[37]

Erhard wrote to Johnson that he fully backed the United States' policy in Vietnam. The Federal Republic would do everything within its constitutional means to support the United States in the endeavor to preserve the freedom of South Vietnam. Bonn promised to continue its political, economic, and cultural aid to Saigon.[38] Johnson was content but demanded a public statement in which Erhard denounced neutralization for Vietnam. Bonn refused to do so because such a declaration would only increase Franco-German tensions without changing anything in South Vietnam. Bonn found a diplomatic solution. Erhard assured Ambassador Nguyen Qui Anh, representing the new government of General Nguyen Khanh, that West Germany endorsed the American position in Vietnam but refused to directly criticize the French plan of neutralization.[39]

The French were angered by the German attitude, and the intense debate over Vietnam between both governments continued. Bonn maintained that the conflict in Vietnam was another chapter in the struggle of the free world against Communist aggression, implicitly acknowledging its own dependence on Washington. The French disagreed. The crisis in Indochina resulted out of an indigenous struggle for self-determination but was further complicated by U.S.-Chinese antagonism.[40] Paris also criticized the German notion of solidarity with the United States on Vietnam, condemning it as uncritical and shortsighted. De Gaulle argued that Western solidarity could be best achieved when any member of NATO was at liberty to express its honest opinions on that matter.[41]

French criticism of Bonn was an obvious consequence of de Gaulle's own foreign policy agenda. The basic component for French influence in the world was its leadership in Europe. The Franco-German treaty promised close cooperation and a shared policy for Europe. Erhard proved reluctant to accept French guidance and oscillated into the American sphere. While firm in its commitment to the United States, Bonn endeavored to maintain a straightforward understanding with Paris in order to preserve its chances for eventual unification. It was difficult for the West Germans to reject the French view on Vietnam outright, given the lack of German expertise in Southeast Asia. Although de Gaulle was unable to convince Erhard fully of his point of view, the general's argument in favor of negotiations did impress the chancellor and his advisors.

Erhard made a tentative attempt to affect American thinking on Vietnam during an encounter with Rusk in the summer of 1964. The chancellor wondered whether Beijing could be persuaded to end its interference in Southeast Asian affairs. Rusk's response was a straight no. The secretary regarded China as the major threat for Southeast Asia as well as for South Korea and India. A liberal policy toward Beijing would only provoke further Communist offensives. If Beijing insisted on its current course, it might lead to another war in Asia. With Americans dying in South Vietnam, Washington contemplated escalation, unless Hanoi and Beijing realized that aggression was futile.[42] Rusk's assertion was revealing to Erhard and left no doubt that

Washington would not back down over Vietnam. Erhard hurried to ascertain that the Federal Republic was not considering diplomatic relations with the PRC but was merely interested in expanding trade relations. Erhard even doubted whether contacts with the PRC could lead to any new approach on the German question.[43] Facing American pressure, the chancellor caved in and retreated from his government's earlier assessment on China and surrendered to the American point of view.[44]

Meeting Erhard in July 1964, Johnson expressed his appreciation over German support, especially since the other European allies did nothing to help the United States in Vietnam. German aid was also beneficial in Johnson's efforts to rally Congress and public opinion behind his Vietnam policy. Nevertheless, the president still faced difficult decisions on his country's future course in Vietnam.[45] Erhard appreciated Johnson's trust and friendship. As another sign of German goodwill, Erhard promised to settle the question of offset contribution to ease the financial burden for American troops in West Germany.[46] Once more, Erhard believed his strategy of unconditional support of Washington correct. He failed to realize that Johnson was mainly interested in European endorsement of his Vietnam policy and had no intention to embark on a campaign for German unification. German and American perceptions of global issues and national self-interest were miles apart.

While Erhard received some approval from Johnson, the chancellor was scorned by de Gaulle during their next encounter in July 1964. De Gaulle used threats as well as the bait of unification to win Erhard to his side. The general accused Erhard of being a deferential vassal to Washington but then invited Bonn to join his *force de frappe* and promised to work for a European solution for the German question. De Gaulle depicted himself as the champion of German unity and maintained that Washington was not at all interested in this vital German issue.[47] Neither intimidations nor promises worked. Erhard desired a stronger European voice in global affairs, but the current crisis in Vietnam required the undivided moral support of the United States.[48]

But Erhard's defiance of de Gaulle only intensified the German dilemma. Bonn needed both the United States and France to sanction German campaigns toward unification. But how could Bonn please both allies when they were at odds over Vietnam and China? Erhard was unable to envision an alternative to his current balancing act between Washington and Paris. The chancellor also harbored serious doubts whether the general's vision of a united Europe could ever be achieved.[49] Washington remained the most important ally because only Washington could completely guarantee the viability of the Federal Republic, even if that meant unification was postponed.

With France's increasing pressure on Bonn to back its policies, Erhard again turned to Washington in search of reassurance, believing that only through close cooperation with the United States could unification become reality.[50] Washington was keener on German assistance in South Vietnam. Johnson hoped that Bonn would publicly endorse Washington's policy, while he was less forthcoming on the German question.[51] By supporting the American Vietnam policy, Bonn invested heavily in the relationship with Washington, simply based on the hope of obtaining further support for unification, yet this hope became more and more unrealistic.[52]

The resulting quandary for Erhard was that, while he made the decision to stand by the United States, he still had to placate Paris to prevent a complete rift with de Gaulle. But the growing disparity in American and French foreign policy aims placed Erhard in an untenable situation. Against all odds, he kept trying to procure some benefit for West Germany. He simply could not lose the support of either Washington or Paris. Undersecretary Karl Carstens put his finger on the German predicament. He argued that German reunification could only be achieved with the full support of all three Western powers. Neither a French-German alliance nor sole dependence on the United States would bring results. Any German initiative toward unification would be futile without American backing. Even if the United States was temporarily less forthcoming on the question of German unity, Bonn had no choice than to maintain close relations with Washington. Bonn simply had to continuously engage Washington to better convey West German policy goals.[53]

Carstens did agree with the French position in regard to China and Vietnam. Germany should improve relations with the PRC to entice Beijing into a more productive attitude toward the German question. Regarding Vietnam, Carstens concurred with the French assessment that chances of an American victory were dim.[54] Although Paris and Bonn were not that far apart in their assessment on the PRC and the discouraging prospect in Vietnam, Bonn believed that it simply could not permit a possible strain in German-American relation by criticizing the American policy in Southeast Asia.

AMERICA'S VIETNAM AND
THE RESULTING QUAGMIRE FOR ERHARD

In December 1964, Bonn received disturbing news from Washington. Johnson was contemplating further escalation of American involvement in Vietnam. Bonn hoped to prevent an escalation of the conflict.[55] Regardless of repeated German declarations supporting the American role in Vietnam as vital to the survival of the free world, to Bonn the conflict in the Far East presented an undesired hurdle in the pursuit of German unity. American escalation in Vietnam would move German interests farther down the list of top priorities in Washington.

American military strikes against North Vietnam after the Pleiku attack in February 1965 increased German apprehension despite assurances that the United States did not intend to escalate the conflict.[56] Intelligence gathered by German diplomats stationed in Asia reaffirmed the French view that the chance of an American victory in Vietnam was discouraging. But an American defeat in Vietnam might result in the collapse of Laos, Cambodia, and Thailand, affecting the entire Pacific rim. The French plan of neutralization was also not very promising since it might quickly lead to a Communist takeover of South Vietnam.[57] More importantly for Bonn, an American withdrawal from Southeast Asia might weaken American determination to defend the Western world, which touched at the core of German security concerns. Bonn was concerned mostly about a possible reduction of U.S. troops in West Germany and, more generally, whether Washington might lose interest in Europe.[58] Erhard saw no other choice than to support Washington's policy. Not unlike the Johnson administration, Bonn could not envision a viable alternative to the current American Vietnam policy.[59]

Deployment of American ground troops to Vietnam in March 1965 was barely noticed in Bonn due to a brewing crisis in the Near East over West German arms deliveries to Israel.[60] Soon, the increasing number of U.S. forces in Vietnam raised German public awareness and concerns about the conflict. Foreign Secretary Schröder sought American advice on how to justify the bloodshed in Vietnam to his constituency at home. He expected that Washington would inform Bonn in detail about the progress in Vietnam, allowing him to give the German people an objective account of American goals in Southeast Asia. Rusk proved understanding but complained about a lack of allied support for the United States in Vietnam. Rusk stressed that the West had to appreciate the gravity of the situation in Vietnam and demanded that America's allies be more forthcoming in their support.[61] Schröder confirmed German allegiance and his country's willingness to contribute financially to American projects along the Mekong River and the founding of an Asian Development Bank.[62] National Security Advisor McGeorge Bundy demanded even more forcefully a greater German effort in Vietnam. Washington was determined to succeed in Southeast Asia despite possible obstacles ahead.[63] Bonn was forewarned that Washington had made its decision to seek victory in Vietnam, even if it required taking a long arduous road to get there.[64] Secretary of Defense Robert McNamara also focused on Vietnam in a meeting with the chancellor, intimating his expectation that Bonn contribute its share by complying fully with offset payments for U.S. troops in Germany.[65]

The Vietnam conflict was no longer an issue that Bonn could disregard. It not only touched the German need for American protection but also exposed a decreasing American willingness to explore new venues in the German situation. While Erhard did not see any alternative but to sanction American escalation in Vietnam, he did worry whether the conflict might lead to U.S. troop withdrawals from West Germany. Hopefully, a sufficient number of GIs would remain to protect the Federal Republic, but would they remain if the war in Vietnam turned badly, as de Gaulle predicted? How could Erhard work for unification if the Cold War intensified over the Vietnam issue? Last, Bonn faced increasing demands by Washington to further contribute to the conflict in Vietnam. What else could Bonn offer if economic and humanitarian aid was not sufficient in the eyes of Washington? France would object to an even stronger German endorsement to the American war effort in Vietnam. Bonn was more and more trapped diplomatically by the conflict in Vietnam.

During a subsequent summit with Johnson in June 1965, Erhard repeated the German litany of loyalty regarding Vietnam. The chancellor hoped that Johnson would show the same commitment regarding the German question as the president demonstrated in his Vietnam policy. Erhard grew more anxious over the implications of the Vietnam conflict. He was concerned whether the United States would stand by its commitment to West German security. An American withdrawal from Southeast Asia, on the other hand, might cause further apprehension among West Germans about whether the United States was truly a reliable ally. Erhard discussed these concerns with General de Gaulle and explained that he could perceive no other path than reassuring Washington of Germany's confidence and loyalty.[66]

De Gaulle sympathized with the German predicament yet deeply regretted the American policy in South Vietnam. But de Gaulle could do nothing to alleviate German fears since, to him, the American effort in Vietnam was doomed.[67] By painting a worst-case scenario, de Gaulle again tried pulling West Germany into his orbit. He masterfully used the conflict in Vietnam as a demonstration to Erhard that Germany was vulnerable in its present reliance on Washington. Bonn would be far better off to follow the general's leadership. Erhard wanted reassurance that German concerns mattered and had no intention of exchanging his reliance on Washington with an open endorsement to de Gaulle.[68]

In July 1965, Ambassador Averell Harriman informed Erhard that President Johnson would increase the number of American troops in South Vietnam. Harriman assured Bonn that no U.S. troops would be withdrawn from Europe.[69] The ambassador also delivered a request by Johnson asking for additional political, psychological, and economic support in Vietnam. Washington was urging Western unity regarding Moscow, Beijing, and Hanoi:

> [Soviet Premier] Kossygin is a hardened Communist and believes that Communism will be victorious also through wars of liberation. This conviction could be dampened if a revolutionary war, like in Vietnam, could not succeed. The war in Vietnam has to be won. The United States [has] to demonstrate that Mao Tse-dong and Giap were wrong. The Soviet Union will then focus more on its internal development and hence be less dangerous. Vietnam is the key to this new direction.[70]

Harriman skillfully reversed de Gaulle's argument on the best course in Vietnam. The ambassador maintained that the American commitment in Vietnam did not endanger the security of West Germany. Instead, victory in Vietnam would further strengthen the free world against Communism.[71]

In August 1965, for the first time, Bonn had the opportunity to discuss the Vietnam situation with London. The meeting revealed the British to be optimistic about the chances of an American victory in Vietnam. Undersecretary Alexander Böker was informed about recent British diplomatic initiatives to establish contacts with Ho Chi Minh, which had unfortunately failed. The British were skeptical about the viability of the Saigon regime and maintained some reservations about American strategy but refused to openly criticize Washington. At least publicly, London fully supported America's Vietnam policy. The Foreign Office deplored the Soviet refusal to cooperate with Britain as cochair in Geneva, further impeding peace talks. According to the British, Beijing profited from the Vietnam conflict but would not intervene unless directly attacked by the United States. Böker was confused about the contradictory assessments of his British colleagues and felt that London lacked any clearly defined plan for future negotiations.[72]

Based on this short discussion, Bonn assumed that the Anglo-American side was generally in agreement over Vietnam policy. The gloomy French scenario on Vietnam had left its mark on Bonn, and British optimism about American chances there came somewhat as a surprise. Bonn was obviously not aware that London, too, had profound doubts about the American Vietnam strategy but chose to keep these concerns secret. Although the diplomatic approach seemed proper for British interest, it deprived Western Europe, and Bonn in particular, of a mediating voice. With British backing, Bonn might have a greater impact on Washington regarding Vietnam. But Erhard did not seek further discussion on the Vietnam conflict with London. He was left in his own quagmire trying to plot a course that brought some progress for unity while Paris and Washington were drifting further apart on Vietnam.

During his election campaign in late summer 1965, Erhard pledged that he would continue economic and humanitarian aid to Saigon. Although most Germans empathized with the plight of the Vietnamese, many became weary of Erhard's overall direction in international affairs. The opposition, media, and even members of the CDU accused Erhard of lacking in leadership and undermining Bonn's influence in world affairs.[73] Paris blamed the Vietnam conflict as being the major reason for increased international tensions and urged a more assertive stance by the European countries. Disregarding European advice, the United States increased its commitment in Vietnam.[74]

Facing British reluctance toward and outright French opposition against American policy in Vietnam, Washington increasingly focused on what the Federal Republic could do to aid the American effort in Vietnam.[75] Rusk asked Schröder for German aid to Saigon in the form of technical engineers, medical personnel, and even police units and also to encourage the private sector to do business in South Vietnam. Otherwise, Congress might reconsider the American commitment to Europe because of growing costs in Vietnam.[76] Schröder was hesitant to comply, pointing to the difficult legal situation in deploying any German nationals beyond the scope of the Western alliance. He had already discussed Vietnam with several aid organizations, and most doctors and the Red Cross were reluctant to deploy to Vietnam.[77] But German constitutional intricacies did not interest Washington. As with Britain, Johnson expected a public gesture of support from Bonn. Johnson was determined to exert additional pressure to receive the desired backing from West Germany.

Vietnam completely overshadowed Erhard's state visit to Washington on December 19–22, 1965, which turned out to be one of the most troubling and eye-opening encounters during Erhard's tenure as chancellor. The treatment Erhard received was a well-organized display of pressure, cajoling, and thinly veiled threats. The bottom line was that Johnson insisted on a greater German contribution in Vietnam, not only in the form of money but also by deploying German troops.[78] Erhard countered by pointing to current German aid to South Vietnam and his record of moral support to Washington.[79] But Washington wanted more. McNamara stated frankly that it was unacceptable for the United States to sacrifice so much for the defense of the free world while the allies hardly did anything. Bonn had to comply in full with the offset purchases to cover the costs of American troops in West Germany, and any additional help would be very welcome.[80]

Johnson demanded German acquisitions of American weaponry as the offset payment for the expenses of American troops in Germany. The president then directly asked for German military contributions in Vietnam. Erhard responded that, according to the German constitution, he could not send any troops or even any engineering or medical corps to Vietnam. Johnson was not ready to concede, and his "good friend" Erhard received the full Johnson treatment of threats and sweet talk. The president reminded Erhard of all America had done for West Germany during the last decades and that it was now time for Germany to pay back its dues. The United States needed concrete and feasible help in Vietnam, and Bonn had to provide whatever it could.[81] Erhard left the meeting deeply shaken and near despair, and his counsel was simply bewildered. They had some idea that Johnson was a passionate "full-blooded" politician, but nobody expected that he would confront Erhard in such a brutal fashion and ask for the impossible. The depressed Erhard soon left for bed, while his team spent the rest of the night deliberating how they could escape "partly unharmed from this crazy situation."[82]

The visit was a debacle for the German leader. Johnson was adamant concerning the offset payments, despite German pleas to consider their current economic difficulties. The president even threatened that American troops might be reduced in Germany if Bonn was not more forthcoming. Most disturbing was the American demand for German troops. McNamara repeated the American request for a construction battalion and a medical company to South Vietnam in January 1966. In addition, Washington badly needed the presence of German military units in Vietnam, which went even beyond the demands made by Johnson.[83]

Erhard was willing to provide more financial aid, and even convened a special government commission to evaluate the conflict in Vietnam, but he could not send armed forces. His reasoning was based on constitutional stipulations that the Bundeswehr was created solely for defensive purposes. Even more disconcerting for Bonn was that German soldiers in Vietnam would seriously undermine the carefully nurtured image of a peaceful and "rehabilitated" Germany. Only twenty years after the Second World War, a German military mission, however justifiable, would cause consternation among Western Europeans and most likely Soviet hostility. The West Germans were disinclined to support such a decision by Erhard. Consequently, German-American friendship on which Erhard had placed so much faith was less amenable than he had thought. For Erhard's advisors and the CDU, debate on whom to trust more, Washington or Paris, became more relevant than ever.[84] Even worse, none of the allies were interested in German unification.[85] By the end of January 1966, Bonn decided that military deployments to Vietnam were impossible because of legal and political concerns.[86]

Neither Washington nor Paris appreciated the German position. While the United States was eager for Bonn to provide additional assistance to Saigon, de Gaulle grew increasingly gloomy over Vietnam and urged Bonn to follow his lead.[87] The Germans worried about their own security, which might be undermined by further escalation in Southeast Asia, leading to the withdrawal of American troops from Europe. In addition, Bonn was also apprehensive of anti-European reactions by the American public and Congress, which could result in a reduced American commitment in Western Europe.[88] Torn between Washington and Paris, Bonn hoped to placate both allies by providing only "moral" support to South Vietnam.

A meeting of Erhard's special cabinet commission for Vietnam revealed in February 1966 that Bonn had no intentions of increasing current aid to Saigon. The most important members of the commission, the foreign secretary and secretary of defense, were absent. Instead, the secretaries of economic cooperation, finances, health, and urban development, Walter Scheel, Rolf Dahlgrün, Elizabeth Schwarzhaupt, and Paul Lücke, respectively, attended the meeting. Only Lücke favored a deployment of personnel to Vietnam. His colleagues emphatically disagreed. Secretary Scheel (Free Democratic Party [FDP]) urged that Bonn distance itself from the war in Vietnam. The dispatch of the hospital ship *Helgoland* sufficed completely in showing West German support of the United States in Vietnam while reaffirming the solely humanitarian character of German aid. They agreed that Bonn should definitely refrain from any action that might be interpreted as being either military or political support for the Saigon regime.[89]

The commission was mostly concerned about the increased financial burden additional aid to Saigon might pose. German business was reluctant to send representatives to Vietnam. Private charity organizations further complicated matters for Bonn. The relief organizations insisted that any assistance be provided equally to both South and North Vietnam, which, of course, would send the wrong signal to the United States. If volunteers were to be recruited, Bonn had to guarantee financial security to their families in case the volunteers were killed in Vietnam. Lücke had a meeting later that day with a representative of German business that, although not promising, was considered a positive gesture in itself.[90] With the exception of Lücke, nobody proved willing to provide more than financial aid to Vietnam, apparently also reflecting the opinion of Germans in general.

Despite official statements that Americans were fighting in Vietnam for German freedom as well, the American policy failed to win unqualified enthusiasm in Germany. Certainly, many Germans empathized with the hardship and suffering of the Vietnamese people. As in the United States, the war entered German living rooms every night during news hour. Body counts, pictures of bombed landscapes, and napalm victims brought back buried memories of the past world war and, with it, a sentiment of solidarity toward the Vietnamese people and growing skepticism about American goals and conduct in the region.[91] A possible deployment of German troops might encounter criticism and opposition at home. The conservative *Frankfurter Allgemeine Zeitung* opposed a Rusk proposal of military contributions by Western Europe and rejected any German military role in Southeast Asia. The burden of German history would not make German military aid a success but rather only undermine the Western effort in Vietnam: "The German predicament, which is a result of the past and its current vulnerability do not have to be explained. Any military aid under such circumstances would not result in a moral advantage to America or the West. Indeed, negative effects would weigh much higher. There must be other venues to provide moral assistance [to South Vietnam]."[92] German constitutional restriction thus provided the Erhard government with the easiest way to reject American demands for military contributions in Southeast Asia.[93] Pressure from Washington continued. Several senators demanded German military deployment, and in a secret Senate hearing, Secretary McNamara again indicated that West Germany might also contribute militarily.[94] However, an official statement of the State Department denied that Washington was urging Bonn to send soldiers.[95] Not surprisingly, news indicating possible negotiations with Hanoi was greeted with relief by the Erhard cabinet.[96] The chancellor also rejoiced over Washington's acceptance that no German military units should be deployed to Vietnam.[97] Yet, this success was short lived.

THE OFFSET PAYMENTS AND THE FALL OF ERHARD

Although Johnson no longer demanded a German military contribution to Vietnam, Bonn had to assist financially. The offset payments were the means to increase German aid to Vietnam. Washington adamantly insisted that Bonn fulfill its obligation. Though willing, Erhard was unable to meet American demands. He faced an economic crisis, resulting in a German budget deficit. American persistence that Erhard pay intensified domestic criticism of the chancellor. His efforts to find a compromise with Washington failed because of American intransigence, hastening Erhard's fall. The offset payments became the principal issue of contention between Bonn and Washington in 1966.[98] Erhard's difficulties with Washington threatened the first pillar of Adenauer's foreign policy paradigm—mutually good relations with the United States. Erhard found himself at odds with not only Paris but also Washington.

American demands that Bonn contribute to the costs of U.S. military commitment in Germany was not a new issue. Since 1960, Bonn faced growing American pressure to financially contribute to the upkeep of U.S. personnel in West Germany. In 1961, and again 1963, Bonn agreed to purchase large quantities of military equipment from the United States.[99] But Bonn remained apprehensive about the potential correlation between American protection and West German offset payments. In 1964, Washington's budget was strained by the intensifying war in Vietnam, and Congress insisted on a larger financial contribution from the Europeans to the Atlantic alliance.[100] Bonn agreed to a new offset settlement in May 1964 that provided for annual weapons purchases of $675 million. This agreement did not include the safeguard of former understandings with Kennedy, which made German purchases dependent on a balanced budget in West Germany. Shortly afterward, West Germany experienced a recession accompanied by inflation, which led to difficulties in balancing the federal budget. Erhard's desire to find consensus in Washington quickly vanished during his fateful December 1965 visit to Washington. Johnson insisted on an immediate offset payment of one hundred million dollars and an additional fifty million dollars for the war in Vietnam. This was not what Erhard had hoped for.[101]

In the spring of 1966, McNamara posed an ultimatum: either Bonn would stand by its financial obligations or face a reduction of U.S. troops in Germany. Bonn was troubled by the unveiled threat and pointed to NATO stipulations, which did not make European security dependent on monetary contributions.[102] But Washington remained adamant. Rusk was angered by constant European pleas for American protection, while the Europeans were unwilling to increase their contributions to Europe's defense. Unless European attitude changed, the United States was forced to cut its expenses in Europe. In Bonn, there was no doubt that American intransigence on the offset question was a result of the Vietnam War.[103]

The offset payments became a burden to the chancellor, attracting media attention in both countries. Diplomatic exchanges between Bonn and Washington grew tenser. The armories of the Bundeswehr were overflowing with American weapons, yet Washington would not accept any delay in recompense and offered Bonn the opportunity to acquire American technology in other areas—as long as the money kept coming. By May 1966, Bonn was $660 million behind in payments but pledged it would fulfill its obligations as soon as possible. Yet Washington did not accept further German shortcomings.[104]

In June 1966, Rusk asked Erhard for a prepayment of one billion deutsche marks, which was urgently needed to contribute to the expanding American budget over Vietnam. Erhard was baffled by the enormous sum and could not comply.[105] McNamara repeatedly singled out Germany in his demand for greater monetary compensation: "I think we can say to the Germans, as we have, that over a reasonable period of time either we must have collective defense of the free world or we are not going to have any defense at all because this country is not going to continue to bear a disproportionate burden of the defense of the free world and we certainly aren't going to defend it alone."[106]

The Vietnam crisis was now deeply affecting Bonn. McNamara was not interested in German security issues or unification. The war in Vietnam had become his overriding concern, and Bonn must contribute financially.[107] German-American relations reached a historic low. Generally, the German media and public were apprehensive about U.S. troop withdrawals but angered by American financial pressure.[108] Johnson was also not in the mood for compromise in the offset question. To Rainer Barzel, head of the CDU/Christian Social Union (CSU) parliamentary representatives, Johnson repeated his uncompromising stand. The United States was stretched to its limits due to the war in Vietnam, and unless the Europeans assisted Washington, his country might turn to isolationism and leave the Europeans to the Soviets.[109]

The American message to Bonn was unmistakable: support us, pay us, or we might abandon you. Was Johnson completely sincere? Of course, he had no intentions of relinquishing the American role and predominance in the Western world. He successfully employed the same strategy of scare tactics during Erhard's visit in December 1965. Johnson's advisors further debated this approach to Germany during the summer of 1966, and they were divided on how much pressure to exert. Ultimately, McNamara prevailed. His strategy of a "tough stand" was aimed at maneuvering Bonn into asking Washington to "cut troops" and "invite us out."[110] McNamara insisted on "100% weapons-offset, regardless of German politics" and stressed that the message had to be delivered instantly, since otherwise the German budget might simply not allow any payments in full for the coming years. While Johnson remained reluctant to issue an ultimatum, it was obvious further confrontation with Bonn was still to come.[111]

McNamara's argument was interesting and revealing. Was Washington so obsessed with Vietnam to risk a loss of influence in Europe by forcing Bonn to ask the United States to abandon Germany? The answer is simple: Washington could pressure Bonn to fall in line. With France pursuing *grandeur* by defying Washington, and London working for a diplomatic settlement on its own, Germany was unable to use the European card in its relations with the United States. Erhard's course had led nowhere in the international arena. Washington demanded money—not kind words of moral support.

Erhard's agony was intensified by domestic criticism on both his foreign and economic policies. The chancellor was blamed for a CDU loss in July 1966 to the SPD in state elections in North Rhine–Westphalia.[112] The press attacked Erhard's failure in maintaining good relations with Washington and Paris. Many journalists and politicians now endorsed Adenauer's close cooperation with Paris, concluding that Bonn, when at odds with France, was always seen with less respect in the United States. Erhard remained defiant and hoped that his upcoming September visit to Washington would bring positive results and a way out of the domestic dilemma.[113]

However, Erhard would travel to the United States empty-handed. He lacked the fiscal means to pay the German dues to Washington for 1966 and 1967.[114] McNamara continued his media attacks on West Germany. Rumors of U.S. troop reductions also did not end.[115] In the middle of this growing storm, Bonn reaffirmed its support for the American role in Vietnam. A German delegation visited South Vietnam during the summer of 1966 and was deeply shocked by the hardship and suffering witnessed there, promising additional humanitarian aid.[116] While this show of goodwill pleased Saigon, it did not change anything for Bonn with the Americans. More urgently than before, Washington needed any possible kind of Western support since it increasingly faced domestic criticism over the war in Vietnam.[117]

September 1966 turned out to be one of the worst months for Erhard as chancellor. His trusted advisor Ludger Westrick resigned, leading media and politicians alike to demand changes in the cabinet, including the office of chancellor. Struggling at home, several advisors cautioned against the scheduled visit to Washington. But Erhard believed the trip might result in a badly needed foreign policy success, allowing him to regain the confidence of the public and party skeptics. His hope was unrealistic given the bad news he had to convey regarding the offset payment. Bonn was 50 percent behind in the scheduled contributions and would be unable to close the gap in the next year.[118]

In Washington, Erhard promised to pay German dues but indicated that he could not meet the 1967 deadline. He planned to increase the defense budget to prevent similar calamities in the future.[119] Erhard reminded Johnson of the American security guarantees for Europe and pointed to anxieties possible U.S. troop reductions caused in Germany. As his last resort, Erhard played the French card. He told Johnson that many Germans, including a growing number of delegates in the Bundestag, preferred closer ties with France. While he was against any bilateral agreement with de Gaulle, Erhard added that he "hoped the President would not misunderstand him but he wanted to say that a different German Government that might succeed his Government might not show the same loyalty and determination to cultivate close ties with the United States." The chancellor hoped that Johnson appreciated his current predicament and that the offset problem could be settled in a manner satisfying both sides.[120]

Johnson fired back that he faced even more serious difficulties, and it was not "clear to him what the essence of the chancellor's remarks was." The president continued that during the past years he had always relied on the

"German word," and if they could not fulfill their commitment, it would "put them in a very serious and disconcerting position" by nullifying the existing offset agreement. Johnson refused to accept any alteration in the current payment schedule and accused Erhard of dishonesty. The chancellor left the meeting near despair, empty-handed, and shamed.[121]

Erhard's vision of a strong American-German friendship, eventually opening the path for German unification, was torpedoed by the American engagement in Vietnam. Yet Erhard remained the loyal soldier by assuring Johnson that the United States was doing the right thing in Vietnam.[122] McNamara remained "hard like Shylock" and did not give an inch toward a compromise in the offset question. The final communiqué at least allowed Erhard to save face by promising to do his best to comply with the scheduled contributions for American troops in Germany.[123]

The visit to Washington only intensified the growing clouds hanging over Erhard's political future in Germany. The budget calamities remained unresolved, and measures to consolidate government spending, including higher taxes, were strongly criticized by the media and by the coalition partner FDP. On October 27, 1966, the FDP ended the coalition, and its ministers resigned from the cabinet. On November 2, Erhard's own party, the CDU, urged him to step down. In the Bundestag, the SPD and FDP intensified their pressure to force Erhard's resignation, and on November 10, the CDU decided to select a successor for Erhard and nominated Kurt Georg Kiesinger. On November 30, 1966, Erhard finally resigned, and Kiesinger was elected chancellor the next day, heading the Great Coalition between the CDU/CSU and the SPD. Foreign Secretary Schröder was replaced by SPD leader Willy Brandt.[124]

Erhard's inability to forcefully convey his concerns to Washington and the increasing American pressure on his government to assist in the Vietnam War contributed to his fall. The conflict in Southeast Asia demolished Erhard's foreign policy agenda. The more South Vietnam preoccupied policy making in Washington, the more the German question became of only secondary importance. Washington was unwilling to risk additional tensions in Europe by challenging the status quo. Kennedy had accepted the division of Germany during the Berlin crisis in 1961, and Johnson did not change this course. Upon assuming office in late 1963, Erhard sincerely believed that German loyalty to the United States would bring greater benefits for the Federal Republic. He pursued this policy partly because he distrusted de Gaulle's ambitions in Europe. Although Erhard's concern about de Gaulle was not unfounded, the chancellor further limited his foreign policy options by refusing to play the European card in negotiations with Washington. During his last encounter with Johnson, Erhard finally used the European angle, but it was far too late.

Unlike Adenauer, Erhard ultimately failed to understand the motivations and self-interest that shape international relations. Erhard also rejected Adenauer's paradigm that a successful German policy had to be built on both good relations with Washington and a solid grounding in Europe. Undoubtedly, both Adenauer and Erhard put German interests first, but they differed profoundly in their respective approaches. Adenauer was a politician of the old school of balanced power. Erhard was more of an idealist, hoping that his loyalty to Washington would be some day rewarded. In hindsight, the limitations placed on German foreign policy making make Erhard's course understandable. The Federal Republic depended on American protection, and unlike France, which even after its withdrawal from NATO command enjoyed a "free-rider" position simply because of its geographical location, Bonn could not afford to alienate the United States.

Perhaps the only opportunity for a more promising German impact on American thinking was a concerted European policy, but Erhard did not even consider this option because he regarded good relations with Washington as paramount for his policy goals of West German security and progress on unification. While Bonn, London, and Paris were doubtful and apprehensive about the growing American commitment in Southeast Asia, they never discussed the possibility of a joint initiative to make their voice heard in Washington. Bonn and Paris repeatedly discussed the Vietnam conflict but did so with their own (not common) interests in mind. Erhard, the "eager ally," supported the American role in Vietnam because he believed it would help his own political agenda. It did not. Instead, he faced increasing American pressure to contribute to the war. Johnson needed European support, but with a defiant France, and a reluctant Great Britain, West Germany was the ideal ally to contribute to the effort in Vietnam, regardless of the domestic costs to Erhard.

Chapter 8

Harold Wilson and the Elusive Search for a Diplomatic Settlement

In October 1964, after thirteen years of Tory rule, the Labour Party won the majority in Parliament by the very slim margin of three seats. Harold Wilson was invited by the queen to form the new government. Born in 1916 in Yorkshire, Wilson studied economics at Oxford and entered government as minister for trade during the Labour cabinet of Clement Attlee from 1945 to 1951. In 1963, Wilson was elected leader of the Labour Party and restored party discipline to exploit the Tory weaknesses and oust the Conservative Party.[1] In terms of British foreign policy, particularly toward the United States, Wilson's election did not represent a departure from the attitudes of his Tory predecessors. Although as opposition leader Wilson urged for a more independent policy from Washington, as prime minister he, too, placed great emphasis on close Anglo-American relations.[2]

The serious economic crisis of the mid- and late 1960s revealed that Britain was far overextended in its international commitments and could no longer play great power politics. Britain depended on American economic support, and Wilson realized that political autonomy could not be achieved without economic strength.[3] Patrick Gordon Walker, Wilson's first foreign minister, outlined Labour foreign policy shortly before the 1964 election victory. The United Kingdom could not afford a "full nuclear armoury" and instead had to rely on the United States for protection, which meant that Britain needed to base its policy on the alliance with Washington. Generally, Walker argued,

The basis of British foreign policy must be to re-think the US alliance and coordinate it. Almost every British policy will react in one way or another upon relations with the US. We must try to co-ordinate them and build a coherent whole out of them. If we are dependent upon the US for ultimate nuclear protection we must so arrange our relations with [the] US that our share in the pattern of this alliance is as indispensable as we can make it. . . . In some matters we must adapt our views to theirs—in exchange for similar concessions by [the] US in matters which greatly concern us.[4]

Britain had to retain its independence but needed to approach foreign policy based on the obvious limitations as a global power. Accordingly, Walker advocated a more active role in Europe and closer ties with West Germany. France would always be a difficult partner, but Britain should work out a "common analysis of Latin America and SE Asian policies" with Paris. Walker recommended consulting with Washington on the Sino-Soviet split and finding a joint position on the "nature of Communism in the new context." He was determined to support the United States in Southeast Asia but suggested that Britain bring about a solution that allowed for American disengagement by leaving a settlement up to the peoples of the region.[5] Undoubtedly, Britain was dependent on the United States' nuclear shield and therefore had to devise foreign policy skillfully to pursue its best interest without causing strains in Anglo-American relations.

The major concern for Wilson was the deteriorating situation in Vietnam. Lyndon B. Johnson remained angry about Alec Douglas-Home's refusal to abide by the American embargo against Cuba. In spring 1964, Johnson told Wilson, then still opposition leader, that he would never again trust a British prime minister.[6] Wilson faced a rather complex challenge. He had to strengthen the special relationship and then try to influence American decision making on Vietnam. But he could and would not commit British forces to the conflict in Southeast Asia despite the British need for continuous American military protection in Europe.

The prime minister also had to fend off domestic criticism, mostly from the ranks of his own Labour Party, on British support for Washington in Vietnam, along with possible complications with members of the Commonwealth who sympathized with the Communist-Nationalist forces in Vietnam. Wilson's solution was to play the role of mediator and work for a political settlement. The British cochairmanship in the 1954 Geneva Conference gave Wilson the political framework in which he could operate. Wilson's goal was to prevent further escalation in Southeast Asia and protect British security in Europe by maintaining close ties with the United States.

THE BRITISH ASSESSMENT OF VIETNAM: 1964

In October 1964, American Secretary of State Dean Rusk emphasized to British Foreign Minister Walker that the United States had no intentions of withdrawing from Vietnam and instead might even expand its commitment.

Shortly afterward, Walker received an assessment of the conditions in South Vietnam from his ambassador in Saigon, Sir Gordon Etherington-Smith. The ambassador criticized the uncoordinated and often misguided American economic aid to Vietnam. The general population saw little of the millions of dollars pouring into the country, while South Vietnamese leaders indulged in costly pet projects such as a four-lane highway leading nowhere. Overall, though, the situation was not hopeless. What was required was a more effective American contribution to the development of South Vietnam, particularly in the countryside.[7]

The Southeast Asia experts in London disagreed with Etherington-Smith by pointing to the lack of overall analysis in the ambassador's report. The problem was not only whether economic aid reached Vietnamese farmers but also if the American effort was sufficient to defeat the Viet Cong. Moreover, the overriding concern in the Foreign Ministry focused on possible escalation of the war by the Americans if their current policy proved futile. London generally regarded the chances of an American victory against the Vietnamese Communists as rather slim.

The Wilson government hoped that the United States might against the greater odds still turn the tide and prevail against the insurgents in South Vietnam. If the effort failed, however, British interests would not be severely harmed by the loss of South Vietnam. London had already been very pessimistic about the survival of South Vietnam in 1954, and despite the dire predictions the country actually still survived. In 1964, no one could foresee how long Saigon might be able to survive. If Saigon fell and the West had to withdraw to its major defense line in Thailand, this would not result in a major catastrophe, at least in the assessment of Whitehall. Nevertheless, it would be detrimental for the West if American international prestige was severely damaged by the failure to save South Vietnam.[8] Ambassador Etherington-Smith challenged this judgment; he saw the dominoes falling in Southeast Asia and even favored the deployment of American combat troops. But he could not with certainty predict future developments in Vietnam that might undermine the American effort. In light of the unstable situation in Vietnam, the ambassador agreed that it was necessary to prepare Washington for the worst-case scenario.[9]

To gather a more detailed estimate about American prospects in Vietnam, London turned to Robert Thompson, head of the British Advisory Mission (BRIAM) in Saigon—the English counterpart to CIA expert Edward G. Lansdale. Thompson was the most seasoned British expert on the region and on guerrilla warfare. He had served in Southeast Asia, particularly Malaysia, since the 1950s. His estimate was similar to the briefings Johnson received from his advisors, but Thompson's conclusions clearly differed from those of his American colleagues. Thompson discerned three options for the United States: continue the war along the current lines, bomb North Vietnam and its supply lines to the south, or withdraw and lose South Vietnam.[10] Options A and B were not very promising. The present course had led only to further deterioration of the situation in South Vietnam, and bombing would not end North Vietnamese aggression either. Attacks on the North might increasingly undermine the will of the South to stand up to aggression, seeing outsiders killing their own people. Moreover, bombings would ultimately not prevent northern infiltration of supplies and men to the South and posed the danger of Chinese and Soviet intervention.[11] Withdrawal was not a pleasant alternative, but Thompson argued that it was "better to accept the consequences of defeat and try to ameliorate the situation than making everything worse" in escalating the conflict. In conclusion, the best solution for Washington was to negotiate with the National Liberation Front (NLF), withdraw American forces, and reach a political settlement with Hanoi. Thompson also maintained that, regardless of the decision made by Washington, Vietnam would eventually be united under Communist rule. Yet this prospect was not as dreadful as many in the West thought because the prime motive of the North Vietnamese was reunification. This nationalist agenda, in addition to the centuries-old enmity with China, precluded Vietnam from ever becoming a mere satellite of Beijing.[12]

The Foreign Office agreed with Thompson's analysis. The task now was to develop a strategy to convince Washington that negotiations were the best choice and to prevent further escalation of the conflict. A peaceful settlement in the near future was recommendable before events in Vietnam destroyed any chances for an American way out. London was not so much concerned about the fate of Saigon as maintaining Western influence in Southeast Asia, where Britain was worried about the safety of Malaysia as well as Singapore. London believed it was important to convey its position to Washington as soon as possible. Wilson did not want to cause Anglo-American tensions over Vietnam and repeat the mistakes of Anthony Eden's vacillating course in 1954, which signaled first support for a united action on Dien Bien Phu and then changed policy.[13]

Another military coup in Saigon made the Wilson mission more difficult. The Americans were deeply angered by the violent infighting among the Vietnamese military, and Ambassador Maxwell Taylor expressed his frustration in no uncertain terms to the new South Vietnamese leader, General Nguyen Khanh. Further Viet Cong attacks on American installations gave the hawks in Washington more ammunition to call for airstrikes against North Vietnam. In light of the recent events in Vietnam, Wilson believed it unwise to propose negotiations to Johnson during his visit to Washington.

Wilson's first visit to Washington in early December 1964 went better than expected. Johnson opened the conversation by restating that he would never trust a British prime minister again, perhaps Johnson's way of checking out what his counterpart was made of. Wilson remembered the president's earlier remark but was determined to hold his ground. The prime minister expressed his understanding of American concerns about British allegiance and promised complete confidentiality of any talks with Johnson. Johnson set the tone of the discussions by complaining that he was tired of being constantly told that it was the United States' "business to solve all the world's problems and do so mainly alone." Obviously, the president was interested in not so much British advice but rather action.[14]

The American desire for a more active British role in Southeast Asia was also apparent in Wilson's conversation with Rusk. The American foreign secretary asked Wilson for British cooperation in Vietnam, even on a token basis. The United States contacted a number of allied states for assistance "both for its practical effect as well as for the political impact" to demonstrate "free world solidarity" to North Vietnam and China. Washington hoped that Britain would deploy both civilians and military advisors to the countryside where support was needed most. Wilson refused to enter such a commitment because Great Britain, as cochairman of the Geneva Conference, was obligated to a peaceful settlement in Vietnam. In addition, Britain was already deeply engaged in Malaysia with fifty-four thousand troops and could not spare any more for Vietnam.[15]

In fact, Wilson opposed not only any British commitment in Vietnam but also any further escalation of the conflict, with or without his government. In his opinion, any Western effort in South Vietnam would prove futile, and additional military engagement by the United States potentially endangered world peace. The threat of a larger conflict with the People's Republic of China (PRC) and even perhaps the Soviet Union directly affected Britain's own self-interest in terms of both its Asian interests and its security in Europe. Britain, like France and West Germany, was strongly against such a perilous course.

Members of Parliament (MPs) were concerned about the events in Vietnam as well. They were appalled by the cruelty of the conflict, including the torture of prisoners of war by all sides involved. They desired better information on the conflict and a British initiative to "call attention to the universal horror and disgust and grief caused to all civilised men" by the current practice of torture in Vietnam. MP Derek Page asked whether Britain, as cochair of the Geneva Conference, was bent on inviting all powers concerned to the conference table as soon as possible to prevent further escalation.[16]

These questions put Wilson between a rock and a hard place. He did not agree with the potentially dangerous American strategy in Vietnam, but he also did not desire to alienate his major ally. It was his government's policy to "support the Republic of Vietnam in their effort to put an end to the Communist insurrection" aided by Hanoi in direct violation of the 1954 agreement.[17] Hence, the Wilson government recognized the effort of the United States to aid the South Vietnamese. Labour MP Konni Zilliacus did not agree with the British government's view and accused the United States of breaking the Geneva agreement and Wilson of further abetting the American transgression:

> Does not my hon. Friend recognise that the American policy in Southern Vietnam is in violation of the 1954 Treaties, to which we are a party, that the Government which they are supporting is a puppet Government which they themselves have imposed, that public opinion will be shocked at the revelation that we are following the policy of the Tories in this matter and that, apart from being a crime, this policy is a blunder because it will make our name stink throughout the Far East, and that this policy is bound to fail anyway?[18]

These strong and divisive words impacted Wilson. As opposition leader, he had taken a similar stand, but as prime minister, he needed to defuse Labour criticism to stay in power. If he endorsed the view of radical Labour on Vietnam, he would cause a crisis in Anglo-American relations. If he favored American strategy in Vietnam, he might lose his slim parliamentary majority. The prime minister needed to find a course that silenced his Labour opponents without creating tensions with Washington.[19]

Under pressure at home, Wilson was determined to urge Washington to consider negotiations and withdrawal from South Vietnam. At the end of December 1964, he consulted with Foreign Secretary Walker about British strategy in Washington. Walker recommended against any initiatives for the time being since Wilson had given his diplomatic support to the American policy during his recent visit to Washington. In addition, Wilson had to appreciate the pressures facing Johnson at home. To abruptly change course, Walker argued, might lead to American accusations of British disloyalty. London could clearly not become the scapegoat for any failure in Washington. In order to avoid possible tensions with the Americans, it was preferable that Johnson make the first move to initiate a political settlement. If Johnson desired British assistance, he would probably not be shy about asking for it.[20] Britain obviously did not want to step right in the middle of the firing line, and though peace in Vietnam was a major goal, amiable Anglo-American relations were of equal importance. Wilson agreed with Walker. He was not willing to risk transatlantic misunderstanding over Vietnam even though it created considerable difficulties in Parliament. It had been easier for him to attack government policy than make it. Like his predecessors, Wilson chose amicable relations with Washington instead of Anglo-American confrontation over the Vietnam question.

WILSON'S EFFORT TO PREVENT
ESCALATION: FEBRUARY–MARCH 1965

Wilson decided to wait for a more opportune moment to present his views to Washington. But the conflict in Vietnam again developed its own momentum. General Khanh resigned, and a civilian government was formed in January 1965 yet, within days, was purged by Marshal Nguyen Cao Ky and General Nguyen Chanh Thi. For the Americans, the coup presented a "real mess." As a result of widespread Buddhist revolts, attacking both the Saigon government and the American presence in the country, the South Vietnamese military finally agreed to cooperate with the civilian government. Conspiracy rumors persisted, and Washington feared that a new government might be willing to negotiate with the Viet Cong and advocate an American withdrawal. In Washington, the supporters of greater military involvement gained the upper hand, waiting only for another incident that justified intensifying the air war and possible troop deployments. The attack on U.S. Army barracks in Pleiku on February 6, 1965, gave Washington the reason to strike back forcefully at North Vietnam.[21]

Wilson endorsed the immediate American retaliation against North Vietnam after the attack on Pleiku and so did his new foreign secretary, Michael Stewart.[22] Understandably, it was impossible for the Americans not to respond to the sustained violence against their personnel. Moreover, following strict interpretation, Washington could not actually be accused of breaking the Geneva agreement, because it was not a party to the settlement, and North Vietnam had repeatedly disobeyed the stipulations of 1954. The British government hoped—against all odds—that the Viet Cong would cease their guerrilla attacks and leave the South Vietnamese in peace. London would then have the opportunity to work for negotiations: "The British government would be glad to see negotiations for a new settlement begin, but until a basis for reasonable negotiations has been achieved, suggestions that a new Geneva conference should be convened are regarded as premature."[23]

Pleiku, and the subsequent attack on Americans at Qui Nhon, profoundly disturbed Wilson because he feared that Johnson might give in to the demand of his hard-liners and escalate the war in Vietnam.[24] Wilson, once more under pressure from Parliament about the implications of American airstrikes, tried to establish contact with Johnson. Late in the evening of February 10, the prime minister met with Stewart after receiving the news of the assault on Qui Nhon. Wilson believed it was urgent to have a personal encounter with the American president to better express British concerns. After several attempts, Wilson reached Johnson by phone.[25] It turned out to be a very unpleasant conversation. Johnson admonished the British leader for getting overexcited, and when Wilson replied that his cabinet suggested he fly to Washington perhaps the next day, Johnson cut him off and harshly rejected the idea:

> I think a trip, Mr. Prime Minister, on this situation would be very misunderstood and I don't think any good would flow from it. If one of us jumps across the Atlantic every time there is a critical situation next week I shall be flying over when Sukarno jumps on you and I will be giving you advice. . . . As far as my problem in Vietnam we have asked everyone to share with us. They were willing to share advice and not responsibility. . . . I won't tell you how to run Malaysia and you don't tell us how to run Vietnam. . . . If you want to help us in Vietnam send us some men and send us some folk to deal with these guerrillas. And announce to the press that you are going to help us.[26]

Wilson was baffled and asked what he could tell the House of Commons; Johnson snapped back that it was actually Wilson who called him. Wilson responded that he had to say something to his constituency and suggested a conference on Vietnam. Johnson was clearly not in the mood to consider a political settlement. Instead, he argued in terms of self-defense; when the Communists attacked in the middle of the night and killed his people, there was only one immediate and appropriate response. If Wilson ever faced a similar challenge, Johnson would expect the same straightforward forceful response and would back him up "one hundred percent."[27]

Johnson's outburst definitely ended the prospect for a peace conference for the time being. Instead, the president preferred to see the Union Jack flying in the Vietnamese countryside. But the prime minister was not ready to back down either. Despite the negative signals coming from Washington, Wilson was determined to initiate negotiations on Vietnam. Whether or not successful, the prime minister could only gain both internationally and domestically. By playing the role of peacemaker, Wilson could neutralize his own Labour opponents in Parliament. After consultations with Washington, Wilson sent a note to Moscow on February 20, 1965, to contact the governments of the Geneva Conference and seek their view "on the circumstances in which a peaceful settlement" might be obtained.[28] London urged Washington to delay further attacks on North Vietnam to allow the Soviets sufficient time to consider the proposal and contact Hanoi. Secretary Rusk concurred but would not delay reprisals against North Vietnam much longer. Ultimately, Moscow and Washington were not interested in the British conference proposal, and

Soviet leaders responded to Wilson's proposal by denouncing the United States' policy in Vietnam and demanding the withdrawal of all American forces and equipment.[29]

Even before Moscow replied to the British proposal, on March 2, 1965, Washington started Operation Rolling Thunder—the air campaign against North Vietnam—and deployed 3,500 marines to South Vietnam. Washington had made its decision to resolve the conflict in Vietnam by military means. Negotiations were relegated to secondary importance and could only take place from an American position of strength. To placate Wilson, Washington continued to signal its eagerness for a peaceful solution. Former Foreign Minister Walker met with Rusk on March 6, 1965, and the American assured Walker that Johnson indeed appreciated the British initiative on Vietnam. Rusk considered two possibilities: a follow-up conference on Laos where Vietnam would be informally discussed, or direct negotiations with the Soviet Union.[30] Rusk had also contacted the Soviets and hoped for a productive dialogue on the Vietnam question. Even if the Soviets did not cooperate, Britain should pursue its role as Geneva cochairman and approach various governments to hear their opinion on possible venues for a settlement.

Walker had sufficient experience to realize that Rusk's overtures were little more than a smoke screen. When Rusk suggested that Johnson was willing to risk war against Indonesia to show loyalty to the British support of Malaysia, it was evident that Washington hoped for British military contributions to Vietnam. Walker remained noncommittal on Vietnam but expressed the willingness of his government to work for a genuine settlement for Vietnam. He emphasized that Britain did not desire the role of a neutral negotiator between Russia and the United States. However, American willingness to settle in Vietnam would strengthen Wilson's control over Labour in Parliament.[31] Britain wanted neither a war over Malaysia nor to be forced to intervene in Vietnam. In order to maintain his narrow majority in Parliament, Wilson needed negotiations, not escalation, in Vietnam.

WILSON UNDER FIRE AT HOME

Wilson's domestic difficulties increased after the Pleiku attack. In several parliamentary debates during March 1965, the Tories generally supported the American strategy in Vietnam and labeled the prime minister's peace initiatives as an attempt at "appeasement." Politically more dangerous to Wilson was Labour's opposition to the American engagement in Vietnam. Labour MPs demanded greater British pressure on Johnson to accept negotiations and even suggested a joint British-French initiative leading to the neutralization of Vietnam. Wilson had no intention of teaming up with Charles de Gaulle, and defended American airstrikes. The culprit was not Washington but Hanoi.[32] Wilson's solution to the complex "Vietnam question" and his domestic problems was negotiations. The British leader hoped to quiet radical Labour MPs and critical Conservatives by playing the role of constructive peacemaker. This approach would also allow continuous good relations with the United States. Wilson argued that Parliament should endorse his policy of a negotiated settlement and refrain from destructive narrow-minded accusations of both his government and the United States: "In the past few weeks I have made our position quite clear about the situation in Vietnam. I have said that we are pursuing these matters through diplomatic channels. I am more concerned with getting the right answer than with getting the right declaration."[33]

Years before a large number of congresspersons began to question the American commitment in Vietnam, British MPs voiced pertinent concerns about the conflict in Vietnam. Certainly, many MPs stood by the United States, but others, refusing to follow the containment theory, squarely blamed Washington for intensifying a civil war and endangering world peace. They demanded that Wilson take action to bring about a peaceful settlement. These politicians were even less willing to send a single British soldier to Vietnam.

Well aware of Wilson's dilemma, former Prime Minister Douglas-Home endorsed the prime minister's course and favored support of the United States, at least for the time being. Once again, Wilson encountered more understanding for his effort to seek negotiations, without alienating the United States, from the Tories rather than his own Labour Party. Regardless of the debate in the House of Commons about the means to restore peace in Vietnam, Wilson was convinced that his way of diplomatic initiatives was the "only way."[34]

The Soviet refusal to cooperate with London in reconvening the Geneva Conference was a setback but did not discourage Wilson. But his chances to convene an international conference on the Vietnam problem became increasingly remote. A visit by Soviet Foreign Secretary Andrei Gromyko to London in March 1965 did not produce any results on Vietnam. Gromyko indicated that Moscow was no longer interested in reconvening the Geneva Conference and supported Hanoi's demand of an immediate American withdrawal from Vietnam. Wilson refused to concede failure. While Moscow stalled on reconvening the Geneva Conference, it might change its mind in the future. Consequently, it was important to maintain contact with the Soviet Union, while Britain also needed to explore further venues to influence Washington. Wilson realized that the political climate, wherein both Washington and Moscow put the blame on each other, was not conducive to creating an atmosphere of trust, yet there was no alternative other than to keep trying to find a political solution.[35] Washington disagreed and hoped for military success to turn things around in Vietnam.

THE STEWART MISSION TO WASHINGTON

"Time is running out swiftly in Vietnam and temporizing or expedient measures will not suffice," summed up a report to President Johnson in March 1965. Before any negotiations could begin, Washington insisted on a program of "graduated reprisals" against Hanoi.[36] On March 22, 1965, American ambassador to Saigon Taylor suggested that the United States might further expand the war in Vietnam. On the same day, the Pentagon admitted that American troops were using a "variety of gas" in Vietnam. Wilson's Labour Party was enraged, and the British public was shocked. In Parliament, Wilson was asked to end his "unconditional" support of the United States and dissociate himself from American actions by pronouncing the "horror and indignation" felt in Britain.

In this charged atmosphere, British Foreign Secretary Stewart arrived in Washington to explore whether the Johnson administration was either willing to work for a political settlement or planning to force Hanoi into submission. Several members of Parliament, led by Labour MPs Michael Foot and Philip Noel-Baker, sent a telegram to Stewart en route to Washington that made it clear that they found the recent escalation simply appalling. In a letter to Wilson, they added to these complaints by pointing out that the ideals of the Labour Party were at risk if London condoned Washington's course in Vietnam. Both the Labour Party and Wilson's government would face a severe crisis unless London issued a strong protest.[37] Vietnam was increasingly threatening the unity of the Labour Party. While Stewart empathized with the American effort in Vietnam, he was determined to confront Rusk and President Johnson to calm the brewing storm at home.

The Americans were prepared for the British charge. A memorandum from National Security Advisor McGeorge Bundy to Johnson revealed that Washington was fully aware of the domestic pressure on Wilson. The British leader needed some cooperation from Johnson to get out of an increasingly untenable situation at home. The question for Washington was whether it was willing to help Wilson out of his dilemma, but Bundy decided not to.[38] According to Bundy, Wilson was responsible for the troubles he was in, and everyone in England was rather misstating the Vietnam situation. Obviously, the prime minister was more interested in saving his own neck than in helping the United States. Given his "outrageous phone call" to the president in

February, it was tempting to let him struggle with his own problems. In the long run, however, Bundy believed it was not wise to "fall out with Prime Ministers" since the blame usually ended up in Washington. Moreover, a strong rebuttal from Washington would probably induce Wilson to "make critical noises about us, thus appealing both to his own party and the natural nationalism of many independent Englishmen."[39]

In the context of the obstinate French attitude on Vietnam, it was not prudent for Washington to alienate another Western ally and reap more damaging criticism for its policy in Southeast Asia. What then was the best way out for Washington? In the end, it was some give and take from both sides. Washington would publicly announce that it was in close contact and fully exchanged views with London on Vietnam, saving some of Wilson's reputation and making the British feel significant. Bundy added,

> Then we can put on some parsley about how glad we are to have Mr. Stewart and how much we look forward to the Prime Minister's visit [planned for April]. In return, the British should undertake not to advocate negotiations and not to go back on their existing announced approval of our present course of action. They should limit themselves to the expression of hope that a path to a peaceful settlement will come, plus expression of alertness, as Co-Chairman of the Geneva conference, to any opportunities for peaceful settlement which may develop in the future.[40]

Wilson would not be exhilarated about the American position, but according to his ambassador, an expression of kind words and mutual understanding was preferable to an open split with the United States. As with de Gaulle's insistence on neutralization of both Vietnams and lack of efficient support by West Germany, Washington was concerned about not the motives of Britain in suggesting negotiations but only the impact divergent European views had on Washington's own success in Vietnam. The British position was another nuisance that might affect European, and perhaps world, opinion, undermining the effort to subdue the Communists in Vietnam. To preempt the accusations of spraying lethal gas in Vietnam, Bundy sent another memo to the president, explaining that no poison was used but that it was simply "riot-control gas" that police forces all over the world employed.[41]

Both sides, ready for the diplomatic battle, met on March 23, 1965. Rusk took some wind out of Stewart's sails by addressing possible diplomatic channels for a settlement. Stewart interrupted and addressed the use of "poison-gas," which Rusk denied. Stewart was not finished and maintained that the use of gas as well as napalm led to inappropriate suffering of civilians and produced only limited military gains. Rusk strongly disagreed and emphasized that napalm was of great value for military progress. He contended that the United States limited the deployment of napalm to attacks on military targets and stressed that Britain had previously used napalm as well. He added that this war "was not a Sunday-school party" but was a "rough business."[42] Rusk was not against British initiatives to explore a diplomatic solution to the conflict as cochair of the Geneva Conference, but he was opposed to any British role as arbiter or intermediary on Vietnam.

President Johnson, too, deflected Stewart's complaints about employing "barbarous and horrible weapons" by explaining that poison gas was in fact never used, yet admitted that London should have been better informed. Then Johnson worked hard to win British sympathy. For an hour, he told Stewart about his own hopes and fears, as well as the fierce domestic pressure he had to face. He impressed Stewart and suddenly changed gear. Johnson favored negotiations "if one could offer a reasonable prospect of their succeeding."[43] In the meantime, he had to pursue a policy of "appropriate and measured response" to aggression in Vietnam. Nobody could expect the United States to abandon South Vietnam, and American withdrawal would lead to the fall of Southeast Asia, perhaps even India. Ambassador to the United Kingdom David Bruce described Johnson's performance as "grand theatre" with the president as forceful as "Niagara Falls." Johnson told Bruce after the meeting that Stewart had offered not a "single practical or helpful suggestion."[44] Like the French, the British complained a great deal but did not provide Johnson with what he really wanted—an unequivocal endorsement of the American policy in Vietnam.

Although Wilson failed to change Johnson's mind on negotiations, the prime minister claimed the Stewart visit was a success. His foreign minister had voiced profound concern and opposition to the American policy in Vietnam. He was pleased with his secretary's comments after the meeting with Johnson, issuing a statement intended to reflect the Labour government's position and also appease Wilson's critics at home. Stewart told the National Press Club in Washington, "In the choice of measures everyone responsible should consider not only what is militarily appropriate for the job in hand but the effect on people around the world. What I am, in fact, asking the United States to display is what your Declaration of Independence called 'a decent respect for the opinions of mankind.'"[45]

De Gaulle used the same argument in his Phnom Penh speech a year later in September 1966. On neither occasion did European opinion make a profound impact on Washington. Far more irritating than British statements, though, was de Gaulle's persistent criticism, which influenced opinions in Southeast Asia and in the third world in general. Wilson felt he scored a point with Stewart's visit, but Johnson saw things otherwise and complained bitterly over the lack of European support. The president was determined to pursue the commitment of his predecessors and respond to North Vietnamese aggression until it ceased. He thought it was "insulting" that all these politicians from Europe came over to see him to use these meetings for solely domestic purposes, although they had no "practicable solutions to offer for American problems."[46] On the same day of the Stewart visit, Johnson emphasized that he was not willing to negotiate and believed his message was "getting through" to both the Europeans and Hanoi. He added, "I don't wanna go to Hanoi. I was a hell of a long time getting into this. But I like it."[47]

The American view was not encouraging to Wilson, coming shortly after the Soviet refusal to reconvene the Geneva Conference. But in the face of his rebellious party members in the Commons, he remained determined that his peace initiatives would lead to an initial first step, some kind of response by any side, however minor, but nevertheless better than further military escalation. Wilson eagerly awaited a memorandum by Rusk, explaining the American policy in Vietnam, which Rusk had promised to Stewart. The British leader hoped he could use a more detailed and encouraging statement by Washington to deflect domestic criticism in Parliament. The position paper never arrived, and Wilson once more took the initiative, publicly reaffirming the British proposal of February 1965 to convene a conference.[48] Since Washington was not responding to British suggestions, Wilson's conference idea was the only face-saving measure left.

In early April, Wilson met with de Gaulle in Paris and discussed the crisis in Vietnam. The French president was openly anti-American and unwilling to modify his neutralization proposal for Vietnam.[49] Wilson defended the United States but could not overcome the intransigence of de Gaulle on Vietnam. Wilson explained to de Gaulle the British peace initiative and the overall difficulty to precisely assess the intentions of Hanoi and Beijing. The North Vietnamese demand of an American withdrawal and the American precondition of an end of North Vietnamese infiltration made any negotiations impossible.[50]

Anglo-French differences in the approach to Vietnam were even more obvious in the meeting between Stewart and Maurice Couve de Murville, the French foreign minister. Couve de Murville reiterated that the conflict in Vietnam was essentially a civil war in which the United States had no right to interfere. The American engagement was only aggravating an already bad situation. Stewart strongly disagreed. He regarded an American withdrawal from South Vietnam as an open invitation to Beijing to intervene directly. Ultimately, negotiations were the only possible way to end the conflict, and Britain was willing to take the lead in organizing a conference. Couve de Murville replied that France had only recently probed the chances for negotiations after the Soviets suggested a conference based on the cessation of

American air attacks on North Vietnam. It was obvious that the Communists were willing to negotiate, while the United States refused to stop its attacks on North Vietnam, which diminished the possibility of a political solution.[51] The entire exchange reflected the inability of both London and Paris to set aside past differences in Anglo-French relations and pursue common goals.

Similar conversations over Vietnam took place between the French and the West Germans and, on one occasion, between the British and the West Germans. The French were increasingly outspoken in their criticism of the United States and also held that the chances for a negotiated settlement faded with every American bomb dropped on North Vietnam. Obviously, Wilson and German Chancellor Ludwig Erhard shared the French skepticism about the possibilities of American success in Vietnam. All three European countries were deeply troubled about further escalation in Vietnam and a potential larger war with the PRC. A larger conflict might result in American troop reductions in Western Europe, which would obviously affect European security. However, Wilson, as well as Erhard, was unwilling to join the French position because neither was ready to follow the French lead and risk complications with the United States (see chapter 7).

Wilson valued good relations with Washington higher than causing further tensions by adopting a common position with de Gaulle. Certainly, de Gaulle's own leadership ambitions in Europe played a significant role in Wilson's analysis, and Britain would not and could not renounce its own voice in global affairs in favor of Paris. The need for American military protection, therefore, outweighed the possibility of a closer alliance with France. While a unified policy by Britain, France, and West Germany regarding the American engagement in Vietnam might have had a greater impact on Washington, a common strategy was never considered by all three countries. Wilson decided to continue his course and work for negotiations, while refraining from publicly condemning the American role in Vietnam.

SECOND WILSON VISIT TO WASHINGTON: SEPARATE FUNCTIONS BUT COMMON COURSE?

In mid-April 1965, Wilson was back in Washington, fully prepared to hold his own on the issue of Vietnam. A few days before his arrival, Johnson had finally publicly outlined his goals for Vietnam at Johns Hopkins University, where he announced his readiness to enter negotiations with Hanoi without preconditions. Wilson regarded the speech as a promising sign and hoped he could facilitate the process by offering British help. At lunch with the prime minister, Johnson was clearly in a better mood than during their phone conversation in February.[52] Undersecretary George Ball prepared Johnson for the meeting by pointing out that British support for the American policy in Vietnam "has been stronger than that of our major allies" and that Wilson, despite increasing domestic opposition to the war, "steadfastly" remained on course. Johnson should express his appreciation for British loyalty.[53] The president followed Ball's advice, and Wilson found the discussion on Vietnam far more constructive than during previous encounters. However, Johnson was still reluctant to address negotiations and instead stressed the three "Ds," determination, development, and discussion. He asked again for a British military contribution, which Wilson politely declined. Johnson then expounded on how he understood discussions, which reassured Wilson that the Americans were at least contemplating a political settlement. The prime minister pledged his full support in urging the Soviet Union to revive the Geneva process and "build on this new American willingness to secure a settlement round the conference table."[54] Undoubtedly, Wilson was pleased with the new attitude in Washington and the appreciation of his efforts for a political solution for Vietnam. He interpreted Johnson's remarks as a division of function between both countries: "The American government would not be deflected from its military task; but equally he [Johnson] would give his full backing to any British initiative which had any chance of getting peace-talks on the move."[55]

Wilson started his initiative even before he met with Johnson by sending former Foreign Secretary Walker on a tour of Southeast Asia as his personal emissary to discuss Vietnam. Walker produced some "useful" reports but was not able to meet with leaders in Hanoi and Beijing.[56] This setback did not discourage Wilson. He hoped to employ a conference proposal by Cambodian leader Prince Norodom Sihanouk, to open discussion on all the issues troubling Indochina. The Soviets agreed to a conference over Cambodia, and Beijing also signaled its willingness to participate. Everything depended now on the American position. Wilson discussed the idea with Rusk on April 15, 1965, and interpreted the favorable response from Moscow as a sign that both Hanoi and Beijing might actually consider talks. Rusk remained skeptical and wanted more details. Any conference had to be well planned to evade a "total disaster." Washington needed more time to evaluate the proposal, but in general terms, the United States was interested in the Soviet offer for a conference.[57]

Soon after Wilson's visit to Washington, Foreign Secretary Stewart received a reply from the Americans that again indicated that Washington required additional time to decide on a conference and for the time being could only endorse Walker's fact-finding mission in Southeast Asia. Stewart was disconcerted by the American response. He simply could not understand the reluctance of Washington to embark on a political initiative, which in fact had been outlined and promoted by Johnson in the Johns Hopkins speech. Stewart argued that American failure to act on any conference proposal would probably be interpreted as lack of sincerity to reach a negotiated solution for Vietnam. The foreign secretary urged his ambassador to Washington, Sir Patrick Dean, to do everything possible to obtain a quick American response.[58] Washington did not comply. Rusk was waiting for an assessment of the top brass in Honolulu. He further argued that the South Vietnamese could not be forced to accept a conference. London was not impressed and regarded American hesitation as a calculated policy to prevent a conference. London felt that time was an issue and the longer Washington waited to agree to talks, the slimmer the chances were for any diplomatic success.[59]

Again, Wilson met with disappointment. Prince Sihanouk distanced himself from his own conference proposal, and the Honolulu meeting of American policy makers recommended a further increase in U.S. troops and continuous aerial attacks on North Vietnam. The division of functions that Wilson had envisioned after his visit with Johnson was far from becoming reality. In fact, Washington fulfilled its part by solely focusing on the military side of the conflict, but it was not willing to allow Britain to play the role of peacemaker. Partly, Washington's intransigence resulted from Hanoi's unwillingness to accept negotiations without preconditions. Hanoi insisted on an American withdrawal and cessation of air attacks, no foreign interference, recognition of the NLF by Saigon, and "peaceful unification" of Vietnam. Only after these conditions were met would Hanoi be interested in a Geneva-type conference.[60]

Washington stressed that the basis for a settlement must be the independence of South Vietnam. Nevertheless, Ball argued that Washington should seek some common ground with North Vietnam. He felt that a peaceful reunification of Vietnam could be achieved, provided it was based on free elections, truly expressing the will of the Vietnamese people.[61] Johnson gave Ball's proposal a try and ordered a short bombing halt in May 1965. In addition, he was willing to explore the diplomatic angle and sent Foy Kohler to present a note to the North Vietnamese embassy in Moscow. The North Vietnamese refused to accept any communication, and the effort to deliver an oral message through Soviet channels also failed.[62]

Wilson, after the disappointment over his Cambodia initiative, was elated by the bombing pause and the American effort to establish direct contact with Hanoi. Once again, he saw an opportunity to act as peacemaker and silence growing criticism at home. This bubble burst due to Hanoi's intransigence to respond to Kohler and the subsequent American resumption of aerial attacks. The Soviets also refused to consider a conference after these recent setbacks.[63]

The prime minister was "extremely concerned about the worsening Vietnam situation," and his cabinet feared a widening of the war that would inextricably draw Great Britain into the fighting. Also, Wilson's failure on the diplomatic front did not ease any of his domestic problems. Adding to Wilson's quagmire was the issue of British credibility in the Commonwealth.

Wilson wondered how the Vietnam problem might affect the upcoming Commonwealth conference in June 1965. It was obvious that the Asian and African members of the Commonwealth would take a strong anti-American line, complicating proceedings within the Commonwealth, and adding further fodder to his domestic critics.[64] Wilson worked hard to find a way out of the dilemma he faced in the Commonwealth and in Parliament, and to obtain additional leverage on Washington. The result was the Commonwealth peace initiative. The Commonwealth represented about a sixth of the UN members, and its political views ranged from strongly pro-American, as in Australia and New Zealand, to neutral or unaligned, and to anti-American. If all of them agreed on a common policy, it would obviously give Wilson a stronger backing vis-à-vis Washington, keep the Commonwealth from disunity, and score valuable points in Parliament.

As soon as the Commonwealth leaders arrived in London, Wilson made his rounds and won the endorsement of most of them. The Commonwealth leaders proposed both an end to American bombing of North Vietnam and infiltration by North Vietnamese troops to the South. The next step would be a cease-fire and an international conference, leading to the withdrawal of all foreign troops from South Vietnam. Vietnam should eventually become a neutral country, and an international force was to guarantee peace. Washington also gave its "warm support," and Wilson promised Johnson to go "into battle" and win endorsement of the Commonwealth.[65]

Domestically, too, Wilson's initiative brought the desired rewards. Both Douglas-Home for the Tories and Jo Grimond for the radical wing of Labour endorsed the prime minister's strategy. The press applauded the Commonwealth initiative, calling it a "bold and imaginative stroke." Johnson responded favorably and so did the government of Saigon. By June 23, 1965, four Commonwealth ambassadors delivered a joint message to Soviet Premier Aleksey Nikolayevich Kosygin, asking for his backing.[66]

But Wilson experienced disappointment once again. Washington did not agree to a bombing pause for the duration of the Commonwealth initiative unless North Vietnam ceased its own aggression in the South. The reactions in Moscow, Beijing, and Hanoi turned out discouragingly as well. Beijing even accused London of supporting American aggression in Vietnam. Hanoi flatly rejected the proposal and restated that peace would be restored only after an American withdrawal and cessation of their "aggressive war."[67]A last-stance effort to personally deliver the peace proposal by British MP Harold Davies, who had maintained good connections with Hanoi, did not succeed.[68] Wilson had tried and failed again. Domestically, he had to suffer through Tory advice that he should not try anything "unless you are sure that it will succeed." But given the domestic and international constraints on Wilson, the question remained, what else could be done?

Britain did not want the war in Vietnam to threaten its own security interests. As a Southeast Asia Treaty Organization (SEATO) member, though, London still faced the possibility of being forced to deploy British soldiers.[69] Wilson would face even more opposition from his Labour Party and might lose his slight majority in Parliament. Given the overextension of British forces, any intervention in Vietnam was far too costly. It would also be too costly in terms of British security interest in Europe. The role of peacemaker was the only alternative left. But any opportunity to reach a negotiated settlement was evaporating quickly with the increasing number of GIs arriving in South Vietnam.

In July 1965, U.S. Secretary of Defense Robert McNamara admitted to Walker that the chances of success in Vietnam were rather small. Joint South Vietnamese and American forces were far from gaining the upper hand. Even additional American troops were unlikely to succeed in a limited war such as in Vietnam. McNamara hoped the Soviet Union would still apply pressure on Hanoi to reach a negotiated settlement. At the same time, he prepared a memorandum asking for a substantial increase of American troops in Vietnam. Three weeks later, Johnson announced he would do precisely what McNamara suggested and increase the number of American soldiers "by a number which may equal or exceed the 80,000" already in Vietnam.[70]

Against growing odds and rising numbers of U.S. soldiers in Vietnam, Wilson still hoped for a negotiated settlement. In December 1965, he met again with President Johnson, and once more Vietnam topped the agenda. Arriving in Washington, Wilson received a telegram from sixty-eight Labour MPs who demanded that the United States cease its bombing raids on North Vietnam. The MPs were appalled that American bombs hit increasingly close to population centers such as Haiphong. They also were apprehensive of a recent McNamara statement alluding to the "near certainty of war with China." Wilson urged Johnson to suspend aerial attacks in order to assess recent hints that Hanoi was in fact willing to begin negotiations. At least, Johnson did not reject outright the British request, and both leaders discussed possible venues for negotiations with North Vietnam. Wilson made it clear that, if U.S. planes directly attacked Hanoi and Haiphong, he would be forced to publicly denounce any such attack.[71] Later that day, Johnson publicly affirmed that he regarded Britain's role as Geneva cochair essential in bringing all sides to the conference table. Furthermore, Johnson promised to support any British initiative leading to negotiation on Vietnam. The British media responded favorably to Wilson's visit. Most importantly, Johnson had not insisted on British troops in Vietnam. Also, the American president was welcoming Wilson's approach to a conference on Vietnam.[72]

THE FAILURE TO URGE "COMMON SENSE"

Wilson's success in Washington was another Pyrrhic victory. By the time he visited Johnson, more than 180,000 American troops were stationed in Vietnam, and their numbers were increasing. The exchange of pleasantries with the American leaders could not disguise the fact that they were not seriously interested in any negotiations. While genuinely trying, Wilson could not prevent further escalation in Vietnam. His Foreign Office was equally pessimistic. Even before the prime minister went to the United States, his advisors at Whitehall regarded any chance of a negotiated settlement as bleak. For the present, negotiations "would achieve precisely nothing."[73] But Wilson could not simply abandon his policy of reaching a negotiated settlement. Facing a rising number of Labour MPs protesting the American policy in Vietnam, domestic challenges added to London's apprehension about the international implications of American escalation in Vietnam. With the extension of the Christmas bombing halt of late 1965, Wilson hoped that another round of diplomatic initiatives might finally bring results. Yet, in late January 1966, Johnson ordered the resumption of air attacks on North Vietnam. The Foreign Office issued a press statement supporting Johnson's decision before it was cleared with Wilson. The result was a major crisis within the Labour Party over Vietnam.[74]

In Parliament, Wilson defended his effort to seek negotiations but also expressed understanding for Washington's position. Hanoi and Beijing had not demonstrated any desire to embark on a peaceful solution. Wilson deplored that his colleagues, while strongly criticizing the Americans, had shown less enthusiasm in urging both Hanoi and Beijing to come to the conference table.[75] But domestic, particularly Labour, opposition could not be denied, and Wilson had to devise an approach that would both reunite the Labour Party and promise results on Vietnam. Again, diplomatic initiatives seemed the best way, since outright criticism of American policy appeared self-defeating.

In Parliament, Wilson pleaded with Labour and Tories alike to consider the consequences of the war in Vietnam both for Britain and the United States. Surely, the conflict was a tragedy for the Vietnamese people. But even more threatening was the possibility of escalation "to the scale of a major land war in Asia." Last, the fighting in Vietnam prevented a lessening of tensions between East and West. Wilson therefore had no other choice but to work for a political solution, pursuing British self-interest. Yet he reminded his colleagues that unilateral withdrawal by the United States was a double-edged sword. American allies might question Washington's word. But an American withdrawal could only be seen as "a humiliating defeat," which would most likely drive the United States into a position of "intransigent isolation."[76] Once again, Wilson walked the tightrope, balancing immediate domestic concerns with the long-term interest of Great Britain. To the British leader, the only possible approach to settle the thorny Vietnam issue was in finding a diplomatic solution.

In February 1966, Wilson visited the Soviet Union but got nowhere on Vietnam. However, Wilson managed to establish private contacts with Hanoi. Soon, too, this prospect evaporated into thin air.[77] Neither the Soviets nor the North Vietnamese were receptive to Wilson's efforts. Wilson agreed with Moscow during the official press conference that "there can be no military solution in the interests of the people of Vietnam." He hastened to assure his allegiance to the United States by explaining that his foremost loyalty was to British allies and friends. Despite the East-West divide, both sides should work to settle the Vietnam issue.[78]

Members of Parliament were not satisfied. In June 1966, Wilson was urged to meet with President Johnson and demand an end to the war in Vietnam. MP David Winnick pressured Wilson to express the view of many British to Johnson: "Is the Prime Minister aware that there are many people in this country who would like him to do precisely what Attlee did in 1950—to urge common sense on the Americans? Will the Prime Minister inform President Johnson that the majority of the British people have no stomach for this colonial war that the Americans are engaged in?"[79] This was a remarkable statement coming from a former colonial power. It summarized the ambiguities of Britain's past and present. Chastened by the loss of empire, Britain could only advise against its own former mistakes. This advice was certainly biased and reflected British self-interest. Wilson rejected the comparison to the Attlee mission on Korea in 1950. Unlike 1950, Britain did not have troops on the battlefield in Vietnam. Wilson had repeatedly explained British views on Vietnam to the Americans. He related his effort to encourage the Soviet Union to participate in the process of finding a peaceful settlement. But neither Moscow nor Beijing proved receptive to British initiatives. Washington also rejected Wilson's concerns regarding the plan to bomb petrol, oil, and lubricant (POL) storage facilities near Hanoi and Haiphong. When the United States did so at the end of June 1966, Wilson declared he had to "dissociate" from the attacks but also explained that the "United States [is] right to assist the millions of South Vietnamese, who do not wish to live under Communist domination."[80]

In an almost quixotic endeavor, Wilson held fast to the approach adopted by his predecessors. Unwilling and unable to commit Britain to the conflict in Vietnam, he tried repeatedly to initiate a negotiated settlement. In early 1967, Wilson was again certain that the United States was earnestly interested in an initiative to end the war in Vietnam. Johnson sent his personal envoy Chester Cooper to London to express the genuine desire to establish contacts with Hanoi. Accordingly, Washington offered to suspend the bombing of North Vietnam. Hanoi would then reduce its troops in the South, leading to gradual de-escalation. Wilson was asked to convince the Soviets that Washington was sincere in the newest initiative. Hopefully, the Soviets would pressure Hanoi to seriously consider negotiations.[81]

Wilson complied. In fact, Soviet Premier Kosygin proved interested as well when he visited Britain in February 1967. Wilson conveyed the so-called phase A/phase B plan to Kosygin and hoped that the Soviets could impress Hanoi, leading to negotiations. Kosygin was receptive and suggested that it should be the task of the two Geneva chairmen "to advise and assist the US and DRV to meet and discuss their problems at the negotiating table."[82] Immediately, Wilson phoned U.S. Ambassador Bruce and Cooper while Kosygin contacted Hanoi. Wilson handed a copy of the American proposal to Kosygin, after the prime minister had cleared the exact wording with Washington. Bruce was elated that Kosygin not only took the proposal seriously but also expressed hope that Hanoi might accept the American plan. Bruce told the prime minister, "I think you've made it. This is going to be the biggest diplomatic coup of the century."[83]

It turned out otherwise. Hours later Wilson was informed that Washington had changed the proposal. Johnson now insisted that Hanoi stop infiltration to the South immediately as a precondition for any negotiations. Only when Washington was assured that infiltration had ceased would the Americans halt bombing of North Vietnam. Wilson fumed but to no avail. To Wilson, Washington's actions were a "total reversal of policy," and it "had been deliberately taken" just when there was a real chance for a settlement. An angry Wilson still could not believe that the White House had taken him and Kosygin "for a ride." Even profound confusion in Washington could not explain this stab in the back. Instead, Wilson deduced correctly, hawks had won the day and changed Johnson's mind. Washington neglected to consider that its reversal put the prime minister in "a hell of a situation" for his remaining talks with Kosygin.[84]

Wilson was determined to salvage the honor of his government and decided to go it alone. Henceforth, he was presenting the views of the British government and insisted on the original two-phase proposal. But Wilson remained in constant contact with Washington, hoping that Johnson would fall in line. Ultimately, the American response lay in between both proposals, insisting that Hanoi respond within hours. Kosygin proved understanding to the British dilemma and forwarded the new American offer to Hanoi. Nothing came of it, and within days the United States resumed the bombing of North Vietnam.[85]

To Wilson, another "historic opportunity" had been missed by a "disastrous" decision in Washington, and his diplomatic approach was in shambles. From Winston Churchill to Wilson, British leaders did not share the American assessment that South Vietnam had to be held at all costs. British dependence on American military protection and London's desire to remain the "special ally" precluded outright criticism of American policy in Vietnam. As reluctant but loyal ally, London chose to initiate diplomatic solutions of the Vietnam conflict and failed in this effort. The "special relationship" also ruled out a joint European initiative. After de Gaulle's veto on the British entry into the Common Market in 1963, London depended even more on a close relationship with the United States. Like Paris and Bonn, London remained limited by its own perceived self-interest and hence lacked the leverage to change American policy making on Vietnam.

Chapter 9

Lessening of Tensions, 1968–1969

The Tet Offensive, launched on January 30, 1968, was a military disaster for the Viet Cong (VC) and North Vietnamese insurgents. Yet the American public and people around the world watching events unfolding on television received a different picture. Everywhere in South Vietnam, it seemed, American and Army of the Republic of Vietnam (ARVN) forces were besieged. VC combatants even reached the premises of the U.S. Embassy in Saigon. Combined American and ARVN forces fought ferociously against the Viet Cong in the old imperial city of Hue for several weeks.[1] In the north of the country, Americans combated regular North Vietnamese and VC units at the fortress of Khe Sanh. Superior American firepower wrought havoc among the North Vietnamese; the battle was won, but Americans abandoned the fortress in June 1968. President Lyndon B. Johnson did his best to assure the nation that the Communist attacks were a "complete failure" yet with little success. As a result, his approval ratings were falling even more rapidly than before the Tet Offensive. Most damaging was the media assessment and particularly CBS anchorman Walter Cronkite's statement that the war in Vietnam was to end "in a stalemate."[2]

Even before the Tet Offensive, Johnson was considering proposals from his counsel to shift strategy in Vietnam. After Tet, Johnson turned to recently appointed Secretary of Defense Clark Clifford to reevaluate the situation in Vietnam. Reports from generals William Westmoreland and Earle Wheeler were deeply pessimistic, calling for an additional two hundred thousand American troops to prevent defeat. Clifford and his civilian advisors at the Pentagon strongly advocated a new approach: U.S. troops should not be augmented further, and the military should switch its strategy of search and destroy to one of attrition of the enemy. The South Vietnamese government and its military had to assume a greater burden in winning the war. Last, Clifford concluded that the ultimate goal was no longer a military victory but rather a negotiated settlement that would guarantee the South Vietnamese peace and leave them "free to fashion their own political institutions."[3] Clifford prevailed. Secretary of State Dean Rusk added to Clifford's recommendations in proposing a bombing halt and a new peace initiative to Hanoi. After years of reluctance to negotiate, Johnson agreed. The president also noted with deep concern the growing opposition within his own party, in Congress, and of course, within the nation to his Vietnam policy.[4]

On March 31, 1968, Johnson announced to an astounded national audience that he had ordered the cessation of American bombing raids against North Vietnam. The president was also willing to enter into peace talks and hoped that Hanoi would respond favorably. Johnson's concluding statement was even more unexpected; he refused to either seek or accept the nomination of the Democratic Party for another term as president. Therefore, it was clear that America's war in Vietnam had entered a new phase in which the United States still maintained hope of saving South Vietnam but finally decided to negotiate directly with Hanoi.[5]

President Lyndon B. Johnson (right) and Secretary of State Dean Rusk shortly before Johnson announced his decision to negotiate with North Vietnam. LBJ Library Photo by Yoichi Okamoto.

While the Vietnam conflict continued, Johnson's decision to pursue negotiations marked a turning point in transatlantic relations. The president's revised approach indirectly validated French and British concerns of Washington's traditional Vietnam policy. The Europeans received the news of American de-escalation in Vietnam with relief. Johnson's decision signaled a major step toward ending a conflict that the British, Frenchs and West Germans had not wanted.

Prime Minister Harold Wilson was surprised by Johnson's announcement not to run for reelection but was pleased that Washington once more called upon the United Kingdom for help in securing peace in Vietnam. An official British statement "warmly welcomed" Johnson's proposals for Vietnam. Within hours, Wilson's foreign secretary Michael Stewart approached the Soviets and urged Moscow to work with London as cochairmen of the 1954 Geneva Accords in facilitating negotiations on Vietnam.[6] Parliamentary debate on the "dramatic change" in America's Vietnam policy revealed almost gleeful satisfaction that Washington had finally agreed with the British Vietnam policy. Both Labour and Tory MPs entreated the Wilson government to initiate another diplomatic effort aimed at the Soviet Union and the United Nations secretary-general, hoping for a truce and eventual peaceful settlement of the conflict in Vietnam. Conservative MPs Eldon Griffith and the previous Prime Minister Sir Alec Douglas-Home, however, reminded the Labour government that Hanoi must also do its part and renounce aggression against South Vietnam.[7] Clearly, the British expected to play a vital role in the restoration of peace in Southeast Asia.

French President Charles de Gaulle was also elated that Johnson had finally accepted the realities in Vietnam and sought a negotiated settlement. After eight years of advising that negotiations were the only solution for Vietnam, de Gaulle, like his British counterparts, felt vindicated. He called Johnson's decision to halt the bombing of North Vietnam "a first step in the direction of peace" and commended Johnson for this act of reason and courage.[8] De Gaulle and his foreign minister, Maurice Couve de Murville, were not only relieved by American concessions to their long-held position vis-à-vis Vietnam but also believed that Johnson had removed a major obstacle in Franco-American relations. Of course, they maintained that, had the Americans listened closer to French advice, peace negotiations might have commenced years earlier.[9]

Johnson's statement met with approval in West Germany as well. While the new government of the Grand Coalition of the Christian Democratic Union (CDU) and Social Democrats (SPD) of Chancellor Kurt Georg Kiesinger and Vice Chancellor and Foreign Minister Willy Brandt initially seemed to reverse Ludwig Erhard's course and turn more toward France, sending signals of alarm to Washington, the Kiesinger government accepted Johnson's policy of détente during 1967.[10] In spring 1968, Bonn once more demonstrated its loyalty to Washington by emphasizing that the United States had proved its willingness to initiate negotiations, and hence it was up to Hanoi to accept Johnson's offer. Chancellor Kiesinger expressed his deep respect for Johnson's decision and his appreciation of the president's desire for peace. Kiesinger hoped that the American initiative would improve chances for a negotiated settlement in Vietnam. The chancellor felt that any talks should first aim at ending hostilities and then hopefully arrive at a just and durable peace in Southeast Asia. Kiesinger also stressed that further progress depended greatly on positive reactions from Hanoi. The German media gave Johnson's speech mixed reviews. Regret over Johnson's decision not to run for another term was met with questions about whether the American president was truly sincere in his decision. Many journalists questioned the chances of the American initiative to end the war in Vietnam.[11]

While the Vietnam War seemed to be winding down, events in Czechoslovakia during the spring of 1968 raised hopes of a further thaw in East-West relations. Yet, like the Hungarian uprising in 1956, the reformist government in Prague was crushed by Soviet tanks. Soviet leader Leonid Brezhnev made it more than abundantly clear that his government would not tolerate any dissension or disloyalty within Soviet-controlled Eastern Europe. The Soviet invasion of Czechoslovakia in August 1968 was a stern reminder of the realities of the Cold War, right in the heart of Europe. Johnson had worked hard to achieve an arms control agreement with Moscow, which was in shambles for the time being. More importantly, though, the Soviet invasion sent "shivers" through Western Europe and crushed any French notion of leading a concert of powers of European states on both sides of the Iron Curtain without the United States. It was more than obvious to Western Europeans that they still deeply depended on America's military might for their own security. As a result, de Gaulle slowly moved toward better relations with Washington. The Kiesinger government increased its military budget and improved the readiness of its forces.[12]

While Johnson's change of course on Vietnam was a first step toward removing the contentious issue in U.S.-European relations, the election of Richard Nixon signaled a fresh beginning in the transatlantic relationship to America's European allies. Nixon understood that the United States needed the support and backing of its European allies to successfully pursue a policy that served America's national interest. Hence, it was important to sound out European opinions before making major American foreign policy decisions. Shortly after his inauguration, Nixon traveled to Europe to demonstrate that he was not "obsessed with Vietnam" and to prove to his domestic audience that he commanded respect abroad.[13] During his first stop at the North Atlantic Treaty Organization (NATO) headquarters in Brussels, Nixon expressed a desire to "listen and learn," and successfully pursued the same strategy subsequently in London. Prime Minister Wilson was obviously impressed that the new president was sincerely interested in considering the British point of view on Vietnam as well as on other issues. Nixon pleased his host, and both leaders regarded their encounter as a significant step forward in improving Anglo-American relations.[14]

President Nixon's encounter with French President de Gaulle was even more beneficial. The de Gaulle he met was certainly no longer the uncontested ruler he had been just two years ago. The year 1968 had not been a good one for the French leader. Student protest erupted in spring 1968 and was crushed by a heavy-handed police response. Soon students were joined by millions of workers. They forcefully and violently voiced their displeasure with the autocratic governing style of de Gaulle. The old general barely retained his office and authority. The Soviet invasion of Czechoslovakia in August left de Gaulle's vision of French leadership of Europe from the Atlantic to the Ural Mountains in shambles and demonstrated that he had no influence on the Moscow government.[15]

Nixon conveyed to de Gaulle that his cooperation "would be vital for ending the Vietnam War." France had already been chosen as the meeting place for U.S.–North Vietnamese negotiations, which finally started amidst the turbulent May of 1968. The American leader also hoped for additional French assistance in establishing a dialogue between Washington and the People's Republic of China. The French undoubtedly interpreted Nixon's visit as initiating a new phase in French-American relations and marking a distinct departure from the policy of the Johnson administration. Nixon acknowledged the new quality in the transatlantic partnership and accepted that America's preponderance over its European allies and their policies had considerably lessened. Concerning the Vietnam question, Nixon proved as interested in successful negotiations with Hanoi as did de Gaulle.[16]

While America's European allies appreciated the increased attention from the Nixon administration, it was clear to them that American motives were based primarily on U.S. national self-interest. But they regarded the Nixon visit as an opportunity to have a greater voice in Washington, thus pursuing their own agendas. Regardless of any doubts about Nixon's sincerity regarding the various interests of the Europeans, the American president's readiness to consider the Europeans' point of view marked an appreciable step toward a mutualistic approach in European-American relations. From the U.S. perspective, restoring good relations with the Europeans would benefit America's global position. In addition, cordial relations with the main

European allies should have a positive impact on domestic opinion. Nixon best summarized his agenda:

> I felt that the European trip had accomplished all the goals we set for it. It showed the NATO leaders that a new and interested administration which respected their views had come to power in Washington. It served [a] warning on the Soviets that they could no longer take for granted—nor advantage of—Western disunity. And the TV and press coverage had a positive impact at home, instilling however briefly, some much needed pride in our sagging national morale.[17]

By adopting a pragmatic foreign policy, Nixon succeeded in improving transatlantic relations. Although Nixon's approach resembled traditional European foreign policy making far more than that of previous administrations and was easier for the Europeans to understand, the new situation was only a partial "victory" for America's allies. Instead of phrasing events as part of the Cold War struggle between freedom and tyranny, he, too, placed individual national self-interest at the core of foreign policy. In adopting the role of honest listener, Nixon worked toward preventing further European criticism of American foreign policy. He was fully aware of the damage an independent European stand could elicit and had already generated for Washington. While the new American president pursued U.S. foreign policy making in the traditional European strategy of national interest, it was precisely this neorealist approach that prevented any collective and effective European response to America's Vietnam policy. The British, French, and West German sentiment of vindication following Johnson's offer to conduct peace negotiations with Hanoi only temporarily obscured serious shortcomings in policies adopted by all three countries. Paris, London, and Bonn had been unable to influence Washington's Vietnam policy from 1961 onward. American domestic opposition and the shock of the Tet Offensive forced Washington to rethink its strategy in Southeast Asia. In the final analysis, London, Paris, and Bonn had little impact on President Johnson's decision to seek negotiations with Hanoi. And they would also have no say in Nixon's decision on how to end the war in Indochina.

New leadership in the Western European countries also lessoned tensions within Europe. The United Kingdom became a member of the European Economic Community (EEC) in 1973. In West Germany, the Brandt government was able to establish friendly relations with its European neighbors. While German unification was still elusive, Brandt's "Ostpolitik" was a major step toward rapprochement with the Soviet Union and Eastern Europe. In France, President Georges Pompidou was instrumental in providing a venue for the U.S.–North Vietnamese peace talks. The French president also encouraged the British entry into the EEC and continued good relations with Bonn.

Conclusion

In retrospect, Paris and London arrived at a more realistic assessment of the Vietnam situation than had Washington and, based on their history of empire, believed that nothing good could come out of the deployment of American troops to the region. West German policy makers also privately shared French and British reservations on the conflict in Vietnam. Yet the three European countries failed in their efforts to affect American Vietnam policy. France, the Federal Republic of Germany, and the United Kingdom were miles apart from accepting a mutual agenda because their self-centered perspectives remained paramount. Paris and London had ample experience in Asia and were both trying to convey the lessons of their past shortcomings to Washington. Certainly, this "history lesson" was guided by French and British self-interest aimed at enhancing their role in global politics. West Germany also pursued its own national agenda. Unlike France and Britain, Germany had the legacy of military aggression in Europe to deal with and hoped to overcome some consequences of total defeat through pursuing German unification. Regardless of their pasts, the three European powers had to acknowledge their status as secondary powers on the international scene and admit the necessity of cooperation with the United States.

In addition, differences among the Europeans concerning European matters were prevalent during the 1960s—a problem that plagues Europe to this day. Britain applied for membership in the European Economic Community (EEC) but was twice rejected by French President Charles de Gaulle's veto. De Gaulle worked toward French leadership in Europe but ultimately failed because other Europeans rejected French dominance. German Chancellor Ludwig Erhard looked to Washington, Paris, and London for support of German unification. His strategy was a failure as well. A divided, contained Germany would not challenge the status quo in Europe and, to the United

States, Britain, and France, was preferable to a unified and potentially power-ful "greater" Germany.

Through its own painful experience in Vietnam, the United States realized its global limitations as well as the importance of undertaking multilateral as opposed to unilateral actions in the future. Historian C. Vann Wood-ward's reflections on America's war in Vietnam provide important insights into American as well as European thinking. Woodward maintained that America's experience since the country's independence led U.S. foreign policy makers to the belief that they would always succeed regardless of any obstacles America might face. France, Britain, and Germany subscribed to similar concepts in their past. As any nation, they valued their role and contribution in global politics. Woodward argued that, based on the notion of "national innocence," America simply could not be blamed for "imperial-ism" in Vietnam. America's record differed from that of the "colonialist" Europeans.[1] The conflict in Vietnam painfully shattered the positive image many Americans had of their country. Woodward addressed a pertinent predicament Americans have had to face ever since the end of the Vietnam War. How could American ideals be reconciled with the real and complex challenges the nation faced globally? America's image and identity were undermined by the tragedy of Vietnam that divided the country to a degree eclipsed only by the Civil War.

The transatlantic debate over the Vietnam problem revealed once again the profound relevance of national pride and identity among all four allies. The historic and cultural legacy of each country and their respective foreign policy decisions were and remain difficult to dismiss. The viability of the transatlantic alliance depended on a better understanding and appreciation of the heritage and past differences among its members.

The consequences of the failed transatlantic dialogue over U.S. policy in Vietnam were twofold. First, presidents John F. Kennedy and Lyndon B. Johnson escalated the war in Vietnam despite European advice to the con-trary and by doing so found themselves fighting Communism without their European allies' support. The United States lost more than fifty-eight thou-sand service men and women in this tragic chapter of American history and also ultimately failed to secure the independence of a non-Communist South Vietnam. Second, the American refusal to listen more closely to European concerns led to a profound strain in transatlantic relations. In the end, the conflict in Vietnam did not escalate into a major Asian or even third world war because that scenario was always clearly rejected by Washington. But America's effort to gain European support by means ranging from friendly coercion to outright pressure left deep scars in U.S.-European relations. In-stead of desired support, the United States faced a Western Europe critical of the U.S. role in Vietnam that further undermined the American claim that Western liberty had to be defended in Vietnam. For Washington, the lack of its European allies' support in Vietnam not only resulted in a setback for American goals in Southeast Asia but caused a fissure in transatlantic relations as well.

The fallout from the Vietnam conflict allowed the European allies after 1968 to assert their agendas with varying degrees of success. But it was also obvious that these short-term achievements of national self-interest could not reap greater benefits in a post–Cold War multipolar world. On the one hand, for France, West Germany, and Britain, the "Vietnam question" served as a lesson that their foreign policy making was constructed under severe limitations. None of the European powers could succeed in the global framework on its own. On the other hand, if the Europeans pursued a more mutualistic policy in the future, these limitations might be overcome. On the other side of the Atlantic, the Americans experienced the inherent limitations of a unilateral strategy in Vietnam. While the United States possessed far greater military capability than its opponents (North Vietnam and the Viet Cong), America could not win a conflict framed to protect a country against a Communist insurgency simply through military means. Equally, despite its military and economic might, the United States could not dictate policy to the Europeans, and conversely, the Europeans could not tell Washington how to proceed in Vietnam.

The transatlantic debate over the right strategy concerning the Vietnam problem served as a difficult and painful lesson that neither the Europeans nor the Americans would benefit by pursuing a state-centered policy. This learning process led to a greater appreciation of their respective views after President Johnson's decision to seek a political solution to the Vietnam conflict. Divergent views and interests between the United States and its European allies persisted in the following decades. As of 2010, a truly mutualistic European policy within the European Union of twenty-seven member states is still elusive since nationalistic policy making still prevails. However, European criticism of American foreign policy making generally stems from genuine concern and not anti-Americanism.[2] The events of September 11, 2001, led to unrivaled European support for the United States. The European allies hurried to contribute to ousting the Taliban from Afghanistan and bringing the culprits of September 11 to justice. But the subsequent decision by President George W. Bush two years later to invade Iraq led to a rift at least as severe as the debate over the Vietnam War. President Barack Obama's approach of listening and reaching out to America's European allies once more healed old wounds, and the charisma of the new American president reminded Europeans of the idealism and common bonds that connect Europe with the United

States. Allied relations will always be difficult, but the more the partners learn about and appreciate one another's point of view, the better they will be able to coordinate policies to face nonstate threats such as al Qaeda that are determined to destroy the shared heritage of liberty and democracy so dearly held on both sides of the Atlantic.

Epilogue

The Allies and the Iraq War

If Schröder and Chirac had joined [the American intervention in Iraq], it would have changed nothing. But if some of our European friends had said, "Let's develop a common European position, without that we can't join," maybe this would have made a difference. Historians will have that discussion.

—Joschka Fischer, former foreign minister, Federal Republic of Germany, 2007[1]

The Iraq War has been compared repeatedly to the Vietnam War by historians and pundits. Certainly, similarities exist between the two conflicts, but there are also profound differences. The situation in Iraq differed greatly from that of Vietnam. As discussed previously, the United States initially proved reluctant to support the French in Indochina but subsequently committed itself to the independence of a non-Communist South Vietnam. In Iraq, however, no Communist threat existed, although the country was ruled by the brutal dictator Saddam Hussein. Saddam was supported by the United States to balance the Islamic Republic of Iran during the 1980s. When Iraq invaded Kuwait in 1990, President George H. W. Bush carefully built an international coalition based on a United Nations mandate to oust Iraq from Kuwait. The American-led coalition performed successfully in the brief Gulf War of 1991. Following the advice of his chief of staff General Colin Powell and Secretary of Defense Richard Cheney, President Bush decided not to oust Saddam from power but instead to impose rigid restrictions on the Iraqi regime to prevent further Iraqi aggression against its neighbors and to establish a monitoring system under UN jurisdiction to prevent Iraq from acquiring, developing, or using weapons of mass destruction (WMD).[2]

At the time of the first Gulf War, the international system was transforming from the bipolar world of the Cold War to a unipolar structure led by the United States. By 2001, the United States was undeniably the sole superpower. However, despite the preponderance of American power, nongovernment actors were organizing against the United States. Most notable was al Qaeda, led by Osama bin Laden, bent on defending its version of Islam by using terror against the United States. September 11, 2001, shattered the American belief that its homeland was relatively secure from terrorist attacks directed from abroad. America's allies were equally shocked and pledged "unlimited solidarity" with the United States. The North Atlantic Treaty Organization (NATO) for the first time since its creation invoked Article 5, which pledged all members to assist another member in mutual defense of the alliance. Within a month, America's allies sent troops and support for the U.S.-led effort to oust the Taliban and al Qaeda from Afghanistan.[3]

But even before 9/11, members of the George W. Bush administration, led by Vice President Cheney and Secretary of Defense Donald Rumsfeld, had pressured the president to replace the Iraqi regime. The president agreed, and for the next two years, the administration built its case for the American public and world opinion that Saddam's Iraq not only possessed but also continued to pursue WMD in violation of UN resolutions. The Bush administration emphasized the Iraqi regime's use of poison gas against its own Kurdish population and also alleged Iraq's complicity in the events of 9/11. It is now clear that the Bush administration embellished information on Iraq's weapons and ties with al Qaeda and deliberately misled the domestic and world audience. Further, while Bush and his advisors were determined to oust Saddam, they developed no concrete plans to deal with the aftermath of the invasion.[4] The administration won over the majority of the American public, but Europeans were either hesitant or outright opposed to any military action against the Saddam regime. Russia and China were also doubtful about the American course. Secretary of State Powell urged the president to take the issue to the United Nations. In close cooperation with the French, Russians, and British, Washington was able to win the necessary Security Council support for UN Resolution 1441, requiring Iraq to surrender any WMD and allow UN inspectors to verify that Baghdad had done so. A second UN resolution would be required for the use of force in case Iraq did not satisfactorily comply with UN Resolution 1441. However, backed by Great Britain, the United States was not willing to wait for a second UN resolution and instead embarked on Operation Iraqi Freedom in March 2003.

France and Germany strongly opposed the U.S.-led invasion of Iraq. Yet Britain's Prime Minister Tony Blair agreed that the attacks of 9/11 were a fundamental threat to Western values and supported President Bush's course in Iraq. Blair hoped that Britain could play a vital role in the decision-making process not only regarding Iraq but also in building lasting peace in the Middle East. Thus, Britain would remain the "special partner" to the United States and continue to play a global role.[5] French President Jacques Chirac and his foreign minister, Dominique de Villepin, were worried that Iraq had WMD but believed a policy of sanctions and containment was preferable to military action. German Chancellor Gerhard Schröder shared French concerns but, facing a possible defeat in federal elections, shamelessly exploited the possibility of a war in Iraq for the sole purpose of retaining the chancellorship.[6]

Once more, the Allies were at odds. Huge protests in major European cities in February 2003 were followed by an inter-European debate on how to respond to America's policies. The German and French philosophers Jürgen Habermas and Jacques Derrida launched a media campaign to forge a common European identity that would counterbalance the United States. The response to their challenge revealed several important points.[7] First was the question of European identity—was it one of "core" Europe, that is, France and Germany, or did it include Danes, Italians, or Hungarians? Second was the question to which Habermas and Derrida directed their opposition. Was it the United States in general or the policies of the Bush administration in particular that should be opposed? The great majority of European contributors to the debate found issue with the Bush administration but not with America itself and emphasized the strong cultural and historic bonds between Europe and the United States. Karl Otto Hondrich framed the issue in more cynical terms: France, Britain, and Germany were "part of the collective hegemony" led by the United States and functioned as "facilitators between supremacy and impotence."[8]

Opinion polls revealed that the issue indeed was the policy of the Bush administration and not anti-Americanism. In March 2003, the majority of Europeans had an unfavorable view of the United States compared with a poll taken in late summer 2002 when a clear majority had a positive view of America.[9] The presidential candidacy and subsequent election of Barack Obama proved that Europeans had an intense dislike of President Bush and his policies but not of the United States. Europeans would have elected Obama with an overwhelming majority, due to his campaign promise to end the war in Iraq and the overall theme of bringing change to Washington. But President Obama reminded his European audience in Strasbourg, France, "America is changing, but it cannot be America alone that is changing." The president added that, in the United States, there had been "a failure to appreciate Europe's leading role in the world." He continued that Europeans had also displayed anti-American attitudes and emphasized that, on "both sides of the

Atlantic, these attitudes have become all too common. They are not wise."[10] From his speech in Berlin as a presidential candidate and his subsequent comments after his election, President Obama made it clear that he would listen to European concerns but would place American security first, insisting that Europe had to do its part to defend the world from the scourge of terrorism.

While the war in Vietnam and Iraq were born out of very different circumstances, in both cases, the United States was unable to gain the support of all its European allies. The simple reason was respective national self-interest. But as recent events have shown again, able and farsighted leadership by the United States has once more affirmed and reinvigorated the bonds between the transatlantic allies. Differences will remain among the United States and its European allies, but common bonds have sustained the transatlantic partnership as well. As former German Foreign Secretary Joschka Fischer lamented, only a truly common European position would and could influence foreign policy making in Washington. Europe is not yet able or willing to reach a common foreign policy. This said, concerns of some European countries about the American intervention in Iraq proved as valid as those made forty years earlier on the Vietnam problem. President Obama admitted that the war in Iraq was a "war of choice that provoked strong differences" in the United States and the world. He added that the solution to end disunity between America and its friends and allies should be to "use diplomacy and build international consensus to resolve our problems whenever possible."[11]

Notes

INTRODUCTION

1. George W. Ball, *Discipline of Power: Essentials of a Modern World Structure* (Boston: Little, Brown, 1968), 26.

CHAPTER 1:
THE UNITED STATES AND THE VIETNAM CONUNDRUM

1. The origins of the American involvement in Vietnam have been discussed in detail in numerous scholarly works. See, for example, George C. Herring, *America's Longest War: The United States and Vietnam, 1950–1975*, 2nd ed. (New York: McGraw-Hill, 1986), 3–30; Marilyn B. Young, *The Vietnam Wars, 1945–1990* (New York: HarperCollins, 1991), 1–59; David L. Anderson, *Trapped by Success: The Eisenhower Administration and Vietnam, 1953–1961* (New York: Columbia University Press, 1991), 21–35, 68–75, 85–90; and Larry Berman, *Planning a Tragedy: The Americanization of the War in Vietnam* (New York: Norton, 1982), 11–16.

2. Herring, *America's Longest War*, 50–64; Young, *Vietnam Wars*, 52–59. For the last year of the Eisenhower policy in Vietnam, see also Anderson, *Trapped by Success*, 175–97; Seth Jacobs, *Cold War Mandarin: Ngo Dinh Diem and the Origins of America's War in Vietnam* (Lanham, Md.: Rowman & Littlefield, 2006); and James M. Carter, *Inventing Vietnam: The United States and State Building, 1954–1968* (New York: Cambridge University Press, 2008), 6–7.

3. Two differing accounts exist on Eisenhower's recommendations. Dean Rusk understood that Eisenhower would favor unilateral intervention if necessary. Robert McNamara remembered that Eisenhower was "deeply uncertain" about what action to take. See Dean Rusk, *As I Saw It* (New York: Norton, 1990), 428. Rusk's report was confirmed by notes taken by Eisenhower; see William Conrad Gibbons, *The*

U.S. Government and the Vietnam War: Executive and Legislative Roles and Relationships, Part II: 1961–1964 (Princeton, N.J.: Princeton University Press, 1986), 4; and Robert S. McNamara, *In Retrospect: The Tragedy and Lessons of Vietnam* (New York: Simon & Schuster, 1995), 36. See also Richard Reeves, *President Kennedy: Profile in Power* (New York: Simon & Schuster, 1993), 31–32. For Clark Clifford's memorandum on the meeting, see Berman, *Planning a Tragedy*, 16–17.

4. Richard M. Nixon, *RN: The Memoirs of Richard Nixon* (New York: Simon & Schuster, 1990), 232–35. Nixon, obviously unhappy with Kennedy's foreign policy, wanted to give a critical speech of the president's actions, but the Bay of Pigs debacle intervened. However, Nixon maintained that more should be done in Laos.

5. "Senator John Kennedy Speech to the Senate, April 6, 1954," 83rd Cong., 2nd sess., *Congressional Record* 100, part 4 (April 6, 1954): S 4673.

6. Gibbons, *U.S. Government*, 5–6; Herring, *America's Longest War*, 43; Lawrence J. Bassett and Stephen E. Pelz, "The Failed Search for Victory: Vietnam and the Politics of War," in *Kennedy's Quest for Victory: American Foreign Policy, 1961–1963*, ed. Thomas G. Paterson (New York: Norton, 1989), 226.

7. Gibbons, *U.S. Government*, 11–12; Herring, *America's Longest War*, 76.

8. Herring, *America's Longest War*, 78–79; Berman, *Planning a Tragedy*, 19–20; Andrew Preston, *The War Council: McGeorge Bundy, the NSC, and Vietnam* (Cambridge, Mass.: Harvard University Press, 2006), 78–83.

9. Johnson's comment is quoted in Gibbons, *U.S. Government*, 45. Johnson was sent to South Vietnam to reassure Diem of the continuous commitment of the United States. Johnson flourished in the assignment; otherwise, he was much overlooked by Kennedy. What he saw obviously impressed the vice president, and he even hailed Diem as the Winston Churchill of Southeast Asia.

10. James N. Giglio, *The Presidency of John F. Kennedy* (Lawrence: University of Kansas Press, 1991), 17.

11. Nixon, *RN*, 236.

12. Gibbons, *U.S. Government*, 72–84, 96–99. American dollars further built up the Army of the Republic of Vietnam (ARVN); Green Berets and U.S. pilots instructed South Vietnamese military and also participated in raids against the VC. Lastly, strategic hamlets and economic programs for Vietnamese peasants were aimed to turn the tide in the rural areas. Berman, *Planning a Tragedy*, 20–23; Jacobs, *Cold War Mandarin*, 135–36; Robert Dallek, *An Unfinished Life: John F. Kennedy, 1917–1963* (New York: Back Bay Books, 2003), 448–53; Preston, *War Council*, 91–96.

13. Herring, *America's Longest War*, 83; Giglio, *Presidency of John F. Kennedy*, 243; Dallek, *Unfinished Life*, 453–55.

14. Gibbons, *U.S. Government*, 15–17, 39–42; Herring, *America's Longest War*, 87–92; Giglio, *Presidency of John F. Kennedy*, 246–47; Dallek, *Unfinished Life*, 457–60, 528–29.

15. Giglio, *Presidency of John F. Kennedy*, 88–89.

16. Chester Bowles, *Promises to Keep: My Years in Public Life, 1941–1969* (New York: Harper & Row, 1971), 407–8. Southeast Asian neutrality should be guaranteed by the United States, Britain, France, the Soviet Union, India, and Japan. By engaging

the Soviets, the United States could utilize the Chinese-Soviet rift to its advantage. Obviously, Moscow was not keen to accept Chinese expansion into Southeast Asia.

17. Bowles, *Promises to Keep*, 408; Preston, *War Council*, 93.

18. Bowles, *Promises to Keep*, 409; Bassett and Pelz, "Failed Search for Victory," 237–38.

19. Giglio, *Presidency of John F. Kennedy*, 93–94. Bowles publicly criticized the Kennedy decision to give a green light to the Cuban expedition that led to the debacle at the Bay of Pigs. His "treason" drew heavy fire from Robert Kennedy and Dean Rusk, and Bowles was replaced by George Ball.

20. Bowles, *Promises to Keep*, 409–10.

21. Bowles, *Promises to Keep*, 410.

22. Bowles, *Promises to Keep*, 410–11. Bowles maintained that his suggestions for Vietnam was actually the implementation of a policy first envisioned by Franklin Roosevelt and that the promise of true independence had clearly not lost any of its appeal in Southeast Asia almost twenty years later.

23. Bowles, *Promises to Keep*, 411.

24. Bowles, *Promises to Keep*, 412–13.

25. Bowles, *Promises to Keep*, 414. The State Department argued that Hanoi had to renounce and cease all aggression first before a political solution could be found. Though Kennedy initially favored a Bowles fact-finding tour to Southeast Asia, it was postponed due to the Cuban missile crisis and then lack of interest.

26. Bowles, *Promises to Keep*, 416–17.

27. John Kenneth Galbraith, *Ambassador's Journal: A Personal Account of the Kennedy Years* (Boston: Houghton Mifflin, 1969), xiv–xv. Kennedy desired friendship with India as a counterbalance to Communist China but was not very successful in gaining a closer relationship with Nehru; Nehru's state visit was a "disaster," as Kennedy put it.

28. Galbraith, *Ambassador's Journal*, 154. Galbraith maintained that this was not the first time the United States simply went by the rulers' account, and he feared that in South Vietnam this "old mistake" resulted in "one more government which, on present form, no one will support."

29. Galbraith, *Ambassador's Journal*, 260–62. Galbraith commented that the briefing was "geared to the mentality of an idiot, or, more likely, a backwoods congressman." The briefing officer excused the discrepancy in VC losses and ARVN forces by referring first to jungle conditions and then stated that several ARVN divisions might not have actually been there.

30. Galbraith, *Ambassador's Journal*, 266–68. Galbraith expressed his confidence in Ambassador Frederick Nolting and complained that Nolting had to learn about the recent Taylor-Maxwell mission through the radio and thus had no impact on the actual report to the president. Galbraith hoped that Kennedy would clarify the entire issue with the State Department.

31. Galbraith, *Ambassador's Journal*, 311. Galbraith was aware that he was "sadly out of step with the Establishment" but hoped that Kennedy was willing to listen to an outsider's advice.

32. Galbraith, *Ambassador's Journal*, 311–12. Galbraith was also worried about too much influence of the American military on decisions over Vietnam. He referred to current differences of opinion between Ambassador Nolting and General Paul Harkins over the best course for South Vietnam.

33. Galbraith, *Ambassador's Journal*, 312. Galbraith also suggested that Kennedy look for a replacement for Diem.

34. Galbraith, *Ambassador's Journal*, 342–44. Galbraith was also apprehensive that the present commitment to South Vietnam might lead to "a major political outburst about the new Korea and the new war the Democrats as so often before have precipitated us." Galbraith also pointed out that the Strategic Hamlet Program was doing more damage than good. He maintained that the Soviet Union actually had no intentions to become involved in Southeast Asia but that the growing American military involvement was driving Hanoi into the arms of Beijing. American support of Diem also required a reappraisal; Galbraith felt the United States would be better off with another civilian leader.

35. Gibbons, *U.S. Government*, 120–21.

36. Gregory Allen Olsen, *Mansfield and Vietnam: A Study in Rhetorical Adaptation* (East Lansing: Michigan State University Press, 1995), 7–27; Don Oberdorfer, *Senator Mansfield: The Extraordinary Life of a Great Statesman and Diplomat* (Washington, D.C.: Smithsonian Books, 2003), 107, 110. Mansfield made several trips to the region, increasing his understanding of local conditions.

37. "Statement before the Subcommittee of the Committee on Appropriations, United States Senate," 83rd Cong., 2nd sess., *Congressional Record* 100 (July 8, 1954): S 9998–10000. Mansfield called for a "reappraisal" of American foreign policy and charged that Eisenhower, both at Dien Bien Phu and the conference table, had committed serious blunders, leading to a diplomatic humiliation. The French had also made serious mistakes, but American lack of support left the French and Vietnamese resistance to the Viet Minh "exposed, undercut, and ready for collapse."

38. "Statement before the Subcommittee," 10001–2.

39. "Statement before the Subcommittee," 10007; Oberdorfer, *Senator Mansfield*, 115–16.

40. Gibbons, *U.S. Government*, 85; Olsen, *Mansfield and Vietnam*, 97; Oberdorfer, *Senator Mansfield*, 184–85.

41. Gibbons, *U.S. Government*, 84–85; Oberdorfer, *Senator Mansfield*, 185–86.

42. Olsen, *Mansfield and Vietnam*, 99–100. Oberdorfer, *Senator Mansfield*, 188–89.

43. Gibbons, *U.S. Government*, 126–30. The deference to executive authority by Congress was evident in the adoption of the Cuba and Berlin resolutions in the fall of 1962, setting a precedent for the Tonkin Gulf Resolution two years later. The 1962 resolution authorized the president to do whatever he deemed necessary, including the use of force, to prevent the spread of Communism. Other Vietnam skeptics included Wayne Morse, Al Gore Sr., and William Fulbright.

44. Oberdorfer, *Senator Mansfield*, 191–92.

45. Olsen, *Mansfield and Vietnam*, 106–7; Gibbons, *U.S. Government*, 131. Ambassador Nolting was dismayed by Mansfield's contacts with American journalists.

Nolting was currently fighting a cold war with the U.S. press, which was depicting events in South Vietnam far too negatively according to the ambassador's assessment. See Frederick Nolting, *From Trust to Tragedy: The Political Memoirs of Frederick Nolting, Kennedy's Ambassador to Diem's Vietnam* (New York: Praeger, 1988), 85–89; David Halberstam, *The Best and the Brightest*, 20th anniversary ed. (New York: Ballantine Books, 1992), 207–8.

46. Gibbons, *U.S. Government*, 133; Oberdorfer, *Senator Mansfield*, 193.

47. Dallek, *Unfinished Life*, 666–67; Oberdorfer, *Senator Mansfield*, 194–95.

48. Olsen, *Mansfield and Vietnam*, 115. Mansfield also criticized the narrow outlook of many American officials in Vietnam who lacked greater perspective. Jacobs, *Cold War Mandarin*, 136–39; Dallek, *Unfinished Life*, 672; Oberdorfer, *Senator Mansfield*, 197–200.

49. Olsen, *Mansfield and Vietnam*, 115–17. Mansfield argued that a unilateral engagement would overextend American forces and hurt American prestige in other nations in Asia.

50. David L. DiLeo, *George Ball, Vietnam, and the Rethinking of Containment* (Chapel Hill: University of North Carolina Press, 1991), 26–27; George W. Ball, *The Past Has Another Pattern: Memoirs* (New York: Norton, 1982), 99–102.

51. George W. Ball, oral history interview by Joseph Kraft, April 12, 1965, John F. Kennedy Library, Boston, 22–23.

52. Ball, *The Past Has Another Pattern*, 171–73, 182–83.

53. Ball, *The Past Has Another Pattern*, 361–63.

54. Ball, *The Past Has Another Pattern*, 363–66.

55. Ball, *The Past Has Another Pattern*, 366; McNamara, *In Retrospect*, 38–39. While McNamara did not mention Ball, he confessed that he, as other advisors, knew little about Vietnam and lacked experience to deal with crisis. As his own probing into the complexity of Vietnam showed, the United States was already facing a dilemma of a no-win situation in 1961. Though McNamara rejected combat forces for the time being, he did not rule out greater American intervention in the future.

56. Ball, *The Past Has Another Pattern*, 366.

57. Gibbons, *U.S. Government*, 88–92. Gibbons quotes William Bundy who stated that Ball's argument had some impact on the president. See Ball, *The Past Has Another Pattern*, 366–68. Ball was uncertain how to interpret Kennedy's response; either the president simply could not imagine a worst-case scenario requiring combat troops or he actually shared some of Ball's concerns and was determined to prevent further escalation.

58. Gibbons, *U.S. Government*, 122.

59. Gibbons, *U.S. Government*, 123. The April 1962 speech in Detroit is not mentioned in Ball's memoirs and serves as additional proof to the personal dilemma of many government officials who doubted privately the policy in Vietnam but out of a number of reasons were unable to stand up to their beliefs in public.

60. Ball, *The Past Has Another Pattern*, 371–74. In August 1963, Ball, after clearance with his superior, gave a green light to Lodge to end American support to Diem unless the Vietnamese leader adopted a more liberal policy. A second request

by Lodge to convey U.S. misgivings about Diem to Vietnamese generals opposed to their head of state was also authorized by Ball. Jacobs, *Cold War Mandarin*, 162.

61. Ball, *The Past Has Another Pattern*, 374.

62. Herring, *America's Longest War*, 95–97; Jacobs, *Cold War Mandarin*, 142–50. See, for example, "Fiery Protest," *Newsweek*, June 24, 1963: the magazine printed photos of the self-immolations and reported that if Diem "wants to remain in power and unify his people against the tortuous struggle against the Communist Viet Cong, he needs the cooperation of the Buddhists," 63. *Time* followed the events closely as well and made the protest its cover story in August, strongly attacking Mme Nhu because she recommended the complete crackdown on the Buddhists. Her ridicule of the immolations as "Vietnamese barbecues" appalled Western observers.

63. Gibbons, *U.S. Government*, 144–59; Herring, *America's Longest War*, 97–99; Giglio, *Presidency of John F. Kennedy*, 248–50; Berman, *Planning a Tragedy*, 24–27; Dallek, *Unfinished Life*, 672–75. In August 1963, Undersecretary Roger Hilsman sent a telegram to Ambassador Lodge alluding that if Diem remained "obdurate" the U.S. would consider his replacement. Hilsman suggested that Lodge inform South Vietnamese military leaders of the American point of view and asked the ambassador to search for political alternatives to Diem.

64. Gibbons, *U.S. Government*, 163.

65. Giglio, *Presidency of John F. Kennedy*, 251; Jacobs, *Cold War Mandarin*, 166–67; Dallek, *Unfinished Life*, 678.

66. McNamara, *In Retrospect*, 75–81. Taylor and McNamara recommended withholding American aid from Diem unless he complied with U.S. demands. Diem, disgusted with U.S. interference, considered a deal with Hanoi. See Jacobs, *Cold War Mandarin*, 164–65.

67. Gibbons, *U.S. Government*, 188–91, 197. Washington cabled to Lodge that it would not actively endorse a coup but the ambassador should convey to potential new leaders that the United States would not interfere but would continue its economic and financial assistance to a new government in Saigon. In October, Kennedy learned that a coup was imminent, but he was more concerned about political repercussion for the United States in case of failure.

68. Jacobs, *Cold War Mandarin*, 175–80; McNamara, *In Retrospect*, 83–85; Giglio, *Presidency of John F. Kennedy*, 252–53; Gibbons, *U.S. Government*, 200–202. See also Stanley Karnow, *Vietnam: A History* (New York: Penguin, 1984), 304–11.

69. Bassett and Pelz, "Failed Search for Victory," 250; see also Arthur Schlesinger Jr., *A Thousand Days: John F. Kennedy in the White House* (Boston: Houghton Mifflin, 1965), 982.

70. Robert F. Kennedy, *To Seek a Newer World* (New York: Doubleday, 1967), 162–63.

71. See Bassett and Pelz, "Failed Search for Victory," 250–52; Giglio, *Presidency of John F. Kennedy*, 253–54; Rusk, *As I Saw It*, 430; and Theodore Sorensen, *Kennedy* (New York: Harper & Row, 1965), 648–49.

72. McNamara, *In Retrospect*, 43–48.

73. Walter Isaacson and Evan Thomas, *The Wise Men: Six Friends and the World They Made* (New York: Simon & Schuster, 1986), 640. Kennedy told an advisor in

the fall of 1963 that, if he tried to "pull out completely now from Vietnam, we would have another Joe McCarthy Red scare on our hands." See also Herring, *America's Longest War*, 106–7. Herring maintains that Kennedy accepted the "assumption that a non-Communist Vietnam was vital to American global interest."

74. Benjamin I. Page and Robert Y. Shapiro, *The Rational Public: Fifty Years of Trends in Americans' Policy Preferences* (Chicago: University of Chicago Press, 1992), 226–27; John E. Mueller, "Trends in Popular Support for the Wars in Korea and Vietnam," in *Public Opinion and Political Attitudes*, comp. Allen R. Wilcox (New York: Wiley, 1974), 26–28.

75. Beverly Deepe, "The Fall of the House of Ngo," *Newsweek*, November 11, 1963, 27–31.

76. "Foreign Relations: Behind the Denials," *Time*, November 8, 1963, 21–22.

77. Bassett and Pelz, "Failed Search for Victory," 251; Giglio, *Presidency of John F. Kennedy*, 244–49; Schlesinger, *A Thousand Days*, 984–86; Olsen, *Mansfield and Vietnam*, 117; Halberstam, *Best and Brightest*, 209, 299–301; Dallek, *Unfinished Life*, 684.

78. Rusk, *As I Saw It*, 434, 442.

CHAPTER 2: FRANCE AND INDOCHINA

1. D. Bruce Marshall, *The French Colonial Myth and Constitution Making in the Fourth Republic* (New Haven, Conn.: Yale University Press, 1973), 7; Rod Kedward, *France and the French: A Modern History* (Woodstock, N.Y.: Overlook Press, 2006), 317–18.

2. Marshall, *French Colonial Myth*, 32.

3. Marshall, *French Colonial Myth*, 35.

4. Marshall, *French Colonial Myth*, 47. Sarraut told a Vietnamese audience in 1917 that, as governor-general of Vietnam, he wanted to give them "the instrument of liberation which will gradually lead you to those superior spheres to which you aspire." See William J. Duiker, *Sacred War: Nationalism and Revolution in a Divided Vietnam* (New York: McGraw-Hill, 1995), 11.

5. Marshall, *French Colonial Myth*, 47.

6. Stanley Karnow, *Vietnam: A History* (New York: Penguin, 1984), 98–104; Duiker, *Sacred War*, 6–9.

7. William J. Duiker, *Ho Chi Minh: A Life* (New York: Theia Books, 2000), 12–13; Karnow, *Vietnam*, 76–88; Duiker, *Sacred War*, 10–11. France's justification of the regional divisions was based on the different cultures and histories, although this cultural division contradicted Vietnamese history. Even the term *Vietnam* was banned from public usage.

8. Duiker, *Sacred War*, 17–18. Phan Dinh Phung pointed out that his country could not even be conquered by neighboring China, "a thousand times more powerful than Vietnam," and hence Vietnam was destined to remain independent.

9. Duiker, *Sacred War*, 28–34; Marshall, *French Colonial Myth*, 65–66; Karnow, *Vietnam*, 124.

10. Karnow, *Vietnam*, 113–15; Duiker, *Sacred War*, 21.

11. Marshall, *French Colonial Myth*, 75–78.

12. Arthur J. Dommen, *The Indochinese Experience of the French and the Americans: Nationalism and Communism in Cambodia, Laos, and Vietnam* (Bloomington: Indiana University Press, 2001), 47–55. Decoux specifically targeted the ICP and ignored Vichy's plea for clemency; some fifty people were guillotined, including Vo Nguyen Giap's sister-in-law. See also Bernard B. Fall, *Street without Joy* (Mechanicsburg, Pa.: Stackpole Books, 1989), 22–24. More than eight hundred French troops were killed resisting the Japanese troops invading Indochina before Petain signed the agreement to station Japanese troops in Indochina.

13. Jacques Dalloz, *The War in Indochina, 1945–54* (London: Gill and Macmillan, 1990), 34–37. In addition to appealing to Vietnamese nationalism, Decoux initially harshly punished any "dissidents," those French who supported de Gaulle.

14. Dommen, *The Indochinese Experience*, 57–79. By early 1945, Decoux had switched allegiance to de Gaulle and the Free French. He and his commanders had made valiant plans to defend Indochina, but Paris was obviously unable to help against the Japanese takeover. See also Martin Shipway, *The Road to War: France and Vietnam, 1944–1947* (New York: Berghahn Books, 2003).

15. Mark Atwood Lawrence, *Assuming the Burden: Europe and the American Commitment to War in Vietnam* (Berkeley: University of California Press, 2005), 23–26. Lawrence demonstrates that the French worried the United States in addition to Roosevelt anticolonialism also had economic and strategic interest to deny France repossession of Indochina. See also Lloyd C. Gardner, *Approaching Vietnam: From World War II through Dienbienphu, 1941–1954* (New York: Norton, 1988), 28–31; Marilyn B. Young, *The Vietnam Wars: 1945–1990* (New York: HarperCollins, 1991), 10–11; Shipway, *Road to War*, 19–20; and Marianna P. Sullivan, *France's Vietnam Policy: A Study in French-American Relations* (Westport, Conn.: Greenwood, 1978), 30–40. Roosevelt even suggested that China should become the trustee for Indochina.

16. Marshall, *French Colonial Myth*, 90–93.

17. Shipway, *Road to War*, 28.

18. Duiker, *Sacred War*, 38–42; Duiker, *Ho Chi Minh*, 245–54.

19. Shipway, *Road to War*, 124; Dommen, *The Indochinese Experience*, 84–93; Lawrence, *Assuming the Burden*, 59–60. Apparently Bao Dai's choice for prime minister was Ngo Dinh Diem, but the Japanese preferred Kim, a respected scholar and Francophile, who had been exiled to Bangkok. See also Dalloz, *War in Indochina*, 42–46.

20. Shipway, *Road to War*, 122. Although Decoux was crushing any opposition to French rule in Indochina, he revived the term of Vietnam to win greater support for the French against the Japanese among indigenous peoples. Decoux was also first to speak about an Indochinese Union—a term that was adopted by the provisional government.

21. Dalloz, *War in Indochina*, 208–10.

22. Marshall, *French Colonial Myth*, 135–36; Shipway, *Road to War*, 128–29; Lawrence, *Assuming the Burden*, 67. The French Union did not yet officially exist

since it was part of the new constitution for the Fourth Republic, which was finally ratified in October 1946.

23. Quoted in and translated by Shipway, *Road to War*, 126 (emphasis in text).

24. Shipway, *Road to War*, 129–30; Marshall, *French Colonial Myth*, 136; Dalloz, *War in Indochina*, 55, 59. De Gaulle instructed Admiral Thierry d'Argenlieu that "nothing will be agreed with the locals as long as we do not have power."

25. Shipway, *Road to War*, 132–33. Mus reported to his government, "We talk of 'malaise.' But this term is a euphemism, given that the local nationals in this country we just lost are claiming independence, or at least not disavowing those who are. We are confronted with a growing crisis characterized by the fact that the Indochinese elite have recognized it more rapidly and thoroughly than we have." Mus was superbly qualified to assess the situation in Indochina. He grew up in Indochina, became an expert scholar on Southeast Asian cultures, and was later chosen as French agent to assess the situation of Indochina under Japanese occupation. See John T. McAlister and Paul Mus, *The Vietnamese and Their Revolution* (New York: Harper & Row, 1970), 7–15.

26. Shipway, *Road to War*, 134–35. Sainteny received a message from the Viet Minh via the American Office of Strategic Services (OSS) also in July that laid out a five-point program: elections by universal suffrage for a new Indochinese parliament; independence within a period of at least and at most ten years; economic reforms; granting all freedoms as defined by the UN charter; and prohibition of opium.

27. Dommen, *The Indochinese Experience*, 93–98. The OSS was obviously not quite aware of Ho Chi Minh's larger agenda but helped train and equip some two hundred Viet Minh. See also Duiker, *Ho Chi Minh*, 292–94, 299–301. Ho was quite successful in deceiving the OSS. Major Allison Thomas reported that the Viet Minh were no "Communist Bogey" and instead stood for freedom and "reforms from French harshness." Gardner, *Approaching Vietnam*, 64–65.

28. Shipway, *Road to War*, 135–36; Duiker, *Sacred War*, 44–48; Sullivan, *France's Vietnam Policy*, 40–41. Sullivan argues that the OSS presence and two American planes flying overhead was a signal of American support in the U.S. anticolonial efforts against France. Frank Giles, *The Locust Years: The Story of the Fourth Republic, 1946–1958* (New York: Carroll & Graf, 1991), 48. Dao Dai urged de Gaulle to recognize Vietnamese independence.

29. Duiker, *Sacred War*, 49; see also Duiker, *Ho Chi Minh*, 322–24.

30. Duiker, *Sacred War*, 50–52; Duiker, *Ho Chi Minh*, 332–37; Dommen, *The Indochinese Experience*, 124–33. The September riots in and around Saigon also resulted in the first American casualty. Major Albert Peter Dewey, an OSS agent, was killed on his way to the airport. The official handover of British authority took place on January 28, 1946, when Gracey and his troops left Saigon. See Shipway, *Road to War*, 163–64; see also Karnow, *Vietnam*, 150–51. Historian Philippe Devillers who served under Leclerc admitted that the French were able to drive the Viet Minh out of Saigon. The picture in rural areas was different, and Devillers estimated it would take at least one hundred thousand troops to end the conflict in Cochinchina alone.

31. Shipway, *Road to War*, 145–52; Lawrence, *Assuming the Burden*, 124–26. Second in command, General Leclerc was actually far more open-minded about the

situation in Indochina than d'Argenlieu. He maintained that the conflict was at least as much a political as a military issue. Dalloz, *War in Indochina*, 59–60, 63.

32. Giles, *Locust Years*, 25–27. De Gaulle resigned due to growing tension with the Assembly over how power in France should be distributed. De Gaulle insisted on a strong, independent executive, whereas the main parties—Socialists, Communists (PCF), and the center Mouvement Republicain Populaire (MRP)—favored a strong legislature. See also William I. Hitchcock, *France Restored: Cold War Diplomacy and the Quest for Leadership in Europe, 1944–1954* (Chapel Hill: University of North Carolina Press, 1998), 18–20; and Marshall, *French Colonial Myth*, 148–49. Marshall argues that de Gaulle might have treated Indochina more decisively and that his departure left Indochina policy making too much in the hands of lower-ranking officials. This point seems to be refuted by Shipway.

33. Shipway, *Road to War*, 172; Dalloz, *War in Indochina*, 69–70. See also Duiker, *Ho Chi Minh*, 353–63. Ho later commented to Paul Mus that is was "better to sniff French shit for a while than to eat China's for the rest of our lives." See also Lawrence, *Assuming the Burden*, 127–29; and Dommen, *The Indochinese Experience*, 149–51.

34. Shipway, *Road to War*, 172–76; Gardner, *Approaching Vietnam*, 74; Duiker, *Ho Chi Minh*, 362–64. Ho was disappointed that he could not gain better terms but confirmed his friendship with Sainteny. It took Ho's personal appeal to calm anger and disappointment of many Vietnamese. He promised he would "rather die than betray my country." See also Karnow, *Vietnam*, 153–54.

35. Duiker, *Ho Chi Minh*, 367–68.

36. Shipway, *Road to War*, 187–88. Vietnamese representative Hoang Xuan Han expressed his hope "that this land will soon be returned to the bosom of our Fatherland 'Vietnam.'" Duiker, *Ho Chi Minh*, 368.

37. Shipway, *Road to War*, 190–93. D'Argenlieu's views would actually make him the first to employ the concept of falling dominoes, years before U.S. President Dwight Eisenhower made his famous comment. Dalloz, *War in Indochina*, 73.

38. Shipway, *Road to War*, 206–7; see also Duiker, *Ho Chi Minh*, 369–73.

39. Duiker, *Ho Chi Minh*, 374–75; Shipway, *Road to War*, 208–10. The "French Union" was still a project for the future since the French had yet to ratify a constitution for the Fourth Republic, which also defined France's relations to her colonies—the French Union.

40. Shipway, *Road to War*, 211–14. Shipway clearly puts the blame for the failure of Fontainebleau on d'Argenlieu. A memorandum by the high commissioner urged the government to suspend the conference, arguing that both the Indochinese and French settlers there felt that Paris was lacking the stamina to remain. If colonial confidence was lost, France could only "prepare to leave or to envisage armed reconquest." See also Duiker, *Ho Chi Minh*, 375–76; Dommen, *The Indochinese Experience*, 159–60; Lawrence, *Assuming the Burden*, 150–52; and Alain-Gerard Marsot, "The Crucial Year: Indochina 1946," *Journal of Contemporary History* 19, no. 2 (April 1984): 341–42.

41. Duiker, *Ho Chi Minh*, 379–80; Shipway, *Road to War*, 218–19; Lawrence, *Assuming the Burden*, 153; Karnow, *Vietnam*, 154–55.

42. Dalloz, *War in Indochina*, 76–77. Although the constitution denounced "colonization based on arbitrary power," the government in Paris was clearly in charge, thus rejecting independence of any member state.

43. Giles, *Locust Years*, 34–37. Giles notes that schoolbooks in use give a good example of general French thinking during the early Fourth Republic. It was France's overseas possessions "which confer on France the rank as great power. European France is a medium sized power, with overseas France she is a great power, the French Union." See also Marshall, *French Colonial Myth*, 173–75.

44. Marsot, "The Crucial Year," 341.

45. Giles, *Locust Years*, 53; Shipway, *Road to War*, 229–33.

46. Duiker, *Ho Chi Minh*, 385–88. Giap was minister of national defense; Dong served as head negotiator at the Fontainebleau Conference and was also undersecretary for economic affairs, and Chinh served as general secretary of the party. While Ho was never publicly criticized and confidence in "First Citizen" Ho was confirmed at the DRV National Assembly, he was clearly under pressure by the radical wing of the Viet Minh.

47. Shipway, *Road to War*, 237–42; Duiker, *Ho Chi Minh*, 388–89; Giles, *Locust Years*, 54. The Haiphong disaster was the result of another example of French authorities in Indochina taking the initiative without consulting Paris first. General Jean-Etienne Valluy, who had replaced Leclerc, ordered Colonel Pierre-Louis Débès to take control over the city and restore law and order, which Débès did with fatal consequences. See also Karnow, *Vietnam*, 156. Paris was partly to blame as well. Pressured by the high commissioner, Prime Minister Bidault authorized d'Argenlieu to use artillery to punish the Viet Minh. Dommen, *The Indochinese Experience*, 163–65; David G. Marr, "Creating a Defense Capacity in Vietnam, 1945–1947," in *The First Vietnam War: Colonial Conflict and Cold War Crisis*, ed. Mark Atwood Lawrence and Fredrik Logevall (Cambridge, Mass.: Harvard University Press, 2007), 96–97.

48. Duiker, *Ho Chi Minh*, 396–97; Shipway, *Road to War*, 262–63. Both authors contend that General Valluy's orders to remove barricades in Hanoi precipitated a Viet Minh reaction. The Viet Minh canceled an attack on French positions after the local French commander ordered his troops to stand down and a fact-finding mission of the Secretary of Overseas Affairs Moutet was announced. But then electricity was cut off, the original signal for the Viet Minh attack, and since most units had not received the new orders, they attacked the French. See also Martin Thomas, "French Imperial Reconstruction," in *The First Vietnam War: Colonial Conflict and Cold War Crisis*, ed. Mark Atwood Lawrence and Fredrik Logevall (Cambridge, Mass.: Harvard University Press, 2007), 132–33.

49. Shipway, *Road to War*, 250–56; Lawrence, *Assuming the Burden*, 153–54; Karnow, *Vietnam*, 159.

50. Marsot, "The Crucial Year," 346. Just days before the violence in Hanoi, Blum wrote an article in the Socialist newspaper *Le Populaire* stating that a war of reconquest would be contrary to France's principles and long-term interest.

51. For Blum's speech to the National Assembly, See "La Déclaration de M. Leon Blum," *Le Monde*, December 25, 1946. Blum was eager to prevent further bloodshed

of both the French and Vietnamese, but France could not sit idly by and tolerate such acts of violence. See also Marsot, "The Crucial Year," 346–47.

52. "Le conflit s'étend a Tout le Tonkin," *Le Monde*, December 22, 1946. Moutet stated to the National Assembly that his government was passionately dedicated to peace but that "we are not disposed to suffer such acts of violence committed to our country men and friends" in Indochina. He hoped that previous agreements with the Vietnamese government could still be implemented and that "peace would triumph." A *Le Monde* editorial on December 26, 1946, urged the French to unity and full support of their soldiers and negotiators. The DRV had to renounce its claim to absolute sovereignty and accept limited autonomy within the French Union.

53. Giles, *Locust Years*, 55–56; Duiker, *Ho Chi Minh*, 397–98. As Duiker points out indirectly, d'Argenlieu was correct that negotiating with the Viet Minh would prove futile. On December 22, 1946, the DRV government announced the Vietnamese strategy to victory based on Mao Zedong's model of a people's war. See also Gardner, *Approaching Vietnam*, 75–76; Lawrence, *Assuming the Burden*, 155–56; and Dalloz, *War in Indochina*, 83–84.

54. Giles, *Locust Years*, 56–57; McAlister and Mus, *The Vietnamese and Their Revolution*, 18–23. Mus made one last effort to find a peace settlement in May 1947. The terms he presented were unacceptable to Ho, and Mus was fully aware of that. Hitchcock, *France Restored*, 57–71.

55. Lawrence, *Assuming the Burden*, 132–38. The following account of how France gained U.S. support draws strongly on Lawrence's detailed and insightful study.

56. Giles, *Locust Years*, 135–36. Giles quoted Paul Auriol, son of the first president of the Fourth Republic, as saying, "France without her colonies is nothing." See also Lawrence, *Assuming the Burden*, 155–59. In 1947, France spent some sixty billion francs and suffered five thousand casualties. Lawrence, *Assuming the Burden*, 180. On the differing position of the French parties, see Thomas, "French Imperial Reconstruction," 135–40. See also Marsot, "The Crucial Year," 350.

57. Lawrence, *Assuming the Burden*, 161, 170–77.

58. Dalloz, *War in Indochina*, 88–90.

59. Giles, *Locust Years*, 115–17; Lawrence, *Assuming the Burden*, 186–89. Bollaert replaced d'Argenlieu who was finally sacked by the Ramadier government after years of pursuing his own policies and, of course, sharing great responsibility for the First Indochina War. Bao Dai insisted that France recognize Vietnam unity and independence. See also Karnow, *Vietnam*, 173–74; and Dommen, *The Indochinese Experience*, 174–75.

60. Lawrence, *Assuming the Burden*, 22–24. As Lawrence points out, Bao Dai's reception in Saigon certainly did not inspire the Vietnamese people, and, of course, his government was not fully independent and certainly not unified. See also Karnow, *Vietnam*, 175. Ho Chi Minh, responding to the March Accords, made another appeal for compromise and promised Vietnam's neutrality in the heightening Cold War conflict. Gardner provides an excellent account of the shift of American policy toward Indochina during the late 1940s and, of course, the pivotal year of 1950.

See Gardner, *Approaching Vietnam*, 76–108; and David L. Anderson, *Trapped by Success: The Eisenhower Administration and Vietnam, 1953–1961* (New York: Columbia University Press, 1991), 9–11. Anderson makes the important point that, although Bao Dai's state was more than flawed, the presence of a non-Communist Vietnam became increasingly important to justify greater U.S. commitment to the French cause in Indochina.

61. Quoted in Lawrence, *Assuming the Burden*, 258–59. See also Lawrence, *Assuming the Burden*, 233–35, 239–44.

62. Dalloz, *War in Indochina*, 119–23, 133–36; Dommen, *The Indochinese Experience*, 202–3; Karnow, *Vietnam*, 181–85; Giles, *Locust Years*, 137–38. Although France only used voluntary metropolitan units and other troops from Africa as well as the Foreign Legion, the conflict took an enormous toll on the French officer corps. Some three-fifths of the average annual graduates of France's version of West Point, St. Cyr, were killed, with two-fifths wounded. In light of the French government's design to create a European Defense Community to control and mitigate West Germany's rearmament, this was a dismal prospect.

63. Quoted in Dalloz, *War in Indochina*, 134.

64. Gardner, *Approaching Vietnam*, 88–97, 102. President Eisenhower regarded Indochina as "holding the line of freedom" against the Communist assault in Asia. See Anderson, *Trapped by Success*, 14, 17; and Lawrence, *Assuming the Burden*, 261–67. The United States substantially increased its aid to the French in 1950 and 1951 when Washington gave some fifteen million dollars in military aid. This number increased further during the remainder of the war along with frustration about French strategy and lack of military success.

65. Dalloz, *War in Indochina*, 138–39. De Lattre won the first "conventional" battle against the Viet Minh at Vinh Yen in January 1951 and was the first to use napalm bombs. De Lattre also worked incessantly to find support for the French efforts, particularly in the United States. But Paris could not comply with his request for more troops.

66. Giles, *Locust Years*, 140–41. See also Karnow, *Vietnam*, 185–87; and Duiker, *Ho Chi Minh*, 441–43. De Lattre's fortunes were reversed with the Viet Minh victory at Hoa Binh in February 1952 at the southern edge of the Red River Delta. A series of French defensive posts to stop the Viet Minh from penetrating the delta toward Hanoi were overrun. See also Gardner, *Approaching Vietnam*, 102–8.

67. Anderson, *Trapped by Success*, 17–18. By 1954, after the conclusion of the Korean armistice, Indochina became the forefront in America's Cold War struggle against Communism in Asia. In April 1954, President Eisenhower designated Indochina as the first "domino" that simply could not fall because if it did the rest of Southeast Asia and the entire Pacific Rim might fall to Communism.

68. Dalloz, *War in Indochina*, 164–67. By late spring 1953, a large majority of French politicians were in favor of a negotiated settlement. See also Karnow, *Vietnam*, 191; and Anderson, *Trapped by Success*, 22–23. Washington had consistently urged the French to pursue the war more aggressively. Although General Navarre was not Washington's ideal candidate to do so, the Eisenhower administration committed $385 million to his plan, increasing Washington's share in financing France's

war to almost 80 percent of France's military costs. See also Fall, *Street without Joy*, 312–29, for a detailed account of the battle of Dien Bien Phu.

69. Giles, *Locust Years*, 200–205; Karnow, *Vietnam*, 189–98. The United States tried to internationalize the conflict by bringing in the British, but Prime Minister Winston Churchill adamantly refused. See also Duiker, *Ho Chi Minh*, 452–55. The Vietnamese victory was largely a result of Chinese military aid. The People's Republic of China shared the DRV goal for a decisive victory to enhance the DRV bargaining position at the upcoming Geneva Conference. See also Gardner, *Approaching Vietnam*, 166–78, for Washington's efforts to keep the French fighting in Vietnam.

70. Dalloz, *War in Indochina*, 171–73. Dien Bien Phu encouraged resistance against the French, especially in the North African colonies. Giles, *Locust Years*, 195–295. French casualties, including the Foreign Legion, Africa Corps, and Vietnamese, totaled nearly ninety-three thousand. Support for the war dropped from 52 percent in 1947 to 7 percent in 1954. By 1954, France had actually committed the once unthinkable number of more than five hundred thousand troops, most of them from Africa, Vietnam, and France (one-third); however, none of the French soldiers were conscripts, with the exception of the officer corps. This was another reason that French interest and opposition to the Indochina war developed so slowly. See Kedward, *France and the French*, 323. For de Gaulle's changed perception toward the value of colonies, see Maurice Vaisse, *La Grandeur: Politique Etrangère du General de Gaulle, 1958–1969* (Paris: Fayard, 1998), 33–34.

71. Duiker, *Ho Chi Minh*, 455–57; Karnow, *Vietnam*, 198–201. Both authors indicate that the Chinese preferred a divided Vietnam to a strong DRV. But clearly, given the recent memory of the Korean War, the PRC was also determined to prevent direct U.S. intervention. See also Chen Jian, "China and the Indochina Settlement at the Geneva Conference of 1954," in *The First Vietnam War: Colonial Conflict and Cold War Crisis*, ed. Mark Atwood Lawrence and Fredrik Logevall (Cambridge, Mass.: Harvard University Press, 2007), 243–48. Pham Van Dong opposed a temporary division of Vietnam, but Zhou Enlai prevailed. See also Giles, *Locust Years*, 206–8. Mendès-France had voiced his opposition to French policy in Indochina consistently since 1950 and argued for a political settlement.

72. Jian, "China and the Indochina Settlement," 252–61; Anderson, *Trapped by Success*, 62; Karnow, *Vietnam*, 201–5; Duiker, *Ho Chi Minh*, 458–61. Ho and his colleagues were obviously disappointed by the outcome of the Geneva Conference. Already in 1950, Ho had realized that the United States had become a "dangerous enemy of the Vietnamese people." But he warned, "The deeper their interference the more powerful is our solidarity and our struggle." Gardner, *Approaching Vietnam*, 101.

73. Anderson, *Trapped by Success*, 44–64. Ngo Dinh Diem was appointed prime minister on June 18, 1954, and given full authority by Bao Dai to conduct government affairs. From the moment Diem took office on June 25, he had one clear agenda: to gain "greater and more direct US assistance." And he received what he wished for. Most American officials believed they could do a much better job than the French in Vietnam and build a successful "free" South Vietnam.

74. Dalloz, *War in Indochina*, 183–85. General Navarre and many French officers felt betrayed by the government and blamed them and the French political system in general for losing the war in Indochina. Many of them soon served in Algeria, determined not to suffer humiliation again.

CHAPTER 3: WEST GERMANY FROM THE 1950S TO 1963

1. Christian Hacke, *Die Außenpolitik der Bundesrepublik Deutschland: Von Konrad Adenauer bis Gerhard Schröder* (Frankfurt: Ullstein, 2003), 27–29; Anthony Glees, *Reinventing Germany: German Political Development since 1945* (Oxford, UK: Berg, 1996), 26–31; Mary Fulbrook, *The Divided Nation: A History of Germany, 1918–1990* (New York: Oxford University Press, 1992), 129–33.

2. Hacke, *Außenpolitik*, 30–49. Kaiser and Schumacher had solid credentials resisting the Nazis. Kaiser was very much shaped by his roots in Berlin and saw the city as the springboard to reconcile East and West and their varying political systems. Schumacher's abrasive personal style and anti-Americanism certainly did not help him in relations with the Western allies. His sole focus on an alliance with socialist or social democratic parties proved unrealistic.

3. Fulbrook, *Divided Nation*, 136–38; Glees, *Reinventing Germany*, 50–57. Backed by the Soviets, the East German Communists used former Nazi concentration camps to detain and execute their opponents—some fifty thousand died there, and more than twenty-five thousand were deported to the Soviet Union.

4. Glees, *Reinventing Germany*, 34–38.

5. Glees, *Reinventing Germany*, 38–40.

6. Glees, *Reinventing Germany*, 57.

7. Glees, *Reinventing Germany*, 58–62; Fulbrook, *Divided Nation*, 162–63. The Constituent Assembly chose the term Basic Law to indicate that East Germany was not represented, and hence the Basic Law was only a "provisional" constitution.

8. Arnulf Baring, *Im Anfang war Adenauer: Die Enstehung der Kanzlerdemokratie*, 2nd ed. (Munich: DTV, 1982), 86–91; see also Willy Brandt, *My Life in Politics* (New York: Penguin, 1992), 27.

9. Baring, *Im Anfang war Adenauer*, 108–9; Kurt Sontheimer, *Die Adenauer Ära: Grundlegung der Bundesrepublik Deutschland* (Munich: DTV, 1991), 26; Alfred Grosser, *Geschichte Deutschlands seit 1945: Eine Bilanz* (Munich: DTV, 1985), 172–74.

10. Wolfram F. Hanrieder, *Germany, America, Europe: Forty Years of German Foreign Policy* (New Haven, Conn.: Yale University Press, 1989), 5; Sontheimer, *Die Adenauer Ära*, 29–31; Baring, *Im Anfang war Adenauer*, 109–11; Grosser, *Geschichte Deutschlands*, 420–25. Economic recovery was greatly aided by the Marshall Plan.

11. Hans-Peter Schwarz, "Adenauer und Europa," *Vierteljahreshefte für Zeitgeschichte* 27, no. 4 (October 1979): 474–75.

12. Hans-Jürgen Schröder, "USA und Westdeutscher Wiederaufstieg (1945–1952)," in *Deutschland und die USA im 20. Jahrhundert: Geschichte der politischen*

Beziehungen, ed. Klaus Larres and Torsten Oppelland (Darmstadt: Wissenschaftliche Buchgesellschaft, 1997), 99–101, 103–5; Hanrieder, *Germany, America, Europe*, 6–7; Wolfram F. Hanrieder, "West German Foreign Policy, 1949–1979: Necessities and Choices," in *West German Foreign Policy, 1949–1979*, ed. Wolfram F. Hanrieder (Boulder, Colo.: Westview, 1980), 16–17.

13. Schwarz, "Adenauer und Europa," 480. In an interview in 1957, Adenauer admitted that his greatest fear was that Germany would again be placed between a rock and a hard place and lose once more to the greater powers. As we have seen, de Gaulle tried to revive that old alliance with Russia in December 1944. If Yalta was de Gaulle's obsession, Potsdam was Adenauer's. Hence, the chancellor watched any allied initiative such as the 1955 Geneva summit, the London disarmament conference of 1959–1957, and British Prime Minister Harold Macmillan's visit to Moscow with utmost skepticism.

14. Schwarz, "Adenauer und Europa," 480–81; Hans-Peter Schwarz, "Adenauer's Ostpolitik," in *West German Foreign Policy, 1949–1979*, ed. Wolfram F. Hanrieder (Boulder, Colo.: Westview, 1980), 131. The Berlin crisis of 1948–1949 made it clear that West Germany could not exist without the protection of the United States.

15. Schwarz, "Adenauer und Europa," 482–85. Adenauer realized that German reunification would take decades, but he was convinced that a democratic, prosperous West Germany firmly tied to the West would ultimately prevail over Soviet-imposed rule in East Germany and result in reunification. Since Great Britain was reluctant to join the European Economic Community (EEC), France remained West Germany's main European partner.

16. Hanrieder, *Germany, America, Europe*, 11, 136–37.

17. Volker Berresheim, *35 Jahre Indochinapolitik der Bundesrepublik Deutschland* (Hamburg: Mitteilungen des Institutes für Asienkunde, 1986), 14–15; Alexander Troche, *Berlin wird am Mekong verteidigt: Die Ostasienpolitik der Bundesrepublik Deutschland in China, Taiwan, und Süd-Vietnam, 1954–1966* (Düsseldorf: Droste, 1999), 219–20.

18. Berresheim, *35 Jahre Indochinapolitik*, 31–32. Troche, *Berlin wird am Mekong verteidigt*, 221–22. Bonn's trade mission in Saigon was a minor affair, but the Foreign Office felt it was important to continue the German tradition of being active in Asian affairs.

19. Berresheim, *35 Jahre Indochinapolitik*, 94–98; Thilo Vogelsang, *Das Geteilte Deutschland* (Munich: DTV, 1995), 132–33, 141, 144–48. West Germany also faced legal problems in trying to restore relations with Indochina because those countries were still officially at war with Germany until the Paris Treaty of 1954.

20. Berresheim, *35 Jahre Indochinapolitik*, 96–97; Vogelsang, *Das Geteilte Deutschland*, 148.

21. Troche, *Berlin wird am Mekong verteidigt*, 238–41. Bonn was also concerned and motivated to work closer with South Vietnam after East Germany established diplomatic relations with Cambodia, Laos, and North Vietnam in 1955.

22. Troche, *Berlin wird am Mekong verteidigt*, 226–27, 233–35.

23. Troche, *Berlin wird am Mekong verteidigt*, 235–36. However, Bonn saw its relations with South Vietnam as a measure to balance East German contacts with Cambodia and Laos.

24. Vogelsang, *Das Geteilte Deutschland*, 154; Berresheim, *35 Jahre Indochinapolitik*, 100–102; Frank R. Pfetsch, *Die Außenpolitik der Bundesrepublik Deutschland, 1949–1992: Von der Spaltung zur Wiedervereinigung*, 2nd ed. (Munich: DTV, 1993), 155–57.

25. Troche, *Berlin wird am Mekong verteidigt*, 243–49. West German economic aid to South Vietnam remained rather paltry; between 1956 and 1963, Saigon received some DM6.64 million in aid, ranking behind most Asian countries that received development money. The main reason was that Saigon used most aid for its military buildup and little went to social reform.

26. Troche, *Berlin wird am Mekong verteidigt*, 252–55. The deputy secretary for East Asian affairs, Hilmar Bassler, described the Diem regime as inefficient and corrupt and therefore made any increase of German development contingent on better security in South Vietnam: "Sicherheit vor Hilfe." In November 1960, five South Vietnamese paratroop battalions tried to overthrow Diem but failed. See Seth Jacobs, *Cold War Mandarin: Ngo Dinh Diem and the Origins of America's War in Vietnam, 1950–1963* (Lanham, Md.: Rowman & Littlefield, 2006), 116–19.

27. Troche, *Berlin wird am Mekong verteidigt*, 255–61. John F. Kennedy's new policy of flexible response added to German apprehension about the U.S. military commitment to Western Europe and the FRG in particular.

28. Berresheim, *35 Jahre Indochinapolitik*, 102–3.

29. Frank A. Mayer, *Adenauer and Kennedy: A Study in German-American Relations: 1961–1963* (New York: St. Martin's Press, 1996), 21–22. Kennedy dispatched Averell Harriman to dispel Adenauer's concerns, but Adenauer retained doubts. Kennedy's strategy was vehemently rejected by then West German Secretary of Defense Franz Josef Strauss. See Franz Josef Strauss, *Die Erinnerungen* (Berlin: Siedler, 1980), 392–98.

30. Mayer, *Adenauer and Kennedy*, 7–9; Joachim Arenth, "Die Bewährungsprobe der Special Relationship: Washington und Bonn (1961–1969)," in *Deutschland und die USA im 20. Jahrhundert: Geschichte der politischen Beziehungen*, ed. Klaus Larres and Torsten Oppelland (Darmstadt: Wissenschaftliche Buchgesellschaft, 1997), 152; see also Arthur M. Schlesinger, Jr., *A Thousand Days: John F. Kennedy in the White House* (Boston: Houghton Mifflin, 1965), 338. Schlesinger maintains that Kennedy first approached Adenauer with great respect, but when Adenauer looked increasingly back to the days with Dulles, who allowed the chancellor a "virtual veto" over American policy, the relations soured.

31. Schlesinger, *A Thousand Days*, 318; Grosser, *Geschichte Deutschlands*, 443; Andreas Wenger, "Der lange Weg zur Stabilität: Kennedy, Chruschtschow und das Gemeinsame Interesse am Status quo in Europa," *Vierteljahreshefte für Zeitgeschichte* 46 (1998): 69–73.

32. Arenth, "Die Bewährungsprobe der Special Relationship," 153–54; Konrad Adenauer, *Erinnerungen, 1959–1963* (Stuttgart: Luebbe, 1968), 91–93; Mayer,

Adenauer and Kennedy, 22–25. Adenauer hoped West Germany would be included into the West Allied Ambassadorial Group and finally achieved that goal after five months.

33. Vogelsang, *Das Geteilte Deutschland*, 248–49; McGeorge Bundy, *Danger and Survival: Choices about the Bomb in the First Fifty Years* (New York: Random House, 1988), 361–62.

34. Arleigh Burke, memorandum for the Joint Chiefs of Staff, June 19, 1961, John F. Kennedy National Security Files, Western Europe, 1961–1963, John F. Kennedy Library, Boston.

35. Walt Rostow, memorandum to the president, July 15, 1961, John F. Kennedy National Security Files, Western Europe, 1961–1963, John F. Kennedy Library, Boston.

36. Senator Hubert Humphrey, memorandum to the president, July 14, 1961, John F. Kennedy National Security Files, Western Europe, 1961–1963, John F. Kennedy Library, Boston.

37. Humphrey, memorandum.

38. Bundy, *Danger and Survival*, 368.

39. Office of the White House Press Secretary, text of the President's Report to the Nation on the Berlin Crisis, July 25, 1961, John F. Kennedy National Security Files, Western Europe, 1961–1963, John F. Kennedy Library, Boston.

40. Department of State Policy Planning Council, United States Objectives, July 29, 1961, John F. Kennedy National Security Files, Western Europe, 1961–1963, John F. Kennedy Library, Boston.

41. Department of State Policy Planning Council, United States Objectives, July 29, 1961, John F. Kennedy National Security Files, Western Europe, 1961–1963, John F. Kennedy Library, Boston.

42. Brandt, *My Life In Politics*, 3–4; Mayer, *Adenauer and Kennedy*, 88; Arenth, "Die Bewährungsprobe der Special Relationship," 152–53.

43. Wenger, "Der lange Weg zur Stabilität," 78.

44. Walter Rostow, memorandum to McGeorge Bundy, August 7, 1961, John F. Kennedy National Security Files, Western Europe, 1961–1963, John F. Kennedy Library, Boston. See also Robert Dallek, *An Unfinished Life: John F. Kennedy, 1917–1963* (New York: Back Bay Books, 2003), 418–25.

45. Bundy, *Danger and Survival*, 366–67.

46. Wenger, "Der lange Weg zur Stabilität," 82–83; Schlesinger, *A Thousand Days*, 326–30; Mayer, *Adenauer and Kennedy*, 39. De Gaulle rejected negotiation under Soviet threats.

47. Memorandum of conversation between the secretary of state and Chancellor Adenauer, August 10, 1961, John F. Kennedy National Security Files, Western Europe, 1961–1963, John F. Kennedy Library, Boston. See also Mayer, *Adenauer and Kennedy*, 32–33. Both Fulbright and Mansfield argued that Berlin should become a "free city" protected by "international guarantees."

48. Mayer, *Adenauer and Kennedy*, 40–41. Kennedy resented Adenauer's "veto" to his efforts in negotiating with Moscow. Khrushchev interpreted Kennedy's ac-

tions as possible weakness and gave Ulbricht the signal to go ahead with building the Berlin Wall.

49. Schlesinger, *A Thousand Days*, 331–32; Arenth, "Die Bewährungsprobe der Special Relationship," 155–56.

50. Hanns-Jürgen Küsters, "Konrad Adenauer und Willy Brandt in der Berlin Krise, 1958–1963," *Vierteljahreshefte für Zeitgeschichte* 40, no. 4 (October 1992): 527–29; Mayer, *Adenauer and Kennedy*, 43–46.

51. Brandt, *My Life in Politics*, 3–4; Küsters, "Konrad Adenauer und Willy Brandt," 529–30; Arenth, "Die Bewährungsprobe der Special Relationship," 156; Vogelsang, *Das Geteilte Deutschland*, 251–53; Bundy, *Danger and Survival*, 370. Bundy, then national security advisor, admits that the American reaction to the wall was slow but stresses that neither the Western powers nor West Germany would have been willing to risk war over Berlin. See also Dallek, *Unfinished Life*, 425–29.

52. Mayer, *Adenauer and Kennedy*, 47–61. Adenauer was clearly unhappy about U.S.-USSR back-channel negotiations over Berlin.

53. Wenger, "Der lange Weg zur Stabilität," 83–84; Mayer, *Adenauer and Kennedy*, 91–94; Karl Carstens, *Erinnerungen und Erfahrungen* (Boppard, Germany: Harold Boldt Verlag, 1993), 288–91.

54. The President's European Trip, West-Germany-Berlin, Eire, Italy, June 1963, John F. Kennedy National Security Files, John F. Kennedy Library, Boston.

55. Arenth, "Die Bewährungsprobe der Special Relationship," 157–60.

56. Arenth, "Die Bewährungsprobe der Special Relationship," 92–99; Wenger, "Der lange Weg zur Stabilität," 95–96; Schlesinger, *A Thousand Days*, 338–39. Schlesinger expressed Washington's irritation over the "chronic discontent" of Bonn and its "endless stream of complaints," particularly by German Ambassador Wilhelm Grewe, which led to his recall in August 1962, after the Germans published a U.S. draft of the Principles Paper. For details, see Mayer, *Adenauer and Kennedy*, 68–73.

57. Adenauer, *Erinnerungen*, 119–21; Mayer, *Adenauer and Kennedy*, 78–80.

58. Adenauer, *Erinnerungen*, 123–27.

59. Adenauer, *Erinnerungen*, 138–40, 149.

60. Adenauer, *Erinnerungen*, 168, 172; Mayer, *Adenauer and Kennedy*, 95; Carstens, *Erinnerungen*, 250–51.

61. Mayer, *Adenauer and Kennedy*, 95–96; Adenauer, *Erinnerungen*, 198; Carstens, *Erinnerungen*, 251–53. Carstens met with Kennedy and tried to assure the president that the relationship with Washington was indispensable [*unverzichtbar*] to West Germany.

62. Adenauer, *Erinnerungen*, 199–200. "Ich bemerkte eingangs, in der jetzigen unsicheren Zeit komme dem Zusammenstehen Frankreichs und Deutschlands noch grössere Bedeutung zu. Ich sei sehr unruhig wegen der Vereinigten Staaten. Ich wisse nicht, welchen Verteidigungskurs man dort habe, denn alles ändere sich dort sehr schnell. . . . Sicherlich wolle Amerika niemanden täuschen, doch keiner könne wissen, wie die Amerikaner morgen dächten. Es bleibe ein unbehagliches Gefühl. Deutschland stehe in unmittelbarer Berührung mit Russland, direkt dahinter komme Frankreich. Die Gefahr für Westeuropa sei sehr groß geworden. Angesichts der

sprunghaften amerikanischen strategischen Auffassungen könne man nie wissen, ob sich nicht auch die politischen Auffasungen änderten, so daß eine allgemeine Malaise übrigbliebe."

63. Adenauer, *Erinnerungen*, 206–7.

64. Mayer, *Adenauer and Kennedy*, 92.

65. Mayer, *Adenauer and Kennedy*, 95–97; Hans-Jürgen Schröder, "Deutsche Aussenpolitik 1963/64: Die 'Akten zur Auswärtigen Politik der Bundesrepublik Deutschland,'" *Vierteljahreshefte für Zeitgeschichte* 43 (July 1995): 525. Ambassador Karl Heinrich Knappstein, Washington, D.C., to Foreign Secretary Gerhard Schröder, January 23, 1963, in *Akten zur Auswärtigen Politik der Bundesrepublik Deutschland*, 1963, vol. 1 (Munich: Oldenbourg, 1997), 162–65.

66. Horst Osterheld, *Aussenpolitik unter Bundeskanzler Ludwig Erhard, 1963–1966: Ein Dokumentarischer Bericht aus dem Kanzleramt* (Düsseldorf: Droste, 1992), 274.

67. "Adenauer für Rückzug aus Vietnam," *Frankfurter Allgemeine Zeitung*, August 8, 1966. Adenauer clearly opposed Erhard's turn to the United States. See Ronald J. Granieri, *The Ambivalent Alliance: Konrad Adenauer, the CDU/CSU, and the West* (New York: Berghahn, 2003), 192–94.

CHAPTER 4: BRITAIN AND INDOCHINA

1. For the discussion of British involvement in Vietnam, see George Rosie, *The British in Vietnam: How the Twenty-Five-Year War Began* (London: Panther, 1970).

2. Mark Atwood Lawrence, *Assuming the Burden: Europe and the American Commitment to War in Vietnam* (Berkeley: University of California Press, 2005), 33–35; David B. Abernethy, *The Dynamics of Global Dominance: European Empires, 1415–1980* (New Haven, Conn.: Yale University Press, 2000), 144–45. Churchill's statement led to strong criticism in British possessions, most notably in India.

3. Lawrence, *Assuming the Burden*, 39–43.

4. Martin Shipway, *The Road to War: France and Vietnam, 1944–1947* (New York: Berghahn Books, 2003), 163–64; Lawrence, *Assuming the Burden*, 75–79, 102–3; Rosie, *The British in Vietnam*, 120–25.

5. Walter L. Arnstein, *Britain, Yesterday and Today, 1830 to the Present*, 7th ed. (Lexington, Mass.: D. C. Heath, 1996), 363–65; William Roger Louis, *Ends of British Imperialism: The Scramble for Empire, Suez and Decolonization*, 2nd ed. (London: I. B. Tauris, 2006), 405–10; Derek W. Urwin, *A Political History of Western Europe since 1945*, 5th ed. (London: Longman, 1997), 114–15; Abernethy, *Dynamics of Global Dominance*, 148–50.

6. Arnstein, *Britain*, 366–67; Norrie MacQueen, *Colonialism* (London: Pearson-Longman, 2007), xx–xxi; Abernethy, *Dynamics of Global Dominance*, 150–51.

7. D. R. Sar Desai, *Southeast Asia: Past and Present*, 3rd ed. (Boulder, Colo.: Westview, 1994), 182–85; Andrew Rotter, *The Path to Vietnam: Origins of the American Commitment to Southeast Asia* (Ithaca, N.Y.: Cornell University Press, 1989), 56–60; Louis, *Ends of British Imperialism*, 563–66.

8. Abernethy, *Dynamics of Global Dominance*, 150.

9. Rosie, *The British in Vietnam*, 102.

10. Lawrence, *Assuming the Burden*, 106–15, 165–70.

11. Rotter, *Path to Vietnam*, 60–61; Lawrence, *Assuming the Burden*, 202–4.

12. Lawrence, *Assuming the Burden*, 204–13; Rotter, *Path to Vietnam*, 62–63.

13. Rotter, *Path to Vietnam*, 103–23; Lawrence, *Assuming the Burden*, 254–61.

14. Lawrence, *Assuming the Burden*, 276–77.

15. Kevin Ruane, "Refusing to Pay the Price: British Foreign Policy and the Pursuit of Victory in Vietnam, 1952–1954," *English Historical Review* (February 1995): 72–75.

16. Ruane, "Refusing to Pay the Price," 75–77.

17. Ruane, "Refusing to Pay the Price," 78–85.

18. Ruane, "Refusing to Pay the Price," 86–87; Arthur Combs, "The Path Not Taken: The British Alternative to U.S. Policy in Vietnam, 1954–1956," *Diplomatic History* 19, no. 1 (Winter 1995): 33–36. On Eden and the Geneva negotiation, see Lloyd C. Gardner, *Approaching Vietnam: From World War II through Dienbienphu, 1941–1954* (New York: Norton, 1988), 256–64, 282–87.

19. On British policy during the First Indochina War, see Anthony Eden, *Full Circle: The Memoirs of Anthony Eden* (Boston: Houghton Mifflin, 1960); Ruane, "Refusing to Pay the Price." See also Richard, *The Macmillan Years, 1957–1963: The Emerging Truth* (London: John Murray, 1996), 377–81. While Churchill and his foreign minister Eden admitted that a French defeat would have serious consequences for Southeast Asia, they ultimately decided that a British intervention would not serve the best interest of the United Kingdom. Eden adamantly refused American pressure to intervene in favor of the French. See also Gardner, *Approaching Vietnam*, 299–306; David L. Anderson, *Trapped by Success: The Eisenhower Administration and Vietnam, 1953–1961* (New York: Columbia University Press, 1991), 71–74.

20. Anderson, *Trapped by Success*, 83–87; Combs, "Path Not Taken," 43–49.

21. Alistair Horne, *Harold Macmillan*, vol. 2, *1957–1986* (New York: Penguin, 1989), 281; Arthur Schlesinger Jr., *A Thousand Days: John F. Kennedy in the White House* (Boston: Houghton Mifflin, 1965), 375; Harold Macmillan, *At the End of the Day, 1961–1963* (London: Macmillan, 1973), 517. Despite their differences, Macmillan and Kennedy developed good personal relations. Macmillan's understanding and support after Kennedy's dreary encounter with Nikita Sergeyevich Khrushchev in Vienna set the pattern for Macmillan's description on his relations with Eisenhower and Kennedy: "I was sort of the son to Ike, and it was the other way around with Kennedy." When Macmillan resigned from office because of bad health, Kennedy sent a "touching" letter, expressing his affection and respect for the prime minister.

22. Ormsby-Gore was an old friend of Kennedy's, dating back to Joseph P. Kennedy's term as ambassador in Great Britain. Kennedy trusted his advice; see Schlesinger, *A Thousand Days*, 335.

23. Lamb, *Macmillan Years*, 386. Kennedy asked Macmillan repeatedly whether Great Britain would "join in" to save Laos, but the prime minister refused to give any firm support.

24. Macmillan, *At the End of the Day*, 223.

25. Macmillan, *At the End of the Day*, 236. The British legacy allowed India under Jawaharlal Nehru and Pakistan's leaders Muhammad Ali Jinnah and Liaqut Ali Khan to maintain law and order and make a "good start."

26. Macmillan, *At the End of the Day*, 236.

27. Macmillan, *At the End of the Day*, 237. Macmillan deplored the fact that the United States did not sign the Geneva agreement and quickly undermined the settlement by backing Ngo Dinh Diem and South Vietnamese independence.

28. Peter Busch, *All the Way with JFK? Britain, the US, and the Vietnam War* (Oxford: Oxford University Press, 2003), 19–21. Busch's contention that Macmillan saw the neutralization of Laos as a blow to the West is clearly at odds with the prime minister's account of events, both on Laos and Vietnam.

29. Macmillan, *At the End of the Day*, 238–39; Lamb, *Macmillan Years*, 385.

30. Horne, *Harold Macmillan*, 293. Macmillan was briefed by his minister of defense, Harold Watkinson, that "military intervention in Laos has always been nonsense" and that Britain could not risk "being drawn into a major war"; Macmillan asked Kennedy whether "the thing was worth doing at all." See Lamb, *Macmillan Years*, 386–87.

31. Horne, *Harold Macmillan*, 293; Lamb, *Macmillan Years*, 386.

32. Macmillan, *At the End of the Day*, 239; Schlesinger, *A Thousand Days*, 334. Macmillan explained to the queen that on Laos "the dualism of American policy is much worse than it is in Europe." He perceived a profound split between Kennedy and Dean Rusk on the one hand and lesser ranks of the State Department, members of the U.S. military, and SEATO members, who urged intervention in Laos, on the other hand. However, the British military strongly advised against such commitment. Macmillan concluded his report, "We are thus threatened with the possibility of being asked to intervene militarily in the Far East, just at the time the European crisis is deepening [i.e., Berlin]."

33. Lamb, *Macmillan Years*, 391. Douglas-Home was more willing than Macmillan to send a token force to Laos in case the Geneva Conference failed, since Anglo-American relations were at stake and Britain could not "back out."

34. Alec Douglas-Home, speech from September 27, 1962, October 12, 1962, Country Files: Great Britain, John F. Kennedy National Security Files, Western Europe, 1961–1963, John F. Kennedy Library, Boston.

35. Lamb, *Macmillan Years*, 394. Douglas-Home urged Macmillan to financially contribute to Laos, despite the objections of the British treasury; good relations with Washington were more important than fiscal concerns.

36. Macmillan, *At the End of the Day*, 240; Busch, *All the Way with JFK?* 40, 44.

37. Macmillan, *At the End of the Day*, 246.

38. Busch, *All the Way with JFK?* 68–79; Sylvia Ellis, *Britain, America, and the Vietnam War* (Westport, Conn.: Praeger, 2004), 2.

39. Busch, *All the Way with JFK?* 85–86, 89.

40. Busch, *All the Way with JFK?* 97–98, 119–21.

41. Ellis, *Britain*, 2–3.

42. Macmillan, *At the End of the Day*, 240.

43. Great Britain, Parliament, House of Commons, *The Parliamentary Debate: House of Commons Official Report* (London: Her Majesty's Stationery Office, 1962), 1318.

44. Great Britain, *Parliamentary Debate*, March 14, 1962, 1318.

45. Great Britain, *Parliamentary Debate*, March 14, 1962, 1318.

46. Great Britain, *Parliamentary Debate*, March 14, 1962, 1319.

47. Busch, *All the Way with JFK?* 54–57.

48. Great Britain, *Parliamentary Debate*, March 26, 1962, 836–37.

49. Great Britain, *Parliamentary Debate*, March 26, 1962, 839.

50. The Soviet note to Her Majesty's Government is printed in Great Britain, *Parliamentary Debate*, July 23, 1962, 114–16. Moscow pointed to previous communications with London in which the Soviets had urged Britain to support the demand for an immediate American withdrawal from South Vietnam. London refused to do so and in Soviet eyes only encouraged the United States in its aggressive course in South Vietnam.

51. Great Britain, *Parliamentary Debate*, July 23, 1962, 116–17.

52. Kenneth O. Morgan, *The People's Peace: British History, 1945–1989* (Oxford: Oxford University Press, 1990), 217–18.

53. See, passim, Kenneth Young, *Sir Alec Douglas-Home* (London: J. M. Dent, 1970), 80–122.

54. Young, *Sir Alec Douglas-Home*, 103–5. Douglas-Home stressed that Britain could not leave "everything to the United States and the Soviet Union" because otherwise Britain would lose her "national soul" and would be unable to preserve peace.

55. Young, *Sir Alec Douglas-Home*, 123–24. Douglas-Home remained suspicious of Soviet policy but was also anxious about American design, which was obvious in Laos. He felt that the American interference in Southeast Asia was misguided and dangerous for Britain. He was relieved when Washington agreed to a diplomatic settlement, removing another obstacle in Anglo-American relations.

56. Young, *Sir Alec Douglas-Home*, 146.

57. Morgan, *The People's Peace*, 226–27.

58. In Cyprus, conflict between the British and Greek radicals seeking a union with Greece proper dated back to the mid-1950s; adding to the problem were claims by the Turkish population of Cyprus. In Rhodesia, the southern half of the country gained independence as the state of Zambia, while in the north, white supremacists led by Ian Smith tried to establish their independence. Malaysia, now a member of the British Commonwealth, suffered from guerrilla activity sponsored by its neighbor Indonesia.

59. "British and American Planners at Variance," *The Times* [London], February 1, 1964, 8; Young, *Sir Alec Douglas-Home*, 197–98; Robert M. Hathaway, *Great Britain and the United States: Special Relations since World War II* (Boston: Twayne, 1990), 88. Anglo-American misgivings surfaced with a visit by Robert Kennedy to London. The attorney general accused the British of colonialism in Malaysia, to which Douglas-Home strongly objected.

60. "Sir A. Home Seeking to 'keep close to U.S.,'" *The Times*, February 13, 1964, 12.

61. Alec Douglas-Home and Lyndon B. Johnson, memorandum of conversation, White House, Washington, D.C., February 12, 1964, in *Foreign Relations of the United States*, vol. 1, Vietnam, 1964–1968 (Washington, D.C.: Government Printing Office, 1992), 69.

62. De Gaulle suggested the neutralization of both Vietnams following the withdrawal of all foreign forces. See chapter 6.

63. Douglas-Home and Johnson, memorandum of conversation, 69–70; quote from "Washington Talks: Next Steps for Peace," *The Times*, February 14, 1964, 8.

64. "Prime Minister Holds to His Cuba Policy—Wide Agreement in Exchanges with Mr. Johnson," *The Times*, February 14, 1964, 10. Britain also insisted on retaining its own nuclear deterrent despite American efforts of nuclear disarmament. Douglas-Home strongly rejected an American proposal to transform British forces into a conscript military. To him, this ran counter to British tradition and was completely unnecessary because UK forces did their job efficiently.

65. "U.S. Strengthens Its Force off Vietnam," *The Times*, August 4, 1964, 8.

66. "Message from President Johnson to Prime Minister Macmillan," Washington, D.C., August 4, 1964, in *Foreign Relations of the United States*, vol. 1, Vietnam, 1964–1968 (Washington, D.C.: Government Printing Office, 1992), 622–23. (The editors obviously missed that Macmillan resigned in October 1963.)

67. "British Support for American Stand," *The Times*, August 7, 1964, 10.

68. "Wide Support for U.S. Action against N. Vietnam," *The Times*, August 7, 1964, 8; Hathaway, *Great Britain and the United States*, 89.

69. "Saving South Vietnam," *The Times*, August 7, 1964, 11.

70. "Saving South Vietnam," 11.

CHAPTER 5: LYNDON B. JOHNSON AND MILITARY ESCALATION IN VIETNAM, 1964–1968

1. For Lyndon B. Johnson's background, see Doris Kearns, *Lyndon Johnson and the American Dream* (New York: Harper & Row, 1976). A good comparison between Kennedy and Johnson is found in Tom Wicker, *JFK and LBJ: The Influence of Personality upon Politics* (New York: Pelican, 1968). For the Johnson presidency, Johnson's own account is a valuable source: Lyndon Baines Johnson, *The Vantage Point: Perspectives on the Presidency, 1963–1969* (New York: New Popular Library, 1971).

2. Wicker, *JFK and LBJ*, 195–97; John L. Bullion, *Lyndon B. Johnson and the Transformation of American Politics* (New York: Longman, 2008), 5–6, 22, 34–35.

3. Quoted in Stanley Karnow, *Vietnam: A History* (New York: Penguin, 1984), 320.

4. Johnson, *Vantage Point*, 435.

5. Kearns, *Lyndon Johnson*, 48–93; Bullion, *Lyndon B. Johnson*, 9–46.

6. Wicker, *JFK and LBJ*, 154–55; Kearns, *Lyndon Johnson*, 144.

7. Kearns, *Lyndon Johnson*, 102–58; John Morton Blum, *Years of Discord: American Politics and Society, 1961–1974* (New York: Norton, 1991), 140.

8. Wicker, *JFK and LBJ*, 153; Robert Dallek, *Flawed Giant: Lyndon Johnson and His Times, 1961–1973* (New York: Oxford University Press, 1998), 12. George Ball recounted that Johnson deplored his lack of influence as vice president. See George W. Ball, oral history interview by Paige E. Mulhollan, July 8, 1971, Lyndon B. Johnson Library, Austin, Tex., I:2.

9. Dean Rusk, oral history interview by Paige E. Mulhollan, September 26, 1969, Lyndon B. Johnson Library, Austin, Tex., 1. Johnson had a State Department officer serving on his staff who provided him with daily reports from Saigon.

10. Ball, interview, I:10.

11. Frank E. Vandiver, *Shadows of Vietnam: Lyndon Johnson's Wars* (College Station: Texas A&M University Press, 1997), 15–16.

12. George C. Herring, *America's Longest War: The United States and Vietnam, 1950–1975*, 2nd ed. (New York: McGraw-Hill, 1986), 108–10; Kearns, *Lyndon Johnson*, 251–53; Robert S. McNamara, *In Retrospect: The Tragedy and Lessons of Vietnam* (New York: Simon & Schuster, 1995), 102; Johnson, *Vantage Point*, 42. Johnson vowed to devote every hour to achieving Kennedy's goals. For Vietnam, that meant "seeing things through."

13. Dallek, *Flawed Giant*, 99–100.

14. Johnson, *Vantage Point*, 43; McNamara, *In Retrospect*, 102–3.

15. Johnson, *Vantage Point*, 45–46; *The Pentagon Papers: The Defense Department History of United States Decisionmaking on Vietnam*, vol. 3, Senator Gravel, ed. (Boston: Beacon, 1971), 18. American officials were expected to achieve better communication with their South Vietnamese counterparts, allowing for a more effective approach against the Communist insurgents.

16. William Conrad Gibbons, *The U.S. Government and the Vietnam War: Executive and Legislative Roles and Relationships, Part II: 1961–1964* (Princeton, N.J.: Princeton University Press, 1986), 210, 212.

17. *Pentagon Papers*, 19–20.

18. McNamara, *In Retrospect*, 104–5.

19. *Pentagon Papers*, 31–32; McNamara, *In Retrospect*, 105–6. According to McNamara, the Minh government was the main culprit since it did nothing to facilitate victory in Saigon. The Army of the Republic of Vietnam (ARVN) strategic operations and deployments proved unsuccessful.

20. Dallek, *Flawed Giant*, 102.

21. Mike Mansfield, letter to the president, January 6, 1964, Lyndon B. Johnson Library, Austin, Tex.

22. Mansfield, letter; Don Oberdorfer, *Senator Mansfield: The Extraordinary Life of a Great Statesman and Diplomat* (Washington, D.C.: Smithsonian Books, 2003), 213–15.

23. McNamara, *In Retrospect*, 107; Gibbons, *U.S. Government*, 216–17.

24. U.S. Congress, *Congressional Record*, February 19, 1964, Washington, D.C., 3114.

25. U.S. Congress, *Congressional Record*, February 19, 1964, 3115. Mansfield, like Charles de Gaulle, could not guarantee that neutralization would work, but it was

still the far better alternative. See U.S. Congress, *Congressional Record*, February 19, 1964, 3277–78.

26. U.S. Congress, *Congressional Record*, March 4, 1964, Washington, D.C., 4359, 4831.

27. Gregory Allen Olsen, *Mansfield and Vietnam: A Study in Rhetorical Adaptation* (East Lansing: Michigan State University Press, 1995), 130–31.

28. *Pentagon Papers*, 36.

29. Vandiver, *Shadows of Vietnam*, 17; *Pentagon Papers*, 38–44; Herring, *America's Longest War*, 111–13. General Minh was overthrown by General Nguyen Khanh in January 1964. The next month, the Viet Cong initiated a new offensive, attacking joint ARVN-U.S. units. A bomb in a Saigon movie theater killed three Americans, leaving fifty wounded.

30. *Pentagon Papers*, 50–51.

31. *Pentagon Papers*, 57; Johnson, *Vantage Point*, 66–67; McNamara, *In Retrospect*, 119.

32. Lyndon B. Johnson, National Security Council Meeting No. 526, April 3, 1964, Lyndon B. Johnson Library, Austin, Tex., 3–4. McNamara presented the gloomy facts on Vietnam and discussed alternatives, excluding negotiations. At that point, the administration rejected direct attack of North Vietnam but knew they might be forced to do so if a stepped-up program of assistance to Saigon failed.

33. Johnson, National Security Council Meeting No. 526, 6. Even Mansfield supported the continuation of a limited U.S. role. Johnson dismissed de Gaulle's plan of neutralization as too vague. The notes of the meeting do not indicate that congressional leaders were informed of current covert operations.

34. Lyndon B. Johnson, National Security Council Meeting No. 532, May 15, 1964, Lyndon B. Johnson Library, Austin, Tex., 1, 4–5. Congressman Jensen expressed explicitly what Rusk phrased diplomatically. While Germany, France, Great Britain, and Australia provided some aid, the United States shouldered most of the burden. McNamara affirmed that combat troops would not play a part of the U.S. role in South Vietnam.

35. Johnson, *Vantage Point*, 68; see also Ball, interview, I:26, 27.

36. Vandiver, *Shadows of Vietnam*, 20. For the time being, Johnson settled on a middle course of gradually increasing pressure against North Vietnam without committing American troops. But it was also clear that instead of reducing American "advisors" their number would have to increase.

37. George W. Ball, *The Past Has Another Pattern: Memoirs* (New York: Norton, 1982), 374–75.

38. Ball, interview, I:14.

39. Ball, interview, I:13–14.

40. Ball, interview, I:20; see also Dean Rusk, oral history interview by Paige E. Mulhollan, July 28, 1969, Lyndon B. Johnson Library, Austin, Tex., 36.

41. Johnson, *Vantage Point*, 68.

42. Frederick Dutton prepared two studies elaborating the advantages of a congressional resolution. Accordingly, congressional backing would further convey American determination to Hanoi and Beijing. A resolution would also preclude do-

mestic repercussions and silence Senate opponents. The downside was that Vietnam would come to the forefront of public opinion, but in the long run a resolution would force the large number of undecided congressmen to endorse the administration. See memorandum to McGeorge Bundy, June 1, 1964, Lyndon B. Johnson Library, Austin, Tex., 1–3; and Rusk, interview, September 26, 1969, 11. Rusk made the same point about potential consequences at home if the president failed to secure congressional support.

43. McNamara, *In Retrospect*, 120; Olsen, *Mansfield and Vietnam*, 133–34.

44. William C. Berman, *William Fulbright and the Vietnam War: The Dissent of a Political Realist* (Kent, Ohio: Kent State University Press, 1988), 19–20; Larry Berman, *Planning a Tragedy: The Americanization of the War in Vietnam* (New York: Norton, 1982), 32.

45. Peter Iverson, *Barry Goldwater: Native Arizonan* (Norman: University of Oklahoma Press, 1997), 92–96.

46. Iverson, *Barry Goldwater*, 109–10; Blum, *Years of Discord*, 156–57; Dallek, *Flawed Giant*, 131.

47. Iverson, *Barry Goldwater*, 109–13; Blum, *Years of Discord*, 158; Dallek, *Flawed Giant*, 131.

48. Richard M. Nixon, *RN: The Memoirs of Richard Nixon* (New York: Simon & Schuster, 1990), 256–58. Nixon visited Asia in early 1964 and found America's Asian allies complaining about the lack of U.S. determination against the Communists.

49. Dallek, *Flawed Giant*, 144–45.

50. Dallek, *Flawed Giant*, 145.

51. *Pentagon Papers*, 64–65; Ball, *The Past Has Another Pattern*, 377; McNamara, *In Retrospect*, 121; Herring, *America's Longest War*, 174.

52. *Pentagon Papers*, 72–76; McNamara, *In Retrospect*, 121–23. Hanoi was not intimidated and remained confident that combined NLF and North Vietnamese forces would be victorious, even if this meant direct confrontation with the United States. See Herring, *America's Longest War*, 118–19.

53. McNamara, *In Retrospect*, 129–31; Herring, *America's Longest War*, 119; Vandiver, *Shadows of Vietnam*, 20–22. The Tonkin Gulf incident has been widely covered in historiography. The second attack is now very much in doubt, and at the time serious questions were raised whether the American ships ever came under fire. The first incident on the *Maddox* at least within twelve miles of the North Vietnamese coastline also raises numerous questions because its patrol followed another Oplan 34A mission, attacking North Vietnamese on their soil.

54. McNamara, *In Retrospect*, 131–32; Vandiver, *Shadows of Vietnam*, 22–23; Johnson, *Vantage Point*, 112–13. McNamara and Rusk briefed the Senate on the event and explained why Johnson did not retaliate.

55. McNamara, *In Retrospect*, 132–35; Ball, interview, I:22–23; Lloyd C. Gardner, *Pay Any Price: Lyndon Johnson and the Wars for Vietnam* (Chicago: Ivan R. Dee, 1995), 137–38.

56. U.S. Congress, *Congressional Record*, 88th Cong., 2nd sess., August 6, 1964, Washington, D.C., 18414.

57. For Gruening's dissent, see U.S. Congress, *Congressional Record*, August 6, 1964, 18413–16. Gruening blamed U.S. escalation of North Vietnamese attacks on the *Maddox*. The U.S. policy was a grave mistake from the beginning, and he urged his colleagues to pressure for American disengagement, concluding that "all Vietnam is not worth the life of a single American boy."

58. U.S. Congress, *Congressional Record*, August 6, 1964, 18399–400. Fulbright and Mansfield both defended the resolution because of North Vietnamese aggression. Putting their own misgivings on America's policy aside for the time being, they accused Hanoi of repeated aggression. Mansfield, though, hoped that a peaceful solution could still be found by employing the United Nations.

59. U.S. Congress, *Congressional Record*, August 6, 1964, 18403, 18406–410. They were also critical of the initial Eisenhower decision to get involved in Vietnam.

60. Senators Allen Ellender (D-LA) and George McGovern (D-SD) did raise the question whether American ships should have been deployed that close to North Vietnam. They also wondered if this deployment was connected to South Vietnamese raids against the North. See U.S. Congress, *Congressional Record*, August 6, 1964, 18403, 18408.

61. U.S. Congress, *Congressional Record*, August 6, 1964, 18415.

62. U.S. Congress, *Congressional Record*, August 6, 1964, 18415–16.

63. *Pentagon Papers*, 84; Herring, *America's Longest War*, 123.

64. *Pentagon Papers*, 85–87.

65. *Pentagon Papers*, 87; Marilyn B. Young, *The Vietnam Wars, 1945–1990* (New York: HarperCollins, 1991), 126; Herring, *America's Longest War*, 124.

66. Gardner, *Pay Any Price*, 140–41.

67. Dallek, *Flawed Giant*, 238–39; McNamara, *In Retrospect*, 151–53, 156. McNamara also harbored doubts whether bombing might work, and he was surprised to learn that General Johnson shared these concerns since the Joint Chiefs did not mention it. Admiral Sharp, commander in chief for the Pacific, judged the situation in Saigon as so volatile that a review of American policy was necessary, indicating that disengagement should be considered.

68. Johnson, *Vantage Point*, 120–21; McNamara, *In Retrospect*, 155; Ball, interview, I:26. Ball stressed that the president never pushed for escalation, that he got dragged along, avoiding to make a final decision. Rusk also doubted that bombing could succeed given the particular situation of the predominantly agricultural North Vietnam. Korea had demonstrated that despite extensive bombing the enemy was still able to supply an army of half a million men. See Rusk, interview, September 26, 1969, 22–23.

69. Ball, *The Past Has Another Pattern*, 376–79.

70. Ball, *The Past Has Another Pattern*, 380–81.

71. Ball, *The Past Has Another Pattern*, 381.

72. Ball, *The Past Has Another Pattern*, 382.

73. Ball, *The Past Has Another Pattern*, 382–83. He reminded Johnson that his predecessors had committed themselves to Vietnam solely to help the Vietnamese defend themselves and not to fight a conflict the Vietnamese might not even want.

74. Ball, interview, I:30–31.

75. Ball, interview, I:29–30; Ball, *The Past Has Another Pattern*, 383; McNamara, *In Retrospect*, 156–58. Interestingly, Rusk did not comment on the Ball memorandum in either the oral history interview or his memoirs.

76. Johnson, *Vantage Point*, 121; McNamara, *In Retrospect*, 159.

77. For the complete memorandum, see *Pentagon Papers*, 657–66.

78. *Pentagon Papers*, 658.

79. *Pentagon Papers*, 658.

80. *Pentagon Papers*, 659.

81. *Pentagon Papers*, 659.

82. *Pentagon Papers*, 270.

83. McNamara, *In Retrospect*, 162; Ball, *The Past Has Another Pattern*, 388–89.

84. Dallek, *Flawed Giant*, 241.

85. McNamara, *In Retrospect*, 163–64; Ball, *The Past Has Another Pattern*, 389; *Pentagon Papers*, 248–53.

86. Olsen, *Mansfield and Vietnam*, 137.

87. Olsen, *Mansfield and Vietnam*, 137–38; Oberdorfer, *Senator Mansfield*, 254–56; Berman, *William Fulbright*, 33.

88. Berman, *William Fulbright*, 33.

89. Dallek, *Flawed Giant*, 244; Kearns, *Lyndon Johnson*, 258–59.

90. *Public Papers of the Presidents of the United States: Lyndon B. Johnson, 1963–1969* (Washington, D.C.: Government Printing Office, 1966), January 4, 1965, 3.

91. McNamara, *In Retrospect*, 168; Johnson, *Vantage Point*, 122–23.

92. Dean Rusk, *As I Saw It* (New York: Norton, 1990), 447.

93. Lyndon B. Johnson, National Security Council Meeting No. 547, February 8, 1965, Lyndon B. Johnson Library, Austin, Tex., 2–3.

94. *Pentagon Papers*, 271–72.

95. *Pentagon Papers*, 389–92.

96. Daniel Ellsberg, "The Quagmire Myth and the Stalemate Machine," *Public Policy* (Spring 1992): 218. Accordingly, the "machine" dictated most policy decisions on Vietnam. Kennedy and Johnson could not overcome the rigidity and self-interest of the bureaucracy. John Kenneth Galbraith, McNamara, and Ball made the same point by pointing to the difficulties of acquiring objective analysis on Vietnam.

97. C. Vann Woodward, *The Burden of Southern History*, 3rd rev. ed. (Baton Rouge: Louisiana State University Press, 1993), 219.

98. On U.S. intervention in the Dominican Republic, see Stephen E. Ambrose, *Rise to Globalism: American Foreign Policy since 1938*, 6th rev. ed. (New York: Penguin, 1991), 218–21.

CHAPTER 6: DE GAULLE'S RESPONSE TO AMERICAN POLICY IN VIETNAM, 1961–1966

1. Don Cook, *Charles de Gaulle: A Biography* (New York: Pedigree Books, 1983), 28–79; Herbert Lüthy, "De Gaulle: Pose and Policy," in *Fifty Years of Foreign*

Affairs, ed. Hamilton Fish Armstrong (New York: Praeger, 1972), 356–57. Lüthy stressed that de Gaulle's family "abhorred" the Third Republic and instead relished the images of France's former glory, the days of Louis XIV and Napoleon Bonaparte. This upbringing instilled in de Gaulle the "sublime idea" of France, that she would again play a major role in world politics.

2. Gordon Wright, *France in Modern Times*, 4th ed. (New York: Norton, 1987), 396–400; Robert Dallek, "Roosevelt and de Gaulle," in *De Gaulle and the United States: A Centennial Reappraisal*, ed. Robert O. Paxton and Nicholas Wahl (Oxford, UK: Berg, 1994), 49–60. De Gaulle suspected that Britain intended to take over the French colonial empire. Even more humiliating to de Gaulle was the fact that Franklin D. Roosevelt questioned the general's claim to represent all French. It took three months after the Normandy invasion for Washington to recognize de Gaulle as the head of the new government in France.

3. Maurice Couve de Murville, *Une Politique Etrangère, 1958–1969* (Paris: Plon, 1971), 18–21, 48–55, 58–65. While Murville gratefully acknowledged American help in rebuilding France, he deeply deplored American intervention in domestic politics in Europe. Using the battle cry of Communism, the United States supervised the policies of Western European countries that were, according to Murville, reduced to a subservient status. Obviously, this situation was unacceptable to de Gaulle. See also W. W. Kulski, *De Gaulle and the World: The Foreign Policy of the Fifth French Republic* (Syracuse, N.Y.: Syracuse University Press, 1966), 25–27; and Stanley Hoffmann, *Decline or Renewal? France since the 1930s* (New York: Viking, 1974), 283–90. Hoffmann provides an excellent analysis of de Gaulle's overall foreign policy goals in the context of France's international limitations.

4. Charles de Gaulle, *Memoirs of Hope: Renewal and Endeavor*, trans. Terence Kilmartin (New York: Simon & Schuster, 1971), 37–39. De Gaulle admitted that nationalism drove the resistance in both Indochina and Algeria. Most of the indigenous leaders had been educated in the West and adopted Western principles of human rights and liberty. Ultimately, imperialism was a policy of the past, but France could still play a global role by actually fostering the independence of its former colonies.

5. Hoffmann, *Decline or Renewal?* 285–86.

6. Couve de Murville, *Politique Etrangère*, 73–79. Membership in NATO might accordingly engulf France in an unwanted and dangerous war in Southeast Asia. NATO membership also undermined French sovereignty, and de Gaulle insisted on developing his own nuclear force to free his country from American control of the nuclear trigger.

7. Marianna P. Sullivan, *France's Vietnam Policy: A Study in French-American Relations* (Westport, Conn.: Greenwood, 1978), 62–65.

8. Jean Lacoutre, *De Gaulle: The Ruler, 1945–1970* (New York: Norton, 1991), 371.

9. De Gaulle, *Memoirs of Hope*, 256.

10. De Gaulle's conception of the transient importance of ideologies is even more apparent in his approach to the Soviet Union. He insisted on using the term "Russia" and regarded Communism as only another chapter in the quest for great power politics that went back to the days of Peter the Great.

11. "De Gaulle, Africa, and Southeast Asia," memorandum for McGeorge Bundy, May 13, 1961, John F. Kennedy National Security Files, Western Europe, 1961–1963, France, Box 70, John F. Kennedy Library, Boston.

12. "De Gaulle, Africa, and Southeast Asia"; "What We Want from Paris," memorandum, May 30, 1961, John F. Kennedy National Security Files, Western Europe, 1961–1963, France, Box 70, John F. Kennedy Library, Boston.

13. John F. Kennedy and Charles de Gaulle, record of conversation, February 17, 1961, and memorandum of conversation, May 6, 1961, John F. Kennedy National Security Files, Western Europe, 1961–1963, France, Box 70, John F. Kennedy Library, Boston. De Gaulle expressed his desire for consultations within weeks of Kennedy's inauguration. French ambassador Hervé Alphand restated de Gaulle's intentions in a meeting with Paul Nitze in May 1961.

14. Walt Rostow and Jean-Claude Winkler, memorandum of conversation, November 29, 1962, John F. Kennedy National Security Files, Western Europe, 1961–1963, France, Box 72, John F. Kennedy Library, Boston.

15. Rostow and Winkler, memorandum of conversation.

16. John F. Kennedy and Maurice Couve de Murville, memorandum of conversation, May 25, 1963, John F. Kennedy National Security Files, Western Europe, 1961–1963, France, Box 73, John F. Kennedy Library, Boston.

17. Charles de Gaulle, "Statement on Vietnam by President Charles de Gaulle on August 29, 1963," in *Major Addresses, Statements, and Press Conferences of General Charles de Gaulle, May 19, 1958—January 31, 1964* (New York: French Embassy, Press and Information Division, 1964), 241.

18. Couve de Murville, *Politique Etrangère*, 114–15; Fredrik Logevall, "De Gaulle, Neutralization, and the American Involvement in Vietnam, 1963–1964," *Pacific Historical Review* 61, no. 1 (February 1992): 79–80.

19. Department of State, telegram to George Ball, September 23, 1963, John F. Kennedy National Security Files, Western Europe, 1961–1963, France, Box 73, John F. Kennedy Library, Boston.

20. Seth Jacobs, *Cold War Mandarin: Ngo Dinh Diem and the Origins of America's War in Vietnam, 1950–1963* (Lanham, Md.: Rowman & Littlefield, 2006), 139–40.

21. McGeorge Bundy, telegram to embassy in Paris, September 25, 1963, John F. Kennedy National Security Files, Western Europe, 1961–1963, France, Box 73, John F. Kennedy Library, Boston.

22. Bundy, telegram.

23. Memorandum for the president, Murville's meeting with the secretary of state, October 7, 1963, John F. Kennedy National Security Files, Western Europe, 1961–1963, France, Box 73, John F. Kennedy Library, Boston.

24. Ambassador Charles Bohlen, telegram to Sherman Kent, October 16, 1963, and Central Intelligence Agency, Office of National Estimates, John F. Kennedy National Security Files, Western Europe, 1961–1963, France, Box 73, John F. Kennedy Library, Boston.

25. Couve de Murville, *Politique Etrangère*, 110–15.

26. Couve de Murville, *Politique Etrangère*, 121. According to Couve de Murville, Dean Rusk described Johnson as "intelligent, authoritarian, and extremely sensitive." Rusk left no doubt that Johnson was determined to take the reins of power.

27. Charles E. Bohlen, *Witness to History, 1929–1969* (New York: Littlehampton Book Services, 1973), 504–5; Cook, *Charles de Gaulle*, 366–67. De Gaulle regarded the previous invitation invalidated by Kennedy's death and expected Johnson to go through protocol procedure again. Johnson believed the visit was a done deal and told this to reporters. De Gaulle, as the statesman already in power, felt slighted by Johnson's comments. Johnson and de Gaulle would meet in person only once more—at the funeral of Konrad Adenauer in April 1967.

28. Lloyd C. Gardner, "Johnson and de Gaulle," in *De Gaulle and the United States: A Centennial Reappraisal*, ed. Robert O. Paxton and Nicholas Wahl (Oxford, UK: Berg, 1994), 258.

29. Lyndon Baines Johnson, *The Vantage Point: Perspectives on the Presidency, 1963–1969* (New York: New Popular Library, 1971), 23.

30. Couve de Murville, *Politique Etrangère*, 99–100; Logevall, "De Gaulle," 79; George W. Ball, *The Past Has Another Pattern: Memoirs* (New York: Norton, 1982), 336. Ball noted the enormous patience Johnson had with de Gaulle—quite against Johnson's character—but it was obvious that he respected the French leader because of "his presumption, cunning, and imperial style."

31. H. W. Brands, "Johnson and de Gaulle: American Diplomacy Sotto Voce," *Historian* 44 (August 1987): 478–79; Maurice Ferro, *De Gaulle et l'Amérique: Une Amitié tumulteuse* (Paris: Plon, 1973), 359.

32. Couve de Murville, *Politique Etrangère*, 125–27; Philippe Devillers, "French Policy and the Second Vietnam War," *World Today*, June 1967, 256; "Le Gouvernement Francaise Serait Décidé A Reconnaitre La Chine Populaire," *Le Monde*, January 18, 1964, 1. Eventually, the United States saw the validity in de Gaulle's approach during the presidency of Richard Nixon, and his understanding with China facilitated the Paris Peace Accords of 1973.

33. Ludwig Erhard and Charles de Gaulle, conversation, Paris, February 14, 1964, in *Akten zur Auswärtigen Politik der Bundesrepublik Deutschland*, 1964, vol. 1 (Munich: Oldenbourg, 1997–), 211–12; Couve de Murville, *Politique Etrangère*, 129–31.

34. "Saigon," *Le Monde*, January 22, 1964, 3.

35. Couve de Murville, *Politique Etrangère*, 125–27; "La Chine Populaire," *Le Monde*, January 25, 1964, 5, January 28, 1964, 1, and January 29, 1964, 1–2; Logevall, "De Gaulle," 85; Gardner, "Johnson and de Gaulle," 265–66. As expected, Taiwan protested and recalled its ambassador in Paris.

36. Logevall, "De Gaulle," 85.

37. "Les Relations Franco-Vietnamiennes," *Le Monde*, February 2–3, 1964, 3.

38. Robert S. McNamara, *In Retrospect: The Tragedy and Lessons of Vietnam* (New York: Simon & Schuster, 1995), 55; Logevall, "De Gaulle," 82–83; Gardner, "Johnson and de Gaulle," 267.

39. Logevall, "De Gaulle," 87.

40. Embassy in Vietnam, telegram to Department of State, Saigon, March 23, 1964, in *Foreign Relations of the United States* (*FRUS*), Vietnam, 1964–1968, vol. 1 (Washington, D.C.: Government Printing Office, 1992), 187.

41. Brands, "Johnson and de Gaulle," 479–80.

42. Charles Bohlen, ambassador to France, memorandum to the president, Washington, D.C., March 12, 1964, in *FRUS*, Vietnam, 1964–1968, vol. 1, 140–41. The CIA also warned of the detrimental consequences de Gaulle's policy had in South Vietnam and on Western unity in general. See Brands, "Johnson and de Gaulle," 482.

43. McGeorge Bundy, president's special assistant for National Security Affairs, memorandum to the President, Washington, D.C., March 15, 1964, in *FRUS*, Vietnam, 1964–1968, vol. 1, 152; the President, message to Henry Cabot Lodge, ambassador to Vietnam, Washington, D.C., March 20, 1964, in *FRUS*, Vietnam, 1964–1968, vol. 1, 185.

44. Embassy in Vietnam, telegram, 188.

45. Embassy in Vietnam, telegram, 188–89.

46. The President, message to Charles Bohlen, ambassador to France, Washington, D.C., March 24, 1964, in *FRUS*, Vietnam, 1964–1968, vol. 1, 191.

47. The President, message to Charles Bohlen, 191–92. Johnson wanted to hear from de Gaulle what French diplomats said in private: an American withdrawal from Vietnam would have disastrous results. The message to Bohlen included a personal note from Johnson to de Gaulle that reiterated the main points in a very straightforward language and was modified to prevent an adverse reaction from the general.

48. Charles Bohlen, ambassador to France, message to the President, Paris, April 2, 1964, in *FRUS*, Vietnam, 1964–1968, vol. 1, 216–17. De Gaulle did not even consider the Khanh regime a real government. Since the fall of Diem, Saigon had been under the rule of military usurpers.

49. Bohlen, message to the President, 217–18.

50. Bohlen, message to the President, 218.

51. Bohlen, message to the President, 218–21. Bohlen could not discern whether de Gaulle was operating on genuine conviction based on the current situation or past French experience in Indochina, yet regardless of the reasons, the general remained firm that neutralization was the only alternative to further escalation. De Gaulle displayed considerable contempt for not only the Khanh government but also the Vietnamese people in general. Khanh's recent behavior might partly account for de Gaulle's view. But, again, it was also obvious that Vietnam served as a means to de Gaulle's end—a greater role for France, independent from the Anglo-Saxons.

52. Logevall, "De Gaulle," 88–89.

53. Dean Rusk and Maurice Couve de Murville, memorandum of conversation, U.S. Embassy Chancery, Manila, April 12, 1964, in *FRUS*, Vietnam, 1964–1968, vol. 1, 234; Ferro, *De Gaulle et l'Amérique*, 362.

54. Rusk and Couve de Murville, memorandum of conversation, 235.

55. Rusk and Couve de Murville, memorandum of conversation, 235.

56. Ferro, *De Gaulle et l'Amérique*, 235.

57. Couve de Murville, *Politique Etrangère*, 129–31.

58. Delegation at the SEATO Ministerial Council Meeting, telegram to the Department of States, Manila, April 15, 1964, in *FRUS*, Vietnam, 1964–1968, vol. 1, 239.

59. Couve de Murville, *Politique Etrangère*, 132–35. At least to Couve de Murville, Rusk never doubted that American strategy in South Vietnam would lead to success. Also, Rusk persistently adhered to the domino theory, further justifying the American role in Vietnam. Couve de Murville stated that Beijing was interested in peace talks but could not tolerate an expanding American presence on the Asian mainland. See also Ferro, *De Gaulle et l'Amérique*, 365–68.

60. Logevall, "De Gaulle," 90. For Rusk's view on Vietnam, see Dean Rusk, *As I Saw It* (New York: Norton, 1990), 441–43.

61. Ball, *The Past Has Another Pattern*, 377.

62. The President, memorandum to George Ball, undersecretary of state, Washington, D.C., June 4, 1964, in *FRUS*, Vietnam, 1964–1968, vol. 1, 449–50. Johnson repeated that he favored a peaceful solution but was determined to see things through if necessary. He stressed that Ball should not mention any contingency planning for South Vietnam because he feared de Gaulle might leak this information to the Chinese. However, he was "open" for any French suggestions to solve the conflict in Vietnam.

63. George Ball, undersecretary of state, telegram to the Department of State, Paris, June 6, 1964, in *FRUS*, Vietnam, 1964–1968, vol. 1, 464–65.

64. Ball, telegram, 465–66.

65. Ball, telegram, 466. Ball argued that the PRC was still in an expansionist and bellicose phase of its revolution that precluded an understanding with Washington.

66. Ball, telegram, 467.

67. Ball, telegram, 467; Ball, *The Past Has Another Pattern*, 378. De Gaulle alluded to Chinese history and pointed to the relative ease with which Western powers had defeated the Boxer Rebellion of 1900. For the time being, nobody could predict the outcome of a war between the West and the PRC.

68. Ball, telegram, 468. De Gaulle dismissed Ball's comparison of the PRC and Soviet Russia in 1917: "Russia had had an intelligentsia, an army, and agriculture. China has none of these things."

69. Ball, telegram, 468. Ball maintained that South Vietnam had to be further strengthened and Hanoi's infiltration had to be reduced before any talks could take place. He also pointed to the repeated transgression by Hanoi in violation of the Laos accords.

70. Ball, telegram, 469.

71. Ball, telegram, 469–70. De Gaulle resented American criticism of his policy that cast him in the role of scapegoat. Ball had privately hoped that de Gaulle's argument might affect and perhaps even change the perceptions of Johnson and his "hawkish" advisors.

72. Logevall, "De Gaulle," 95; Dean Rusk and Hervé Alphand, memorandum of conversation, Department of State, Washington, D.C., July 1, 1964, in *FRUS*, Vietnam, 1964–1968, vol. 1, 533.

73. Rusk and Alphand, memorandum of conversation, 534.

74. Rusk and Alphand, memorandum of conversation, 535.

75. Rusk and Alphand, memorandum of conversation, 535.

76. Rusk and Alphand, memorandum of conversation, 535–36. Rusk maintained that the loss of Saigon would undermine American credibility in the West. Alphand did not share this view and affirmed European confidence in the United States.

77. Rusk and Alphand, memorandum of conversation, 536–37.

78. Rusk and Alphand, memorandum of conversation, 537.

79. "Sur L'Indochine," *Le Monde*, July 25, 1964, 3.

80. Logevall, "De Gaulle," 95–96.

81. Logevall, "De Gaulle," 96–97; "Après La Conférence de Presse de L'Elysée," *Le Monde*, July, 26, 1964, 1–2; "La Situation en Indochine," *Le Monde*, July 29, 1964, 3. Paris was concerned by these developments and feared that Hanoi would increase its activity in the South. American comments that Washington would respond "appropriately" to such aggression intensified French anxiety.

82. Couve de Murville, *Politique Etrangère*, 131–34.

83. Gardner, "Johnson and de Gaulle," 271.

84. Couve de Murville, *Politique Etrangère*, 133–34; Gardner, "Johnson and de Gaulle," 270–71. Johnson's intimidation strategy and threat to withdraw American troops from Europe certainly worked with Bonn and, to a lesser degree, also with London. But Paris was far from being impressed. Two years later, it was France that withdrew from NATO command, citing the war in Vietnam as one of the reasons for this decision.

85. Couve de Murville, *Politique Etrangère*, 136–39. Couve de Murville also pointed to recent French contacts with the PRC that revealed that Beijing favored a peace conference. Paris received similar signals from Hanoi.

86. Gardner, "Johnson and de Gaulle," 271–72. Couve de Murville partly blamed the influence of the CIA and some advisors for Johnson's intransigence. Accordingly, the American president received too many "facts" that were not based on realities in Vietnam.

87. Gardner, "Johnson and de Gaulle," 272.

88. "Washington accuse Hanoi," *Le Monde*, March 1, 1965, 2.

89. "Washington accuse Hanoi," 2.

90. "La Crise Vietnamienne," *Le Monde*, March 2, 1965, 2. The paper commented on a recently published "White Paper" that alleged that most Americans were insufficiently informed on the complicated situation in Vietnam or why the United States was involved in that country. On the CIA White Paper, see also Marilyn B. Young, *The Vietnam Wars, 1945–1990* (New York: HarperCollins, 1991), 141–42. A few critics within the United States argued along similar lines as Paris by stating that the pace of escalation had accelerated not because of Vietnamese action but rather due to increased American pressure.

91. Couve de Murville, *Politique Etrangère*, 142; "Paris réaffirme qu'une Conférence Internationale est la Seule Voie Possible de La Paix au Vietnam," *Le Monde*, March 4, 1965, 1; "La Situation dans Le Sud-Vietnam," *Le Monde*, March 9, 1965, 1.

92. "Les Réncontres Franco-Americaines," *Le Monde*, September 1, 1965, 1–2.

93. "Les Déclarations de M. Couve de Murville ont récueilli une large approbation aux Nations unies," *Le Monde*, October 1, 1965, 1.

94. Couve de Murville, *Politique Etrangère*, 135–36; "Les Déclarations," 1.

95. Couve de Murville, *Politique Etrangère*, 136.

96. Gardner, "Johnson and de Gaulle," 272–73.

97. Guy de Carmoy, *The Foreign Policies of France, 1944–1968*, trans. Elaine P. Halperin (Chicago: University of Chicago Press, 1970), 477. De Gaulle also used economic pressure to defy the United States. He decided to convert U.S. currency into gold, to not only diminish American gold reserves but also drain American financial resources at a time when the U.S. government experienced the growing expenditures caused by the commitment in Vietnam. Couve de Murville, *Politique Etrangère*, 218–23.

98. President Charles de Gaulle, letter to President Lyndon B. Johnson, Paris, March 7, 1966, in *FRUS*, Western Europe Region, 1964–1968, vol. 13 (Washington, D.C.: Government Printing Office, 1995), 325.

99. Francis M. Bator, President's deputy special assistant for National Security Affairs, memorandum to President Lyndon B. Johnson, March 7, 1966, in *FRUS*, Western Europe Region, 1964–1968, vol. 13, 327. Washington was clearly angered by de Gaulle's decision but would not criticize him in public because it might lead to detrimental reactions by other European countries. Most frustrating was the fact that France did enjoy the status of "free rider" because its geography guaranteed NATO protection.

100. French government, aide-mémoire to U.S. government, Paris, March 11, 1966, in *FRUS*, Western Europe Region, 1964–1968, vol. 13, 333.

101. Couve de Murville, *Politique Etrangère*, 79–84; Gardner, "Johnson and de Gaulle," 273–75; Brands, "Johnson and de Gaulle," 488–90.

102. Embassy in France, telegram to Department of State, Paris, March 31, 1966, in *FRUS*, Western Europe Region, 1964–1968, vol. 13, 352.

103. Couve de Murville, *Politique Etrangère*, 73–79. Murville emphasized that, while Paris had repeatedly asked for a revision of NATO, Washington considered its predominance in the alliance as the "easiest and most efficient way."

104. U.S. Congress, Senate, *Hearings before the Committee on Foreign Relations*, 89th Cong., 2nd sess., June 20, 1966, Statement of McGeorge Bundy, 4–5.

105. Anne Sa'adah, "Idées Simples and Idées Fixes: De Gaulle, the United States, and Vietnam," in *De Gaulle and the United States: A Centennial Reappraisal*, ed. Robert O. Paxton and Nicholas Wahl (Oxford, UK: Berg, 1994), 295–98.

106. Couve de Murville, *Politique Etrangère*, 137; Ferro, *De Gaulle et l'Amérique*, 370. De Gaulle urged Johnson in February 1966 to accept a negotiated settlement, worried over the renewed bombing of North Vietnam after a short break during the Christmas holidays.

107. "Vietnam et L'Evolution du Conflit," *Le Monde*, September 1, 1966, 1. Sihanouk deplored the failure of recent initiatives by France and Canada to Hanoi. His country was certainly anxious to prevent any further escalation of the Vietnam conflict.

108. "La Visite de Général De Gaulle au Cambodge," *Le Monde*, September 1, 1966, 2. De Gaulle met with representatives from Hanoi and the NLF before he addressed the Cambodians.

109. "La Visite," 2.

110. "La Visite," 2.

111. "La Visite," 2.

112. "La Visite," 2; Sa'adah, "Idées Simples and Idées Fixes," 307–11.

113. Couve de Murville, *Politique Etrangère*, 137–38; Gardner, "Johnson and de Gaulle," 275–76.

114. Brands, "Johnson and de Gaulle," 490–91; Ferro, *De Gaulle et l'Amérique*, 372–73.

115. Couve de Murville, *Politique Etrangère*, 137–38. Murville blamed the United States for the escalation in Vietnam and demanded that Washington initiate a diplomatic settlement.

116. Couve de Murville, *Politique Etrangère*, 137–38. Johnson gave a similar speech to Erhard, leading to the question of whether the American president just needed an outlet to voice his own doubts about Vietnam or if he used the "teary eyes" approach to win approval for his policy.

117. Ferro, *De Gaulle et l'Amérique*, 374.

118. Department of State, circular telegram to the embassy in France, Washington, D.C., October 28, 1966, in *FRUS*, Western Europe Region, 1964–1968, vol. 13, 490.

119. Sa'adah, "Idées Simples and Idées Fixes," 310–11; Hoffmann, *Decline or Renewal?* 284.

120. Gardner, "Johnson and de Gaulle," 277–78; Brands, "Johnson and de Gaulle," 491.

121. Couve de Murville, *Politique Etrangère*, 139–42.

CHAPTER 7: LUDWIG ERHARD

1. For Adenauer's statement and the reaction to it, see "Adenauer für Rückzug aus Vietnam," *Frankfurter Allgemeine Zeitung*, August 8, 1966. Erhard headed a coalition government of the Christian Democrats (CDU) and liberals (Free Democratic Party [Freie Demokratische Partei, or FDP).

2. Christian Hacke, *Die Außenpolitik der Bundesrepublik Deutschland: Von Konrad Adenauer bis Gerhard Schröder* (Frankfurt: Ullstein, 2003), 100–103; Alfred Grosser, *Geschichte Deutschlands seit 1945: Eine Bilanz* (Munich: DTV, 1985), 177; Alfred C. Mierzejewski, *Ludwig Erhard: A Biography* (Chapel Hill: University of North Carolina Press, 2004), 2–19.

3. Grosser, *Geschichte Deutschlands*, 256–58. By 1948, Erhard had fully developed his theory of a social market economy (Soziale Marktwirtschaft), combining free market competition with safeguards for the individual from the excesses of capitalism. Mierzejewski, *Ludwig Erhard*, 27–41.

4. Hacke, *Außenpolitik der Bundesrepublik*, 101–5; Frank R. Pfetsch, *Die Außenpolitik der Bundesrepublik Deutschland, 1949–1992: Von der Spaltung zur Wiedervereinigung*, 2nd ed. (Munich: DTV, 1993), 158–61. Erhard's success in rebuilding West Germany earned him the nickname "father of the economic miracle."

5. For Erhard's approach toward unification, see Peter Bender, *Die "Neue Ostpolitik" und ihre Folgen: Vom Mauerbau bis zur Wiedervereinigung*, 4th ed. (Munich: DTV, 1996), 105–6. For Erhard's attitude toward de Gaulle prior to his election as chancellor, see Volker Hentschel, *Ludwig Erhard: Ein Politikerleben* (Berlin: Ullstein, 1998), 588–94; and Mierzejewski, *Ludwig Erhard*, 167–72. Foreign Secretary Schröder shared Erhard's reservations toward de Gaulle. Torsten Oppelland, *Gerhard Schröder (1910–1989): Politik zwischen Staat, Parteien, und Konfessionen* (Düsseldorf: Droste, 2002), 541–43.

6. Great Britain was consulted as well on issues of the common market, arms control, nuclear sharing, and the German question, but neither side faced as intense pressure to constantly find common ground as Erhard experienced in his interactions with Washington and Paris.

7. Waldemar Besson, *Die Außenpolitik der Bundesrepublik Deutschland: Erfahrungen und Maßstäbe* (Munich: R. Piper Verlag, 1970), 310–14, 329; Hacke, *Außenpolitik der Bundesrepublik*, 114–16; Pfetsch, *Außenpolitik der Bundesrepublik*, 162–64. For criticism on Erhard's new course, see Horst Osterheld, *Aussenpolitik unter Bundeskanzler Ludwig Erhard, 1963–1966: Ein Dokumentarischer Bericht aus dem Kanzleramt* (Düsseldorf: Droste, 1992), 18–20. Ronald J. Granieri, *The Ambivalent Alliance: Konrad Adenauer, the CDU/CSU, and the West* (New York: Berghahn, 2003), 167–75, 182–83.

8. Ludwig Erhard and Dean Acheson, conversation, October 19, 1963, in *Akten zur auswärtigen Politik der Bundesrepublik Deutschland (AAPD)*, October 1–December 31, 1963, vol. 3 (Munich: Oldenbourg, 1997), 1337–40. Erhard criticized the current French policy, most notably the de Gaulle veto against the British entry to the EEC. Foreign Secretary Schröder painted a similar picture and stressed that the U.S. commitment was vital to West Germany. See Gerhard Schröder and Dean Acheson, conversation, October 19, 1963, in *AAPD*, October 1–December 31, 1963, vol. 3, 1343–44.

9. Ludwig Erhard and U.S. ambassador George McGhee, conversation, October 22, 1963, in *AAPD*, October 1–December 31, 1963, vol. 3, 1363–64. Erhard was very much concerned about suggestions from members of Congress and former president Dwight Eisenhower to withdraw more GIs from Europe. See also Ludwig Erhard and Dean Rusk, conversation, October 25, 1963, in *AAPD*, October 1–December 31, 1963, vol. 3, 1385–86. Erhard assured Rusk of German allegiance and loyalty. Rusk pointed out that the United States not only had to protect Germany but also so far had sacrificed more than one hundred thousand men in the struggle against Communism. Gerhard Schröder and Dean Rusk, conversation, October 26, 1963, in *AAPD*, October 1–December 31, 1963, vol. 3, 1392. Rusk complained that West Germans were extremely sensitive to any rumor about American troop withdrawals while obviously nobody bothered that the French reduced their forces in West Germany.

10. Osterheld, *Aussenpolitik unter Bundeskanzler Ludwig Erhard*, 37–41. Osterheld was highly critical of the American involvement in Vietnam and its complicity in the overthrow of Diem. He maintained that coup was a grave mistake that further drew the United States into the quagmire of Vietnam and destroyed a chance for victory.

11. Undersecretary Alexander Böker, memorandum, November 7, 1963, in *AAPD*, October 1–December 31, 1963, vol. 3, 1415–16. Böker pointed out that Great Britain, like the United States, was reluctant to recognize the new regime. France refused to acknowledge any government coming to power illegally, but France would maintain its already established ties with South Vietnam.

12. Böker, memorandum, 1417. Böker feared that any negotiation between Saigon and Hanoi might lead to the same chaos that already existed in Laos and Cambodia, and fully accepted the American domino theory for Southeast Asia.

13. Ambassador York Alexander von Wendland, letter to Foreign Ministry, December 16, 1963, in *AAPD*, October 1–December 31, 1963, vol. 3, 1647. Bonn increased its economic aid but could do little to change de Gaulle's policy of neutralization.

14. Wendland, letter, 1648. West Germany gave a fifteen-million-dollar credit to Saigon; Wendland remained ambiguous in his advice to Bonn—he leaned toward de Gaulle's idea of neutralization but feared a Communist sweep over Southeast Asia.

15. Ambassador Karl Heinrich Knappstein, letter to Foreign Ministry, November 19, 1963, in *AAPD*, October 1–December 31, 1963, vol. 3, 1453.

16. Ambassador Karl Heinrich Knappstein, letter to Foreign Ministry, January 22, 1964, in *AAPD*, 1964, vol. 1, 110–12. Knappstein elaborated on the different status of France and West Germany in the United States. France's aid to American independence and alliances of two world wars gave Paris a freedom of action that Bonn could only dream of. Accordingly, France could be "unfaithful" from time to time, but Germany did not enjoy such tolerance (112–14).

17. Ulrich Wickert, "Wickert Memorandum: Relations between the FRG and the PRC," December 11, 1963, in *AAPD*, October 1–December 31, 1963, vol. 3, 1617–19. Wickert pointed out that Washington should be informed of any German approach to Beijing and that even economic relations could be voided by Washington, given its concern about Chinese military support of Hanoi.

18. Senior official Franz Krapf, memorandum to Foreign Ministry, May 19, 1964, in *AAPD*, 1964, vol. 1, 542–43.

19. Krapf, memorandum, May 19, 1964, 543.

20. Krapf, memorandum, May 19, 1964, 545–47.

21. Senior official Franz Krapf, memorandum to Foreign Ministry, May 30, 1964, in *AAPD*, 1964, vol. 1, 585–88.

22. Krapf, memorandum, May 30, 1964, 589.

23. Niels Hansen, consul in Bern, memorandum, July 21, 1964, in *AAPD*, 1964, vol. 1. The Japanese government was also worried about Sino-German contacts. Bonn downplayed the issue by stating it was only interested in better trade conditions. See Undersecretary Karl Carstens, message to embassy in Tokyo, July 18, 1964, in *AAPD*, 1964, vol. 1, 863–64. See also Alexander Troche, *Berlin wird am Mekong verteidigt: Die Ostasienpolitik der Bundesrepublik Deutschland in China, Taiwan, und Süd-Vietnam, 1954–1966* (Düsseldorf: Droste, 1999), 158–70.

24. Ludwig Erhard and Lyndon B. Johnson, conversation, June 12, 1964, in *AAPD*, 1964, vol. 1, 653–54.

25. Ludwig Erhard and Lyndon B. Johnson, conversation, Stonewall, Tex., December 28, 1963, in *AAPD*, October 1–December 31, 1963, vol. 3, 1672–74.

26. Undersecretary Karl Carstens, memorandum, December 30, 1963, in *AAPD*, October 1–December 31, 1963, vol. 3, 1712–13; Osterheld, *Aussenpolitik unter Bundeskanzler Ludwig Erhard*, 44–48. The Germans were quite happy about the good start at Johnson's ranch and felt that both leaders had established an agreeable relationship. See also George McGhee, *At the Creation of a New Germany: From Adenauer to Brandt, an Ambassador's Account* (New Haven, Conn.: Yale University Press, 1989), 128–30.

27. Foreign minister Gerhard Schröder, memorandum, January 6, 1964, in *AAPD*, 1964, vol. 1, 15–18. Schröder reminded the German ambassadors that they had to continue pressing arguments for German unification. Although some countries grew tired of and oblivious to this German concern, the diplomats had to keep the issue alive.

28. Undersecretary Karl Carstens, memorandum, January 15, 1964, in *AAPD*, 1964, vol. 1, 42–45. Of course, Paris hoped that Washington would eventually recognize the validity of the French course both toward Vietnam and China.

29. Ludwig Erhard and Charles de Gaulle, conversation, February 14, 1964, in *AAPD*, 1964, vol. 1, 208, 211–12. De Gaulle maintained that, while the United States was unwilling to disengage from South Vietnam, it could not possibly succeed with its current strategy. Since Washington rejected all-out war against North Vietnam and China, the United States could only sink deeper into a quagmire. Given the domestic problems in China, Beijing might be willing to accept a settlement over Vietnam.

30. Erhard and de Gaulle, conversation, February 14, 1964, 213–14; Osterheld, *Aussenpolitik unter Bundeskanzler Ludwig Erhard*, 64–68.

31. For a more in-depth debate about Franco-German difference over the recognition of the PRC and Vietnam, see Gerhard Schröder and Maurice Couve de Murville, conversation, February 14, 1964, in *AAPD*, 1964, vol. 1, 224–25. Murville blamed the United States for the crisis within the alliance and stated that Paris was willing to openly discuss the problems in Southeast Asia with other NATO members. Both secretaries agreed that bilateral talks were in fact quite helpful to resolve the thorny issue and current divergence of opinion on Vietnam between Bonn and Paris.

32. Ludwig Erhard and U.S. ambassador George McGhee, conversation, February 18, 1964, in *AAPD*, 1964, vol. 1, 257–59. Erhard restaged his recent encounter with de Gaulle for the American ambassador. This time, it was Erhard who lectured his French counterparts on the pitfalls of neutralization in Vietnam and strongly denounced the PRC as the true aggressor in the region. De Gaulle was trying to play the "angel of peace," undermining American effort. Of course, Erhard fully supported the American commitment to Vietnam. On the German-French agreement about the worrying prospects in Vietnam, see Karl Carstens, *Erinnerungen und Erfahrungen* (Boppard, Germany: Harold Boldt, 1993), 255, 265.

33. Ambassador Klaus-Peter Klaiber, Paris, letter to Foreign Ministry, March 6, 1964, in *AAPD*, 1964, vol. 1, 316–20. Klaiber argued that the cause of French-American tensions was de Gaulle, who since 1958, did everything possible to increase

the independence of France vis-à-vis the United States. De Gaulle disregarded allied concerns and instead relished the role of defender of the third world.

34. Klaiber, letter, 323 [author's translation].

35. Conference of ambassadors, April 21, 1964, in *AAPD*, 1964, vol. 1, 467–69. Undersecretary Carstens wondered why the United States did not take advantage of the current economic problems within the Soviet Union and external difficulties resulting out of the Sino-Soviet split. The ambassadors argued that Washington was unwilling to adopt "classical power-politics" and hoped for evolutionary changes within the Eastern bloc to improve the situation in Europe. The West Germans were unwilling to realize and accept that Washington, at least for the present, was not interested in challenging the status quo in Europe.

36. Ludwig Erhard, letter to Lyndon B. Johnson, May 8, 1964, in *AAPD*, 1964, vol. 1, 517. Bonn adopted a "Deutschland Initiative" in January 1964 that prescribed several steps for the reunification of Germany, which was debated with no results. In 1964, Erhard regarded the initiative as a first hopeful sign that the Western allies were willing to work harder for a solution regarding Germany.

37. Ludwig Erhard, letter to Lyndon B. Johnson, May 5, 1964, in *AAPD*, 1964, vol. 1, 515; Ambassador York Alexander von Wendland, Saigon, letter to Erhard, May 5, 1964, in *AAPD*, 1964, vol. 1, 515. Wendland's assessment is documented as a footnote to Erhard's letter, which includes a report by the ambassador to Washington, Knappstein, describing the determination of Johnson to prevent the fall of South Vietnam at all costs.

38. Erhard, letter, May 5, 1964, 515–16. Erhard maintained that South Vietnam was a symbol for Western determination against the Communist threat. He also subscribed to the "domino theory," fearing that the fall of Saigon would have serious repercussions for all of Southeast Asia. Neutralization would only accelerate a Communist takeover.

39. Gerhard Schröder, letter to Ludwig Erhard, May 17, 1964, in *AAPD*, 1964, vol. 1, 541–42. Erhard expressed his sympathy with and admiration for the "heroic struggle" of the South Vietnamese against Communist aggression. He hoped that General Khanh remained firm to save his country's independence, which was in the best interest of not only Southeast Asia but also the world.

40. See, for example, Gerhard Schröder and Maurice Couve de Murville, conversation, June 8, 1964, in *AAPD*, 1964, vol. 1, 622–23. Murville presented to Bonn the same argument the French used in Washington: The war in Vietnam was a civil war, and in order to prevent further escalation, the U.S. should reach an understanding with the PRC. For Vietnam, the best solution was the return to the Geneva Settlement of 1954 by neutralizing the entire country.

41. Schröder and Couve de Murville, conversation, June 8, 1964, 624.

42. Ludwig Erhard and Dean Rusk, conversation, June 12, 1964, in *AAPD*, 1964, vol. 1, 646–48.

43. Erhard and Rusk, conversation, 648. Erhard clearly told Rusk a different story than his own advisors' assessment on possible contacts with Beijing; he discarded the China card to placate Washington.

44. Erhard and Johnson, conversation, June 12, 1964, 653–54. Johnson scorned those countries that did have diplomatic ties with the PRC since it undermined the U.S. effort in South Vietnam. Erhard did not even attempt to discuss possible German-PRC relations and hinted that Bonn was working to send a hospital ship, the *Helgoland*, to relieve the suffering of the South Vietnamese.

45. Erhard and Johnson, conversation, June 12, 1964, 655–57. Johnson complained about domestic pressure on Vietnam, with Republicans urging him to do more, while the left was against further engagement. The lack of European support made it even more difficult for Johnson to justify his policy at home and obtain the needed financial support from Congress. Johnson also hinted at the far-reaching decisions he still had to make on Vietnam, which would have repercussions beyond the United States. While he did not provide details, he was referring to the possible deployment of ground troops.

46. Erhard and Johnson, conversation, June 12, 1964, 658–59. The offset payments would come to haunt Erhard two years later, when, caught in an economic crisis, West Germany had difficulties complying with American demands. See also Osterheld, *Aussenpolitik unter Bundeskanzler Ludwig Erhard*, 91; and McGhee, *At the Creation*, 145–49.

47. Ludwig Erhard and Charles de Gaulle, conversation, July 3, 1964, in *AAPD*, 1964, vol. 1, 714–16. However, de Gaulle made it clear to Erhard that he was not willing to conduct his foreign policy in mere deference to American wishes. For participation in the *force de frappe*, see undersecretary of state Karl Carstens and Charles de Gaulle, conversation, July 4, 1964, in *AAPD*, 1964, vol. 1. De Gaulle told Carstens that the Multilateral Nuclear Force (MLF) would not give Germany control over atomic weapons and offered a German participation in the *force de frappe*.

48. Ludwig Erhard and Charles de Gaulle, conversation, July 3, 1963, in *AAPD*, October 1–December 31, 1963, vol. 3, 718–21. Erhard refused to accept de Gaulle's position on NATO, China, and Southeast Asia.

49. Erhard and de Gaulle, conversation, July 3, 1963, 774–75.

50. On continuous French pressure on Germany to follow de Gaulle's lead, see Gerhard Schröder and Maurice Couve de Murville, conversation, July 4, 1964, in *AAPD*, 1964, vol. 1, 762–64; Ludwig Erhard and U.S. ambassador George McGhee, conversation, July 6, 1964, in *AAPD*, 1964, vol. 1, 788. Erhard bitterly resented that de Gaulle called him a "mere vassal" of the United States, probably hoping for American sympathy.

51. Erhard and McGhee, conversation, July 6, 1964, 794–95. McGhee promptly presented Erhard with a list of projects in South Vietnam that required foreign aid. He also assured Erhard that Washington would never regard de Gaulle as the sole voice of the Europeans. McGhee, *At the Creation*, 147–49.

52. Osterheld, *Aussenpolitik unter Bundeskanzler Ludwig Erhard*, 101–2. Osterheld was dismayed that Erhard refused to participate in the *force de frappe*, but Erhard had made his choice in favor of the United States. Yet he encountered increasing criticism by Adenauer and other members of his party.

53. Undersecretary Karl Carstens, memorandum, July 27, 1964, in *AAPD*, 1964, vol. 1, 887–88.

54. Carstens, memorandum, July 27, 1964, 891–93. Carstens was also worried that de Gaulle might adopt an openly unfriendly course toward Bonn and recommended that his government refrain from any public criticism of de Gaulle.

55. Ambassador Karl Heinrich Knappstein, letter to the Foreign Ministry, December 30, 1964, in *AAPD*, 1964, vol. 1, 1571, 1573.

56. Ludwig Erhard and Ambassador George McGhee, conversation, February 8, 1965, in *AAPD*, 1965, vol. 1, 274.

57. Gerhard Schröder and secretary-general of NATO Manlio Brosio, conversation, March 25, 1965, in *AAPD*, 1965, 617. See footnote 20 about ambassador conference.

58. Gerhard Schröder and Dean Rusk, conversation, May 13, 1965, in *AAPD*, 1965, 823, 831–34. Rusk, as well as Robert McNamara, assured Bonn that despite the growing number of ground troops in Vietnam no forces would be withdrawn from Germany. Rusk also downplayed the German concern that Beijing might intervene. He suggested that the situation in Vietnam would come to a conclusion more quickly if "the other side engaged in large scale military action," which remained puzzling to Schröder.

59. Schröder and Brosio, conversation, 617.

60. Osterheld, *Aussenpolitik unter Bundeskanzler Ludwig Erhard*, 149–57, 168–73, 188–89. West Germany exported military equipment to Israel in secret, albeit sanctioned by Washington. The export of weaponry was a very sensitive matter in terms of both constitutional restriction in West Germany and the delicate relations to Israel as a result of the Holocaust. The crisis eventually led to diplomatic relations with Israel and the cessation of ties with Egypt and other Arab countries. Mierzejewski, *Ludwig Erhard*, 193–94.

61. Gerhard Schröder and Dean Rusk, conversation, June 2, 1965, in *AAPD*, 1965, 922–28. Moscow, Beijing, and Hanoi were unwilling to engage in a constructive dialogue. Rusk admitted that Hanoi profited from the struggle between Moscow and Beijing and continued its policy of infiltration.

62. Schröder and Rusk, conversation, June 2, 1965, 927–28.

63. Gerhard Schröder and National Security Advisor McGeorge Bundy, conversation, June 3, 1965, in *AAPD*, 1965, 942.

64. Schröder and Bundy, conversation, 943. Though Bundy gave the usual reassurance that Washington was working to solve the German question, he was much more worried about the French opposition to the American role in Vietnam and hoped that Bonn could influence de Gaulle.

65. Schröder and Bundy, conversation, 945–46; Ludwig Erhard and secretary of defense Robert McNamara, conversation, June 4, 1965, in *AAPD*, 1965, 947–53. France's obstinate policy toward NATO was also discussed in depth. McNamara bombarded Erhard with the number game on Vietnam. Erhard was concerned about Soviet intervention in Vietnam, but McNamara replied that such a scenario was very unlikely unless the PRC was directly attacked. McGhee, *At the Creation*, 176–78.

66. Ludwig Erhard and Charles de Gaulle, conversation, June 11, 1965, in *AAPD*, 1965, 1002–5.

67. Erhard and de Gaulle, conversation, June 11, 1965, 1007–8. De Gaulle felt that events in Vietnam proved his continuous warning to Washington correct. De Gaulle also regarded the possibility of a political solution as more than dim, because the United States had missed the chance to do so and "it was now too late." He also suggested that failure in Vietnam might induce the United States to adopt an isolationist position and abandon Western Europe as well. De Gaulle proposed modifications of the NATO obligations, which would require mutual assistance in case of Soviet aggression, but did not apply in case of a Chinese or North Vietnamese attack on the United States (1018).

68. Moscow also showed no interest in negotiations with Bonn; East Berlin caused further headaches by impeding East-West transit and killing refugees at the inner German border. See Ambassador Karl Heinrich Knappstein, letter to Foreign Ministry, reporting on bilateral talks regarding prospects of German unification, June 17, 1965, in *AAPD*, 1965, 1055. Rusk met with Erich Mende, minister for Inner German Affairs, and both were concerned about the renewed intransigent attitude in Moscow on the German question. Rusk admitted that the American role in Vietnam clearly strained U.S.-Soviet relations. Ambassador Herbert Blankenhorn, letter to Foreign Ministry, reporting from the meeting of the West European Union (WEU) in Luxembourg, June 30, 1965, in *AAPD*, 1965, 1097.

69. Ludwig Erhard and Ambassador Averell Harriman, conversation, July 24, 1965, in *AAPD*, 1965, 1250–51.

70. Erhard and Harriman, conversation, 1251.

71. Erhard and Harriman, conversation, 1251. See also Osterheld, *Aussenpolitik unter Bundeskanzler Ludwig Erhard*, 217–19. Osterheld commented on the remarkable skills of persuasion in Harriman's delivery. The American eloquently praised German support for Vietnam, which even surpassed that of the British.

72. Senior official Alexander Böker, memorandum on German-British consultation regarding problems in Africa, the Near and Middle East, and South and Southeast Asia, August 18, 1965, in *AAPD*, 1965, 1372–73. Böker was clearly surprised by the British response that the United States could win the war in Vietnam. His surprise reflects the doubts of the Erhard government that Washington could indeed succeed in Southeast Asia. The documents of the *AAPD* to the end of 1966 include no other evidence on German-British consultation over the Vietnam conflict. Like the Americans, the British insisted on greater financial contribution for the upkeep of their troops in Germany.

73. Osterheld, *Aussenpolitik unter Bundeskanzler Ludwig Erhard*, 220–27, 237–38. Adenauer reproached Erhard for not cooperating closer with de Gaulle; the CDU was increasingly polarized as well between the Adenauer and Erhard camp by favoring either Washington or Paris as the principal ally. Granieri, *Ambivalent Alliance*, 205–10. Schröder defended the chancellor by arguing that the American commitment to South Vietnam was proof of the U.S. determination to fight Communism and hence protect the interests of West Germany.

74. Gerhard Schröder and Maurice Couve de Murville, conversation, November 12, 1965, in *AAPD*, 1965, 1704.

75. McNamara pressured European NATO allies to do more in Vietnam and threatened the redeployment of U.S. troops in Europe. He met with no success. No country volunteered to send forces to Vietnam. See Mission to the North Atlantic Treaty Organization, telegram to Department of State, December 18, 1965, in *Foreign Relations of the United States* (*FRUS*), Western Europe Region, 1964–1968, vol. 13 (Washington, D.C.: Government Printing Office, 1995), 287.

76. Gerhard Schröder and Dean Rusk, conversation during NATO conference in Paris, December 15, 1965, in *AAPD*, 1965, 1899–1900. Rusk explained to the German that he and McNamara were doing their best to prevent troop withdrawals from Europe, but Congress demanded greater contributions from the NATO partners.

77. Schröder and Rusk, conversation, December 15, 1965, 1900.

78. Ludwig Erhard, Dean Rusk, and Robert McNamara, conversation, December 20, 1965, in *AAPD*, 1965, 1915–17.

79. Erhard, Rusk, and McNamara, conversation, 1917–18. Rusk pointed out that Johnson was deeply worried about how the Vietnam conflict would affect his domestic program. Johnson had his heart and soul set on his "Great Society" while he felt damned by whatever choice he made in Vietnam. Erhard should follow through his commitment as well.

80. Erhard, Rusk, and McNamara, conversation, 1918–19. McNamara relayed that two hundred thousand Americans would be in South Vietnam by the end of 1965, with more to be deployed in 1966. The war already cost ten billion dollars per year, which would further increase. McNamara indicated that the United States had reached the end of the line in its duty to Western freedom, while its allies remained complacent. Erhard's first encounter with Johnson appeared to be a short relief from Vietnam. See Ludwig Erhard and Lyndon B. Johnson, conversation, December 20, 1965, in *AAPD*, 1965, 1920–25.

81. Osterheld, *Aussenpolitik unter Bundeskanzler Ludwig Erhard*, 268–70; German-American government consultation, December 20, 1965, in *AAPD*, 1965, 1929–31. Rusk and McNamara made it abundantly clear that the United States would stand by South Vietnam. Hanoi was unwilling to negotiate, and hence the bombing of North Vietnam would continue until it broke their will to fight. McNamara admitted that success could not be achieved quickly, since North Vietnam was basically an agricultural country. To Erhard, it was clear that Vietnam would be on the agenda for a long time.

82. Osterheld, *Aussenpolitik unter Bundeskanzler Ludwig Erhard*, 270; McGhee, *At the Creation*, 183–86. Ambassador McGhee was critical of Johnson's treatment of Erhard, stating that the president "had greatly overplayed his hand."

83. Ambassador Karl Heinrich Knappstein, letter to Foreign Ministry, January 11, 1966, in *AAPD*, 1966, vol. 1, 7–9. Knappstein commented on McNamara's request for German troops that the secretary was under political pressure to find allied support for Vietnam. Knappstein asked for further guidance from Bonn on how to respond to the question of a German military contribution to Vietnam. For Erhard's public statement, see footnote 1 of Knappstein document. U.S. ambassador McGhee also asked for a German contribution in every way possible. See Gerhard Schröder and

George McGhee, conversation, January 14, 1966, in *AAPD*, 1966, 21–22. Schröder maintained that Bonn was already doing more than most Western allies. As another sign of support, Bonn sent the hospital ship *Helgoland* to South Vietnam.

84. Erhard and Johnson, conversation, December 20, 1965, 1938–42; Osterheld, *Aussenpolitik unter Bundeskanzler Ludwig Erhard*, 271–72; Kurt Sontheimer, *Die Adenauer Ära: Grundlegung der Bundesrepublik Deutschland* (Munich: DTV, 1991), 35–37.

85. Undersecretary Karl Carstens, memorandum, January 27, 1966, in *AAPD*, 1966, 77–78, 80, 93. All German allies were preoccupied with problems they deemed more important than German unification. Vietnam forced Moscow to adopt a more aggressive policy against the United States. But the Soviets had no intention to intervene militarily. For Bonn, this new ice age crushed any possibility of even beginning meaningful discussions on unification.

86. Senior official Franz Krapf, letter to Ambassador Karl Heinrich Knappstein, Washington, D.C., January 28, 1966, in *AAPD*, 1966, 111–12. Krapf pointed to the past difficulties to even establish the Bundeswehr and argued that any military role in Southeast Asia would leave the FRG more vulnerable to Soviet pressure.

87. Osterheld, *Aussenpolitik unter Bundeskanzler Ludwig Erhard*, 286. McNamara, in particular, became the black sheep for German policy makers. Gerhard Schröder and Maurice Couve de Murville, conversation, February 7, 1966, in *AAPD*, 1966, 159. Couve de Murville maintained that the war in Vietnam was far more complicated than the Americans perceived, and he was still concerned about Chinese interference. It was American intransigence than prevented a peaceful settlement in Vietnam. Only negotiations could prevent further deterioration.

88. Schröder and Couve de Murville, conversation, February 7, 1966, 161–64.

89. Senior official Rudolf Thierfelder, head of the legal division of the Foreign Ministry, memorandum regarding cabinet commission on aid to South Vietnam, February 14, 1965, in *AAPD*, 1965, 187–88.

90. Thierfelder, memorandum, 188–89. All ministers were worried about insufficient and unseasoned personnel at the German embassy in Saigon and were happy to hear that, with Wilhelm Kropf, an experienced diplomat was taking over. Further discussion of the topic was postponed and immediate responsibility handed over to their department heads.

91. See Joachim Arenth, "Die Bewährungsprobe der Special Relationship: Washington und Bonn (1961–1969)," in *Deutschland und die USA im 20. Jahrhundert: Geschichte der politischen Beziehungen*, ed. Klaus Larres and Torsten Oppelland (Darmstadt: Wissenschaftliche Buchgesellschaft, 1997), 163.

92. *"Soldaten für Vietnam?" Frankfurter Allgemeine Zeitung*, January 25, 1966, 1 [author's translation].

93. For the constitutional restraints of the FRG, see Luitpold Werz, head of cultural affairs section, Foreign Ministry, memorandum to embassy in Washington, D.C., April 18, 1966, in *AAPD*, 1966, 506–10. Werz presented a lengthy memorandum discussing the clauses of the Basic Law; Article 26 condemned aggressive actions and made them a punishable offense, which of course, could be used by Washington. Nevertheless, the overall intent of the Basic Law, along with the fact that no

branch of government could even declare a state of war, made it abundantly clear that Bonn could not deploy German troops beyond the narrowly and purely defensively defined scope of NATO.

94. Ambassador Karl Heinrich Knappstein, letter to Undersecretary Karl Carstens, February 21, 1966, in *AAPD*, 1966, 204–5. Knappstein was deeply concerned about statements of Democratic senators John Stennis and Richard Russell in favor of a West German military contribution to Vietnam. The *Baltimore Post* claimed that McNamara had made the same proposal in a Senate hearing, which sent Knappstein on a frantic search to find out what McNamara had actually told the committee. While the actual statement was classified, the ambassador finally received a shortened version that acknowledged the constitutional restriction preventing Bonn from deploying military units. However, McNamara expressed his hope to convince Bonn "to come in" and contribute more in Vietnam.

95. Knappstein, letter, February 21, 1966, 205–6. Knappstein was told that only a few senators were actually demanding a German military contribution. The entire affair made Knappstein quite apprehensive, and he hoped that a meeting with McNamara could better clear the air. Bonn hoped that further discussions would be held in secret in order to avoid anti-American sentiments in Germany.

96. Ludwig Erhard, letter to President Lyndon B. Johnson, February 25, 1966, in *AAPD*, 1966, 225. The *Frankfurter Allgemeine Zeitung* followed the American initiative closely; see, for example, "Die Friedensoffensive," *Frankfurter Allgemeine Zeitung*, January 3, 1966, 1; and "Das Weiße Haus bestätigt die Aufnahme eines direkten Kontaktes zu Hanoi," *Frankfurter Allgemeine Zeitung*, January 12, 1966, 1.

97. Karl Carstens and Alfred Puhan, conversation, March 14, 1966, in *AAPD*, 1966, 298–99.

98. On Erhard's economic difficulties, see Mierzejewski, *Ludwig Erhard*, 195–99; and Hubert Zimmermann, *Money and Security: Troops, Monetary Policy, and West Germany's Relations with the United States and Britain, 1950–1971* (Washington, D.C.: German Historical Institute, 2002), 189–94. Until 1955, West Germany covered the cost of U.S. troops as part of the occupation payment. From 1955 onward, Washington covered all cost, but money spent by GIs led to a dollar glut in Europe. This situation was further worsened by the economic recovery of Europe, reversing the trade balance to Europe's favor.

99. Zimmermann, *Money and Security*, 194–99. In 1960, Bonn refused a monetary settlement, arguing it would be regarded by Germans as occupation costs. In light of the construction of the Berlin Wall, Bonn was more malleable to the American demands, and in October 1961, Bonn agreed to order military equipment for $1.425 billion during the next two years, which covered the foreign exchange of U.S. troops; at that time, the Bundeswehr needed the ordered matériel, and in 1963, the agreement was renewed for two more years.

100. Zimmermann, *Money and Security*, 199–201.

101. Zimmermann, *Money and Security*, 201–5; Osterheld, *Aussenpolitik unter Bundeskanzler Ludwig Erhard*, 271.

102. Ambassador Karl Heinrich Knappstein, Washington, D.C., letter to Foreign Ministry, May 24, 1966, in *AAPD*, 1966, 680.

103. Knappstein, letter, May 24, 1966, 681–82. Congress was openly disgusted with European failure to play their part. Some congressmen charged that Europeans had forgotten the hardships of the previous world wars and focused solely on their self-interest, which made them "fat and lazy." British demands for a greater German contribution to their army of the Rhine made matters worse for Erhard. He refused to pay more to Britain, but McNamara would not tolerate the same approach. See Ludwig Erhard and British chancellor of the treasury James Callaghan, conversation, May 24, 1966, in *AAPD*, 1966, 683–85.

104. Zimmermann, *Money and Security*, 201–2; Ambassador Karl Heinrich Knappstein, Washington, D.C., letter to Gerhard Schröder, June 2, 1966, in *AAPD*, 1966, 744–46; McGhee, *At the Creation*, 189–93.

105. Ludwig Erhard and Dean Rusk, conversation, June 9, 1966, in *AAPD*, 1966, 785–86.

106. Ambassador Karl Heinrich Knappstein, Washington, D.C., letter to Gerhard Schröder, June 10, 1966, in *AAPD*, 1966, 802–8. Congress also demanded greater financial contributions by the Europeans to cover American global commitments.

107. "Zwei amerikanische Reserve-Divisionen weniger für Europa bereit," *Frankfurter Allgemeine Zeitung*, July 29, 1966, 1. McNamara adopted the position that a Soviet attack was unlikely and announced that two reserve divisions would be no longer available for Europe and redeployed to South Vietnam.

108. Knappstein, letter, June 10, 1966, 808. Knappstein suggested that Bonn work on alternatives for the possible withdrawal of GIs. He was also deeply concerned that the frequent leaks from Washington to the American media on the offset question would severely damage the image of the United States in West Germany.

109. Rainer Barzel and Lyndon B. Johnson, conversation, Washington, D.C., June 16, 1966, in *AAPD*, 1966, 825–26. Johnson pointed out that the United States had lost more than two thousand Americans in Vietnam. If America behaved as selfishly as the Europeans and simply quit Europe, it would mean war in Europe, Africa, and Latin America.

110. Francis M. Bator, president's deputy special assistant for National Security Affairs, memorandum to President Johnson, August 11, 1966, in *FRUS*, Western Europe Region, 1964–1968, vol. 13, 444–45. George Ball and McGhee cautioned against too much pressure on Erhard, risking the collapse of his government.

111. Bator, memorandum, 446–47.

112. Adenauer certainly did not spare Erhard either. In August 1966, the former chancellor embarked on a public campaign criticizing his successor. Adenauer recommended the American withdrawal from Vietnam and urged Erhard to improve French-German relations. Many CDU/CSU members agreed, and the CSU (the Bavarian faction of the CDU) officially endorsed Adenauer's criticism of the United States. See "Adenauer dringt auf außenpolitische Diskussion in der CDU," *Frankfurter Allgemeine Zeitung*, August 11, 1966; and Granieri, *Ambivalent Alliance*, 219–20.

113. Osterheld, *Aussenpolitik unter Bundeskanzler Ludwig Erhard*, 337–39. The press speculated about changes in the cabinet and demanded a new course. Public opinion polls regarded the international situation of the Federal Republic as worse

than ever. The SPD and some members of the coalition partner FDP demanded Erhard's resignation.

114. Undersecretary Karl Carstens, memorandum, July 22, 1966, in *AAPD*, 1966, 977–78. Germany would pay its nationals working on American bases and provide free storage facilities and free maintenance of U.S. training facilities.

115. Carstens, memorandum, July 22, 1966, 979–81. Knappstein complained to Rusk that McNamara's press campaign seriously undermined German-American understanding. Rusk assured the ambassador that the United States had no intention of reducing troops in West Germany but also pointed to congressional pressure to receive German offset payments in full. McNamara and his British colleague Denis Healey threatened substantial troop withdrawals unless Bonn met its financial obligations. See senior official Ruete, memorandum, August 5, 1966, in *AAPD*, 1966, 1039–40.

116. Ludger Westrick and General Nguyen Huu Co, conversation, August 12, 1966, in *AAPD*, 1966, 1061–63. Erhard reaffirmed his support for the American policy in a meeting with Swedish Prime Minister Tage Erlander. Unlike Erlander, Erhard was against any negotiations on Vietnam at the present time. The United States fought in South Vietnam because of contractual obligations, and Bonn relied on a similar American commitment for its viability. See German-Swedish government consultation, September 2, 1966, in *AAPD*, 1966, 1127–28, 1131.

117. Undersecretary Karl Carstens, memorandum on conversation with Ambassador McGhee for upcoming visit in Washington, D.C., August 25, 1966, in *AAPD*, 1966; Arenth, "Die Bewährungsprobe der Special Relationship," 163–64; Osterheld, *Aussenpolitik unter Bundeskanzler Ludwig Erhard*, 346.

118. Osterheld, *Aussenpolitik unter Bundeskanzler Ludwig Erhard*, 350; memorandum of section 3 A4, Offset Payments, September 21, 1966, in *AAPD*, 1966, 1234–35.

119. Ludwig Erhard and Dean Rusk, conversation, Washington, D.C., September 26, 1966, in *AAPD*, 1966, 1237–38. Rusk was relatively understanding, but obviously it was left to Johnson to forcefully debate the issue.

120. Ludwig Erhard and Lyndon B. Johnson, conversation, Washington, D.C., September 26, 1966, in *FRUS*, Western Europe Region, 1964–1968, vol. 13, 471–73; Ludwig Erhard and Lyndon B. Johnson, conversation, Washington, D.C., September 26, 1966, in *AAPD*, 1966, 1242–45.

121. Memorandum of conversation, 476–77; Osterheld, *Aussenpolitik unter Bundeskanzler Ludwig Erhard*, 354. Johnson was obviously determined to force Erhard to pay. The chancellor swallowed the verbal abuse and invited Johnson to visit Germany. Erhard also agreed to tripartite (U.S./UK/FRG) negotiations on offset payments. McGhee, *At the Creation*, 191–93.

122. Ludwig Erhard and Lyndon B. Johnson, conversation, Washington, D.C., September 27, 1966, in *AAPD*, 1966, 1266–67.

123. Osterheld, *Aussenpolitik unter Bundeskanzler Ludwig Erhard*, 356–58. Mostly critical of Erhard, Osterheld had to give him credit for gaining a little more time in the offset payments and not breaking under pressure.

124. Thilo Vogelsang, *Das Geteilte Deutschland* (Munich: DTV, 1995), 279–80; Grosser, *Geschichte Deutschlands*, 178–79; Mierzejewski, *Ludwig Erhard*, 203–4.

CHAPTER 8: HAROLD WILSON AND THE ELUSIVE SEARCH FOR A DIPLOMATIC SETTLEMENT

1. Kenneth O. Morgan, *The People's Peace: British History, 1945–1989* (Oxford: Oxford University Press, 1990), 239, 243–44.

2. Sylvia Ellis, *Britain, America, and the Vietnam War* (Westport, Conn.: Praeger, 2004), 14–15.

3. Chris Wrigley, "Now You See It, Now You Don't: Harold Wilson and Labour Foreign Policy, 1964–1970," in *The Wilson Governments, 1964–1970*, ed. Richard Coopey, Steven Fielding, and Nick Tiratsoo (London: Pinter, 1993), 128.

4. Patrick Gordon Walker, *Political Diaries, 1932–1971*, edited with an introduction by Robert Pearce (London: Basic Books, 1991), 298–99; Wrigley, "Now You See It," 127.

5. Walker, *Political Diaries*, 299–302.

6. Harold Wilson, *The Labour Government, 1964–1970: A Personal Record* (London: Weidenfeld & Nicholson, 1971), 46; Rolf Steininger, "Grossbritannien und der Vietnamkrieg," *Viertelsjahreshefte für Zeitgeschichte* 45, no. 4 (October 1997): 591; Wrigley, "Now You See It," 123–25, 128. Wrigley maintains that Wilson was determined to maintain a voice in world affairs and tried to master the crisis with multifaceted initiatives.

7. Gordon Etherington-Smith, letter to Edward H. Peck, Foreign Office, October 10, 1964, Public Records Office, in Steininger, "Grossbritannien und der Vietnamkrieg," 593–94.

8. J. E. Cable, Foreign Office, memorandum, October 30, 1964, and Edward H. Peck, Foreign Office, letter to Ambassador Gordon Etherington-Smith, October 30, 1964, Public Records Office, in Steininger, "Grossbritannien und der Vietnamkrieg," 594–95. London was also concerned that failure in South Vietnam would affect the neutrality of Cambodia and Laos.

9. Gordon Etherington-Smith, letter to Edward H. Peck, Foreign Office, November 11, 1965, Public Records Office, in Steininger, "Grossbritannien und der Vietnamkrieg," 595.

10. Robert Thompson to Edward H. Peck, November 25, 1964, Public Records Office, in Steininger, "Grossbritannien und der Vietnamkrieg," 595–97. For more detail on Thompson, see Robert Thompson, *No Exit from Vietnam*, updated ed. (New York: David McKay, 1970). Thompson argues that generally the United States misunderstood the nature of the conflict and Vietnamese conditions. Instead of responding to indigenous problems, the United States perceived the conflict solely in terms of containment of Communism and was step-by-step drawn into an undefined commitment.

11. Steininger, "Grossbritanien und der Vietnamkrieg," 596. See also Thompson, *No Exit from Vietnam*, 120. Thompson held that the United States should have stuck to its limited commitment, even after Ngo Dinh Diem's fall, instead of assuming full responsibility for the outcome of the war. The former approach would have placed the blame for failure on the South Vietnamese, allowing Washington an honorable way out.

12. Steininger, "Grossbritanien und der Vietnamkrieg," 597.

13. Steininger, "Grossbritanien und der Vietnamkrieg," 596.

14. Wilson, *Labour Government*, 47; memorandum for the record, Washington, D.C., December 7, 1964, in *FRUS*, Western Europe Region, 1964–1968, vol. 13, 137. Johnson emphasized that he did not want to become bogged down as Franklin D. Roosevelt was in 1937 when totalitarianism was on the rise and the American people and Congress were opposed to an active foreign policy.

15. Harold Wilson and Dean Rusk, memorandum of conversation, Washington, D.C., December 8, 1964, in *FRUS*, Vietnam, 1964–1968, vol. 1, 985–87; Wilson, *Labour Government*, 48; Ellis, *Britain, America, and the Vietnam War*, 25–31.

16. Great Britain, Parliament, Houses of Commons, *Parliamentary Records* (London: Her Majesty's Stationery Office, 1965), December 14, 1964, 7–8.

17. Great Britain, *Parliamentary Records*, December 14, 1964, 7–10.

18. Great Britain, *Parliamentary Records*, December 14, 1964, 10.

19. Great Britain, *Parliamentary Records*, December 22, 1964, 1049–50. Zilliacus reminded Wilson of his previous statements on Vietnam as opposition leader. Wilson affirmed what he had said, but an outright attack on the U.S. Vietnam policy was no longer an option for a sitting prime minister.

20. Patrick Gordon Walker, memorandum for Harold Wilson, December 29, 1964, Public Records Office, in Steininger, "Grossbritanien und der Vietnamkrieg," 600. British ambassador to Washington Lord Harlech (David Ormsby Gore) agreed with Walker. Nobody in Washington was willing to talk about retreat, and Britain had to be very cautious in proposing negotiations. Ellis, *Britain, America, and the Vietnam War*, 47.

21. George C. Herring, *America's Longest War: The United States and Vietnam, 1950–1975*, 2nd ed. (New York: McGraw-Hill, 1986), 127–31.

22. Walker had lost his seat in Parliament and was forced to resign his position as foreign secretary.

23. "Britain Supports America," *The Times* [London], February 9, 1965, 9.

24. On February 10, 1965, a bomb killed twenty-three Americans at the coastal city of Qui Nhon, wounding thirty more. David Bruce, ambassador to the United Kingdom, diary entry, Washington, D.C., February 10, 1964, in *FRUS*, Vietnam, 1964–1968, vol. 2 (Washington, D.C.: Government Printing Office, 1996), 213. Bruce reported that Johnson was by now clearly obsessed with events in Vietnam.

25. Wilson felt the situation was comparable to 1950 when the United States considered the use of nuclear weapons in Korea. Then Prime Minister Clement Attlee flew immediately to Washington to consult with Harry Truman. Wilson's effort in 1965 turned out to be far more quixotic. His ambassador Harlech reached Bundy on

the phone, but Bundy rejected Wilson's travel plans. Johnson also rejected Wilson's travel plans but finally accepted Wilson's phone call. See Steininger, "Grossbritanien und der Vietnamkrieg," 602; and Ellis, *Britain, America, and the Vietnam War*, 47–51.

26. Wilson, *Labour Government*, 79–80.

27. Steininger, "Grossbritanien und der Vietnamkrieg," 601–3; Ellis, *Britain, America, and the Vietnam War*, 53–55.

28. Wilson, *Labour Government*, 80–88.

29. Harold Wilson and Lyndon B. Johnson, conversation, Washington, D.C., February 21, 1965, in *FRUS*, Vietnam, 1964–1968, vol. 2, 343–45; Steininger, "Grossbritanien und der Vietnamkrieg," 604–8.

30. Walker, *Political Diaries*, 302–3.

31. Walker, *Political Diaries*, 303–4. Walker quickly got the impression that Rusk's readiness to negotiate was far from being decided policy. Hence, he refused to commit Britain to either Vietnam or a futile role of intermediary between Washington and Moscow.

32. Great Britain, *Parliamentary Records*, February 22, 1965, 4–6; Great Britain, *Parliamentary Records*, March 1, 1965, 166–68; Great Britain, *Parliamentary Records*, March 9, 1965, 236–41. MPs wondered whether Britain was willing to reconvene the Geneva Conference in achieving the peaceful reunification and neutralization of Vietnam or at least work to convene any type of high-level conference in an "attempt to stop the war in Vietnam"; Zilliacus favored de Gaulle's plan of neutralization, but Wilson obviously preferred his own approach of international diplomacy. See also Wilson, *Labour Government*, 83.

33. Great Britain, *Parliamentary Records*, March 16, 1965, 1069–70; Great Britain, *Parliamentary Records*, March 9, 1965, 239–41. Wilson fought a valiant battle mainly against his own party. He admonished his colleagues to put aside their self-righteousness that made his job even more difficult. Wilson also had to answer to charges by Labour MP Sydney Silverman that American action in Vietnam was an "act of plain, naked war."

34. Great Britain, *Parliamentary Records*, March 16, 1965, 1071.

35. Wilson, *Labour Government*, 85; Ralph B. Smith, *An International History of the Vietnam War*, vol. 3: *The Making of a Limited War, 1965–1966* (New York: St. Martin's Press, 1991), 59. Moscow faced strong pressure by Hanoi and Beijing: Hanoi demanded more support, while Beijing accused Moscow of doing too little.

36. Johnson report outline, March 14, 1965, in *FRUS*, Vietnam, 1964–1968, vol. 2, 438; Joint Chiefs of Staff, memorandum to Robert McNamara, secretary of defense, March 15, 1965, in *FRUS*, Vietnam, 1964–1968, vol. 2, 440–41. Washington insisted that Hanoi end its infiltration into South Vietnam before any talks could commence.

37. Wilson, *Labour Government*, 85; Steininger, "Grossbritanien und der Vietnamkrieg," 611–12.

38. McGeorge Bundy, president's special assistant for National Security Affairs, memorandum to President Lyndon B. Johnson, Washington, D.C., March 22, 1965, in *FRUS*, Vietnam, 1964–1968, vol. 2, 468. U.S. ambassador to Great Britain David Bruce fully related the criticism Wilson faced from within the Labour Party.

39. Bundy, memorandum, March 22, 1965, 468.

40. Bundy, memorandum, March 22, 1965, 469.

41. McGeorge Bundy, president's special assistant for National Security Affairs, memorandum to President Lyndon B. Johnson, Washington, D.C., March 23, 1965, in *FRUS*, Vietnam, 1964–1968, vol. 2, 470.

42. Michael Stewart, secret record of conversation between the foreign secretary and Dean Rusk, to Harold Wilson, Washington, D.C., March 23, 1965, Public Records Office, in Steininger, "Grossbritanien und der Vietnamkrieg," 612.

43. David Bruce, ambassador to the United Kingdom, diary entry, Washington, D.C., March 23, 1965, in *FRUS*, Vietnam, 1964–1968, vol. 2, 471–72. Johnson explained that some Americans wanted to quit the war while others demanded that he bomb China and destroy Hanoi.

44. David Bruce, ambassador to the United Kingdom, diary entry, Washington, D.C., March 23, 1965, in *FRUS*, Vietnam, 1964–1968, vol. 2, 471–72. Bruce remarked that Johnson "is power sublimated" and served the British "oratorical sandwiches, with layers of gravity and levity." Stewart would probably never forget these ninety minutes with Johnson. Ellis, *Britain, America, and the Vietnam War*, 70–72.

45. Wilson, *Labour Government*, 85–86.

46. Bruce, diary entry, March 23, 1965, 472.

47. Luncheons with the President, Files of McGeorge Bundy, Lyndon B. Johnson National Security Files, Western Europe, 1963–1968, vol. 1, March 23, 1965, Lyndon B. Johnson Library, Austin, Tex. The issue of gas warfare almost led to an open skirmish between Washington and London. Stewart condemned the American use of gas in Vietnam in his Washington press conference. Johnson was enraged and was ready to send a note of protest to Wilson but decided otherwise. McNamara charged that Britain had used gas in Cyprus and was one of the leading manufacturers of tear gas. Now the British felt insulted. See in *FRUS*, Vietnam, 1964–1968, vol. 2, 481–82.

48. Steininger, "Grossbritanien und der Vietnamkrieg," 614–15.

49. Wilson, *Labour Government*, 92–93.

50. Harold Wilson and Charles de Gaulle, conversation, April 2, 1965, Public Records Office, in Steininger, "Grossbritanien und der Vietnamkrieg," 615.

51. Michael Stewart and Maurice Couve de Murville, the French foreign minister, record of meeting, April 2, 1965, Public Records Office, in Steininger, "Grossbritanien und der Vietnamkrieg," 616.

52. Wilson, *Labour Government*, 94–95; Ellis, *Britain, America, and the Vietnam War*, 76–80. Johnson told the British ambassador Sir Patrick Dean that he was still angry about British criticism of the use of gas and napalm and angry that all complaints attacked American bombing, neglecting to condemn the atrocities committed by the Communists.

53. Harold Wilson and Lyndon B. Johnson, conversation, April 15, 1965, in *FRUS*, Vietnam, 1964–1968, vol. 2, 557.

54. Wilson, *Labour Government*, 95.

55. Wilson, *Labour Government*, 96.

56. Wilson, *Labour Government*, 96; Walker, *Political Diaries*, 302. Walker was in the region from April 14 to May 4 and visited Saigon, Phnom Penh, Tokyo, and Delhi. Smith, *International History of the Vietnam War*, 61.

57. Steininger, "Grossbritanien und der Vietnamkrieg," 617–19; Smith, *International History of the Vietnam War*, 61–62, 108–9. China was interested in the conference to increase its own role in Southeast Asia and curb growing North Vietnamese influence in Laos and Cambodia. Washington did not want to reject a conference on Cambodia outright, fearful that Sihanouk might completely break relations with the United States and drift toward the Communist side.

58. Michael Stewart, letter to embassy in Washington, April 18, 1965, Public Records Office, in Steininger, "Grossbritanien und der Vietnamkrieg," 619.

59. Steininger, "Grossbritanien und der Vietnamkrieg," 619–20. Both administrations also disagreed about the conference format. London hoped for an extended discussion to give Hanoi and Beijing time to accept serious talks. Washington insisted on a detailed agenda on which a conference would put a stamp of approval.

60. Danney, deputy director, Bureau of Intelligence and Research, intelligence memorandum to secretary of state Dean Rusk, April 15, 1965, in *FRUS*, Vietnam, 1964–1968, vol. 2, 558–59; Smith, *International History of the Vietnam War*, 109–10. Sihanouk demanded that Saigon not be represented at the conference, knowing that this request would be unacceptable to the United States; Sihanouk was primarily interested in settled issues on Cambodia. In addition, the prince was angry over a *Newsweek* article insulting his wife and the incidental bombing of a Cambodian village by the Americans.

61. George Ball, undersecretary of state, memorandum to President Lyndon B. Johnson, April 18, 1965, in *FRUS*, Vietnam, 1964–1968, vol. 2, 586–89. Ball early on criticized the growing American involvement in Vietnam and eventually gained the position of "devil's advocate" during the Johnson administration. Ball's position is discussed in chapter 5.

62. McGeorge Bundy, president's special assistant for National Security Affairs, memorandum to President Lyndon B. Johnson, Washington, D.C., May 13, 1965, in *FRUS*, Vietnam, 1964–1968, vol. 2, 651–52. In June 1965, Johnson again asked for international pressure to bring Hanoi to the conference table. See also Smith, *International History of the Vietnam War*, 154.

63. Michael Stewart and Soviet foreign minister Andrei Gromyko, record of conversation at the Imperial Hotel, Vienna, May 15, 1965, Public Records Office, in Steininger, "Grossbritanien und der Vietnamkrieg," 623. Gromyko rejected any conference for the time being and was "singularly negative, even by his own standards" on any prospect in Vietnam.

64. Wilson, *Labour Government*, 108.

65. Wilson, *Labour Government*, 108–10; Ellis, *Britain, America, and the Vietnam War*, 101–6; Steininger, "Grossbritanien und der Vietnamkrieg," 625; Smith, *International History of the Vietnam War*, 154. Julius Nyerere of Tanzania proved the greatest obstacle to the Commonwealth initiative. He was strongly anti-American and also very much concerned about his image as an independent African leader in an upcoming African Third World Conference in Algiers. In the end, Nyerere was forced to accept the majority view of the Commonwealth countries.

66. Wilson, *Labour Government*, 111–13.

67. Wilson, *Labour Government*, 121–22; Steininger, "Grossbritanien und der Vietnamkrieg," 625–26; Smith, *International History of the Vietnam War*, 154.

68. Wilson, *Labour Government*, 122. Davies met an adamant Ho Chi Minh and returned to London empty-handed. Ellis, *Britain, America, and the Vietnam War*, 109–11.

69. Smith, *International History of the Vietnam War*, 154–55. Britain stated that the defense of Malaysia already strained its resources and hence it could not commit combat forces to Vietnam. Yet Commonwealth members Australia and New Zealand were willing to do so, although as allies to the United States.

70. Steininger, "Grossbritanien und der Vietnamkrieg," 628; see also Robert S. McNamara, *In Retrospect: The Tragedy and Lessons of Vietnam* (New York: Simon & Schuster, 1995), 192–200.

71. Wilson, *Labour Government*, 187.

72. Wilson, *Labour Government*, 188; Ellis, *Britain, America, and the Vietnam War*, 132–34.

73. Steininger, "Grossbritanien und der Vietnamkrieg," 628.

74. Wilson, *Labour Government*, 204–5.

75. Wilson, *Labour Government*, 205–6; Great Britain, *Parliamentary Records*, February 8, 1966, 253–57.

76. Great Britain, *Parliamentary Records*, February 8, 1966, 250–52.

77. Wilson, *Labour Government*, 213–14; Ellis, *Britain, America, and the Vietnam War*, 154–55.

78. Wilson, *Labour Government*, 214.

79. Great Britain, Parliament, Houses of Commons, *The Parliamentary Debate: House of Commons Official Report* (London: Her Majesty's Stationery Office, 1966), June 21, 1966, 282.

80. Ellis, *Britain, America, and the Vietnam War*, 160–62, 172–75. Of course, the decision to dissociate angered Johnson but was received favorably by the Labour Party.

81. Wilson, *Labour Government*, 345–46.

82. Wilson, *Labour Government*, 347–48; see also Marilyn B. Young, *The Vietnam Wars, 1945–1990* (New York: HarperCollins, 1991), 181; and Ilya V. Gaiduk, *The Soviet Union and the Vietnam War* (Chicago: Ivan R. Dee, 1996), 102–3. Soviet contacts with Hanoi indicated some North Vietnamese willingness to talk; Moscow was clearly interested in establishing contact between the United States and North Vietnam.

83. Wilson, *Labour Government*, 356.

84. Wilson, *Labour Government*, 357–59; Young, *Vietnam Wars*, 181–82; Gaiduk, *Soviet Union and the Vietnam War*, 103–6. Kosygin was as disappointed as Wilson. He felt that Washington destroyed a real chance to open negotiations. Ellis, *Britain, America, and the Vietnam War*, 216–32.

85. Wilson, *Labour Government*, 363–65.

CHAPTER 9: LESSENING OF TENSIONS, 1968–1969

1. Stanley Karnow, *Vietnam: A History* (New York: Penguin, 1984), 523–34; George C. Herring, *America's Longest War: The United States and Vietnam, 1950–1975*, 2nd ed. (New York: McGraw-Hill, 1986), 189–92.

2. Karnow, *Vietnam*, 539–47; Herring, *America's Longest War*, 201–3.

3. *The Pentagon Papers: The Defense Department History of United States Decisionmaking on Vietnam*, vol. 4, Senator Gravel, ed. (Boston: Beacon Press, 1971), 558–68. See also Lyndon Baines Johnson, *The Vantage Point: Perspectives on the Presidency, 1963–1969* (New York: New Popular Library, 1971), 393–99.

4. Herring, *America's Longest War*, 198–202. The Senate Foreign Relations committee questioned Rusk for eleven hours and made it clear that Congress wanted a greater role in decision making for Vietnam in the future. Senator Eugene McCarthy and Robert Kennedy announced in March 1968 that they would run against Johnson on a platform to end the Vietnam conflict.

5. Johnson, *Vantage Point*, 435; Herring, *America's Longest War*, 206–13.

6. Harold Wilson, *The Labour Government, 1964–1970: A Personal Record* (London: Weidenfeld & Nicholson, 1971), 519–20. Johnson called on Britain and the Soviet Union as Geneva cochairmen to "do all they can" to encourage "genuine peace in south-east Asia." Wilson was worried that Johnson's resignation might induce Hanoi just to play a waiting game in search of better conditions from another president. See also "Johnson Orders Halt in North Vietnam Bombing," *The Times*, April 2, 1968, 2, on Stewart's talk with the Soviet ambassador to the UK.

7. "Vietnam: New Doors Opening," *The Times*, April 2, 1968, 5.

8. "Surprise Générale aux Etats-Unis et dans le Monde," *Le Monde*, April 2, 1968.

9. Maurice Couve de Murville, *Une Politique Etrangère, 1958–1969* (Paris: Plon, 1971), 153–57; Maurice Vaisse, *La Grandeur: Politique Etrangère du Général de Gaulle, 1958–1969* (Paris: Fayard, 1998), 366.

10. Thomas Alan Schwartz, *Lyndon Johnson and Europe: In the Shadow of Vietnam* (Cambridge, Mass.: Harvard University Press, 2003), 147–65. The Germans finally agreed to a trilateral agreement with the United States and the United Kingdom to settle troops and offset payments.

11. "Réactions en France et dans le Monde," *Le Monde*, April 3, 1968, 8; Wolf Schneider, "Der ungeliebte Kaiser von Amerika," *Stern*, April 14, 1968, 17. Commentator Wolf Schneider acknowledged Johnson's far-reaching achievements in domestic politics but squarely blamed Johnson for escalating civil strife in Vietnam to a full-blown war. Hence, Johnson profoundly damaged the international credibility and reputation of the United States.

12. Schwartz, *Lyndon Johnson and Europe*, 219–20.

13. Richard M. Nixon, *RN: The Memoirs of Richard Nixon* (New York: Simon & Schuster, 1990), 370.

14. Wilson, *Labour Government*, 619–21. Wilson pointed out that the visit had already begun positively when Nixon expressed his hope for better Anglo-American

relations. Wilson was particularly impressed by Nixon's willingness to listen, and the prime minister certainly liked to hear Nixon's appreciation of the Commonwealth.

15. Don Cook, *Charles de Gaulle: A Biography* (New York: Pedigree Books, 1983), 398–411. During the height of the revolt in May 1968, de Gaulle even sought refuge in Baden-Baden, West Germany, for some twenty-four hours. German asylum laws had always been lenient to refugees from revolutionary upheaval in France.

16. Couve de Murville, *Une Politique Etrangère*, 154–59; Nixon, *Memoirs*, 370–73; Cook, *Charles de Gaulle*, 412. The violence in Paris totally overshadowed the commencement of U.S.–North Vietnamese peace talks, robbing de Gaulle of the limelight to assure his country and the world that he had been vindicated at last.

17. Nixon, *Memoirs*, 375.

CONCLUSION

1. C. Vann Woodward, *The Burden of Southern History*, 3rd rev. ed. (Baton Rouge: Louisiana State University Press, 1993), 221–22.

2. Max Paul Friedman, "Anti-Americanism and U.S. Foreign Relations," *Diplomatic History* 32, no. 4 (September 2008): 497–514.

EPILOGUE: THE ALLIES AND THE IRAQ WAR

1. Joschka Fischer, "Between Kosovo and Iraq: The Process of Redefining the Transatlantic Relationship," *Bulletin of the German Historical Institute* 41 (Fall 2007): 16.

2. Lloyd C. Gardner and Marilyn B. Young, eds., *Iraq and the Lessons of Vietnam, or, How Not to Learn from the Past* (New York: New Press, 2007), 9.

3. Philip H. Gordon and Jeremy Shapiro, *Allies at War: America, Europe, and the Crisis over Iraq* (New York: McGraw-Hill, 2004), 59–65; Wilfried Mausbach, "The Forlorn Superpower: European Reactions to the American Wars in Vietnam and Iraq," in *Iraq and the Lessons of Vietnam, or, How Not to Learn from the Past*, ed. Lloyd C. Garner and Marilyn B. Young (New York: New Press, 2007), 57–87.

4. Lloyd C. Gardner, "Mr. Rumsfeld's War," in *Iraq and the Lessons of Vietnam, or, How Not to Learn from the Past*, ed. Lloyd C. Gardner and Marilyn B. Young (New York: New Press, 2007), 174–200.

5. See Daniel Coates and Joel Krieger, *Blair's War* (Cambridge, UK: Polity Press, 2004).

6. Gordon and Shapiro, *Allies at War*, 104–28.

7. See Daniel Levy, Max Pensky, and John Torpey, *Old Europe, New Europe, Core Europe: Transatlantic Relations after the Iraq War* (London: Verso, 2005).

8. Karl Otto Hondrich, "The Organizing Power," in *Old Europe, New Europe, Core Europe: Transatlantic Relations after the Iraq War*, ed. Daniel Levy, Max Pensky, and John Torpey (London: Verso, 2005), 89.

9. Gordon and Shapiro, *Allies at War*, 3. The poll conducted in 2002 and then in March 2003 showed that support for the United States fell from 75 to 48 percent in Britain, from 70 to 34 percent in Italy, from 63 to 31 percent in France, and from 61 to 25 percent in Germany.

10. Helene Cooper, "Obama Connects with Young Europeans," *New York Times*, April 3, 2009.

11. Barack Obama, "Text: Obama's Speech in Cairo," *New York Times*, June 4, 2009.

Bibliography

PRIMARY SOURCES

Unprinted Archival Sources

Ball, George W. Oral history interview by Joseph Kraft. April 12 and 16, 1965. John F. Kennedy Library, Boston.

———. Oral history interview by Larry J. Hackmann. February 16, 1968. John F. Kennedy Library, Boston.

———. Oral history interview by Paige E. Mulhollan. July 8 and 9, 1971. Lyndon B. Johnson Library, Austin, Tex.

———. Papers. Vietnam. Lyndon B. Johnson Library, Austin, Tex.

Bundy, William P. Oral history interview by Paige E. Mulhollan. May 26, 1969. Lyndon B. Johnson Library, Austin, Tex.

Johnson, Lyndon B. National Security Council Meetings. Vols. 1–4, 1963–1965. Lyndon B. Johnson Library, Austin, Tex.

———. National Security Files. Western Europe, 1963–1968. Lyndon B. Johnson Library, Austin, Tex.

Kennedy, John F. National Security Files. Western Europe, 1961–1963. John F. Kennedy Library, Boston.

Memoranda to President Lyndon B. Johnson. National Security Council. Vols. 5–8, 1963–1965. Lyndon B. Johnson Library, Austin, Tex.

Rusk, Dean. Oral history interview by Paige E. Mulhollan. July 28 and September 26 and 29, 1969. Lyndon B. Johnson Library, Austin, Tex.

Printed Primary Sources

Akten zur auswärtigen Politik der Bundesrepublik Deutschland. Vols. 1–3. Munich: Oldenbourg, 1997.

Die Auswärtige Politik der Bundesrepublik Deutschland. Cologne: Auswärtiges Amt der Bundesrepublik Deutschland, 1972.

Department of State Bulletin. Washington, D.C.: Government Printing Office, 1939–.

Foreign Relations of the United States (FRUS). Vols. 1, 2, and 13. 1964–1968. Washington, D.C.: Government Printing Office, 1992–1999.

Gallup, George, Jr., ed. *The Gallup Poll: Public Opinion.* Wilmington, Del.: Scholarly Resources, 1961–1968.

Gaulle, Charles de. "Statement on Vietnam by President Charles de Gaulle on August 29, 1963." In *Major Addresses, Statements, and Press Conferences of General Charles de Gaulle, May 19, 1958—January 31, 1964.* New York: French Embassy, Press and Information Division, 1964.

Gibbons, William Conrad. *The U.S. Government and the Vietnam War: Executive and Legislative Roles and Relationships.* Parts I and II. Congressional Research Service. Washington, D.C.: Government Printing Office, 1984.

Great Britain. Parliament. Houses of Commons. *The Parliamentary Debate: House of Commons Official Report.* London: Her Majesty's Stationary Office, 1962, 1966.

———. Parliament. Houses of Commons. *Parliamentary Records.* London: Her Majesty's Stationery Office, 1965.

Johnson, Lyndon B. *Lyndon B. Johnson's Vietnam Papers: A Documentary Collection,* edited by David M. Barrett. College Station: Texas A&M University Press, 1997.

The Pentagon Papers: The Defense Department History of United States Decisionmaking on Vietnam. Vols. 3 and 4. Senator Gravel, ed. Boston: Beacon, 1971.

Public Papers of the Presidents of the United States: John F. Kennedy, 1961–1963. Washington, D.C.: Government Printing Office, 1961–1964.

Public Papers of the Presidents of the United States: Lyndon B. Johnson, 1963–1969. Washington, D.C.: Government Printing Office, 1964–1970.

Schwarz, Hans Peter, ed. *Akten zur Auswärtigen Politik der Bundesrepublik Deutschland, 1963–1966.* Vols. 1 and 3. Munich: Oldenbourg, 1989–1990.

U.S. Congress. Senate. Committee on Foreign Relations. *Background Information Relating to Southeast Asia and Vietnam.* 7th ed. Washington, D.C.: Government Printing Office, 1966.

———. Senate. Committee on Foreign Relations. *Causes, Origins, and Lessons of the Vietnam War.* 92nd Cong., 2nd sess., May 9, 10, and 11, 1972. Washington, D.C.: Government Printing Office, 1973.

———. Senate. Committee on Foreign Relations. *Conflicts between United States Capabilities and Foreign Commitments.* 19th Cong., 1st sess., February 21, 1967. Washington, D.C.: Government Printing Office, 1967.

———. *Congressional Record.* 1954–1964. Washington, D.C.

———. Senate. Committee on Foreign Relations. *Supplemental Foreign Assistance, Fiscal Year 1966—Vietnam.* 89th Cong., 2nd sess. Washington, D.C.: Government Printing Office, 1966.

———. Senate. Committee on Foreign Relations. *United States Policy toward Europe and Related Matters.* 89th Cong., 2nd sess. Washington, D.C.: Government Printing Office, 1966.

———. Senate. *Hearings before the Committee on Foreign Relations*. 89th Cong., 2nd sess., June 20, 1966, Statement of McGeorge Bundy.

Personal Accounts

Adenauer, Konrad. *Erinnerungen, 1959–1963*. Stuttgart: Luebbe, 1968.

Ball, George W. *The Past Has Another Pattern: Memoirs*. New York: Norton, 1982.

Bohlen, Charles E. *Witness to History, 1929–1969*. New York: Littlehampton Book Services, 1973.

Bowles, Chester. *Promises to Keep: My Years in Public Life, 1941–1969*. New York: Harper & Row, 1971.

Brandt, Willy. *My Life in Politics*. New York: Penguin, 1992.

Carstens, Karl. *Erinnerungen und Erfahrungen*. Boppard, Germany: Harold Boldt, 1993.

Clifford, Clark. *Counsel to the President*. New York: Random House, 1991.

Couve de Murville, Maurice. *Une Politique Etrangère, 1958–1969*. Paris: Plon, 1971.

Eden, Anthony. *Full Circle: The Memoirs of Anthony Eden*. Boston: Houghton Mifflin, 1960.

Galbraith, John Kenneth. *Ambassador's Journal: A Personal Account of the Kennedy Years*. Boston: Houghton Mifflin, 1969.

Gaulle, Charles de. *Memoirs of Hope: Renewal and Endeavor*, translated by Terence Kilmartin. New York: Simon & Schuster, 1971.

Johnson, Lady Bird. *A White House Diary*. New York: University of Texas Press, 1970.

Johnson, Lyndon Baines. *The Vantage Point: Perspectives on the Presidency, 1963–1969*. New York: New Popular Library, 1971.

Kennedy, Robert F. *To Seek a Newer World*. New York: Doubleday, 1967.

Macmillan, Harold. *At the End of the Day, 1961–1963*. London: Macmillan, 1973.

McGhee, George. *At the Creation of a New Germany: From Adenauer to Brandt, an Ambassador's Account*. New Haven, Conn.: Yale University Press, 1989.

McNamara, Robert S. *In Retrospect: The Tragedy and Lessons of Vietnam*. New York: Simon & Schuster, 1995.

Nixon, Richard M. *RN: The Memoirs of Richard Nixon*. New York: Simon & Schuster, 1990.

Nolting, Frederick. *From Trust to Tragedy: The Political Memoirs of Frederick Nolting, Kennedy's Ambassador to Diem's Vietnam*. New York: Praeger, 1988.

Osterheld, Horst. *Aussenpolitik unter Bundeskanzler Ludwig Erhard, 1963–1966: Ein Dokumentarischer Bericht aus dem Kanzleramt*. Düsseldorf: Droste, 1992.

Rusk, Dean. *As I Saw It*. New York: Norton, 1990.

Strauss, Franz Josef. *Die Erinnerungen*. Berlin: Siedler, 1980.

Walker, Patrick Gordon. *Political Diaries, 1932–1971*, edited with an introduction by Robert Pearce. London: Basic Books, 1991.

Wilson, Harold. *The Labour Government, 1964–1970: A Personal Record*. London: Weidenfeld & Nicholson, 1971.

Newspapers and Journals

Der Spiegel
Frankfurter Allgemeine Zeitung
Le Monde
Newsweek
New York Times
Stern
The Nation
Time
The Times [London]

SECONDARY SOURCES

Monographs

Abernethy, David B. *The Dynamics of Global Dominance: European Empires, 1415–1980.* New Haven, Conn.: Yale University Press, 2000.

Ambrose, Stephen E. *Rise to Globalism: American Foreign Policy since 1938.* 6th rev. ed. New York: Penguin, 1991.

Anderson, David L. *Shadow on the White House: Presidents and the Vietnam War, 1945–1975.* Lawrence: University Press of Kansas, 1993.

———. *Trapped by Success: The Eisenhower Administration and Vietnam, 1953–1961.* New York: Columbia University Press, 1991.

Armstrong, Hamilton Fish, ed. *Fifty Years of Foreign Affairs.* New York: Praeger, 1972.

Arnstein, Walter L. *Britain, Yesterday and Today: 1830 to the Present.* 7th ed. Lexington, Mass.: D. C. Heath, 1996.

Ball, George W. *Discipline of Power: Essentials of a Modern World Structure.* Boston: Little, Brown, 1968.

Baring, Arnulf. *Im Anfang war Adenauer: Die Enstehung der Kanzlerdemokratie.* 2nd ed. Munich: DTV, 1982.

Bark, Dennis L., and David R. Gress. *A History of West Germany.* Vol. 2, *Democracy and Its Discontent.* Oxford, UK: Blackwell, 1992.

Bender, Peter. *Die "Neue Ostpolitik" und ihre Folgen: Vom Mauerbau bis zur Wiedervereinigung.* 4th ed. Munich: DTV, 1996.

Berman, Larry. *Planning a Tragedy: The Americanization of the War in Vietnam.* New York: Norton, 1982.

Berman, William C. *William Fulbright and the Vietnam War: The Dissent of a Political Realist.* Kent, Ohio: Kent State University Press, 1988.

Berresheim, Volker. *35 Jahre Indochinapolitik der Bundesrepublik Deutschland.* Hamburg: Mitteilungen des Institutes für Asienkunde, 1986.

Besson, Waldemar. *Die Außenpolitik der Bundesrepublik Deutschland: Erfahrungen und Maßstäbe.* Munich: R. Piper Verlag, 1970.

Blasius, Rainer A. *Von Adenauer zu Erhard: Studien zu auswärtigen Politik der Bundesrepublik Deutschland*. Munich: DTV, 1994.

Blum, John Morton. *Years of Discord: American Politics and Society, 1961–1974*. New York: Norton, 1991.

Bullion, John L. *Lyndon B. Johnson and the Transformation of American Politics*. New York: Longman, 2008.

Bundy, McGeorge. *Danger and Survival: Choices about the Bomb in the First Fifty Years*. New York: Random House, 1988.

Busch, Peter. *All the Way with JFK? Britain, the US, and the Vietnam War*. Oxford: Oxford University Press, 2003.

Califano, Joseph A., Jr. *The Triumph and Tragedy of Lyndon Johnson: The White House Years*. New York: Texas A&M University Press, 1991.

Carmoy, Guy de. *The Foreign Policies of France, 1944–1968*, translated by Elaine P. Halperin. Chicago: University of Chicago Press, 1970.

Carter, James M. *Inventing Vietnam: The United States and State Building, 1954–1968*. New York: Cambridge University Press, 2008.

Castigliola, Frank. *France and the United States: The Cold War Alliance since World War II*. New York: Twayne, 1992.

Coates, Daniel, and Joel Krieger. *Blair's War*. Cambridge, UK: Polity Press, 2004.

Cook, Don. *Charles de Gaulle: A Biography*. New York: Pedigree Books, 1983.

Dallek, Robert. *Flawed Giant: Lyndon Johnson and His Times, 1961–1973*. New York: Oxford University Press, 1998.

———. *An Unfinished Life: John F. Kennedy, 1917–1963*. New York: Back Bay Books, 2003.

Dalloz, Jacques. *The War in Indochina, 1945–54*. London: Gill and Macmillan, 1990.

Daum, Andreas W., Lloyd C. Gardner, and Wilfried Mausbach, eds. *America, the Vietnam War, and the World: Comparative and International Perspectives*. Washington, D.C.: Cambridge University Press, 2003.

DiLeo, David L. *George Ball, Vietnam, and the Rethinking of Containment*. Chapel Hill: University of North Carolina Press, 1991.

Dommen, Arthur J. *The Indochinese Experience of the French and the Americans: Nationalism and Communism in Cambodia, Laos, and Vietnam*. Bloomington: Indiana University Press, 2001.

Duiker, William J. *Ho Chi Minh: A Life*. New York: Theia Books, 2000.

———. *Sacred War: Nationalism and Revolution in a Divided Vietnam*. New York: McGraw-Hill, 1995.

Ellis, Sylvia. *Britain, America, and the Vietnam War*. Westport, Conn.: Praeger, 2004.

Fall, Bernard B. *Street without Joy*. Mechanicsburg, Pa.: Stackpole Books, 1989.

Ferro, Maurice. *De Gaulle et l'Amérique: Une Amitié tumulteuse*. Paris: Plon, 1973.

Fulbrook, Mary. *The Divided Nation: A History of Germany, 1918–1990*. New York: Oxford University Press, 1992.

Gaiduk, Ilya V. *The Soviet Union and the Vietnam War*. Chicago: Ivan R. Dee, 1996.

Gardner, Lloyd C. *Approaching Vietnam: From World War II through Dienbienphu, 1941–1954*. New York: Norton, 1988.

——. *Pay Any Price: Lyndon Johnson and the Wars for Vietnam.* Chicago: Ivan R. Dee, 1995.

Gardner, Lloyd C., and Ted Gittinger, eds. *International Perspectives on Vietnam.* College Station: Texas A&M University Press, 2000.

Gardner, Lloyd C., and Marilyn B. Young, eds. *Iraq and the Lessons of Vietnam, or, How Not to Learn from the Past.* New York: New Press, 2007.

Gibbons, William Conrad. *The U.S. Government and the Vietnam War: Executive and Legislative Roles and Relationships, Part II: 1961–1964.* Princeton, N.J.: Princeton University Press, 1986.

Giglio, James N. *The Presidency of John F. Kennedy.* Lawrence: University of Kansas Press, 1991.

Giles, Frank. *The Locust Years: The Story of the Fourth Republic, 1946–1958.* New York: Carroll & Graf Publishers, 1991.

Glees, Anthony. *Reinventing Germany: German Political Development since 1945.* Oxford, UK: Berg, 1996.

Gordon, Philip H., and Jeremy Shapiro. *Allies at War: America, Europe, and the Crisis over Iraq.* New York: McGraw-Hill, 2004.

Granieri, Ronald J. *The Ambivalent Alliance: Konrad Adenauer, the CDU/CSU, and the West.* New York: Berghahn, 2003.

Grosser, Alfred. *Geschichte Deutschlands seit 1945: Eine Bilanz.* Munich: DTV, 1985.

Hacke, Christian. *Die Außenpolitik der Bundesrepublik Deutschland: Von Konrad Adenauer bis Gerhard Schröder.* Frankfurt: Ullstein, 2003.

Halberstam, David. *The Best and the Brightest.* 20th anniversary ed. New York: Ballantine Books, 1992.

Hanrieder, Wolfram F. *Germany, America, Europe: Forty Years of German Foreign Policy.* New Haven, Conn.: Yale University Press, 1989.

——, ed. *West German Foreign Policy, 1949–1979.* Boulder, Colo.: Westview, 1980.

Hathaway, Robert M. *Great Britain and the United States: Special Relations since World War II.* Boston: Twayne, 1990.

Hentschel, Volker. *Ludwig Erhard: Ein Politikerleben.* Berlin: Ullstein, 1998.

Herbst, Ludolf. *Option für den Westen: Vom Marshallplan bis zum deutsch-französischen Vertrag.* 2nd ed. Munich: DTV, 1996.

Herring, George C. *America's Longest War: The United States and Vietnam, 1950–1975.* 2nd ed. New York: McGraw-Hill, 1986.

——. *LBJ and Vietnam: A Different Kind of War.* Austin: University of Texas Press, 1995.

Hitchcock, William I. *France Restored: Cold War Diplomacy and the Quest for Leadership in Europe, 1944–1954.* Chapel Hill: University of North Carolina Press, 1998.

Hoffmann, Stanley. *Decline or Renewal? France since the 1930s.* New York: Viking, 1974.

Holsti, Ole R., and James N. Rosenau. *American Leadership and World Affairs: Vietnam and the Breakdown of Consensus.* Winchester, Mass.: Unwin & Hyman, 1984.

Horne, Alistair. *Harold Macmillan*. Vol. 2, *1957–1986*. New York: Penguin, 1989.

Hunt, Michael H. *Ideology and U.S. Foreign Policy*. New Haven, Conn.: Yale University Press, 1987.

Irving, R. E. M. *The First Indochina War: French and American Policy, 1945–54*. London: C. Helm, 1975.

Isaacson, Walter, and Evan Thomas. *The Wise Men: Six Friends and the World They Made*. New York: Simon & Schuster, 1986.

Iverson, Peter. *Barry Goldwater: Native Arizonan*. Norman: University of Oklahoma Press, 1997.

Jacobs, Seth. *Cold War Mandarin: Ngo Dinh Diem and the Origins of America's War in Vietnam, 1950–1963*. Lanham, Md.: Rowman & Littlefield, 2006.

Karnow, Stanley. *Vietnam: A History*. New York: Penguin, 1984.

Kattenburg, Paul. *The Vietnam Drama in American Foreign Policy, 1945–1975*. New Brunswick, N.J.: Transaction, 1980.

Kearns, Doris. *Lyndon Johnson and the American Dream*. New York: Harper & Row, 1976.

Kedward, Rod. *France and the French: A Modern History*. Woodstock, N.Y.: Overlook Press, 2006.

Kissinger, Henry. *Diplomacy*. New York: Simon & Schuster, 1994.

Kraslow, D., and Stuart H. Loory. *The Secret Search for Peace in Vietnam*. New York: Random House, 1968.

Kulski, W. W. *De Gaulle and the World: The Foreign Policy of the Fifth French Republic*. Syracuse, N.Y.: Syracuse University Press, 1966.

Kunz, Diane B., ed. *The Diplomacy of the Crucial Decade: American Foreign Relations during the 1960's*. New York: Columbia University Press, 1994.

Lacoutre, Jean. *De Gaulle: The Ruler, 1945–1970*. New York: Norton, 1991.

Lamb, Richard. *The Macmillan Years, 1957–1963: The Emerging Truth*. London: John Murray, 1996.

Larres, Klaus, and Torsten Oppelland, eds. *Deutschland und die USA im 20. Jahrhundert: Geschichte der politischen Beziehungen*. Darmstadt, Germany: Wissenschaftliche Buchgesellschaft, 1997.

Lawrence, Mark Atwood. *Assuming the Burden: Europe and the American Commitment to War in Vietnam*. Berkeley: University of California Press, 2005.

Lawrence, Mark Atwood, and Fredrik Logevall, eds. *The First Vietnam War: Colonial Conflict and Cold War Crisis*. Cambridge, Mass.: Harvard University Press, 2007.

Levy, Daniel, Max Pensky, and John Torpey. *Old Europe, New Europe, Core Europe: Transatlantic Relations after the Iraq War*. London: Verso, 2005.

Linsel, Knut. *Charles de Gaulle und Deutschland, 1914–1969*. Sigmaringen, Germany: Thorbecke Verlag, 1998.

Logevall, Fredrik. *Choosing War: The Lost Chance for Peace and the Escalation of War in Vietnam*. Berkeley: University of California Press, 1999.

Louis, William Roger. *Ends of British Imperialism: The Scramble for Empire, Suez and Decolonization*. 2nd ed. London: I. B. Tauris, 2006.

MacQueen, Norrie. *Colonialism*. London: Pearson-Longman, 2007.

Marshall, D. Bruce. *The French Colonial Myth and Constitution Making in the Fourth Republic*. New Haven, Conn.: Yale University Press, 1973.

Mayer, Frank A. *Adenauer and Kennedy: A Study in German-American Relations, 1961–1963*. New York: St. Martin's Press, 1996.

McAlister, John T., and Paul Mus. *The Vietnamese and Their Revolution*. New York: Harper & Row, 1970.

Mierzejewski, Alfred C. *Ludwig Erhard: A Biography*. Chapel Hill: University of North Carolina Press, 2004.

Morgan, Austen. *Harold Wilson: A Life*. London: LPC Group, 1992.

Morgan, Kenneth O. *The People's Peace: British History, 1945–1989*. Oxford: Oxford University Press, 1990.

Newhouse, John. *De Gaulle and the Anglo-Saxons*. New York: Viking, 1970.

Nicholas, H. G. *The United States and Britain*. Chicago: University of Chicago Press, 1975.

Oberdorfer, Don. *Senator Mansfield: The Extraordinary Life of a Great Statesman and Diplomat*. Washington, D.C.: Smithsonian Books, 2003.

Olsen, Gregory Allen. *Mansfield and Vietnam: A Study in Rhetorical Adaptation*. East Lansing: Michigan State University Press, 1995.

Oppelland, Torsten. *Gerhard Schröder (1910–1989): Politik zwischen Staat, Parteien, und Konfessionen*. Düsseldorf: Droste, 2002.

Page, Benjamin I., and Robert Y. Shapiro. *The Rational Public: Fifty Years of Trends in Americans' Policy Preferences*. Chicago: University of Chicago Press, 1992.

Paterson, Thomas G. *Kennedy's Quest for Victory: American Foreign Policy, 1961–1963*. New York: Norton, 1989.

Paxton, Robert O., and Nicholas Wahl. *De Gaulle and the United States: A Centennial Reappraisal*. Oxford, UK: Berg, 1994.

Pfetsch, Frank R. *Die Außenpolitik der Bundesrepublik Deutschland, 1949–1992: Von der Spaltung zur Wiedervereinigung*. 2nd ed. Munich: DTV, 1993.

Preston, Andrew. *The War Council: McGeorge Bundy, the NSC, and Vietnam*. Cambridge, Mass.: Harvard University Press, 2006.

Reeves, Richard. *President Kennedy: Profile in Power*. New York: Simon & Schuster, 1993.

Rosie, George. *The British in Vietnam: How the Twenty-Five-Year War Began*. London: Panther, 1970.

Rotter, Andrew. *The Path to Vietnam: Origins of the American Commitment to Southeast Asia*. Ithaca, N.Y.: Cornell University Press, 1989.

Sar Desai, D. R. *Southeast Asia: Past and Present*. 3rd ed. Boulder, Colo.: Westview, 1994.

———. *Vietnam: The Struggle for National Identity*. Boulder, Colo.: Westview, 1992.

Schlesinger, Arthur, Jr. *A Thousand Days: John F. Kennedy in the White House*. Boston: Houghton Mifflin, 1965.

Schwartz, Thomas Alan. *Lyndon Johnson and Europe: In the Shadow of Vietnam*. Cambridge, Mass.: Harvard University Press, 2003.

Shipway, Martin. *The Road to War: France and Vietnam, 1944–1947*. New York: Berghahn Books, 2003.

Smith, Ralph B. *An International History of the Vietnam War*. Vols. 2 and 3. New York: St. Martin's Press, 1985, 1991.

———. *Vietnam and the West*. Ithaca, N.Y.: St. Martin's Press, 1968.

Sontheimer, Kurt. *Die Adenauer Ära: Grundlegung der Bundesrepublik Deutschland*. Munich: DTV, 1991.

Sorensen, Theodore. *Kennedy*. New York: Harper & Row, 1965.

Sullivan, Marianna P. *France's Vietnam Policy: A Study in French-American Relations*. Westport, Conn.: Greenwood, 1978.

Thompson, Robert. *No Exit from Vietnam*. Updated ed. New York: David McKay, 1970.

Tint, Herbert. *French Foreign Policy since the Second World War*. New York: Palgrave Macmillan, 1973.

Touchard, Jean. *Le Gaullisme, 1940–1969*. Paris: Plon, 1978.

Troche, Alexander. *Berlin wird am Mekong verteidigt: Die Ostasienpolitik der Bundesrepublik Deutschland in China, Taiwan, und Süd-Vietnam, 1954–1966*. Düsseldorf: Droste, 1999.

Urwin, Derek W. *A Political History of Western Europe since 1945*. 5th ed. London: Longman, 1997.

Vaisse, Maurice. *La Grandeur: Politique Etrangère du Général de Gaulle, 1958–1969*. Paris: Fayard, 1998.

Vandiver, Frank E. *Shadows of Vietnam: Lyndon Johnson's Wars*. College Station: Texas A&M University Press, 1997.

Vogelsang, Thilo. *Das Geteilte Deutschland*. Munich: DTV, 1995.

Wicker, Tom. *JFK and LBJ: The Influence of Personality upon Politics*. New York: Pelican, 1968.

Woodward, C. Vann. *The Burden of Southern History*. 3rd rev. ed. Baton Rouge: Louisiana State University Press, 1993.

Wright, Gordon. *France in Modern Times*. 4th ed. New York: Norton, 1987.

Young, Kenneth. *Sir Alec Douglas-Home*. London: J. M. Dent, 1970.

Young, Marilyn B. *The Vietnam Wars, 1945–1990*. New York: HarperCollins, 1991.

Ziegler, Philip. *Wilson: The Authorised Life of Lord Wilson of Rievaulx*. London: Weidenfeld & Nicholson, 1993.

Zimmermann, Hubert. *Money and Security: Troops, Monetary Policy, and West Germany's Relations with the United States and Britain, 1950–1971*. Washington, D.C.: German Historical Institute, 2002.

Selected Articles

Arenth, Joachim. "Die Bewährungsprobe der Special Relationship: Washington und Bonn (1961–1969)." In *Deutschland und die USA im 20. Jahrhundert: Geschichte der politischen Beziehungen*, edited by Klaus Larres and Torsten Oppelland. Darmstadt, Germany: Wissenschaftliche Buchgesellschaft, 1997.

Arnold, Hugh M. "Official Justification for America's Role in Indochina, 1949–1967." *Asian Affairs: An American Review* 3, no. 1 (1975).

Bassett, Lawrence J., and Stephen E. Pelz. "The Failed Search for Victory: Vietnam and the Politics of War." In *Kennedy's Quest for Victory: American Foreign Policy, 1961–1963*, edited by Thomas G. Paterson. New York: Norton, 1989.

Bourget, Claude. "Indo-China: Black Market War." *The Nation*, May 16, 1953.

Brands, H. W. "Johnson and de Gaulle: American Diplomacy Sotto Voce." *Historian* 44 (August 1987).

Buchan, Alistair. "The Indochina War and World Politics." *Foreign Affairs* 58, no. 4 (1975).

Combs, Arthur. "The Path Not Taken: The British Alternative to U.S. Policy in Vietnam, 1954–1956." *Diplomatic History* 19, no. 1 (Winter 1995).

Conze, Eckart. "Hegemonie durch Integration? Die amerikanische Europapolitik und ihre Herausforderung durch de Gaulle." *Vierteljahreshefte für Zeitgeschichte* 43, no. 2 (April 1995).

Costigliola, Frank. "The Failed Design: Kennedy, de Gaulle, and the Struggle for Europe." *Diplomatic History* 8, no. 3 (Summer 1984).

Dallek, Robert. "Roosevelt and de Gaulle." In *De Gaulle and the United States: A Centennial Reappraisal*, edited by Robert O. Paxton and Nicholas Wahl. Oxford, UK: Berg, 1994.

Devillers, Philippe. "French Policy and the Second Vietnam War." *World Today*, June 1967.

Ellsberg, Daniel. "The Quagmire Myth and the Stalemate Machine." *Public Policy* (Spring 1992).

Fischer, Joschka. "Between Kosovo and Iraq: The Process of Redefining the Transatlantic Relationship." *Bulletin of the German Historical Institute* 41 (Fall 2007).

Friedman, Max Paul. "Anti-Americanism and U.S. Foreign Relations." *Diplomatic History* 32, no. 4 (September 2008).

Gardner, Lloyd C. "Johnson and de Gaulle." In *De Gaulle and the United States: A Centennial Reappraisal*, edited by Robert O. Paxton and Nicholas Wahl. Oxford, UK: Berg, 1994.

———. "Mr. Rumsfeld's War." In *Iraq and the Lessons of Vietnam, or, How Not to Learn from the Past*, edited by Lloyd C. Gardner and Marilyn B. Young. New York: New Press, 2007.

Herring, George C. "America and Vietnam: The Debate Continues." *American Historical Review* 92 (April 1987).

Hondrich, Karl Otto. "The Organizing Power." In *Old Europe, New Europe, Core Europe: Transatlantic Relations after the Iraq War*, edited by Daniel Levy, Max Pensky, and John Torpey. London: Verso, 2005.

Hyland, William G. "The Soviet Union and West Germany." In *West German Foreign Policy, 1949–1979*, edited by Wolfram F. Hanrieder. Boulder, Colo.: Westview, 1980.

Jian, Chen. "China and the Indochina Settlement at the Geneva Conference of 1954." In *The First Vietnam War: Colonial Conflict and Cold War Crisis*, edited by Mark Atwood Lawrence and Fredrik Logevall. Cambridge, Mass.: Harvard University Press, 2007.

Kaplan, Lawrence S. "Western Europe in 'The American Century': A Retrospective View." *Diplomatic History* 6, no. 2 (Spring 1982).

Küsters, Hanns Jürgen. "Konrad Adenauer und Willy Brandt in der Berlin Krise, 1958–1963." *Vierteljahreshefte für Zeitgeschichte* 40, no. 4 (October 1992).

Livingston, Robert G. "West Germany: A Favorite Ally." *German Politics and Society* 9 (October 1986).

Logevall, Fredrik. "De Gaulle, Neutralization, and the American Involvement in Vietnam, 1963–1964." *Pacific Historical Review* 61, no. 1 (February 1992).

Lüthy, Herbert. "De Gaulle: Pose and Policy." In *Fifty Years of Foreign Affairs*, edited by Hamilton Fish Armstrong. New York: Praeger, 1972.

Marr, David G. "Creating a Defense Capacity in Vietnam, 1945–1947." In *The First Vietnam War: Colonial Conflict and Cold War Crisis*, edited by Mark Atwood Lawrence and Fredrik Logevall. Cambridge, Mass.: Harvard University Press, 2007.

Marsot, Alain-Gerard. "The Crucial Year: Indochina 1946." *Journal of Contemporary History* 19, no. 2 (April 1984).

Mausbach, Wilfried. "The Forlorn Superpower: European Reactions to the American Wars in Vietnam and Iraq." In *Iraq and the Lessons of Vietnam, or, How Not to Learn from the Past*, edited by Lloyd C. Gardner and Marilyn B. Young. New York: New Press, 2007.

Mayer, Frank A. "Adenauer and Kennedy: An Era of Distrust in German-American Relations?" *German Studies Review* 17, no. 1 (February 1994).

Mueller, John E. "Trends in Popular Support for the Wars in Korea and Vietnam." In *Public Opinion and Political Attitudes*, compiled by Allen R. Wilcox. New York: Wiley, 1974.

Ruane, Kevin. "Refusing to Pay the Price: British Foreign Policy and the Pursuit of Victory in Vietnam, 1952–1954." *English Historical Review* (February 1995).

Sa'adah, Anne. "Idées Simples and Idées Fixes: De Gaulle, the United States, and Vietnam." In *De Gaulle and the United States: A Centennial Reappraisal*, edited by Robert O. Paxton and Nicholas Wahl. Oxford, UK: Berg, 1994.

Schröder, Hans-Jürgen. "Deutsche Aussenpolitik 1963/64: Die 'Akten zur Auswärtigen Politik der Bundesrepublik Deutschland.'" *Vierteljahreshefte für Zeitgeschichte* 43 (July 1995).

———. "USA und Westdeutscher Wiederaufstieg (1945–1952)." In *Deutschland und die USA im 20. Jahrhundert: Geschichte der politischen Beziehungen*, edited by Klaus Larres and Torsten Oppelland. Darmstadt, Germany: Wissenschaftliche Buchgesellschaft, 1997.

Schwarz, Hans-Peter. "Adenauer's Ostpolitik." In *West German Foreign Policy, 1949–1979*, edited by Wolfram F. Hanrieder. Boulder, Colo.: Westview, 1980.

———. "Adenauer und Europa." *Vierteljahreshefte für Zeitgeschichte* 27, no. 4 (October 1979).

———. "West German Foreign Policy, 1949–1979: Necessities and Choices." In *West German Foreign Policy, 1949–1979*, edited by Wolfram F. Hanrieder. Boulder, Colo.: Westview, 1980.

Steininger, Rolf. "Grossbritanien und der Vietnamkrieg." *Vierteljahreshefte für Zeit-geschichte* 45, no. 4 (October 1997).

Thomas, Martin. "French Imperial Reconstruction." In *The First Vietnam War: Colo-nial Conflict and Cold War Crisis*, edited by Mark Atwood Lawrence and Fredrik Logevall. Cambridge, Mass.: Harvard University Press, 2007.

Wenger, Andreas. "Der lange Weg zur Stabilität: Kennedy, Chruschtschow und das Gemeinsame Interesse am Status quo in Europa." *Vierteljahreshefte für Zeitge-schichte* 46 (1998).

Wrigley, Chris. "Now You See It, Now You Don't: Harold Wilson and Labour Foreign Policy, 1964–1970." In *The Wilson Governments, 1964–1970*, edited by Richard Coopey, Steven Fielding, and Nick Tiratsoo. London: Pinter, 1993.

Index

About the Author

Eugenie M. Blang earned master's degrees in history and in English and American literature from the University of Konstanz, Germany. She received her PhD in American history from the College of William and Mary, Virginia. Blang is currently assistant professor of history at Hampton University, Virginia.